T0119492

Endless Summers

Endless Summers

The Fall and Rise of the Cleveland Indians

Updated Edition

by Jack Torry

Diamond Communications, Inc.
South Bend, Indiana
1996

ENDLESS SUMMERS
The Fall and Rise of the Cleveland Indians
Copyright ©1995, 1996 by Jack Torry

10 9 8 7 6 5 4 3 2 1

Manufactured in the United States of America

Diamond Communications, Inc.
Post Office Box 88
South Bend, Indiana 46624-0088
Editorial: (219) 299-9278
Orders Only: (800) 480-3717
FAX (219) 299-9296

Library of Congress Cataloging-in-Publication Data

Torry, Jack, 1952—
    Endless summers : the fall and rise of the Cleveland
Indians / by Jack Torry.
          p.   cm.
    Includes bibliographical references (p.   ) and
    index.
    ISBN 0-912083-98-0
    1. Cleveland Indians (Baseball team)–History.   I. Title.
GV875.C7T67   1996
796.357'64771'32–dc20   96-7935
                                                   CIP

Contents

Foreword

Like my father before me, my baseball allegiance traveled north and south. Growing up between Ohio's major league meccas, Cleveland and Cincinnati, it was only natural to develop a rooting interest in both, and so, for as long as I can remember, the Indians have been my American League team; the Reds my National League team. These were not so much divided loyalties as complementary ones; my friends and I might indulge in what-if fantasies about the two teams meeting in the World Series — Robby vs. Rocky! — but in reality it never came close to happening. Even in the spring, the teams trained several time zones apart. Thus I was spared the pain of ever having to choose and gave myself totally to both.

I can't honestly say that I remember the 1954 World Series between the Indians and New York Giants. I was five years old, and have a vague recollection of something exciting going on, but I have no independent memory of Willie Mays robbing Vic Wertz, no first-hand sense of how frustrating it must have been to watch the best team in baseball get swept by what most considered an inferior Giants club.

I have no trouble remembering the next time one of my teams made it to the big show, however. It was 1961, and an over-achieving Reds team made it into the World Series against the mighty Maris-Mantle Yankees. The Reds managed one victory at home; the Yankees pounded them in four other games.

Back then, there was no sense that the Indians were already sliding into the unrelenting mediocrity that would become the franchise's hallmark for decades to come. They had continued to contend more often than not in the years following 1954; even if they hadn't won another pennant, and there was no reason not to believe that with a little retooling and tinkering, they would be back atop the American League standings.

That's just the way baseball is. It's cyclical. Teams are up for a while, then they are down, and then they reload. The Reds' experience after 1961 followed the model precisely. Injuries, old age and one horrendous trade — the deal that sent Frank Robinson to the Orioles — shattered the nucleus of the pennant-winning team and led to a few bleak seasons. But by patiently developing talented young players such as Pete Rose, Tony Perez, and Johnny Bench, the Reds had by the end of the decade built a team that over the next seven years would win five National League West titles, four pennants and two world championships.

Granted, that would have been a tough act for anyone to follow, but the Indians didn't even come close. No real stars emerged to replace the stalwarts of those great 1950s teams, and the team seemed to slip a little too comfortably into its role as the perennial doormat of the American League. By the 1970s, the image was set, and the team was pretty much a joke. Being a downstate Indians fan became a much lonelier pursuit, but for those of us who remained true, our loyalty took on a fierce (if somewhat perverse) quality.

I belonged in the mid-1970s to a Dayton-area group of fans called TRIBE — Totally Rabid Indians Boosters Extraordinaire — who would make occasional excursions to Cleveland to see the team play. On one such trip, a small plane we chartered developed mechanical trouble and we had to make a terrifying emergency landing. Ever since, I have been able to say in all honesty that being an Indians fan damn near killed me.

It got so bad that some years I couldn't even muster up any optimism in the spring, that magical period when anything seems possible. Maybe, if the rookie pans out, and the starting pitching holds up, and we catch a few breaks . . . then maybe. Every baseball fan knows that feeling, but with the Tribe you usually knew how forlorn a hope it was.

And we were right, year after miserable year. In retrospect it is now apparent that the Indians never had a prayer of being successful.

In this book, Jack Torry examines four decades of futility and offers a sober, clear-eyed, and ultimately persuasive explanation of how it came to be. Failure, he demonstrates, cannot be blamed on bad trades or untimely injuries or a fired manager putting a hex on the team. The decisions that condemned the Indians to 40 years in the wilderness were not made in the first-base dugout at Municipal Stadium. They were made in the Greenbrier Suite in the Terminal Tower and at Stouffer's Restaurant on Shaker Square. They were made by wealthy men in suits and ties. And luck had nothing to do with it.

I can think of no one better suited for this project than Torry. I have known him since we worked together at the *Columbus Citizen-Journal* in the early 1980s. Back then, he was a baseball writer with a passion for politics and government. Now, he is the Washington correspondent for the *Pittsburgh Post-Gazette* and *Toledo Blade*, but he never lost his love for the game in general and the Indians in particular. Most summer evenings, he can be found leaning over the balcony of his Washington condominium with a portable radio in his hand, the only position in which he can pull in the distant Indians' broadcasts from Cleveland.

In approaching this subject, Jack followed one of the basic tenets of good reporting: Follow the money. What he found was a succession of owners unwilling or unable to make the financial investment necessary to make the franchise successful on the field. The farm system, once one of baseball's best, was gutted; the scouting staff was decimated and player development all but ignored. This foolish, short-sighted economy doomed the Indians to lasting mediocrity far more than did the trade of Rocky Colavito. Only now, under the ownership of Richard Jacobs, is the team finally emerging from the crushing handicap imposed by previous front-office regimes.

The change has been striking. The Indians began play in Jacobs Field — their stunning new home — with a powerful, young team that captured the attention of the baseball world in 1994 and stayed in contention until the players went on strike and the season abruptly ended in August. After 40 years, Indians fans have come to expect such cruel twists of fate.

But even the strike could not wipe out the new sense of optimism. Once again, the revitalized farm system is producing talented young players. Once again, the Indians are respected around the league.

Once again, there is hope.

Joe Dirck
Cleveland, Ohio
November 1994

For my mother and father

Acknowledgments

This book, reported and written during a one and one-half year period between July 1993 and November 1994, is largely based upon 77 interviews. To conduct research, I traveled to California, Florida, Indiana, New York City, Baltimore, as well as a number of times to Cleveland.

In particular, I want to thank Al Rosen, Nate Dolin, Ted Bonda, and Gabe Paul for their patience. Rosen sat through two lengthy interviews at his home in Rancho Mirage, California, as he described in vivid detail the great Indian teams of the 1950s, his feud with Hank Greenberg, and his effort in 1971 to buy the franchise.

Nate Dolin not only put up with repeated telephone interviews, but he and his wife, Mollie, graciously provided my wife and me with several hours of time at their home in Rancho Mirage. Gabe Paul also agreed to several interviews, including one at his condominium in Tampa. Paul's memory is meticulous and he still seems to understand the golden rule that no reporter should leave without a good story. Ted Bonda, who performed financial miracles in keeping the Indians alive in the 1970s, agreed to a long interview at his office in Cleveland and gave up time for follow-up questions by telephone.

I also want to thank Kathleen Daley who spent hours providing details about the life of her remarkable father; Tom Chema, who offered valuable insight into the building of Jacobs Field; Hank Peters, who in two long interviews at his home in Baltimore gave me crucial information on both the collapse of the Cleveland farm system and the efforts to rebuild it; and Herb Score, who during an early interview in Baltimore pointed to the team's finances as the real problem during the past four decades.

Others who gave of their time for long interviews were Joe Altobelli, Armond Arnson, Dick Atkinson, Peter Bavasi, James Biggar, Scott Boras, Mary Boyle, Harry Dalton, Bing Devine, Bob Dykes, Michael Fetchko, Margaret Mitchell Gannon, Bernard Goldfarb, Sheldon Guren, Tim Hagan, John Hart, Andy Kundtz, Hal Lebovitz, David LeFevre, Al Lopez, Howard Metzenbaum, Art Modell, George Moscarino, Peter Shimrak, James Stanton, and Steve Zayac. David Griffiths and Shirley Kvet recalled details about Nick Mileti's years in high school. Nick Mileti declined two telephone requests for interviews, although he made no effort to stop friends from cooperating.

Steve Greenberg kindly made available tapes that Hank Greenberg recorded for his autobiography, including material not used by Ira Berkow in the book, *Hank Greenberg, The Story of My Life*. The unused tapes provided invaluable clues to explaining why the Indians did not transfer to Minneapolis or Houston in 1958. Aviva Kempner who is producing a film on Hank Greenberg, provided invaluable help.

I also deeply appreciate the following people who provided interviews: Jan Allen, Bobby Bragan, Eric Bremner, Steve Brogan, Vincent Campanella, Donald Carmichael, U.S. District Judge Anthony Celebrezze, former Ohio Governor Richard F. Celeste, Rocky Colavito, Billy Connick, Alvin Dark, David Dixon, Ted Garver, Sid Hartman, Oliver Henkel, George Hering, Bob Kennedy, Joe Klein, Dennis Lafferty, Patrick McCartan, Don McNeely, Myron Medinger, William Milkie, Dick Moss, Tom Mulligan, Lee Powar, Shirley Povich, Bill Sears, Al Smith, Tal Smith, Dewey Soriano, Max Soriano, Bob Sudyk, Jim Turner, Ohio Governor George Voinovich, Emmett Watson, Bob Weber, David Weiner, and Helen Williams.

Roy Meyers, former political reporter for the *Cleveland Press* and one-time press secretary to Senator Metzenbaum, volunteered names of people to contact.

Bob DiBiasio of the Cleveland Indians helped immeasurably by locating telephone numbers and addresses of former Indians. My only regret is that Dick Jacobs declined repeated requests for an interview, beginning in September 1993. In a July 1994 letter to DiBiasio, I informed Jacobs that I would fly to Cleveland at any time to interview him between August and the end of September. After agreeing to an interview in August, Jacobs cancelled the session. Through DiBiasio, he cited the baseball strike as the reason, but I suspect Jacobs' inclination to avoid reporters won out.

Archives provided a wealth of information. The lease allowing the Indians to use Cleveland Stadium from 1950 to 1964 is on file at Cleveland city government. The personal papers of William R. Daley, Cyrus Eaton, and William Hopkins are at the Western Reserve Historical Society in Cleveland, and the University of Notre Dame permitted me to examine its files on William Daley and Ignatius O'Shaughnessy. The archives of the 2nd U.S. Circuit Court of Appeals offered the complete trial testimony of the 1951 lawsuit between Kaiser-Frazer and Otis.

William Becker, who runs the *Cleveland Press* collection at Cleveland State University, saved me countless hours with his kind help and provided me with marvelous photographs. The

Acknowledgments

Library of Congress offered access to every newspaper and magazine I could want, particularly the *Cleveland Plain Dealer* and *Cleveland Press*. The reporters who covered the Indians through this period — Russell Schneider, Chuck Heaton, Hal Lebovitz, Paul Hoynes, Terry Pluto, Harry Jones, and Gordon Cobbledick of the *Plain Dealer*, and Frank Gibbons, Whitey Lewis, Bob Sudyk, and Bob August of the *Press* — deserve special praise. They had the misfortune of covering a terrible baseball team, yet they were indefatigable reporters who had excellent sources.

My wife, Saundra Torry of the *Washington Post*, proved an exceptional editor who labored long weekends with me at the word processor. Without her encouragement and help, I never could have finished this book.

Rem Rieder and Jack Schnedler offered excellent suggestions after reading through the manuscript and Ronald Saperstein provided invaluable help. I particularly want to thank Michael Woods, science editor of the *Toledo Blade*, for his encouragement. John Robinson Block, publisher of the *Blade*; Ron Royhab, managing editor of the *Blade*; and Pat Griffith, bureau chief of the *Blade*'s Washington bureau, provided me with the extra time to finish the book. I also owe a debt to Bill Mayer, who constantly encouraged me to stay with writing.

The success of the Indians made a new edition for 1996 an imperative. I want to thank John Craig, executive editor of the *Pittsburgh Post-Gazette*, Fritz Huysman, sports editor of the *Post-Gazette*; and Bob Kinney, sports editor of the *Toledo Blade*, for obtaining press credentials for the Cleveland games of the American League Championship Series and the World Series. During post-season play, John Hart, Mike Hargrove, Mark Wiley, Dave Nelson, Orel Hershiser, John Schuerholz, Charlie Manuel, Dennis Martinez, Charles Nagy, and Paul Assenmacher all were available for impromptu interviews.

I also want to thank Mickey White, Dan O'Dowd, Phil Regan, and John Moag for their time. More importantly, I want to thank Sheldon Zoldan, Tom Bendycki, and Wayne Harer for their encouragement.

Jack Torry
Washington, D.C.

"Teams don't finish down this low by accident."
— Gabe Paul, 1978

Chapter 1

A Catch in Coogan's Bluff

"The Yankees have been caught and stopped."
— Hank Greenberg

Sharp pain shot through Al Rosen's right leg as he struggled to reach first base. He had just slapped a groundball to the right of New York Giants' shortstop Alvin Dark. Dark grasped the ball with his bare hand, but his off-balance toss was too late to force Larry Doby at second base. Now, as the late-afternoon shadows of the Polo Grounds covered Rosen at first base, his leg ached from the hamstring muscle he had pulled two weeks earlier.

Rosen squinted toward the Cleveland dugout to see if manager Al Lopez would replace him with a fresh runner. It would make sense. Rosen's leg was so heavily taped that even on an extra-base hit he might not score. But Lopez didn't make a move. Typical of Lopez, Rosen thought. Lopez knew how badly Rosen wanted to play, especially on this fall afternoon of 1954. It was the eighth inning of the first game of the World Series, and the Cleveland Indians and New York Giants were locked in a 2-2 tie.

Rosen was a major reason that Lopez and the Indians were in the World Series. After winning the league's Most Valuable Player Award in 1953, Rosen batted .300 and drove in 102 runs in 1954. He overpowered the same curveballs that baffled ordinary hitters. Although a plodding runner, he developed into a competent third baseman by doggedly insisting that Indians coach Tony Cuccinello hit him scores of groundballs every day.

More than anything, he reveled in winning. Early in the season when Lopez was without a first baseman, he asked Rosen to switch. Rosen agreed without complaint. Although the Cleveland sportswriters regularly contended that the Indians collapsed in the most crucial games, they always were careful to exclude Rosen from their barbs. They liked him; most called him by his nickname, "Flip."

1

All that season, Rosen played in pain. In a game in Chicago in May, he fractured his right index finger. Less than a month later, he returned to the lineup and smacked two long home runs in the All-Star Game. Although he hit 24 home runs that season, Rosen entered the World Series dissatisfied. The hamstring pull forced him to watch the team's final games from the bench. He felt tentative at the plate. Just hours before the Indians boarded an evening train for New York City, Rosen took extra batting practice in the empty Cleveland Stadium. "I can't seem to get that ball up in the air," he complained.[1]

Rosen may have been the only worrier in a city gripped with euphoria. The Indians and their fans were convinced the team would handle the Giants with ease. The three games scheduled for cavernous Cleveland Stadium were sold out, and scalpers were demanding $100 for a $25 box seat. Comedian Bob Hope, a part owner of the Indians, was deluged with requests. "Everybody in Hollywood except Crosby has hit me for tickets," he joked.[2]

Hotel rooms were scarce even in the nation's seventh largest city; officials fretted because Cleveland had to accommodate as many as 40,000 visitors with just 3,300 rooms. Furniture, appliance, and drug stores mounted television sets in their windows, while two electricians from the Cleveland Electric Illuminating Co. brought a radio to their manhole on Superior Avenue. There was only one ominous sign. When the Indians pulled out of Union Station for New York, they left on Track 13. Not to worry, one railroad official said. "Why, a dozen or more trains leave on Track 13 daily — and they seem to be all right."[3]

Now, from first base in the ancient Polo Grounds, Rosen watched Giants pitching coach Freddie Fitzsimmons walk past him to talk to pitcher Sal Maglie. Left-handed swinging Vic Wertz knelt in the on-deck circle and examined his bat. The odd-shaped Polo Grounds, its right-field wall looming less than 260 feet from homeplate, was perfectly suited for a power hitter like Wertz. A single would produce a run. The way Cleveland's Bob Lemon was pitching, Rosen thought, one would be enough. At the very worst, Rosen figured the Indians would split the first two games in the Polo Grounds before going back to Cleveland. With any luck, the Indians might win the World Series without ever returning to New York City.

Such a triumph would be a fitting conclusion for an extraordinary baseball team and a skilled front office. Not only had the

Indians established an American League record by winning 111 games, but, for that one year, Rosen believed they were the best team ever assembled. Even the substitutes contributed. Rosen remembered an August game in Boston when the Indians were losing to the Red Sox. But Hank Majeski, an aging reserve third baseman, delivered a three-run home run in the seventh inning to give Cleveland a crucial victory.

There was every reason to believe the Indians would produce their own dynasty. Most of the key players, Rosen included, were in their late 20s or early 30s. They would be productive for years to come. The Indians' minor league system was methodically churning out superior young prospects. At Cleveland's minor league team in Indianapolis, 21-year-old Herb Score was throwing his smoking fastball past startled Triple-A batters. At a luncheon at the Colonial Hotel, Lopez predicted that "Score is going to be great." [4]

Since 1948, the Indians had produced one outstanding team after another. They had averaged 95 victories a year, regularly attracted well over one million customers to their home games, negotiated lucrative television and radio contracts, and reaped a substantial profit every year. When Cleveland swept a late- season doubleheader from the second-place Yankees, some of the Indians taunted their defeated rivals. *Sports Illustrated* called it "The Twilight of the Gods." It was now Cleveland's time.

The Indians' great baseball success was no accident. The Indians developed into a winning and profitable team solely through the energetic efforts of two men—Bill Veeck and Hank Greenberg. Veeck organized a syndicate to buy the Indians in 1946 and a year later he recruited Greenberg to help direct the front office. They swiftly transformed a pathetic sixth-place ballclub into a powerful contender by trading shrewdly, pouring vast resources into the minor league system, and aggressively integrating the team.

Rosen's arrival in Cleveland in 1947 coincided with that of Veeck and Greenberg. When the Indians first called Rosen up from Oklahoma City, Veeck asked the young third baseman to fly to Chicago so he could personally meet him. As Rosen walked off the plane at six in the morning, he was astonished to see Veeck, "peg leg and all," waiting. Veeck paid for breakfast, returned Rosen to his plane, and handed him a check for $1,000. Rosen had never seen $1,000 before. [5]

But Bill Veeck spent his life doing the unexpected. When Veeck bought the Indians in 1946, he was just 33 years old and had little money of his own. But he was accustomed to defying the odds. Veeck's right leg was crushed by an anti-tank gun on Bougainville in World War II, and he was confined to a hospital bed for 18 months. On November 1, 1946, he was forced to return to a hospital where doctors amputated the leg. Ten weeks later, Veeck was fitted with an artificial leg in time for a party in his honor at the Hollenden House in Cleveland. He partied hard, worked hard, and rarely slept. Often, he could be found at Gruber's in Cleveland, hoisting drinks with the city's most influential newspapermen—Whitey Lewis and Frank Gibbons of the *Cleveland Press*, Gordon Cobbledick of the *Cleveland Plain Dealer*, and Ed McAuley of the *Cleveland News*. Hank Greenberg marveled at Veeck's ability to drink until four in the morning, run back to the stadium for a few hours' sleep on a trainer's table, and be ready for business at eight in the morning.

He refused to wear a tie and insisted upon being called "Bill." He hobbled through the stands during games, chatting with fans, ushers, and restroom attendants. He hired circus performers, set off fireworks, and gave away orchids and nylons to women. He switched Cleveland's home games from antiquated League Park to Cleveland Stadium, and erected a temporary screen fence to make it easier for players to hit home runs. His style offended most baseball executives, particularly George Weiss of the Yankees and Clark Griffith of the Washington Senators. But by 1948, the Indians won the World Series and established a major league attendance record of 2.6 million.

Veeck clearly was far more than a frantic entertainer. He grew up in a solid baseball family; his father ran the Chicago Cubs' pennant winners of 1929. Both Veeck and Greenberg recognized that baseball was just like any other business. General Motors and Ford invested in developing new products, then marketed them to attract customers. It was the same for baseball. It took money to develop great teams, but great teams attracted fans and produced profits. Veeck constructed a first-rate baseball organization in Cleveland, and ultimately put Greenberg in charge.

Because Veeck often operated as his own general manager, farm director, promotions manager, and treasurer, Greenberg had little to do at first. But by the end of 1948, Veeck asked him to direct the sprawling Cleveland minor league system with its 400 young players. Within a year, Greenberg advanced to become general manager and assume control of the entire baseball team.

Rosen owed his starting job at third base to Greenberg. Rosen's career with the Indians had been stalled because Cleveland had one of the game's best third baseman, Ken Keltner. On a July evening in 1941, Keltner's two back-handed stops of scorching groundballs ended Joe DiMaggio's 56-game hitting streak. Keltner's three-run home run in the playoff against the Boston Red Sox gave the Indians the 1948 pennant. He was popular with the Cleveland fans and the team's veteran players, who had no interest in having the brash, young Rosen take his job. In spring training, when Rosen would run out to third base to take groundballs, Keltner would shoo him aside. During batting practice, Rosen rarely saw a pitch he could hit. "They were protecting their guy," Rosen said years later.

Throughout the summer of 1949, though, it was evident that Keltner's skills were eroding. Greenberg complained that all Keltner could do was "drink and smoke with the rest of the boys." [6] By 1950, Greenberg handed Keltner his release and ordered Rosen into the Cleveland lineup. Greenberg knew that replacing Keltner with a young Jewish ballplayer would be controversial. But Greenberg concluded that Rosen was immune to pressure. Rosen led the league with 37 home runs and drove in 116 runs. The Indians finished just six games behind the Yankees, and appeared poised to contend for the next decade.

Rosen was one of the few Jewish players throughout baseball in 1950, and players and fans ruthlessly taunted him. Pitchers often aimed fastballs at his ribs, but Rosen refused to rub the spot where he'd been hit. Why give the pitcher that satisfaction? he asked. He took it as a compliment; pitchers never threw at mediocre hitters. But verbal taunts enraged him. At San Diego in 1949, pitcher Lou Tost smacked him with a fastball and added a few insults as Rosen jogged to first. Rosen charged the mound and delivered a powerful punch to Tost's jaw. During a game against Boston, one of the Red Sox reserves gave him "the Jew stuff." Finally, Rosen called time and marched toward the Boston dugout. Before he got there, Johnny Pesky and Bobbie Doerr grabbed the reserve player and shut him up. Rosen's temper was so explosive that his teammates kiddingly called him "Blowtop."

Rosen could also turn the tables. During batting practice one afternoon, Rosen took aim at Yankee lefthander Ed Lopat, who baffled power hitters with his assortment of slow curveballs. "Eddie," Rosen joked, "I could hit you falling right out of bed. I don't understand how you get by." An annoyed Lopat snapped, "OK, Big Shot. Someday, I'm going to throw three fastballs right by you and I'm going to tell you each time they're coming." Rosen laughed. "The day that happens, Eddie, I'll give you a half-hour to make the announcement, and then I'll kiss your ass at home-plate." Lopat waited nearly two years until a key game when Rosen was at bat. From the Yankee dugout, Rosen heard the loud voice of Hank Bauer. "Hey, Rosie, this time." Lopat heaved three fastballs past the startled Rosen who stormed away from the plate. Lopat pointed toward his pants and shouted, "Hey, Flipper, you forgot something." [7]

Rosen ended up in Cleveland by pure chance. Born in South Carolina, he grew up in Miami, where he boxed, played football at Florida Military Academy, and pitched for a softball team. His flipping the ball toward homeplate earned him the nickname "Flip." His passion was baseball, and the Red Sox offered him a tryout and sent him to one of their farm clubs in Virginia. The manager, Elmer Yoter, a one-time Chicago Cubs' infielder, was not impressed with the 18-year-old Rosen. "Get a lunch pail and go on home," Yoter told him. Crushed, Rosen nearly went back to Florida when the local director of the YMCA, Frank Stein, took pity on him. Stein told Rosen that a friend of his, Jimmy Gruzdis, was managing a Class D team in Thomasville, North Carolina, and needed a third baseman. Rosen took a four-and-a-half hour bus ride to Thomasville and, within minutes, signed a contract for $90 a month on the glove compartment of Gruzdis' car. That night, Rosen singled in his first trip to the plate, and Gruzdis quickly recognized his new third baseman had major league talent. After long night games in the intense North Carolina heat, Gruzdis would summon Rosen to the ballpark the next morning for extra batting practice.

At the end of the season, Rosen entered the Navy and earned the rank of lieutenant. When World War II ended, Rosen was property of the Cleveland Indians, which had a working agreement with Thomasville. Rosen quickly advanced through the Cleveland system, hitting .349 at Oklahoma City in 1947 and .327 with 25 home runs at Kansas City in 1948. The Indians sent Rosen back to the minor leagues in 1949, a decision he later thought cost them the pennant. Keltner was slipping rapidly and Boudreau often had to play himself at third base. The Indians finished eight games behind the pennant-winning Yankees. A year later, Keltner was gone, and third base in Cleveland belonged to Rosen.

A prime reason for Cleveland's success was that Veeck and Greenberg—alone among American League team officials in the late 1940s—recognized that the quickest way to build a contending team was to sign black players. While most teams were hesitant to integrate in 1948, Veeck and Greenberg knew perfectly well that the teams that aggressively recruited blacks would probably emerge as the strongest.

Veeck's choice as the first black player in Cleveland was Larry Doby, a young second baseman for the Newark Eagles of the Negro Leagues. A frightened failure in 1947, Doby developed into one of baseball's finest center fielders by the next season. Doby batted .318 in the 1948 World Series and won the fourth game in Cleveland Stadium with a home run. Doby was only the beginning. At the height of the 1948 pennant race, Veeck and Greenberg signed Satchel Paige, then approaching his 50th birthday and a legend in the Negro Leagues. That same season, they signed outfielders Al Smith, Dave Hoskins, and Minnie Minoso, the latter a 23-year-old black Cuban. During the winter, Veeck made a special trip to Puerto Rico in search of 6-foot-4 first baseman Luke Easter. By advertising for him on radio, Veeck located —and signed—the powerfully built home run hitter. [8]

By 1950, the Indians, Brooklyn Dodgers, and New York Giants were the most integrated teams in baseball. "The Dodgers and Indians selected Negro talent in a non-competitive market," writes Jules Tygiel. [9] Effa Manley, co-owner of the Newark Eagles, was astonished that most major league teams failed to "get wise to the gold mine which lies in the Negro baseball talent." [10] Watching other American League teams shun black players,

Greenberg thought they were being directed by "imbeciles." [11]

The Indians also sought the best players from Latin America. In 1948, they signed Roberto Avila of Mexico, whom the Dodgers declined to sign after a tryout. In Cleveland, he developed into a .300 hitter. Nicknamed "Beto" by his teammates, Avila was such a clever bunter that he and lead-off hitter Al Smith devised a special play. Whenever Smith was on first, Avila would lay down a bunt to third base and beat the throw to first. Instead of stopping at second, Smith employed his great speed to outrun the shortstop, who had to cover third base. [12]

This swift integration was not painless. Easter, Doby, and Smith were ritually thrown at by opposing pitchers. Easter, a miserable flop as a 1949 rookie, was booed mercilessly. There were suggestions in Cleveland that the reason the Indians did not quickly win another pennant after 1948 was because of the large number of blacks. Actually, the opposite was true. The Indians' great success in the 1950s was largely due to the team's willingness to integrate.

To direct this team on the field, Greenberg personally selected Al Lopez, a move even his harshest critics conceded was brilliant. Lopez became one of the league's most coveted managers, a shrewd handler of the talent that Greenberg and Veeck assembled.

As a teenager growing up in Tampa, Al Lopez earned $5 a week catching Walter Johnson of the Washington Senators during spring training. He was the best defensive catcher in the National League throughout the 1930s and 1940s, once catching an entire season in Pittsburgh without allowing a passed ball. By the time he finished his playing career in Cleveland in 1947, he could not hit at all, but the Indian coaches valued his advice on pitchers. When the Indians wanted to convert outfielder Bob Lemon into a pitcher, Cleveland coach Bill McKechnie asked Lopez for help. "Bill, the only thing with him is control," Lopez told McKechnie. "If he can get the ball over the plate, he'll be all right." Determined to put his skills to managing, Lopez moved to Indianapolis in 1948 to direct the Pirates' top farm team. The very first year, Lopez' team won 100 games and the American Association pennant and followed with strong second-place finishes in 1949 and 1950. The following year, Lopez advanced to Cleveland.

Lopez was quiet and professional. "He never said much, but he knew every damned thing that was going on," Al Smith later said.[13] He rarely called clubhouse meetings because he thought they were a waste of time. Having watched John McGraw ruthlessly drive his New York Giants, Lopez concluded players were more likely to lose confidence "if somebody is hollering [at them] to do better." He loathed having to fine his players; in his first four years in Cleveland, Lopez issued just one fine. He later handed back half the money to the pitcher whose offense had been to miss a train.[14]

His favorites were players like Rosen. They came to the park, put on their uniforms, and never complained about injuries. Years later, Lopez recalled in 1951 when Walt Dropo smashed a line drive off Rosen's face. Although Rosen went to the hospital that night with two swollen eyes, he insisted upon joining the Indians the next day when they traveled by train to Philadelphia. Cleveland trainer Wally Bock applied ice to Rosen's face and by gametime, his black eyes opened and he played. Lopez would tell the Indians, "Look, if I put your name in the lineup, I expect 100 percent effort. If you can't give that to me, all you have to do is tell me that you're not able to play that day."

For all his success directing the Indians, Lopez disliked managing. "Hell no," he barked when a reporter asked if managing was fun. He suffered from chronic insomnia and after night games often read Westerns or detective novels before dozing off at four in the morning. The tense Yankee-Indian pennant races were murder on his stomach, and doctors warned him to avoid raw foods and ice cream at night. He took defeat hard. "There's only one thing worse than losing a game," said Bob Lemon, "and that's watching Al sit there in the clubhouse and stare at his toes after you've lost one." [15]

Although Lopez managed for American League teams, he preferred the National League's swifter style, with players who could catch the ball, bunt, hit behind the runners, and steal a base. He had no interest in heavy-legged sluggers, such as Jim Lemon, Ralph Kiner, and Roy Sievers. Greenberg finally traded Jim Lemon to Washington because Lopez refused to play him. Later in 1959, when Lopez managed Veeck's Chicago White Sox, he advised Veeck to quit wasting time trying to buy Sievers from the Senators. Sievers was so slow afoot, Lopez would tell Veeck, that he would have to hit .330 with 40 home runs to help the team at all. "This is my kind of team," Lopez said of a White Sox club that featured stolen bases, clever bunting, and air-tight defense. [16]

Lopez' greatest strength was handling pitchers. And few managers had better pitching to handle. He could call upon righthanders Bob Lemon, Early Wynn, Mike Garcia, and Bob Feller. Lemon had the game's best sinker; often it darted so wildly that he had trouble keeping it in the strike zone. Feller had lost the steam off his fastball, but developed a sharp slider to go with a curveball that Rosen regarded as the best in baseball. Wynn earned a reputation as the only pitcher who would knock down Ted Williams with a pitch. Sometimes, he even threw at his teammates. Wynn enjoyed pitching batting practice, but refused to stand behind a protective screen. Any hitter unfortunate enough to scorch a line drive near Wynn could be certain that Wynn would hit him with the next pitch. But Wynn also protected his teammates. When pitchers regularly threw at Smith and Doby, Wynn growled in a clubhouse meeting, "We can't score any runs with Al and Doby on their backs." Everybody knew what that meant. [17]

When his starting pitchers tired, Lopez turned to a bullpen dominated by two rookies—lefthander Don Mossi and righthander Ray Narleski. They joined the Indians in the spring of 1954 as starting pitchers, but Lopez already had five starters. What he needed were dependable relief pitchers who could enter the game in the eighth or ninth inning and stop a rally. During a spring training game in Las Vegas against the New York Giants, Lopez planned to let Feller pitch the first five innings and then turn the game over to Mossi and Narleski. As Lopez munched on a sandwich before the game, a friend told him he wanted to place a small bet on the Indians. Lopez shook his head. "Don't bet on ballgames, especially in the spring. I'm looking at two kids and Feller. And Feller stinks in the spring." The friend changed his mind and bet on the Giants. It proved to be a bad bet: Feller, Mossi, and Narleski combined to hold the Giants to one run. [18]

Although Giants manager Leo Durocher described Mossi that spring as a "good-looking lefthander," Lopez preferred to use Narleski in the ninth inning of a close game.[19] His reasoning was simple: Nobody on the Cleveland staff that year threw harder than Ray Narleski. The 25-year-old righthander used his terrifying fastball to save 13 games in 1954—two more than the entire Cleveland staff saved in 1953.

Lopez' first team in 1951 nearly won the pennant. Feller, Wynn, and Garcia each won 20 games, and the Indians led the league in home runs. Greenberg thought the Indians should have won the pennant, but the Yankees prevailed by five games because of crisper infield defense and a deeper bench. A year later, the Yankees edged the Indians by two games. Following a third consecutive second-place finish in 1953, even Lopez was discouraged. His insomnia was worse, he confided to Greenberg. Cincinnati had contacted him about managing. Maybe it was time for a change, Lopez suggested. Greenberg would not hear of it. The Indians were winning 90 games a season. Lopez was his man. Finally, Lopez relented, "If you want me back, I'll be back." [20]

Both Lopez and Greenberg entered 1954 squarely on the spot. The Indians looked like a team that could not win the games that counted. Gordon Cobbledick, predicting a sixth consecutive pennant for the Yankees, wrote that the Indians would have to demonstrate "this year they can win the 'big one.' They've been a long time earning a reputation as a team that looks like a champion until the chips are down." Harry Jones, the baseball writer for the *Plain Dealer*, offered an even harsher assessment: "You find little team spirit on the Indians. The Indians are not a team at all, but a crowd of players, each striving for personal achievement." [21]

But Greenberg had traded judiciously. He obtained right-handed starting pitcher Art Houtteman from Detroit, and signed his old friend, Hal Newhouser, as a left-handed relief pitcher. He added Dave Philley and Wally Westlake to a talented bench. On June 1, he culminated his work by trading an obscure pitcher to Baltimore for Wertz, a powerful, 200-pound left-handed hitting outfielder who had played most of his career in Detroit.

Wertz joined the team in Boston, but the last thing Lopez needed was another outfielder. "Can you play first base?" Lopez asked him. Wertz' answer was not reassuring: Detroit manager Fred Hutchinson let him play a few games at first base in spring training. "I dropped a fly ball and he took me out and wouldn't let me play there again," Wertz said. But Lopez was desperate for a first baseman so he could return Rosen to third base. He penciled Wertz in at first. [22]

It was the key move. In June and July, the Indians won 41 of 58 games. They crushed second-division teams, winning 89 and losing just 21 to the league's five worst teams. But the Yankees hung close. When the Yankees took two out of three from the Indians in early September in New York, the Cleveland lead had been cut to three and a half games. Would the Indians collapse again? Two weeks later, in a doubleheader against the Yankees before 84,587 people in Cleveland Stadium, that question was answered. Rosen doubled home two runs off Allie Reynolds to help Lemon win the first game, 3-1. Wynn won the second game. One week later the Indians clinched the pennant in Detroit.

The Indians were heavy favorites to beat the Giants. The bookmakers set the odds at 9-5. Privately, Lopez believed the Indians would win in five games. Even the writers had turned around. Harry Jones and Cobbledick predicted the Indians would win in six games. Many compared Cleveland to the 1927 Yankees, who won 110 games. "Before I granted the superiority of the 1927 Yanks, I would want to see them hitting against today's pitching," Cobbledick wrote. "More specifically, I would want to see them hitting against the Indians' pitching." [23]

The Indians were relaxed. Just before they boarded a train for New York City, they took a final workout in Cleveland Stadium. Al Smith lined to right field and chortled, "Home run in the Polo Grounds." Batting against Lemon, Rosen kept asking the righthander to throw a different pitch. "What are you after?" Lemon finally complained. Rosen laughed, "I just want to see what you can throw. I may be hitting against you next year." [24]

The Giants, meanwhile, were surprisingly confident. They knew they had a fine team; Durocher believed it was stronger than his 1951 pennant winner. Outfielder Don Mueller batted .342, third baseman Henry Thompson and left fielder Monte Irvin combined to hit 45 home runs, while Alvin Dark was a far better shortstop than his Cleveland counterparts. Willie Mays hit 41 home runs, led the league with a .345 average, and was the game's most gifted center fielder. "All you have to do is make them hit the ball in the park," explained relief pitcher Marv Grissom. "Willie will catch it anywhere." [25]

Grissom, Maglie, Johnny Antonelli, Ruben Gomez, Don Liddle, and Hoyt Wilhelm formed a pitching staff that in 56 games that season held opponents to two runs or less. In Arizona where the teams trained together, the Giants beat the Indians in 13 of 21 exhibition games. "There really wasn't a question in our minds that we'd win," Giants second baseman Davey Williams later said. [26]

The Indians also were suffering from a variety of bumps and bruises. Doby's shoulder was sore, and Rosen's leg was showing no sign of improvement. When the Indians concluded their last workout in the Polo Grounds the day before the World Series, Rosen asked coach Red Kress to pitch extra batting practice. Rosen knocked six line drives into the upper deck of the Polo Grounds. Sore leg or not, Rosen was set to play in his second World Series.

Rosen watched Fitzsimmons motion to the bullpen. Durocher, playing the percentages, wanted the left-handed Liddle to pitch to Wertz, who had stroked three singles off Maglie. As Maglie left for the center-field clubhouse, catcher Wes Westrum patted him on the back.

With Doby and Rosen taking their leads, Liddle fired his first pitch. The ball jumped off Wertz' bat; Wertz later said he never hit a ball harder. As it rose sharply in the air over second base, Wertz was convinced it would reach the center-field bleachers 460 feet away. At second base, Doby took a few steps to his right, turned, and watched Mays in center field. Doby played it correctly. If the ball fell in for extra bases, he had plenty of time to score. If Mays caught it, Doby could tag up for third. Rosen instinctively knew the mammoth drive would reach the wall for extra bases, and he broke for second. [27]

Mays already had turned; all anyone could see was the black numeral 24 on the back of his white jersey. But Mays could clearly see the ball and knew he had a chance. [28] Davey Williams at second base noticed that Mays began slowing down. To Williams, it meant he was going to catch the ball. Mays glanced over his left shoulder and stretched out his glove hand. Just a few steps from the wall, he grasped the drive — 445 feet away from homeplate.

Mays swerved to his left, his hat flew off, and he fired a bullet to Williams, who crisply turned and threw to Westrum covering home. The throws were so accurate that Doby barely had time to tag second and reach third safely. Rosen scampered back to first base. The crowd roared in delight. Rosen and the Indians were stunned. After the game, a disconsolate Lopez said, "Wertz hits the ball as far as anybody ever will, and it's just an out." [29]

The Indians, however, still had runners at first and third and only one out. Durocher's first order of business was to replace Liddle with the right-handed Grissom. Durocher knew perfectly well it was still advantage, Cleveland. Lopez countered by sending left-handed hitting Dale Mitchell to pinch hit for Majeski. Grissom walked Mitchell to load the bases. Lopez summoned pinch-hitter Dave Pope. A flyball would give the Indians the lead. A slow groundball. A wild pitch. But Pope took a called third strike, and catcher Jim Hegan swatted a deep flyball to the 315-foot sign in left field. When Irvin grasped the ball, the Indians were through.

They never would recover. In the bottom of the 10th inning, with Mays on second and Henry Thompson on first, Durocher called for his best pinch-hitter, Dusty Rhodes. Rhodes had homered 15 times that year, usually with the game on the line. Lemon threw a curveball, and Rhodes lifted a high pop fly to right field. Mickey Grasso, who had replaced Hegan, saw Rhodes hit the ball on the bat's trademark, and was certain it was an easy out. Avila thought it was so shallow that he raced out to right field to make the play. But the ball, shoved forward by a breeze, fell into the hands of a fan and beyond the reach of Pope at the 260-foot mark in right field. "The darn thing just barely made it even with the wind helping it," Pope said after the game. In any other park in America, Wertz would have homered and Rhodes would have flied out. [30]

Mays was jubilant. Clapping his hands in delight, he leapt past Rosen, who dejectedly stared at the right-field wall with his hands on his hips. The Giants poured from their dugout to surround Rhodes. A disgusted Lemon tossed his glove so high in the air that it landed behind homeplate. Shocked, the Indians walked to their clubhouse in center field. Wertz slumped in despair at his locker. "They were throwing me a lot of stuff and I was hitting all of it," he said. "It doesn't mean a thing, though. We lost the game." [31]

And the series. Years later, Rosen said that "there's no doubt the game changed" after Mays' catch. "The series changed right there. If we go ahead, you never have the opportunity for Rhodes to come up and do what he did."

The next day, Wynn gave up four base hits. One was a home run by Rhodes and the Indians lost, 3-1. For the first time in anybody's memory, a frustrated Lopez lost his temper when a reporter asked him what the turning point was in the game. "There wasn't any turning point," Lopez said. The reporter persisted. Finally, Lopez snapped, "What are you trying to do? Ask your questions and answer them?" [32]

The Indians boarded a train for Cleveland, while the Giants chartered a plane. Rosen's leg was so sore that Lopez benched him. It would not have mattered had he played. Before 71,555 people in Cleveland Stadium, the Giants knocked Garcia from the mound and won, 6-2. On the fourth day, a sunny Saturday afternoon, Indians Vice President Nate Dolin was fretting that a Giants' sweep would force the Indians to return $750,000 worth of tickets to the fifth game in Cleveland. When he saw Giants owner Horace Stoneham, Dolin joked, "I hope you don't beat us today. It will be a disaster." Stoneham, Dolin knew, needed the World Series money badly. [33]

Rosen tried to play. "Sure the leg still is tender, but I can swing a bat and hitting is what we need," Rosen gamely told reporters. [34] Lopez, admitting his back was "up to the wall," called on Lemon to pitch on two-days' rest. The Giants won, 7-4. The World Series was over.

It was a crushing blow to the Indians. A team that won 111 games had fallen in four. A team that never knew a serious losing streak had been humiliated. Early Wynn, serving as guest columnist for the *Cleveland News*, asked Cobbledick, "What can you write about a thing like this?" [35] A pall hung over the team that autumn and winter. By the following spring, the team was still shaken. Rosen thought an ominous feeling pervaded the clubhouse. It was time to trade some of the players, he thought. Things would never be the same.

There would be no Cleveland dynasty. In 1955, the Indians finished three games behind the Yankees and by 1956 attendance dipped below one million. Rosen quit in a salary dispute with Greenberg, Feller retired, and Lopez left for Chicago. Score's elbow gave out. Bad luck gave way to bad management. Greenberg was fired. The players so carefully trained in Greenberg's farm system were recklessly traded away by his successor. The team owners did little to sustain the player development system.

By doing so, they ignored the basic rule of business: It takes money to build a winner. As attendance declined and financial losses mounted, the owners nearly moved the Indians to another city. The Indians produced just 10 winning teams in the four decades after Mays' catch.

As the New York Giants pounded each other with delight on the Cleveland infield, Rosen went to the Indians' clubhouse and telephoned his in-laws, who were staying at his home. Could they take care of the Rosens' young son for an extra day? Then he borrowed a couple of sleeping pills from the trainer and checked into the Statler Hotel at the corner of Euclid Avenue and 12th Street. Rosen swallowed the pills and slept for 18 hours.

"Nobody will ever know," Rosen said nearly four decades later. "For years, we had been the bridesmaids of the Yankees. We finally beat the Yankees. And in what should have been a glorious year, we wound up absolutely in the depths of despair. We felt like we were the laughing stock. It was just a horrible, horrible experience. And to this day, it's a real downer when I think about it, when I try to recall it. And I try not to. You remember that you were part of something that could have been, and wasn't."

Chapter 2

Rocky, the Howitzer, and the Home Run King

"That kid in center, Maris, I like him." — Casey Stengel

Everybody knew how good Herb Score was. His left-handed fastball was so overpowering, that his minor league manager called him "The Howitzer." Even before he pitched a game in the major leagues, *Sports Illustrated* described him as "so good you can't believe it." Ted Williams said Score was the best left-handed pitcher he ever faced, and Hank Aaron told Score he threw harder than any pitcher he had seen. When the Boston Red Sox offered the Indians $1 million for his contract, Hank Greenberg said no thanks. "If nothing happens to him," said Hall-of-Fame outfielder Tris Speaker, "this kid has got to be the greatest."

As a rookie in 1955, Score won 16 games and led the league in strikeouts. A year later, he increased his victory total to 20 and once again struck out more batters than any American League pitcher. At 23, he was the best pitcher in baseball.

Regarded universally as a left-handed Bob Feller, Score had the same searing fastball and sharp curveball. The same scout, Cy Slapnicka, had signed them both. As the general manager of the Indians in 1935, Slapnicka criss-crossed Iowa in search of the 16-year-old Feller. Fifteen years later, a policeman in Lake Worth, Florida, advised Slapnicka to check out a hard-throwing lefthander at the local high school. "One look was all I needed," Slapnicka said. Three years later, Slapnicka signed Score to a staggering $60,000 bonus. [1]

When he joined the Indians' farm system in 1952, Score had grown to 6-foot-2, weighed slightly over 180 pounds, and had boyishly good looks. He delivered his fastball with a straight, overhand motion, and a follow-through so powerful that he often brushed his left elbow against his right knee. Eventually he had to buy a pad to protect the knee. When he concluded his delivery, he was so twisted around that he no longer could see the plate. To find out if the pitch was a ball or strike, he would whirl toward the center-field scoreboard.

Early on as a professional, Score's control was erratic. Warming up at Reading in 1953, Score heaved a pitch over the catcher's head and into the fender of a parked car. Score once battered catcher Birdie Tebbetts with so many wild fastballs that Tebbetts finally shouted, "Hey kid, I've had enough if you have." [2] Knowing he had to do something, Greenberg asked Ted Wilks, a one-time big winner with the St. Louis Cardinals, to work with Score full time. "You've got a good arm," Greenberg told Score. "I want you to listen to Ted Wilks." Wilks changed Score's leg kick, refined his curveball, and nagged him into throwing strikes. The results were obvious. At Indianapolis in 1954, Herb Score won 22 games, lost just five, struck out 330 batters, and wore out two of Hank Foiles' thick catcher's mitts. Teammate Joe Altobelli thought that if Indianapolis had scored a few extra runs, Score would have been 25-2. [3]

Even though the 1954 Indians had the game's best pitching staff, they knew they had to find room the following spring for Score. He instantly dominated American League hitters. Yogi Berra once told Al Lopez that when Score threw his curveball for strikes, "you might as well have walked away from the plate." [4]

As good as he was, Score was dogged by freak illnesses and injuries. When he was three years old, a bakery truck smacked into him, shattering both his legs. As a young boy, he suffered from pneumonia and rheumatic fever, the latter so serious he spent months in bed recovering. At age 15, he broke an ankle and was operated on for an appendicitis. The illness and injuries followed him to the major leagues: A dislocated left collarbone in 1953, pneumonia again in 1954, a bad stomach in 1956. A neighborhood priest was so worried about the young Score that he gave him a relic of St. Jude, the patron saint for lost causes. Throughout his life, Score prayed to St. Jude, although he joked, "I guess in my case he's got his hands full." [5]

Score's development into a premier major league pitcher happened by careful design. He was just one part of an elaborate player production system designed by Hank Greenberg. The cost? One hundred thousand dollars to locate, sign, and develop just one player. Greenberg's goal? To end the Yankee dynasty and replace it with one of his own in Cleveland.

From his corner office overlooking the West Third Street entrance of Cleveland Stadium, Indians General Manager Hank Greenberg made a daily check on his far-flung minor league empire. By telephone, wire, and mail, he stayed in constant touch with the Indians' nine minor league teams, scattered in small towns such as Reading, Pennsylvania, and Fargo, North Dakota. Eager for any scrap of information, Greenberg instructed his private secretary, Bob Gill, to comb newspapers from across the country. Throughout that summer of 1956, he could chart the progress of the players he was convinced would help the Indians win and make money for the next decade.

Greenberg's favorites were players like himself; hitters with powerful home run swings. At the Indians' Triple-A team in Indianapolis, 21-year-old outfielder Roger Maris was hitting 17 home runs and batting .293. Rocky Colavito, a 6-foot-3 outfielder whom Greenberg loaned to San Diego of the Pacific Coast League, was hitting 12 home runs in just 35 games. At Mobile of the Southern Association, left-handed-hitting first baseman Gordy Coleman was driving in 118 runs with 27 home runs, and catcher Dick Brown was hammering 24 home runs. Catcher Russ Nixon wasn't showing much power at Indianapolis, but he had a .319 batting average and displayed the skill to handle major league pitchers.

Nixon's catching ability was a must because quality pitchers were scattered at every level of Greenberg's system. Bob Lemon, Early Wynn, and Mike Garcia were aging, but Greenberg's system had already produced Herb Score, Don Mossi, and Ray Narleski, and more were on the way. At Indianapolis, lefthander Bud Daley was winning 11 of 12 games and 6-foot-4 lefthander Hank Aguirre was showing a good fastball. Greenberg's pitchers at Mobile led the Southern Association in team earned run average, and at Reading they shattered a league record with 49 consecutive scoreless innings, including a five-hit shutout by righthander Bobby Locke over the Yankees' Double-A team at Binghamton. Locke was leading the Eastern League in victories, 19-year-old righthander Gary Bell was tops in strikeouts, and

20-year-old righthander Jim Grant was winning a dozen games. Jim Perry, whom Greenberg had just signed for $4,000 out of a junior college in North Carolina, was striking out 124 batters in 120 innings at North Platte in the Nebraska State League. At Vidalia, 6-foot-3 lefthander Dick Stigman outclassed opposing hitters as he led the Georgia State League in strikeouts, earned run average, and complete games. Righthander Wynn Hawkins was winning 16 games for Fayetteville of the Carolina League and righthander Ron Taylor, who had just turned 18, was producing 17 victories for Daytona Beach of the Florida State League.

The Cleveland farm system with its 368 players was Hank Greenberg's passion. Although *Cleveland Press* sports columnist Whitey Lewis denounced Greenberg as a flop when it came to trades, Greenberg never believed he could overtake the Yankees with glitzy deals. The Indians would have to beat them at their own game—developing better players in the farm system. [6]

Before Greenberg took control of the Indians' minor league system in 1949, player development was haphazard. The Indians owned seven minor league teams and had working agreements with nine more, but that's where the coordination ended. Each team trained separately and the individual team managers taught the game's fundamentals to the young players as they saw fit.

Greenberg instituted massive changes in his effort to build the best farm system in baseball and convinced the Indians' owners to spend lavishly on it. In 1950, they spent more than $1 million on their farm system when all of organized baseball budgeted only $5 million for player development. In 1951 and 1952, the Indians spent $600,000 on bonuses for young high school and college players, including $75,000 for left-handed pitcher Billy Joe Davidson and $35,000 apiece for infielders Billy Moran and Jerry Del Gaudio. Greenberg insisted that the Indians' minor leaguers train every spring at one central facility. He personally selected a site at Daytona Beach with a large set of barracks, a mess hall, and a spacious recreation area for ping-pong, pool, and movies.

But by day, the players lived baseball. On the diamonds behind the barracks, the minor league managers would teach each player the fundamentals Greenberg's way. At the end of a long day, Greenberg joined his managers, coaches, and scouts in a meeting room to chart the progress of each player on a blackboard. When spring training ended and the Indians' farm teams headed north, Greenberg was confident each player had been assigned to the right team.

He hired a horde of minor league managers and scouts, many of whom he had known during his playing days in Detroit—Jo Jo White, Merrill May, Spud Chandler, Red Ruffing, Kerby Farrell, Mike McNally, Clyde McCullough, and Pinky May. He instructed his minor league managers to develop future major leaguers and not worry about winning baseball games. "We're here to find players to star for the Cleveland Indians," Greenberg told his managers. "Your jobs for next year and the year after don't depend on whether you win or lose pennants. [We] want our players studied and taught in uniform fashion." He would remind them of his chief goal: "We're in this for one reason—to make Cleveland the best baseball club in the country. Not for one year, but forever." [7]

Greenberg's scouts outhustled their rivals in their pursuit of talent. Rocky Colavito was a 16-year-old outfielder who grew up just 20 minutes from Yankee Stadium. Often he waited outside the stadium to collect the autographs of Joe DiMaggio and other Yankee stars. But the Yankee scouts were not impressed, leaving Colavito to choose between the Indians and Philadelphia Phillies. The Phillies wanted him as a pitcher, but McNally liked his powerful swing. On a rainy December afternoon in 1950, Colavito signed with the Indians for $4,500. [8]

Greenberg had to compete with college football to sign Maris, who in high school in Fargo, North Dakota, once ran four kickoffs back for touchdowns in a single game. Bud Wilkinson wanted him to play tailback for Oklahoma. But the left-handed batting Maris also pounded American Legion pitching, and Greenberg's scouts were convinced that young Maris was more interested in baseball than four years of college. Greenberg asked Maris and his father to fly to Cleveland in 1952 for a workout. Greenberg quickly recognized Maris' talents: He ran well, had a strong arm, and a graceful swing. Forget football and sign with the Indians, Greenberg told Maris and his father. Greenberg pointed out that the National Football League paid less than major league baseball. Why waste time in college? Greenberg asked Maris, when he could be learning to play the game in the Indians' farm system.

Maris signed with Cleveland for $15,000 and was assigned to the Indians' Class C team in Fargo. Maris advanced quickly, hitting 32 home runs and stealing 25 bases for Keokuk in the Three-I League in 1954. [9]

Greenberg's insistence upon building a strong farm system was a product of his own experience. As a home run-hitting first baseman for the Detroit Tigers in the 1930s, Greenberg watched the Yankees outspend their American League rivals on player development. He never forgot the Yankees' top farm club at Newark in 1937, which included outfielder Charlie Keller, second baseman Joe Gordon, and pitcher Atley Donald. The Yankees produced a succession of stars to win seven pennants from 1936 to 1943.

Greenberg did his best to allow his Tigers to keep pace. Powerfully built, standing over 6-foot-3, Hank Greenberg was one of the most dominant hitters of the 1930s. Only Jimmie Foxx of the Boston Red Sox and Lou Gehrig of the Yankees could match Greenberg for brute power. "When this Greenberg hits a ball on the nose, it stays hit," wrote Shirley Povich of the *Washington Post*. He hit 58 home runs for the Tigers in 1938 and just missed breaking Babe Ruth's record on the final day of the season in Cleveland. Pitchers loathed facing him with the game on the line. He drove in a staggering 183 runs in 1937 and, to show that was no fluke, drove in 150 runs for the pennant-winning Tigers in 1940.

In an era in which baseball was dominated by players with Italian, Germanic, or Irish names, Greenberg was the first great Jewish ballplayer. Al Rosen, growing up in Florida, revered Greenberg. Actor Walter Matthau fondly remembered years later how excited he had been as a youth when Greenberg made a fundraising appearance at a Jewish settlement house in New York City. [10]

Fiercely competitive, he could not stand to lose. More than 30 years after he played his last baseball game, he met young Detroit pitcher Mark Fidrych at the Beverly Hills Tennis Club. Later, Fidrych heckled Greenberg as the old home run hitter played tennis. An infuriated Greenberg stormed up to Fidrych and snapped, "I can hit anything you pitch—down the middle, outside, inside, curveball, slider." Greenberg later explained his outburst: "You got to intimidate pitchers." [11]

Although Greenberg was the only one of four children not to graduate from college, he was bright, charming, and knew the right people; his close friends included Louis Marx, the toy manufacturer. He married Caral Gimbel, the dark-haired heiress to the family that owned Saks Fifth Avenue and Gimbels. He sported the uniform of lawyers and bankers—expensive pinstripe suits—and combed his black hair straight back off his face.

He was determined to prosper. As a young minor leaguer for the Tigers, he wrote Detroit owner Frank Navin and threatened to quit unless Navin increased his $400 per month salary. Later when he was making $75,000 a year, Greenberg became the first player to have the team defer part of his salary to save income taxes. Unlike other players, he was frugal. By his own reckoning, he saved $300,000 of the $447,000 he made during his career.

Greenberg had retired as an active player when he met Bill Veeck during the 1947 Yankee-Dodger World Series. Dining after one of the games at Toots Shor's, Greenberg and Veeck argued about baseball from 7:30 in the evening until the closing hour of four in the morning. Then Veeck asked Greenberg if he wanted to play or coach. Neither, Greenberg said. But he might be interested in working for Veeck in the Cleveland front office. Veeck took him up on the offer at a salary of $15,000 and by 1949 promoted him to farm director. [12]

Greenberg assumed complete control of the team after Veeck sold the Indians in 1949. Now his personality dominated the team. Where Veeck was gregarious and outgoing, Greenberg was aloof and intellectual. Veeck had counted many of the Cleveland sportswriters as his friends and flattered them by seeking their advice. Before Veeck hired Rogers Hornsby as his manager with the St. Louis Browns, he checked with Gordon Cobbledick. Veeck regarded Whitey Lewis of the *Press* as the "most cutting and caustic" writer in Cleveland. But no matter what Lewis wrote in the afternoon paper, Veeck would hoist a drink with him that evening at Max Gruber's in suburban Cleveland. [13]

Greenberg not only refused to drink with reporters, he could barely stand to talk to them. Even during baseball games, he avoided the press box, preferring to sit with Indians Vice President Nate Dolin in a small box that hung below the right-field upper deck. [14] Greenberg knew more about baseball than the sportswriters and made little effort to hide his disdain for the press, which he described as "miserable." Lewis complained about Greenberg's "seeming inability to make love with the press," and chided him for being "unskilled in public relations."

Greenberg was convinced the Cleveland writers disliked him because in 1950 he had fired one of their favorites, player manager Lou Boudreau. Neither Greenberg nor Veeck ever thought much of Boudreau's ability as a manager. But Veeck, fearful of the reaction from writers and fans, never had the courage to make the change. Greenberg decided to replace Boudreau with Al Lopez, and he concocted an elaborate scheme to mislead the *Plain Dealer* and *Press.* He called a press conference at Cleveland Stadium and arranged to have Lopez fly into Cleveland under an assumed name. To guarantee secrecy, Greenberg had Lopez stay at his Shaker Heights home. They ate a late breakfast and drove to the ballpark. [15]

Reporters had been expecting Greenberg to rename Boudreau. Harry Jones of the *Plain Dealer* reported that salary questions were "the only cause of delay" in the announcement that Boudreau would return. When Greenberg announced Lopez would replace Boudreau, the Cleveland writers were livid. They'd been had.

Lewis, in particular, delighted in tormenting the thin-skinned Greenberg. A talented writer relentlessly on the attack, Lewis was the city's most controversial columnist. Nobody escaped his barbs. As far as he was concerned, he knew more about Cleveland sports than Hank Greenberg and was enraged by Greenberg's put-downs.

Lewis was 52 in 1956, and, although his blond hair—always carefully parted down the middle—was turning gray, he was still known by the nickname "Whitey" instead of his real name, "Franklin." He grew up on the city's east side and as a teenager shot pool with his friend Bob Hope. Lewis later played halfback on the same Glenville High School team as Benny Friedman and moved on for a year of college at Purdue. Bored by academics, he dropped out of school to work as a lifeguard in Florida, then quickly joined an Orlando newspaper. He loved covering sports and in 1929 returned to Cleveland as a boxing writer for the *Press.* By 1939 Lewis was the paper's No. 1 sports columnist, free to write on the Indians, football, or boxing. During World War II, he accompanied Yankee outfielders Johnny Lindell and Tuck Stainback and former Cleveland catcher Steve O'Neill on a 30,000-mile trip throughout the South Pacific. They regaled the

American soldiers with baseball stories, leading one officer to tell Lewis, "Nobody except the Japanese ever held these kids' interest that long." [16] Lewis covered the pennant-winning Indians in 1948, wrote a book about the team's history, and persuaded close friends Bill Veeck and Lou Boudreau to join him at a book-autographing session in downtown Cleveland.

Within a year, Veeck sold the team, Boudreau was fired, and Greenberg was in charge. Lewis savaged Greenberg's trades, particularly a 1951 fiasco in which Greenberg sent Minnie Minoso to the White Sox for a washed-up relief pitcher. When the Indians rehired Greenberg for the 1954 season after three consecutive second-place finishes, Lewis was outraged. "If you judge a front office executive on his accomplishments in…player-juggling and talent-handling, Greenberg is a failure," Lewis wrote. "If you add the delicate field of public relations, both with the press and fandom, Greenberg is a flop." [17] Greenberg retorted: "I cut down on my newspaper reading. You'd be surprised how much that improved my digestion and disposition." [18]

By early 1956, the daily newspapers were openly writing about the Lewis-Greenberg feud. After Lewis wrote that the Indians were poised to dump Bob Feller, Greenberg attacked the columnist at a City Club Forum that included Lewis, Gordon Cobbledick, and Ed Bang of the *News*. "You don't base your stories on fact, Franklin," Greenberg said, deliberately avoiding Lewis' nickname. "You base them on personal opinion." [19] When Nate Dolin asked Lewis to back off, Lewis snapped, "I just want to kill that guy." [20]

The other Cleveland writers showed little mercy in questioning Greenberg's abilities. Gordon Cobbledick described the Indians as a "dull team," and suggested Greenberg should break up the club that finished a strong second to the Yankees in 1955. Frank Gibbons of the *Press* complained that Greenberg's record "as a trader" was "never distinguished."

Greenberg fumed. He loathed Whitey Lewis and thought that Jim Schlemmer of the *Akron Beacon Journal* was a "mean, vicious sonofabitch." [21] But he could afford to ignore his critics. By 1956, Hank Greenberg was at the height of his power. He had the confidence of the team owners, commanded a salary in excess of $65,000 a year, and owned 20 percent of the team which he bought at the bargain price of $50 a share. He lived in a lavish home in Shaker Heights with two acres of land, tennis court, and swimming pool. His dynasty was beginning.

❖

Greenberg was eager to push the graduates of his farm system to Cleveland. By 1953, outfielder Al Smith had moved into the regular lineup, and a year later he was joined by pitchers Don Mossi and Ray Narleski. That same summer, Greenberg repeatedly pressed Al Lopez to promote Herb Score from Indianapolis.

Score clearly was overmatching American Association hitters, throwing five shutouts and shattering a league strikeout record that had stood for half-a-century. In a game in Kansas City, he held the Yankee farm team without a hit for the first eight and two-thirds innings. He threw two quick strikes past Art Schult before firing what appeared to be strike three. But the umpire called it a ball and Schult homered on the next pitch.

Score and Colavito had become buddies, rooming together on the road and buying an aging Chevrolet for $125. The car lasted almost to season's end, before it gave out as they drove to dinner. They sold it for $10 and split the proceeds. Years later, Colavito still referred to Score as "Roomie" and described him as "the best friend I ever had in baseball." [22]

Lopez, however, would not hear of promoting Score. The Indians were winning the pennant and had more than enough pitchers. "Hank, we don't want to bring Score up in the middle of the season," Lopez told Greenberg. "You're going to put a lot of pressure on the kid. Let him stay in Indianapolis, have a good year, and I'll guarantee you next spring he'll be the first pitcher on the mound in spring training." [23]

Greenberg relented, but it was an argument that would be repeated during the next two years when he urged Lopez to play his favorite, Rocky Colavito. Since signing with the Indians, Colavito had steadily advanced through the Cleveland system: hitting 28 home runs at Reading in 1953, 38 at Indianapolis in 1954, and 30 more with the same team in 1955. Greenberg loved to stand by the batting cage to watch Colavito brandish a bat. Colavito worked hard, often pestering Bob Feller and the other Cleveland pitchers to throw him extra batting practice. Joe Altobelli, who for four years roomed with Colavito in spring training at the Cleveland minor league camp, admired Colavito's eye at the plate. Unlike most power hitters, Colavito refrained from swinging at bad pitches.

Lopez installed Colavito in right field to begin the 1956 season, but within a month he regretted the decision. Veteran pitchers fooled him and Lopez finally went to Greenberg. "He's not going to learn anything sitting on the bench," Lopez told him. "Let's send him to San Diego." [24] Greenberg reluctantly broke the news to Colavito, who was infuriated at the demotion. But he responded with what he later described as the "hottest batting streak" of his life. In one month, he hammered 12 home runs, 10 doubles, drove in 32 runs, and batted .368.

As Colavito assaulted Pacific Coast League pitching, Greenberg accompanied the Indians on a trip to Washington. Once there, he persuaded Lopez to join him for a meeting with members of the Ohio congressional delegation. In the middle of the reception, Greenberg excused himself to take a phone call. He came back a few minutes later laughing: Rocky Colavito had called him and wanted to know when he could return to Cleveland. "How in the hell did he find you?" Lopez asked in amazement. Greenberg smiled. "He knows where I am every time. He calls me at least once a day." [25]

Colavito rejoined the Indians in July and finished the year with 21 home runs and a .276 batting average. Greenberg was so happy with Colavito's year that he promised him a bonus if he played more than 100 games in 1957. Just before appearing in his 100th game, Colavito went to Greenberg's office. Before Colavito said a word, Greenberg instructed his secretary, "Write this fellow a check." [26]

Tall, muscular, with dark good looks, Colavito quickly became a favorite in Cleveland. Before every at bat, he would grasp both ends of his bat, lift it behind his back, and stretch his muscles. Young boys on the Cleveland sandlots liked to imitate Colavito's stretch.

Baserunners quickly learned not to challenge Colavito. Once, Detroit's Earl Torgeson was on second base when a Tiger batter flied deep to Colavito in right field. Assuming that "no man can throw me out from that distance," Torgeson tagged for third. Halfway to the base, Torgeson saw the third-base coach frantically motioning him to slide. Colavito's powerful throw reached third base in time and Torgeson was tagged out. [27] Hank Sauer once jokingly bet Colavito that he could not throw a ball from homeplate to the center-field wall in El Paso, Texas. Colavito took the bet and fired the ball over the wall—400 feet away.

By 1957 Greenberg's young farmhands were needed because many of the older Indians were departing. Bob Feller retired after a winless season in 1956. Hal Newhouser quit, his left arm aching from pain. Larry Doby was traded to the White Sox. They were followed by Al Lopez, who quit in exhaustion after another second-place finish to the Yankees in 1956. Whitey Lewis insisted that Greenberg drove Lopez out of Cleveland by constantly second-guessing his strategy.

But Lopez had been drained by an Indian collapse in the fall of 1955 that had been every bit as disastrous for the team as the four-game sweep in the 1954 World Series. With Al Rosen slowed by injuries, and Mike Garcia, Bob Feller, and Art Houtteman slipping rapidly, the Indians were seven games out of first place on July 1. But they won 37 of 59 games in July and August, and when they headed east in early September, they held a half-game lead over the second-place Yankees.

They won five consecutive games before playing a doubleheader in New York before 65,310 people. The Yankees won the first game, 6-1, to cut the Cleveland lead to one-half game. But in the second game, Herb Score limited the Yankees to two runs in six innings before leaving for a pinch hitter. The Indians took a 3-2 lead in the eighth when Bobby Avila homered and Hoot Evers scored on a wild pitch. Through three tense innings, Don Mossi shut down the Yankees with his sharp curveball. When Evers caught Elston Howard's flyball for the final out, the jubilant Indians swarmed over Mossi. "My insides are practically worn out," Lopez laughed afterwards. "I'm now working on the outside of my stomach." [28]

The Indians returned home September 16, leading the Yankees by one game with just eight left. They announced that World Series tickets would go on sale that week. The city's hotels were overwhelmed with requests for rooms for the series against the Brooklyn Dodgers. [29]

Then, inexplicably, they collapsed. The fifth-place Tigers swept three games in Cleveland in which the Indians scored only four runs. The Yankees roared ahead and won the pennant by three games. Lopez put on a brave face. "It's no disgrace to lose to that team," he told reporters. But the Detroit sweep struck him as hard as the 1954 World Series, and he wanted to quit. A horrified Nate Dolin, the Indians' vice president, pleaded with Lopez to stay. "Al, you can't do this," Dolin told Lopez. "I want you to stay for my sake."

Lopez reluctantly gave in. "I'll stay for one more year." [30]

The Indians finished second again in 1956, but this time the Yankees won by a comfortable nine games. The Associated Press reported in August that Lopez would resign at the end of the season. When Lopez finally told Greenberg he was leaving, Greenberg made no effort to talk him out of it, instead volunteering to recommend Lopez to Spike Briggs in Detroit. [31] But Lopez' departure left Greenberg puzzled. In a bizarre about-face the day Lopez resigned, Greenberg actually sought out Gordon Cobbledick at the stadium to ask why Lopez was leaving. "On account of you," Cobbledick harshly replied. Greenberg threw back the insult: Lopez was leaving "because of the newspapers and all the tensions you fellows have created." Lopez quickly signed to manage the White Sox and Greenberg replaced him with Kerby Farrell, one of his minor league managers. [32]

Gone too was Al Rosen. At age 32, he announced in the winter of 1957 that he would retire. He had been playing in greater pain since the 1954 triumph. The day before he was to fly to Tucson for spring training in 1955, an old Model A plowed into the rear of his car. Rosen did not need to be hospitalized, but he suffered a neck and back injury. As the season got underway, he pulled a hamstring and his batting average tumbled to .244.

He had vowed as a young player "never to go over the hill. I'll quit before that time. There's nothing worse in sports than a fellow trying to do what his legs and arms and eyes won't let him do." [33] Nor did Rosen have any desire to coach or manage after he retired. Instead, armed with a degree from the University of Miami and a talent for investments, he joined Bache & Co. in Cleveland in the off-season. Soon, he earned more money with Bache than with the Indians.

Moreover, he and Greenberg sparred over salary. Although Greenberg was the one who pushed Rosen into the Cleveland starting lineup in 1950, the two had a strained relationship.

Greenberg seemed to resent Rosen's popularity with the same fans and reporters who always picked on him. The Oakwood Country Club, a posh Jewish club, admitted Rosen as a member. "How can you get into Oakwood and I can't?" Greenberg once snapped. Rosen responded by privately questioning some of Greenberg's trades, such as first baseman Mickey Vernon to Washington for "the infamous Dick Weik." [34]

Even though Rosen batted .300 in 1954, Greenberg slashed his $42,500 a year salary by $5,000. "You're the highest paid infielder in the American League," Greenberg scoffed. Rosen replied, "Well, I don't know any other infielder who has those kinds of numbers." [35] After the 1955 season, Greenberg cut Rosen's salary by another $5,000. Rosen steamed, but agreed to play. At a luncheon in Cleveland, Greenberg suggested that Rosen had "lost his confidence and needed a change of scenery." [36] Greenberg already had a location in mind; he planned to trade Rosen to Boston.

When Greenberg offered Rosen only $27,500 for 1957, an infuriated Rosen announced he would retire and concentrate his energies at Bache. Nobody took him seriously, least of all Greenberg. That December, Rosen and his wife joined the Greenbergs for dinner. As Rosen danced with Caral Greenberg, she urged him to play in 1957. "Hank is in a lot of trouble with his board of directors," she said. "It would be a terrible thing for you to retire now because it would be a terrible thing for him." Rosen politely explained that his decision was final, adding "things never worked out" between him and Greenberg.

"I know," Caral said sadly. "It's just too bad that you and Hank couldn't have been closer." [37]

But by February, it became obvious that the Indians had no plausible replacement for Rosen. Over lunch at the Hollenden House in downtown Cleveland, Kerby Farrell pleaded with Rosen to change his mind. "I need someone like you to get me over the rough spots. If you don't come along with me, I don't think I can succeed here." Rosen yielded on one condition: He wanted more than $27,500.

Because Rosen and Greenberg were barely speaking, Bill Veeck offered to act as an intermediary. Veeck drove to Rosen's home in Shaker Heights and suggested the Indians might pay Rosen $40,000 for the 1957 season. That was fine, Rosen said. He told Sam Sampliner, his boss at Bache, that he would play one more year. "Don't worry about it," Sampliner assured him. "Your business will be here when you get finished. You go right ahead."

Whether Veeck was making an offer on behalf of Greenberg or himself is not clear. A few days later, Veeck telephoned Rosen and told him to "call Henry. He's on his high horse." Rosen tracked Greenberg down at the Indians' minor league complex. "You'll play for $27,500," Greenberg said firmly, "or you won't play." No, Rosen said. I'm finished. [38] An annoyed Greenberg told reporters, "I couldn't allow Rosen to pressure me into offering him what amounted to a bribe to come back and play another year." [39]

From his new job in Chicago, Al Lopez telephoned Greenberg. He wanted Rosen for his White Sox. "Hank, if you let me talk to Rosen, he's willing to come back," Lopez said. "I'd like to make a deal for him." Greenberg rejected the offer out of hand. "If he doesn't play for me, Al, he doesn't play for anybody." [40]

The Cleveland newspapers, which once fawned over Rosen, treated him brutally. The *Plain Dealer*'s editorial page produced a poem that declared, "And when you say: 'I've quit,' stay quit; don't do as Al has done." Gordon Cobbledick, in a rare defense of Greenberg, wrote that had Greenberg relented, the entire team would have been demoralized. Cobbledick claimed that privately, the players were glad Rosen was gone, and he insisted that Al Smith, Billy Harrell, or Bobby Avila could play third base just as effectively. Cobbledick's argument was nonsense. In the next four years, the Indians used 34 different players at third base.

Rosen attended a luncheon for the Indians at the Statler Hotel the day before the season opened. When he was introduced, a group of musicians in the ballroom struck up, "You're in the money." [41] On a Tuesday evening in April, Bob Lemon invited his old friend to the stadium for batting practice. Rosen's swing was as powerful as ever; on the very first pitch he drilled a line drive off the left-field fence. "I came down to lend a rooting interest and couldn't resist the temptation to put a uniform on," Rosen said. [42] But Rosen felt unwanted by the team. He later confided that it was the longest summer of his life. "Nobody will ever know how much I miss baseball," he said after the season.

At the frigid 1957 opener against the White Sox in Cleveland, Score, Colavito, and Maris started. Maris singled three times, leading White Sox manager Al Lopez to say, "He's swinging that bat much better." Score struck out 10 Chicago batters. But Score, unable to control his curveball, walked 11 batters as the Indians lost, 3-2, in 11 innings. "I had to stick to fastballs," Score said. "I didn't know where the curveball was going." [43]

A week later against the same White Sox, Score threw his curveball for strikes, Maris made a diving somersault catch of Sherman Lollar's line drive, and Colavito homered. When Score struck out Lollar in the ninth, he had 10 strikeouts and a 5-0 shutout. In his next start against Detroit, Score struck out 10, allowed just three hits, and won, 2-1. Detroit's Jay Porter wondered after the game how many games Score would win if he pitched for the Yankees. He'd probably be 40-2, Porter concluded. Tiger infielder Ron Samford said, "I batted against Score in the American Association, but it wasn't like today. He didn't have that curveball then." [44] Against Washington, Score struck out 12 in the first six innings. But the Senators knocked him from the game with four runs in the seventh.

Maris was having a torrid spring, too. In the Indians' final spring game in Arizona, Maris homered, singled off Baltimore's Ray Moore, and crushed a 410-foot flyball to center field. He also displayed skill in the field. In the sixth inning, Baltimore's Bob Nieman lined a ball off the left-field wall. As Nieman raced for second base, Maris scooped up the ball and fired a perfect throw to second. Nieman was out, and the Indians had a left fielder. Harry Jones of the *Plain Dealer* wrote that if "Maris is given the left-field job, by the end of the season he will be considered one of the rising stars of the American League."

By the end of May, Maris was batting .313, and sportswriters were calling him the "Fargo Express." He stole the first base of the season for the Indians. Lawrence Hawkins, editor of the *Plain Dealer*'s *Sunday Pictorial Magazine*, was so impressed that he asked sports columnist Gordon Cobbledick if he should put Maris on the cover of his magazine and declare him the "Rookie of the Year." [45] Vic Wertz confided to Herb Score that Maris had great talent. Lou Boudreau, now managing Kansas City, said that "when he gets under the ball, he'll give it a long ride." During a private dinner, Casey Stengel urged Yankee General Manager George Weiss to get Maris in a trade with Cleveland. Weiss ordered Tom Greenwade, who signed Mickey Mantle off the Oklahoma sandlots, to personally scout Maris. [46]

❖

Score's next scheduled start was in a night game against the first-place Yankees in Cleveland. The Yankees had won six consecutive games, but were only three and a half games ahead of the Indians. "Herb Score will fire his southpaw rockets" at the Yankees, Frank Gibbons predicted that afternoon in the *Cleveland Press*. That very morning, the *Saturday Evening Post* ran an advertisement in the *Plain Dealer* to promote a story on Score for the following weekend. The ad teased the readers: "Is Herb Score just another promising pitcher with a great fast ball, or is the Cleveland Indians' young southpaw destined for the Baseball Hall of Fame?"

The newspapers and magazines that chronicled Score's phenomenal rise that spring were dominated by news of Wisconsin Senator Joe McCarthy's death, the Cold War, and the terrors of the nuclear bomb. An Associated Press story assured readers that if the Soviet Union launched an attack upon Western Europe, the United States could retaliate with two billion tons of nuclear explosives. The day before the game, Massachusetts Senator John F. Kennedy won the Pulitzer Prize for his book, *Profiles In Courage*. In Cleveland that afternoon, employees of the Cleveland Electric Illuminating Co., ended their week-long strike by accepting a 15-cent per hour wage increase.

Cleveland newspapers still devoted equal space to TV and radio listings. WDOK Radio offered a selection of Benny Goodman's hits at noon, while WERE had Jimmy Dudley and Bob Neal broadcasting the Indians' game at eight in the evening. But Clevelanders were rapidly tuning out radio and switching on their black-and-white TV sets to watch Rosemary Clooney sing on KYW or see folks like themselves win a fortune on WJW's "$64,000 Question."

Those wishing to avoid baseball or television could head for a movie theater. At the Allen on Euclid Avenue, it was the last night for James Stewart in the *Spirit of St. Louis*. The theater already was promoting its next show, *Abandon Ship* with Tyrone Power and Stephen Boyd, warning that the ending was "so startling, we urge you not to reveal it to your friends."

❖

Score was in his typical good-natured mood. Before warming up, he teased Early Wynn for being a graceless loser. "You kick the trash cans, banging up your toes, and upset everybody in the place," Score joked. "When I get knocked out, I come in like a gentleman. Oh, maybe I throw my glove into the locker before I get to it. But I try not to give anybody any trouble." [47]

Daylight was fading on what had been a pleasant spring afternoon in Northern Ohio. The Indians expected a crowd of 18,000 at the stadium, including 1,200 cab drivers for a special promotion. The Indians planned to transport relief pitchers to the mound in cabs. But with Score pitching for the Indians and Tom Sturdivant for the Yankees, nobody expected many cab rides.

Score retired the Yankee leadoff hitter, Hank Bauer, on a groundball to Al Smith at third. Gil McDougald, the hard-hitting Yankee shortstop, worked the count to 2-and-2. As Bob Neal described the game from the radio booth, Score took his cap off and wiped his brow with his left hand. The next pitch—Score's 12th of the game—was a fastball, low and away. McDougald's bat flashed and he smacked a vicious line drive up the middle. In right field, Rocky Colavito thought the ball would land in center field, and he ran to make the play. But from the dugout, Joe Altobelli saw Score throw his glove up in self-defense. He was too late. The ball smashed his right eye, and he toppled to the ground in agony. One writer sitting in the press box recalled a cracking sound, as if a human face was coming apart at the bones. Mickey Mantle heard two loud "pows"—the sounds of the ball hitting McDougald's bat and Score's eye. [48]

The ball trickled toward Smith at third base, who scooped it up. Seeing that McDougald had stopped running, Smith held the ball for a second. When he heard someone shout, "Throw him out," Smith tossed the ball to Vic Wertz at first base. Then he dashed to Score, crumpled on his left side, with his glove covering his face. [49] Blood rushed from Score's right eye, ears, and nose. McDougald took one look and almost vomited. [50] Al Smith thought Score looked like the loser of a bout with Joe Louis, while Mantle was certain Score had lost his eye. Yet, despite the force of the impact, Score remained fully conscious, even asking Smith to remove his mouthguard.

Players from both teams hovered around him; Colavito, Farrell, Casey Stengel, catcher Jim Hegan, and Indians coach Eddie Stanky. Colavito elevated Score's head by gently slipping his own glove underneath the stricken pitcher. Trainer Wally Bock tried to stop the bleeding. At one point, someone shoved a towel in Score's mouth, and he nearly choked. The public address announcer asked for doctors. Score was lifted gingerly onto a stretcher, and Bock, Mike Garcia, Jim Busby, and Bob Usher carried him from the field. Not wanting to look, Altobelli walked to the other end of the dugout as the Indians carried Score into the Cleveland clubhouse. Bock gently placed him on a rubbing table and joined the team's physician, Dr. Don Kelly, in applying a thick, white bandage around Score's eye and head. They called an ambulance.

A stream of visitors entered the clubhouse: Greenberg, Tris Speaker, and Nate Dolin. When Colavito poked his head into the trainer's room, Score jokingly asked, "What are you doing here? Get out there and get me a couple of base hits." Reminding Score of the Sugar Ray Robinson-Gene Fullmer fight of a week earlier, a reporter tried to ease the tension. "You look as if you'd just gone 10 rounds." Score replied, "Now I know how Fullmer felt." [51] When somebody casually mentioned that he would see Score at the hospital, Score joked, "I hope I can see you."

Greenberg clambered into the ambulance and both raced off to Lakeside Hospital, followed in another car by Tris Speaker. Fortunately for Score, one of the leading eye specialists in the country, Dr. Charles Thomas, lived in Cleveland. He rushed to Lakeside and determined that Score suffered from a broken nose, a slashed eyelid, and swelling and hemorrhaging in the right eye. But Dr. Thomas concluded that Score would regain his vision.

An intrepid reporter for the *Cleveland Press* snuck into Score's third-floor hospital room the next morning. As Score munched on breakfast, he said, "I just heard on the radio that I spent a restful night. That's a laugh. I didn't get any sleep at all. No, I take that back. I got about an hour." [52]

McDougald was stricken. After the game, McDougald asked for Dr. Kelly's telephone number. McDougald tried to visit Score, but physicians shooed him and other well-wishers away. The next day, a photographer caught McDougald gazing at a *Cleveland News* headline, "Score Won't Lose Eye." When a Cleveland reporter told McDougald, "I hope you got more sleep than I did last night," the Yankee infielder replied, "If you closed your eyes at all, you got more than I did." [53]

Hundreds of people, including Baseball Commissioner Ford

Frick, telephoned the hospital. Mother Raymond of Holy Cross grade school in Euclid asked hospital officials to "tell Mr. Score that all the nuns and children out here are praying for him." Vice President Richard Nixon, comedian Phil Silvers, and Larry Doby sent telegrams, while the *Cleveland Press* ran a front-page editorial declaring that "thousands of Clevelanders earnestly—and prayerfully—hope and believe that [Score] will come back again." Score's fiance, Nancy McNamara, a senior at St. Mary's College in Indiana, rushed by train to Cleveland with her college roommate. After mulling it over for a day, Greenberg ordered Score on the disabled list.

Two weeks later, Score met with reporters in his hospital room. With a disk attached to the right eye of his reading glasses, and wearing a red robe, he sat on the edge of the bed. He had no idea when he would pitch again. "At least I can see the wall," Score said. "I couldn't six days ago." [54]

Herb Score would not pitch the rest of the season. Many baseball people are convinced the injury finished him, that he spent the rest of his playing days fearful of another line drive. Bobby Bragan, the new Cleveland manager in 1958, thought Score was leery on the mound the following spring. [55] But Score was determined to pitch. He was the first Indian to show up in 1958 at the team's spring training site in Arizona and pitched batting practice. Score was confident his fastball was just as explosive, and he had no fear of another line drive. On March 5, he struck out four of the first five batters he faced in an intrasquad game. "I felt perfectly natural out there," Score said. [56]

Cleveland officials began to think the impossible: Score as good as ever. He threw 11 consecutive scoreless innings during the exhibition season. His return thrilled the country. Dave Garroway interviewed him for NBC's "Today Show." Before the Indians played the Giants in an exhibition game in El Paso, fans hounded Score in the lobby of the Hilton Hotel clamoring for his autograph. They roared when he struck out eight Giants in five innings.

The Indians were so confident, they chose Score to pitch Opening Day against the Kansas City Athletics. Score lost, 5-0. But four days later, he struck out eight and beat Detroit, 7-5. The huge crowd of 46,698 in Briggs Stadium erupted with cheers as Score ended the game by striking out Billy Martin. Score followed with a 13-strikeout, three-hit shutout of the White Sox. Al Smith, traded to Chicago that winter, said it "was the first time I've ever batted against Herb, and I'm not looking forward to the next one." [57]

Rain washed out Score's next two scheduled starts, and he did not pitch until the Indians went to Washington. That night, he felt tightness in his left elbow. By the ninth inning of a 2-2 tie, his elbow ached so badly that he bounced a pitch to homeplate. Although nobody realized it at the time, Score had ripped a tendon in his elbow. A fragile elbow, not a dramatic line drive to his eye, ended his career. [58]

His fastball faded. Nobody knew that better than Score. He realized he "never had the same stuff" again. In the first inning of an exhibition game against Washington in 1960, he walked four, allowed two hits, and yielded three runs. "This is no fun for anybody," he said in exasperation. Five days later, the Indians traded him to Chicago, and, by the following year, his fastball had deteriorated to the point where he ruefully joked it could be timed with an hour glass. [59]

He quit playing and became a broadcaster for the Indians. Other left-handed pitchers, Sandy Koufax and Steve Carlton, won Cy Young awards. But those who saw Herb Score at his best did not soon forget. "There probably never would have been a left-handed pitcher who would have been better," Al Rosen said years later. "I would not do anything to denigrate the great career of Sandy Koufax. But I've got to tell you: I can't believe that Sandy Koufax was any better than Herb Score would have been." [60]

The Cleveland Indians began 1957 with three young superstars, Herb Score, Roger Maris, and Rocky Colavito. Three years later they were gone; Score felled by injury, Maris and Colavito traded. Their loss was a catastrophe for the team, and the Indians began their descent into what Rosen described as "this terrible period of Cleveland baseball."

Chapter 3

The Man Who Couldn't Say No

"A man in motion is Mr. Lane, and sometimes he moves so fast that he meets himself coming back." — Gordon Cobbledick

Frank Lane was at it again. This time as general manager of the St. Louis Cardinals, he dreamed of trading Stan Musial. Never mind that trading Musial was like the New York Yankees trading Mickey Mantle. Lane already had traded one St. Louis favorite, Red Schoendienst, and he seemed perfectly capable of giving up another. August Busch, Jr., the owner of the Cardinals, Anheuser-Busch, and much of St. Louis, was aghast. He delivered a stern warning to Lane: "Don't you deal Musial." [1]

It was one of the rare times in his life that Frank Lane did not get his way in a trade. He loved to deal: The bigger the names, the more complicated the transaction, the better. Lane was the architect of the only trade of team managers in baseball history. When Lane ran the Indians, Mollie Dolin jokingly told friends she feared that she would pick up the paper one morning and discover that Lane had traded her husband, Nate, an Indians' vice president. Gabe Paul thought his trading was compulsive. Al Rosen called him a "tradeaholic." Bill Veeck put it more pointedly: If offered a trade, Frank Lane could not say no.

Lane traded so often that his frazzled public relations people could not keep pace. Gordon Cobbledick discovered in spring training one year that Lane had already traded away 15 of the players listed in the team's newest press guide. [2] During Lane's 55 years in baseball, he is credited officially with more than 300 trades involving 700 players. "Frank Lane is the first general manager I've known who you have to check with before sending out your laundry," joked Cleveland pitcher Bob Lemon. [3]

He could trade brilliantly. He once gave the Philadelphia Athletics an obscure reserve catcher for second baseman Nellie Fox. He dealt an aging catcher to Detroit for left-handed starting pitcher Billy Pierce. Even when a trade turned out badly, he never looked back. "If you make a bad one, forget it and make two more," he liked to say.

Lane loved complicated transactions involving more than one team. As general manager of the White Sox in 1952, Lane pressed for a three-way deal involving Cleveland and the St. Louis Browns that would have given him first baseman Vic Wertz and hard-hitting infielder Ray Boone. Lane proposed trading shortstop Chico Carrasquel to the Indians for Boone and Larry Doby. Then, he hoped to ship Doby to the Browns for Wertz. When Hank Greenberg rejected the offer, Lane goaded him by proclaiming the Indians as "the most cowardly traders in the business." [4]

Lane would go to any lengths to make his trades, even misleading his own bosses. In 1953 when Bill Veeck was struggling to keep the Browns solvent, he offered pitcher Virgil Trucks to Lane's White Sox for $100,000. Lane desperately wanted Trucks, but the Comiskey family insisted that he spend no more than $50,000. That did not stop Lane. He gave Veeck $50,000 for Trucks and promptly added $15,000 for a pitcher the Browns had planned on releasing. Every time Lane and Veeck agreed to a trade that summer, Lane added a few extra thousand dollars. By year's end, Lane had Trucks and Veeck had $95,000 of the Comiskeys' money. [5]

Lane was loud, brash, and aggressive. He roamed through the stands, screeching at umpires, players, and his own managers. In St. Louis, Lane often screamed so loudly that his embarrassed chief assistant, Bing Devine, would quietly excuse himself and leave. When Gabe Paul was running the Cincinnati Reds, he enjoyed calling Frank Lane after an Indians' defeat. "How is everything?" Paul would innocently ask. Then, holding the phone a few inches from his ear, Paul waited for the inevitable Lane eruption. Lane once stormed into the private box of Chuck Comiskey to complain to American League President Will Harridge about the league's umpires. He denounced umpire Eddie Rommel as a "rockhead" after Rommel called a game in Cleveland because of rain. [6]

He showered abuse on his own players, even those he personally liked. In his first spring training with Cleveland, Lane would pull up his chair near the Indians' dugout. During one at-bat by Minnie Minoso, Lane tossed compliments to Minoso every time the Cleveland outfielder took a ball. When the pitcher fired two strikes past Minoso, Lane shouted, "Hey, don't take too many." A third strike whizzed past Minoso and Lane exploded in rage, "You look like a big bag of shit with a cherry on top." [7]

He ruthlessly second-guessed his field managers' strategy. His first manager in Chicago, Jack Onslow, grew so weary of Lane's complaining, that he snapped, "As far as I'm concerned, Lane can manage the team." In the ninth inning of a close game in Cleveland, Indians Manager Bobby Bragan sent catcher Jay Porter to pinch hit. Up in the press box, Lane grumbled that Porter was "an automatic strikeout." Moments later, Porter homered to win the game and Lane was gloating, "That's my boy." [8]

He liked players who reflected his personality. His favorites were Jimmy Piersall, Billy Martin, Alvin Dark, and Nellie Fox. They were tough, experienced veterans who did not make mistakes. He wanted brassy managers as well; he once tried to hire Leo Durocher. Frank Lane hated to lose and he wanted players intolerant of defeat.

He was a man of limitless energy, who, according to one story he enjoyed telling, talked on his hotel telephone for 36 consecutive hours as he orchestrated a three-way trade with Cleveland and the Philadelphia Athletics. He loved to call friends and associates early in the morning and announce, "Rise and shine. The only ones who make money in bed are whores." [9] Although he was 61 when he took the Cleveland job, he could easily have passed for 40. He neither smoked nor drank, and stayed in shape with a rigorous exercise program, once spending $400 for a special chair that jiggled while he sat in it. [10] He personally answered critical fan letters. He prided himself on reading the sports pages of 65 different newspapers every day and memorizing the daily box scores. Harry Dalton, who served in the front office of the Baltimore Orioles, thought he was a "walking collection of statistics."

He maintained a deep tan and enjoyed driving a white Cadillac convertible, although in typical Lane style, he insisted upon shouting at other drivers, smacking the car horn, and weaving from one lane to another. Once during spring training, a baseball writer noticed that John Carmichael of the *Chicago Daily News* appeared unusually nervous as he sat in a Tampa hotel. "I have just agreed," Carmichael glumly explained, "to let Frank Lane drive me to Lakeland." [11]

Newspaper reporters loved him. "Any time they needed a story, they'd pick up the phone and call Frank," Bing Devine said. "Frank loved publicity and attention. He'd run to it." There were no secrets on Lane's teams. Any reporter wishing inside information on a trade only had to telephone Lane. After his hiring in Cleveland, Lane promptly announced: "It's time I made my first deal with the Yankees." [12] But the very traits that endeared him to reporters made baseball officials cringe. Lane talked so openly about private trades that Commissioner Ford Frick threatened to fine him. Some baseball executives thought he was a sucker. Lane clearly earned his nicknames, "Trader Lane" and "Frantic Frankie."

This was the man who at the end of 1957 assumed control of the Cleveland Indians with its rich minor league system that promised a limitless future. He ran the Indians for just three years, but his legacy was felt for decades. He wanted to be remembered as the man who created an exciting pennant winner in Cleveland. Instead, he is remembered chiefly for two things: Trading Roger Maris and Rocky Colavito.

As a young man, Frank Lane wanted to play baseball. He earned tryouts with minor league teams in Reading and Marion, Ohio, but never won full-time employment. "I couldn't hit a curve," Lane said, prompting Tim Cohane to write that the curve was "one of the few things he could neither outtalk nor outhustle." Determined to remain in sports, Lane played for an early professional football team in his hometown of Cincinnati, and later served as a basketball and football referee in the Big Ten. While other referees bundled up in sweaters and jackets, Lane delighted in wearing only shirtsleeves during frigid football games. He was tougher than the rest.

In 1933, Lane accepted a front-office job with the Cincinnati Reds. There, he worked under Larry MacPhail, who became his mentor. Both men were aggressive, energetic, and volatile. MacPhail once took a punch at the co-owner of the New York Yankees. But MacPhail was a brilliant innovator. He introduced night games to baseball, built powerful pennant winners in Cincinnati and Brooklyn, and elevated Leo Durocher from the playing ranks to manage the Dodgers to the World Series.

Lane worked his way up to direct the Cincinnati farm system. When Japanese bombs fell on Pearl Harbor, Lane enlisted in the Navy even though he was over 40. He rose to the rank of lieutenant commander. After the war, Lane rejoined MacPhail with the Yankees, who assigned him to run the front office of New York's Triple-A team in Kansas City. Within a year, Lane advanced to the presidency of the American Association, before accepting an offer from the Comiskey family to breathe life into the all-but-embalmed Chicago White Sox.

For three decades after the Black Sox scandal of 1919, the White Sox were a hopeless second-division team. In one four-year span from 1929 through 1933, the White Sox averaged 93 losses and never rose above seventh place. Lou Comiskey, the son of the team's founder, Charles Comiskey, hated spending money and his frugality showed on the field. The White Sox consistently lost while their crosstown rivals, the Cubs, appeared in five World Series from 1929 to 1945.

By 1948, Lou Comiskey was dead, and his widow, Grace, and their son, Chuck, were anxious to win. Following 101 losses and an eighth-place finish in 1948, the Comiskeys sacked the team's general manager, Leslie O'Connor, and the manager, Ted Lyons. They issued the call for Frank Lane.

The story goes that Lane immediately announced that every player was on the trading block and there were "no sacred cows" on the team. Actually, White Sox manager Jack Onslow said it, not Lane. [13] But Lane intended to act that way. At the 1948 winter meetings in Minneapolis, Irving Vaughan of the *Chicago Tribune* wrote that Lane was "eager to indulge in barter without undue waste of time." [14]

Lane acquired pitchers Billy Pierce and Dick Donovan from Detroit, Nellie Fox from Philadelphia, Trucks and catcher Sherman Lollar from the St. Louis Browns, and shortstop Chico Carrasquel from Brooklyn. In a complicated three-way trade that he orchestrated with Cleveland and Philadelphia, Lane walked away with swift outfielder Minnie Minoso. He fired Onslow and called in brainy Paul Richards to manage the team. He spent vast sums on a farm system that eventually produced shortstop Luis Aparicio, first baseman Norm Cash, catcher John Romano, and pitcher Barry Latman.

He proved in Chicago to be a keen judge of talent. If he did not like a player's ability, he would scribble on a scouting report, "Won't hurt you unless you play him." [15] When Al Rosen flew out to spring training in 1950, he saw Lane on the same plane. Lane motioned him over to an empty seat. Even though Rosen had not yet become a full-time starter for the Indians, Lane told him that Chicago would hire him if Cleveland released him. "Let me tell you something," Lane said. "There are two players who will never get waived out of this league, you and Ray Boone." [16]

Lane's teams in Chicago won on speed rather than brawn; the White Sox consistently led the league in stolen bases. They bunted, took the extra base, and played superior defense. In 1955, the White Sox won 91 games and finished a strong third, only five games behind the pennant-winning Yankees and two behind the second-place Indians. During his seven years as general manager, the franchise's value doubled to $6 million; from 1953 through 1955 the White Sox earned a profit of $610,000. [17]

But Lane's insistence upon complete control brought him in conflict with Chuck Comiskey. While Mrs. Comiskey was happy with Lane's performance, Chuck was anxious to assume greater control of the team. At age 29, Chuck Comiskey believed he was the brilliant heir to his legendary grandfather. "Frank is one of our capable executives," Chuck Comiskey said in a speech in 1955, "but there can only be one person whose orders are final in any business, and in the case of the White Sox, I am in charge." [18] Lane shot back in the newspapers, "I don't think Chuck Comiskey will change. He hasn't liked me in the past." [19] He privately warned Comiskey that the average fan would not identify with the clubowner. "Remember Chuck," Lane said, "no millionaire is ever going to be popular with the masses. The fans trust me because they know I'm just a working stiff." [20]

Mrs. Comiskey was annoyed at the public row and feared Lane was on the "verge of a nervous breakdown." [21] On September 21, even though he had five years remaining on his contract, Lane resigned. He accepted the general manager's post with the St. Louis Cardinals, assuming control of another failing team. Although St. Louis and the Dodgers dominated the National League in the 1940s, by 1955 the Cardinals tumbled to seventh place, and accumulated three-year losses of $1.3 million. [22] Gussie Busch wanted decisive changes, and Lane promised to deliver.

Lane rapidly constructed a team to suit his tastes. He traded away popular Cardinals, such as Schoendienst and pitcher Harvey Haddix. St. Louis fans were particularly enraged with the trade of Schoendienst, but Lane could not care less. "The stories about this poor, freckle-faced kid being cruelly treated curled my ears," he said with contempt. [23] But he obtained shortstop Alvin Dark to improve the infield defense, outfielder Del Ennis to provide power, and pitcher Sam Jones to stabilize the starting rotation. He even changed the St. Louis uniforms, removing the cherished pair of cardinals perched on a bat from the jersey because it "wasn't a uniform; it was a costume." [24] Lane also got lucky; he arrived as the Cardinal minor league system added third baseman Ken Boyer, outfielder Wally Moon, and pitchers Larry Jackson, Lindy McDaniel, and Vinegar Bend Mizell. The Cardinals climbed to second place in 1957 and turned an $800,000 profit. [25]

But, again, Lane clashed with the team owner. Busch, a man used to getting his way, wanted advance knowledge of major trades. Lane not only resisted, he went to great lengths to mislead Busch. When Lane arranged to trade outfielder Bill Virdon to Pittsburgh, Dick Meyer, the Cardinals' executive vice president and a Busch confidant, was hesitant. During a night game at Sportsman's Park, Lane worked feverishly to persuade Meyer and Assistant General Manager Bing Devine that the trade made sense. Virdon had poor eyesight, Lane argued. In a few years, he would not be able to see well enough to play. As they left the ballpark, Meyer said, "Well, I'm not the one who thinks we ought to tell our general manager what to do. But you wait. I'll see Mr. Busch in the morning."

At six the next morning, Devine's home phone rang. It was Meyer. "Turn on the radio," Meyer told him. "The deal's been made." [26]

Lane chafed under any restrictions and scouted about for another team. His luck held. In Cleveland, the Indians had plunged to sixth place in 1957. There was turmoil and feuding between the majority stockholders and Hank Greenberg. The owners were poised to dump the conservative Greenberg in favor of a more dynamic general manager. That would provide an opening for Frank Lane.

The Man Who Couldn't Say No

❖

The men who had owned and operated the Indians since 1949 were known as the "Big Seven." They were powerful businessmen, longtime residents of Greater Cleveland, with all the right political connections. They also happened to be close friends who often dined at each other's Tudor mansions in Shaker Heights. In the fall of 1949, they got together to buy the Indians.

Nate Dolin, a member of the Big Seven and head of the Cleveland Arena, initiated the purchase one night when Bill Veeck stopped by his table at Gruber's. Veeck was in the middle of a costly divorce with Eleanor Raymond, and all his money was tied up in the team. Not only would he have to give Eleanor half the club, but he needed to raise cash for himself.

"What's the price?" Dolin finally asked.

"Two million, two hundred thousand dollars," Veeck replied.

When Veeck left the table to mingle with other customers, Mollie Dolin turned to her husband: "Where will you get that kind of money?" [27] Dolin called his banker, Harry Small, the executive vice president of the Bank of Ohio. Small wanted a share of the team, and he and Dolin rapidly assembled a group that included five other major investors: Ellis Ryan, president of the W. F. Ryan Insurance Co.; Jack B. John, an associate in Ryan's insurance company; George Medinger, the president of the Fostoria Pressed Steel Co.; Donald W. Hornbeck, a partner with the Cleveland law firm of Miller & Hornbeck; and Guy W. Waters, president of the Rausch Nut & Manufacturing Co.

The Big Seven named the 45-year-old Ryan as president. In addition to running the insurance firm his father founded in 1905, Ryan developed a passion for sports, serving for many years as executive vice president of the Cleveland Arena. He chain-smoked and developed an annoying cough. Well tailored, with thinning hair that formed a widow's peak, Ryan gave the appearance of a successful businessman. He owned 20 percent of the team's 3,000 shares of stock and announced, "I hope to be connected with the Indians for the rest of my life." [28]

Ryan was less an authoritarian figure than a first among equals. One member of the Big Seven liked to joke that the group picked Ryan as president because he was a member of the prestigious Union Club where Cleveland's elite regularly lunched with each other and conducted business. Medinger, Dolin, and

Hornbeck had as much say in running the Indians as Ellis Ryan.

The 46-year-old Medinger became one of the team's two vice presidents. After starting his career in banking and investments in New York City, Medinger moved to Cleveland in 1932. He became president of Fostoria Steel, bought a white two-story home in Shaker Heights just down Claythorne Road from Harry Small, and married Margaret Breckenridge, a handsome woman with black hair and a poised manner. Medinger, outgoing with a keen sense of humor, often invited Hank and Caral Greenberg over for dinner. As the years went by, he devoted more time to the Indians, negotiating the team's lucrative radio and television contracts and visiting the Indians' minor league teams.

Hornbeck brought valuable political connections and shrewd legal skills to the team. Born in 1903 in London, Ohio, Hornbeck earned a law degree from Ohio State and developed a lifelong friendship with Republican John W. Bricker, who won a series of statewide elections for attorney general, governor, and senator. Whenever Bricker ran for office, he asked Hornbeck to manage his campaign in Greater Cleveland. But Hornbeck never let ideology get in the way of making money. In 1940, he formed a law firm with Ray Miller, the former Democratic mayor of Cleveland, which quickly became one of the most influential firms in northern Ohio. Hornbeck loved to play golf and enjoyed martinis. That was his flaw; after a few drinks he became rude, abusive, and disoriented. Once while the family was vacationing in Florida, a drunken Hornbeck wandered onto the wrong train and ended up in Chicago. He promised his wife he would quit his drinking, a pledge he did not keep.

Dolin assumed the title of vice president of baseball operations, but he was the most important member of the Big Seven. Short and lacking the natural grace of his partners, Dolin ruefully conceded that he was the "world's worst left-handed golfer." But he possessed the nimblest business brain among the Big Seven. It was Nate Dolin who concluded that the tax laws would permit baseball owners to write off their players like any other asset. He directed the business operations of the team, approved players' salaries, and developed the team's daily promotions.

He was born to Jewish parents on Cleveland's east side and rose to become a wealthy businessman. As a boy, he peddled the *Cleveland News* at the corner of East 79th Street and Quincy

Avenue and liked to boast that he sold more than 200 newspapers every day. He picked up spare change by selling popcorn and ice cream at League Park, and, after graduating from Glenville High School in 1931, he put himself through two years of accounting classes at Cleveland College. He sold tickets for boxing matches at the Jewish Recreation Council and from there moved to direct the box office of the Cleveland Arena, where he managed the ticket operation for the Cleveland hockey team, ice shows, and boxing. By his own count, he distributed 15 million tickets during a 10-year span before he turned his savings into a share of the Indians.

Dolin preferred to remain in the background and allow Ryan to assume the most visible role. He rarely gave interviews to reporters and avoided publicity. His shyness was in part natural, in part imposed. Like many American cities in 1950, Cleveland was a hostile environment for Jewish people. Real estate agents advised home buyers that large areas of suburban Cleveland were off-limits to Jews, and most golf clubs prohibited Jewish members. Dolin was so offended at the overt anti-Semitism at the Union Club, he refused to allow the team's board of directors to meet there. [29]

The Big Seven knew little about the inner workings of baseball and were frank to admit it. Acting on Veeck's suggestion in late 1949, they signed Greenberg to a three-year contract as general manager and provided him with what was described as a "free hand" in player transactions.

The Indians continued to attract huge crowds and reap large profits. But by 1952, Ryan was growing increasingly worried. Even though the Indians finished a strong second to the Yankees, home attendance slid by 300,000 to 1.44 million. What would happen, Ryan wondered, if the Indians fell to the second division? "You can lose your shirt in one season," he warned associates. [30] Ryan grew disenchanted with Greenberg's direction of the team and determined to assert greater control. Ryan engineered the purchase of a farm club in Indianapolis, placed a trusted friend in charge, and concocted plans to dismiss Greenberg and assume the general manager's duties himself.

Dolin, Hornbeck, and Medinger were appalled by their friend's plans. They liked Greenberg and doubted Ryan had the experience to be a skilled baseball trader. During the winter meetings in Phoenix in 1952, a board meeting was called in Cleveland. Ryan left Phoenix by train, smoking one cigarette after another in his parlor car. Warned that photographers waited for him in Cleveland, Ryan straightened his tie and hat and joked, "Guess people just want to see the gore." [31]

At the meeting, Dolin, Medinger, and Hornbeck ousted Ryan as president. Ryan sold his shares of stock for a tidy $250,000 profit to the wealthy investment banking brothers, Wing and Andy Baxter. Although Louis Seltzer, the powerful editor of the *Cleveland Press* privately urged Dolin to replace Ryan with former Cleveland mayor Tom Burke, the Big Seven settled upon 65-year-old Myron "Mike" Wilson as the new president. [32] A graduate of Yale, member of Kirtland Country Club, and partner in the Cleveland insurance firm of Wilson, McBride & Co., Wilson met the obligatory requirement of being a WASP. Wilson characterized himself as a typical baseball fan, admitting, "I don't know much about picking ballplayers." [33] The real winner in the board dispute was Hank Greenberg. Wilson was not going to interfere with Greenberg's direction of the team.

Under Greenberg's hand, the Big Seven racked up enormous profits: $157,288 in 1953, $583,283 in the pennant-winning season of 1954, and $89,756 in 1955. [34] In 1956, Greenberg solidified his authority by buying 20 percent of the stock when the Big Seven reorganized. The Big Seven still controlled a large voting bloc on the board—Medinger and Dolin as vice presidents, Small as treasurer, and Hornbeck as secretary. William R. Daley, president of the powerful Cleveland investment banking house, Otis & Co., emerged as chairman of the board and Wilson remained president. But Greenberg was the respected baseball man, and as long as the team won and turned a profit, his supremacy was unquestioned.

Within a year, however, the fears Ryan expressed in 1952 were realized. The sixth-place Indians attracted less than 750,000 people to their home games in 1957 and reported a loss on paper of $150,000. Wilson warned that the Cleveland ownership was "not set up to stand losses for a long time." Greenberg was under constant attack from the fans and press, and the Big Seven entertained the thought of replacing him. [35]

In reality, the Big Seven panicked with little cause. There was reason to believe that Greenberg's strong minor league system would quickly restore the Indians to their old winning ways. The 1957 dip was easily explained by injuries to Herb Score and Bob Lemon. Two pitchers who combined to win 40 games in 1956 won only eight in 1957. On the financial side, the Indians had consistently shown they could perform. Throughout the 1950s, the Indians, Yankees, and Dodgers were the most profitable teams in baseball. In 1956, the Indians grossed $2.7 million, an amount exceeded in the American League only by the Yankees. While attendance in Cleveland had declined sharply from 1948, broadcast revenues were skyrocketing from $452,650 in 1952 to $1 million in 1956, the largest in baseball. People were not coming to the stadium; they were staying home and watching the Indians on television. [36]

The Big Seven's decision to fire Hank Greenberg in 1957 remains something of a mystery. In his memoirs published after his 1986 death, Greenberg wrote that the Big Seven dismissed him because he was pressing to move the Indians to Minneapolis. Greenberg concluded that Minneapolis newspapers would be kinder than Cleveland's, and, unlike the nervous Big Seven, he knew the Indians were still a strong team with a vibrant farm system. He was convinced that the Indians—operating in another city filled with enthusiasm—would quickly win another pennant.

Teams were on the move elsewhere. At the end of 1952, the Boston Braves left for Milwaukee, where in 1954 they attracted 2.1 million customers to their home games and turned a profit of $457,110. The Browns abandoned St. Louis for Baltimore after the 1953 season, while the Athletics moved from Philadelphia to Kansas City and outdrew the Indians in 1955 by 170,000 people. Los Angeles, San Francisco, and Minneapolis hankered for their own teams.

Giants owner Horace Stoneham, unhappy with the aging Polo Grounds, had all but decided to transfer his team to Minneapolis until Walter O'Malley, owner of the Brooklyn Dodgers, intervened. Why not move the Dodgers and Giants to Los Angeles and San Francisco, O'Malley asked Stoneham. The Dodger-Giant rivalry would survive, and the two teams would leave obsolete stadiums for new ballparks on the West Coast. When Stoneham agreed, Minneapolis was without a team.

But Greenberg may have inadvertently confused the sequence of events in his memoirs. Although he wrote that he urged the Indians to move at the time of his firing in 1957, he appears to be referring to events in the summer of 1958 when Daley was considering a transfer to Minneapolis. It is easy to understand how Greenberg may have become confused because in 1958 he was still a major stockholder and urged Daley to move to Minneapolis.

What is not at all clear is whether either Greenberg or the Big Seven was considering a move one year earlier in 1957. The day Greenberg was fired, he said that any talk of "moving the franchise is ridiculous. It has never been discussed at any meeting." Neither the *Cleveland Press* nor the *Minneapolis Star* in the autumn of 1957 seriously mentioned the Indians as a likely candidate for Minneapolis. *Star* sports columnist Charles Johnson, who had exceptional sources, focused exclusively on the possibility of luring the Washington Senators to Minneapolis. The only major story in the *Star* referring to Cleveland is a wire service report on September 18, 1957, suggesting that the Indians might move to Los Angeles if the Dodgers remained in Brooklyn. Greenberg quickly knocked that story down, saying that "as far as I know, there has been absolutely no talk in league councils about anybody moving anywhere." [37]

Nor is there any evidence to suggest that the Big Seven wanted to move the team in the fall of 1957. From all accounts, Dolin, Hornbeck, Small, and Medinger preferred to remain in Cleveland. Instead, it appears they fired Greenberg after concluding it was the only way to demonstrate to Cleveland fans that they were serious about improving the team. The Big Seven worried that Greenberg's war with the Cleveland writers was hurting attendance. On a plane flight from Washington to Cleveland, Dolin urged Greenberg to end his feud with the local reporters. Dolin bluntly warned Greenberg that despite their friendship "the club and the stockholders come first. If things don't change, I'm going to fire you." [38]

During a three-hour meeting on October 16, 1957, in the Terminal Tower's Greenbrier Suite, Daley and the Big Seven fired Greenberg. Now just another stockholder, Greenberg left the meeting smiling, but inwardly he was bitter. "I feel my work here has been my greatest achievement in the game," Greenberg said. [39]

With Greenberg gone, the Big Seven wanted change. They wanted a quick fix. They wanted excitement. They wanted Frank Lane.

❖

Even as he was handing in his resignation to Gussie Busch, Lane was making plans for Cleveland. Lane thought that Greenberg's Indians were sluggish and needed to improve their speed and defense. He knew exactly who he wanted: Minnie Minoso of the White Sox, Vic Power of the Kansas City Athletics, Bobby Richardson of the Yankees, and Harvey Kuenn of the Tigers. When Detroit General Manager John McHale telephoned him to wish him well, Lane joked, "Never mind the congratulations. Just tell me: Do I get Harvey Kuenn?" Lane was obsessed with Kuenn. Kuenn sprayed the ball to all fields, rarely struck out, and could play either shortstop or right field. To get his favorites, Lane was more than willing to offer Greenberg's favorites, Rocky Colavito and Roger Maris. [40]

At the winter meetings, he acquired Minoso for Early Wynn and Al Smith. "I wanted Minoso and I wanted him bad," Lane said of the outfielder who called the general manager his "Daddy No. 2." [41] For the next two years, Lane followed the same pattern. He traded Wertz to Boston for swift, fiery outfielder Jimmy Piersall. He sent Bud Daley to Baltimore for Larry Doby, only to trade Doby to Detroit for Tito Francona. He dealt Ray Narleski and Don Mossi to the Tigers for Billy Martin. Piersall and Martin had been difficult for managers to handle, but Lane always was confident that he could tame players he called "bad boys." He admitted that Piersall "does act goofy," but he told reporters that "there aren't many who can play center field any better." [42]

Lane got his chance for Vic Power in 1958. Power was only 26, a strong, right-handed hitter whom Herb Score said was the best defensive first baseman he had ever seen. Power had a flair for the game, delighting in one-handed catches of even the most crucial pop flys. Kansas City offered to deal Power and shortstop Woodie Held, but their pricetag was high: Colavito or Maris. Lane was willing to trade Maris, with whom he had a cool relationship. After the 1957 season, Lane wanted Maris to play winter ball, but Maris returned to Fargo to work for a radio station. "I guess you could say we never got along after that," Lane conceded later. [43] Bobby Bragan, whom Greenberg hired at the end of 1957 to manage the Indians, thought Maris was "surly." Maris once walked off a Cleveland minor league team after he quarreled with the manager. Maris resented it when a coach would fiddle with his swing.

Maris also had provoked a quarrel with Nate Dolin. Because the Indians kept Maris through the 1957 season and did not return him to the minor leagues, they owed him a bonus. Dolin called Maris into his office and suggested that Maris could save taxes by having the team pay half the bonus immediately, and the rest the following January. Maris said he would consider it. The next day, a lawyer from Fargo telephoned Dolin and demanded the entire bonus immediately. Dolin sent Maris the check, but vowed not to speak to Maris again. [44]

But the men who directed the Indians' minor league system, Hoot Evers and Bob Kennedy, adamantly opposed trading Maris. Kennedy thought Maris was tough, a good outfielder, and eventually would be a great home run hitter. Even Lane recognized that Maris had talent. The presence of Tom Greenwade at Cleveland games was enough to convince him that the Yankees wanted Maris. By sending Maris to Kansas City, Lane was all but guaranteeing that the outfielder would eventually play in New York. Kansas City owner Arnold Johnson was a close business associate of Yankee owners Dan Topping and Del Webb. It was a common joke throughout baseball that the Athletics served as a Yankee farm team; they would develop young players and trade them to New York. But Lane would not allow Roger Maris to stand in the way of getting Vic Power. Moments before the trading deadline of June 15, 1958, Roger Maris was gone from Cleveland.

Bill Veeck was astonished. A left-handed pull hitter like Maris might hit 50 home runs in Yankee Stadium. Veeck telephoned Lane. "I know I'm handing him over to the Yankees," Lane told Veeck. "But it's a trade I have to make for my own ballclub." [45]

By the spring of 1959, Lane had assembled a team more to his liking. He had an outfield of Minoso, Piersall, Francona, and Colavito, and an infield of Power, Martin, Held, and George Strickland. But Lane's trades carried a high price. Gone were Early Wynn, Bud Daley, and Don Mossi, who in 1959 combined to win 55 games. The Indians did not have enough pitchers to replace them.

Still, it was the strongest Cleveland team since 1956. Rocky Colavito hit 42 home runs, Minnie Minoso drove in 92 runs, Tito Francona batted .363, and Vic Power scored 102 runs. When

Gary Bell beat the Red Sox, 5-1, on June 15, the Indians moved into first place. The team was on its way to its best home attendance since 1951, and the Cleveland sportswriters could hardly restrain themselves. Gordon Cobbledick hailed Lane as a "trading genius." [46]

Even with the Indians in first place, Lane had trouble controlling himself. He toyed with trading Minoso and 19-game winner Cal McLish to the White Sox for starting pitcher Bob Shaw and third baseman Bubba Phillips. He listened to a Yankee offer for Held. But Lane held firm and rejected both possibilities.

As well as the Indians played, they could not keep pace with Lane's old White Sox. The Indians had more power, but the White Sox had stronger pitching, better infield defense, and sturdier catching. The White Sox had one other advantage: Their manager, Al Lopez, was more than a match for Cleveland's Joe Gordon. The White Sox beat the Indians 15 of 22 times that year and were at their best when the two teams met for a crucial four-game series in Cleveland in late August.

The Indians had won six consecutive games through an unusually humid August. They trimmed Chicago's hold on first place to just two games on August 25 when Colavito homered twice to beat the Yankees, 6-3, before 36,143 roaring fans in Cleveland. The next night, the Indians increased their winning streak to eight as Colavito broke a 4-4 tie with the Yankees in the eighth inning when he smacked a soaring home run that cleared the wire fence and reached the center-field bleachers on the second bounce. As Colavito reached the dugout to grasp Joe Gordon's hand, the fans along the first-base line stood and thunderously applauded. In the top of the ninth, Enos Slaughter led off with a double against Jim Perry, who had relieved Gary Bell in the eighth. But Perry retired Norm Siebern on a flyball to Minoso in left field and struck out Johnny Blanchard on a 3-and-2 fastball. Bobby Richardson ended the game with a flyball to left. An emotionally exhausted Frank Lane could only say, "I sure got a thrill out of [Perry's] work in that ninth." [47]

The city had not seen such baseball excitement since 1954. By nine in the morning of the Friday night opener against the White Sox, long lines had formed outside the Cleveland Stadium ticket office. A weary switchboard operator, smoking a cigarette during a quick break, said that the phone lines had "been lit up like a Christmas tree since early morning." Then she gamely plunged back to the phones, telling late callers, "The only seats we have are in the outfield—out near Minnie Minoso and Rocky Colavito." [48] By five in the evening, people began pouring into the huge stadium, oblivious to 90-degree heat so intense it shattered a window in a car parked in one of the sweltering suburbs. An astonished photographer for *Sports Illustrated* climbed to the very top of the upper deck in right field to shoot a wide-angle photo of 70,398 people jammed into their seats and behind the temporary wire fences. Frank Lane had apparently succeeded.

But Chicago's pitching and speed and Al Lopez' brainpower more than compensated for a crowd that drowned out with cheers the announcement of the Cleveland starting lineup. Bob Shaw retired Tito Francona and Rocky Colavito in the fifth inning with two men on base and pitched his way to a 7-3 victory. The next day before 50,290, righthander Dick Donovan shut out the hard-hitting Indians and Jim Landis scored from first base on a single. Colavito had ducked twice to avoid menacing fastballs from Shaw and Donovan. He had just one bad-hop hit to show for the first two games, leading White Sox coach John Cooney to crow, "We've got Rocky Colavito's number." [49]

The Indians were now three and a half games behind and needed to sweep the Sunday doubleheader before 66,586. In a cruel turnabout, Early Wynn, judged too old to pitch in 1957 by Frank Lane, defeated the Indians, 6-3. In the second game, Al Smith, whom Lane traded to the White Sox with Wynn, scored from second base on a flyball to deep right field, as the White Sox won, 9-4. "There's that speed again," Gordon muttered about the swift White Sox. [50] The White Sox finished the season five games ahead of the second-place Indians.

Lane did not handle defeat gracefully and looked for someone to blame. First he pointed to Colavito's performance against the White Sox. Next, he complained about Gordon. Lane insisted that Piersall and Martin play regularly, while Gordon urged Lane to trade Martin to Washington for second baseman Ken Aspromonte. "Joe, you don't understand values," Lane snapped, arguing that Martin was the better player. Gordon refused to back down. "You can't play values," he told Lane. "I look for ability." Lane was particularly enraged in late August in Boston when Gordon failed to call for a sacrifice bunt when the Indians had runners on first and second with nobody out. "Finishing second with a good chance for first isn't good in my opinion," Lane grumbled. [51]

Gordon told Lane on September 18 that he was fed up, and Lane abruptly fired him. Lane wanted to replace him with Leo Durocher, a commentator for NBC's "Game of the Week," but anxious to return to baseball. Dolin drove to Pittsburgh, where he met Durocher at the Penn Sheraton Hotel. Durocher later insisted that Dolin handed him an offer in writing: A $35,000 salary, a $10,000 nontaxable expense account, and the opportunity to buy $360,000 of the team's debentures for $270,000. The Indians promised to buy back Durocher's debentures in three years for the full $360,000. Dolin disputed that, saying that Durocher proposed a deal that would have guaranteed him $50,000 a year after taxes. That was far more than Dolin wanted to pay any manager. Dolin withdrew the offer, returned to Cleveland, and drove to the stadium to see Lane.

"Forget about this guy," Dolin told Lane. "I wouldn't hire this guy if my life depended on it. Now, you have a job. You've got to rehire Joe Gordon." [52]

Before dawn on September 23, Lane telephoned Joe Gordon at his hotel room in Cleveland and woke him from a sound sleep. "Good Lord, don't you ever sleep?" Gordon muttered. Lane invited him over for breakfast. Gordon refused, rolled over, and went back to sleep. Later, he confided to a friend that "maybe [Lane] forgot that he fired me last night, and wants to fire me again."

An hour later, Lane called back. "Joe, you've slept long enough. Come on over."

Lane offered him a two-year contract at $40,000 a year and called reporters to his office to introduce the team's new manager. In walked Gordon, prompting one reporter to ask, "Is this a gag?" The *Plain Dealer* described Gordon's rehiring as a "bizarre and startling development." The entire incident suggested that the Cleveland front office was on an erratic course. [53]

The team that nearly won the pennant needed only minor tinkering. But during the winter, Lane initiated a major overhaul. He traded Martin and McLish to Cincinnati, and sent Minoso to the White Sox for three young players—first baseman Norm Cash, catcher John Romano, and third baseman Bubba Phillips. Then he abruptly sent Cash to Detroit for an unknown third baseman. Unlike the Frank Lane of 1949, who traded aging veterans for exciting young ballplayers, the Frank Lane of 1960 seemed to be trading for the sake of it.

Lane also was thinking the unthinkable—trading Rocky Colavito. Few players ever were more popular in Cleveland than Colavito. There were scores of Rocky Colavito fan clubs. Thousands of people went to games in Cleveland Stadium simply to watch the powerful right-handed home run hitter. Lane, however, was not one of Colavito's fans. He thought Colavito's .257 batting average was far too low, and he later confided to a friend that Colavito was slow and "flat footed." [54] Frank Lane had no room on his teams for slow power hitters who batted .257. He was even less amused when Colavito held out for more money in the spring of 1960.

It was not the first time the two clashed over money. Before the 1958 season, Lane promised Colavito a $3,000 bonus for a good year. "You won't have to come to me," Lane said. "I'll call you up here." By late September, Colavito had 35 home runs and more than 100 runs batted in. He telephoned Lane, who told him to stop by the office. When Colavito asked for the bonus, Lane told him, "I never said that."

Colavito exploded in anger, "You're a liar." [55]

Early in 1960, Detroit General Manager William O. DeWitt telephoned Lane and proposed swapping 1959 batting champion Harvey Kuenn for Colavito. Lane badly wanted Kuenn to play right field. Lane was convinced that the Indians had plenty of power and could win the 1960 pennant if young pitchers Gary Bell, Jim Grant, and Jim Perry improved. Harvey Kuenn would be the final piece to the puzzle. At Daytona Beach, Lane asked Bob Kennedy and Hoot Evers about the trade. As they had with Roger Maris, both objected. They pointed out that Colavito barely had reached his peak, and he gave the team power and a strong arm. But Kennedy concluded that Lane was determined to make the deal. [56]

Lane's only obstacle was Nate Dolin, who was horrified by the idea. Colavito was a magnet in Cleveland and guaranteed the Indians would attract well over one million fans in 1960. But that spring, Dolin entered a Cleveland hospital for throat surgery. Lane telephoned the hospital and told Dolin's wife Mollie that he wanted to trade Colavito. Unable to speak, Dolin wrote a note and asked Mollie to read it to Lane: "Under no conditions can you trade Colavito." [57]

The next day, the Indians played their final exhibition game in Memphis, Tennessee, against the White Sox. Lane telephoned DeWitt at his home in St. Louis and agreed to the trade. He planned an announcement that afternoon to the Cleveland reporters. Lane knew the Colavito trade would be front-page news in Cleveland and Detroit.

In the second inning of the exhibition game, Colavito crushed a line drive over the 350-foot left-field wall. His next time up, Colavito forced a runner at second. As he stood on first base, Colavito saw Gordon walking toward him. Gordon probably was planning on giving him the rest of the day off, Colavito thought. He could get back to the hotel, shower, shave, and be packed when the team left for Cleveland. He was anxious to get home for the opener against Detroit.

"Rocky," Gordon said, "I want to tell you that's the last time you'll bat in a Cleveland uniform. You've been traded to the Detroit Tigers for Harvey Kuenn. I want to wish you all the luck in the world."

Colavito did not know what to say. Finally, he mumbled, "Same to you." Then he walked down the right-field foul line to the Cleveland clubhouse. He passed Herb Score and Johnny Klippstein, who both were relaxing near a light tower. "Roomie," Colavito said to Score, "I've been traded to the Detroit Tigers." Score thought Colavito was joking. Colavito repeated the news two more times before Score believed him. [58]

Cleveland was stunned. Telephone calls poured into the *Plain Dealer* and *Press*. "My teeth almost fell out," said Marvin Jones of South Euclid. Carol Kickel, an eighth-grader in Cleveland, said, "I just want to tell you this: I belong to one of the Rocky Colavito fan clubs. It's all over. We're going to start a new one; the Lane Haters." [59]

The Indians arrived at Hopkins Airport late that evening, and Lane, wearing a rain coat and sunglasses, stepped off the plane. The first thing he saw was a sign, "Up with Rock. Down with Trader Lane." Three hundred angry baseball fans were waiting. They allowed Lane to pass, but they burst into cheers and begged Colavito for autographs.

Baseball executives were aghast. Gabe Paul in Cincinnati thought Lane had made a terrible mistake. William Daley's wife

Cassie protested the trade to her husband. [60] Dolin vowed that Frank Lane's days in Cleveland would soon end. Years later, Hank Peters still could not explain it. "There was no need to make that deal," Peters said. "That's the thing about it. Why would you make that deal? What is the purpose of that deal?" [61]

The trade was a calamity for the Cleveland Indians. Kuenn reported to Cleveland, pulled a muscle in his leg, and played as if he had aged prematurely. The Indians never were a factor in the 1960 race and finished a weak fourth. Attendance fell by more than 500,000 from the previous year as discouraged Cleveland fans simply refused to go to the games. They would not return for years. "That deal took something out of their insides," Gabe Paul said. "Kuenn never did for Cleveland what they thought he could do. They never got over the trading of Rocky." [62]

By the late summer of 1960, Lane knew he was in trouble with Cleveland and with Nate Dolin. Once again, he rooted about for another job. As Lane looked, Dolin telephoned Charles O. Finley, who, as the new owner of the Kansas City Athletics, was in the market for a general manager. "You owe me a favor, Charlie," Dolin said. "You need a general manager. Frank will help you learn the business." When Finley agreed to take Lane, Dolin called Lane to his office. Lane balked. "Frank, you don't hear me right," Dolin snapped. "I'm trying to tell you that your days are numbered and to take that job." [63]

The Indians announced a few days after New Year's in 1961 that Lane left on his own. Cobbledick, who had defended Lane for years, angrily denounced him. "Frank Lane is obsessed with a passion for security," Cobbledick wrote. "The fear of being fired is always with him. That explains why in three terms as general manager—the White Sox, Cardinals and Indians—he has never served out a contract." [64]

The panic-stricken Big Seven had foolishly turned over the Indians in 1957 to an emotional gambler. They knew Lane would engage in endless trades, scream at the umpires, and argue with his players. They wanted a sharp contrast to Hank Greenberg, and, in that, they succeeded. Frank Lane's trades set the team back for years. In 1961, Roger Maris broke Babe Ruth's record with 61 home runs, while Rocky Colavito hit 45, and Norm Cash 41. That same season, Bud Daley pitched for the pennant-winning Yankees, while Don Mossi and Hank Aguirre were key factors for the second-place Tigers.

But Frank Lane does not deserve all the blame for the rapid decline of the Indians. Had the Indians maintained Hank Greenberg's powerful farm system, they would have survived even the loss of Colavito, Cash, Mossi, Daley, and Aguirre. But as Lane made headlines with his trades from 1958 through 1960, Bill Daley and the Big Seven were slashing spending on the farm system that had produced so many talented players. That decision had far greater long-range implications for the Cleveland Indians than Herb Score's injury or Frank Lane's trades.

Lane lasted less than a year in Kansas City. He discovered to his consternation that Finley wanted to make all baseball decisions. One week after moving to Kansas City, Lane told Finley, "I can't understand why you hired a general manager. You don't need one." In late August, Finley fired Lane, who learned of his dismissal from a cab driver. "Gee, that's tough luck, Mr. Lane," the driver told him. Puzzled, Lane asked the driver if he had heard of a player being injured. "No," the driver replied. "You got fired. Didn't you know that?" [65]

Lane became general manager of the Chicago Zephyrs of the National Basketball Association and later served as a consultant for the Baltimore Orioles, Milwaukee Brewers, and Texas Rangers. Nobody seemed to know what to do with him. When he worked for the Texas Rangers, he befriended the visiting clubhouse attendant, Bill Milkie. Milkie would drive Lane from the airport to the Cibola Inn in Arlington. There, in a small coffee shop, Lane would eat a hearty breakfast of poached eggs and bacon, and reminisce about his trades. "I'm a great talker, and you're a great listener," Lane would say. [66]

Lane died alone in 1981, in a small rest home in Richardson, Texas. Baseball Commissioner Bowie Kuhn asked Bobby Bragan to attend the funeral. A quarter of a century earlier, Bragan had been fired as manager of the Indians by Lane. When Bragan arrived at the Restland Memorial Cemetery in Dallas, he saw only seven other people. One was Lane's daughter. Another was Bill Milkie. As Milkie looked about on this cloudy Texas day, he could not help feeling empty. An extraordinary baseball man was gone, but nobody seemed to care. [67]

The minister realized there was no one to deliver a eulogy. He asked Bobby Bragan to say a few words. Bragan thought for a moment. Then he told the seven mourners about Frank Lane and his trades.

Chapter 4

One Tiny Clause

"Don't ever, ever sneer at bookkeeping; that's where the fortunes are made." — Bill Veeck

High up Cleveland's landmark Terminal Tower, Nate Dolin was hunting big-time investors for the Cleveland Indians in a deal with an innovative tax twist. At a private lunch in the Greenbrier Suite, with its richly burnished paneling and commanding view of downtown, Dolin made his pitch to one of the nation's greatest industrialists, Cyrus Eaton, and investment banker William Daley, Eaton's longtime business partner. Daley, who worked in the shadow of the towering Eaton, was enamored with the idea of owning a baseball team, but Eaton had absolutely no interest. "We don't need anything like that," Eaton grumbled.

Nate Dolin had a quick response. "Mr. Eaton," Dolin explained, "you can make a $100 million deal and you'll get four lines on the financial pages of the *Plain Dealer*. When Mr. Daley becomes the head of the Indians, every time he sneezes he'll be on the front pages."

It was a story that Bill Daley relished repeating after he became chairman of the Indians in the winter of 1956. Years later, Daley and Eaton flew down to West Virginia to inspect part of their financial empire, the stately Greenbrier resort in the mountains of White Sulphur Springs. As the aristocratic, silver-haired Eaton and the short, balding Daley emerged from their plane, a group of reporters approached. "Can I help you gentlemen?" Eaton asked expansively. But the reporters weren't interested in Eaton: They wanted to talk baseball. Daley laughed. "Cy, remember that luncheon we had. That fellow was right. Nobody wants to talk to you. I'm the big shot." [1]

Bill Daley had waited a long time to buy his hometown team. In the summer 1949, when Bill Veeck wanted to sell the Indians, Daley had quietly approached him. Daley even planned on elevating Hank Greenberg to the general manager's chair and giving him a share of the team's stock. But Daley's offer fell short of what Veeck wanted for the team, and Veeck sold the Indians to the Big Seven for $2.2 million. [2] Still, Daley did not give up his dream of eventually controlling the Indians. His friends described him as a "bulldog" because of his persistence. Someday, the tenacious Daley would have his chance.

William Raymond Daley, the son of a railroad engineer, had used his drive and perseverance to become an owner of one of the leading investment houses in the United States. He conducted business with Cyrus Eaton, Henry J. Kaiser, and Egyptian President Gamal Abdel Nasser; maintained a close friendship with Father Theodore Hesburgh, the president of the University of Notre Dame; corresponded with Abe Fortas; and gave glittering dinner parties for actress Bette Davis and educator Milton Eisenhower.

Bill Daley's success certainly wasn't built on style or stunning looks. He was short and slight, barely 5-foot-7. He had light brown hair, but his hairline rapidly receded and the few remaining strands turned gray. Daley spoke in a quiet voice and worked best in the background. He was so good at keeping a low profile that when he bought the Indians, one Cleveland newspaper referred to him as James R. Daley.[3] In 1954, when Daley donated $10,000 to Notre Dame for an investment fund at the school's commerce college, he included a letter declaring "it is a mistake to connect my name with the fund. I would rather expect that some of the other members of [Notre Dame's] advisory council might desire to contribute money or securities to the fund from time to time, and I am sure that they would be more likely to do so if my name were not connected with it." [4]

But he more than compensated for his reserved style with a methodical determination and a devotion to hard work. "I find I work best when I'm very busy," he would say, "when I really have too much to do." Like any good lawyer, he prevailed by being better prepared than his competitors. For years, he eschewed driving to work: Too big a waste of time. Instead, every morning he would grab a fistful of newspapers, walk to the Shaker Rapids' stop at Coventry Road, and read voraciously during the 12-minute ride to his office in the Terminal Tower. He was an early convert to flying because he could reach his destination much more quickly than by train. Even as he approached the age of 80, he remained as restless as ever. Shortly before he suffered the stroke that would end his life, he flew from Seattle to Cleveland, dashed off to Chicago, returned home, and then flew to New York City. [5]

He did not make big money until he was past his 40th birthday. He used to joke to his daughter Kathleen that he never suffered through the Great Depression because, "I didn't have any money before it, so I didn't lose it." But he quickly made up for his slow start, and, in 1968, when Daley and Eaton sold most of their interests in iron ore, steel, and shipping, they split the vast sum of $20 million. Bill Daley was a remarkable businessman whose career was marred by only two failures. One was his ownership of the Seattle Pilots in 1969. The other was when he owned the Cleveland Indians.

Bill Daley was born in Ashtabula, Ohio, in 1892, the son of Irish immigrants. Proud of his Irish-Catholic heritage, Daley joined a group in the 1950s to buy the lakes of Killarney in Ireland from an English family of earls. Michael Francis Doyle, the Philadelphia lawyer who arranged the sale, had defended Sir Roger Casement at his 1916 treason trial. Doyle boasted that the lakes were "now free forever from any English rule or control for the first time since the reign of Queen Elizabeth I."

Philanthropy was a big part of Daley's life, often with a focus on his heritage. He served as president of Catholic Charities in Cleveland, and contributed $100,000 in 1957 to the building campaign of Marymount College in Tarreytown, where his daughter Kathleen taught. His happiest moments were at Notre Dame, where he served on the university's advisory board. There, he developed a lifelong friendship with another wealthy Irish Catholic, Ignatius O'Shaughnessy, an oilman from St. Paul.

Daley's father, Flory, worked for 50 years as an engineer on the New York Central Railroad between Cleveland and Buffalo. He once survived a harrowing accident when his train plunged off a trestle in Pennsylvania. Tough Flory Daley emerged from the water with just "a few scratches on my head." [6]

The elder Daley was self-educated and passed on to his son a passion for reading. When Bill Daley wanted to send his father a gift, he invariably chose a book. The younger Daley leaned to history and biography, poring time and again over Winston Churchill's six-volume history of the Second World War and Albert J. Beveridge's 1919 biography of Chief Justice John Marshall. Daley kept his cherished collection of books spotless, warning his two daughters against marking them with pens or pencils.

His friends called him Bill, a nickname he began using in high school when a teacher admonished him, "If you ever want to amount to anything, drop the name 'Willie' and stop parting your hair in the middle." Willie Daley obeyed. He was a gifted, hard-working student with ambitions to be a lawyer. After the family moved to Cleveland in 1910, young Daley earned a law degree at Western Reserve University in 1917.

To earn extra money for school, Daley worked as an usher at League Park for a dollar a game. The Naps, as the Cleveland baseball team was known before adopting the nickname Indians in 1915, were a weak team that generated little interest in the city. In both 1914 and 1915, the team attracted fewer than 200,000 paying customers to its home games. The 1914 Naps lost 102 games and finished last in the American League. But Bill Daley loved working at the ballpark. His favorite players were outfielder Joe Birmingham, a player-manager in 1913 and 1914; and catcher Steve O'Neill, a tough Irishman who caught the brilliant pitchers of the 1920 pennant-winning Indians—Jim Bagby, Stan Coveleski, Ray Caldwell, George Uhle, and Duster Mails.

After working his way through law school, Daley joined the Cleveland law firm of Bulkley, Hauxhurst, Inglis and Saeger, whose name partner was U.S. Senator Robert Bulkley of Ohio. But like thousands of young Americans, Daley enlisted in the Army in 1917 and was assigned to a machine gun company in the 331st Infantry Division. A year later, he was promoted to second lieutenant in the field artillery. Following his discharge in January 1919, he returned to Bulkley, Hauxhurst, where he was promoted to partner in 1925. He married a woman he had known since high school, settled down in the suburbs to raise a family, and had every reason to believe that he could make a comfortable living practicing law in one of the fastest growing cities in America. But Daley was bored with the law, he confided years later to his daughter Kathleen. America in the 1920s was enjoying a decade of unmatched prosperity, and Daley was eager to earn his share.

In 1928, he had his chance: Richard Inglis, his law partner, took a job at the powerful Cleveland investment house, Otis & Co. Inglis asked Daley to join Otis as counsel for its buying department. Daley, then 36, accepted. At Otis he met the man who would change his life—Cyrus Stephen Eaton.

Cyrus Eaton was a man in motion. He played ice hockey until he was 70, snow skied until his eighth decade, and up to age 90 rode a horse about his sprawling farm south of Cleveland. He boasted that he never needed an aspirin. Like William Daley, he was energetic, tough, and relentlessly ambitious. Unlike Daley, he had soaring dreams and imagination. With those, he built an empire of railroads, steel, coal, and electric power.

In a way, it was the Great Depression that brought Daley and Eaton together. Eaton, a partner at Otis since 1916, used the banking house to merge a group of sickly steel companies into Republic Steel, which by 1929 had $350 million in assets. By then, Eaton had assembled a private fortune in excess of $80 million. But within two years, Eaton had lost virtually everything under the crushing weight of the Great Depression and a bitter legal battle with Charles M. Schwab of Bethlehem Steel. Except for his partnership at Otis, Eaton had little, a memory that haunted him for years. "I have found that when you are broke, nobody cares a hang for you," Eaton once said. [7]

With little else in his life but Otis, Cyrus Eaton developed a friendship with Bill Daley, who had advanced to manager of the buying department. Like Eaton and much of the nation, the investment firm was crippled by the Depression. Daley reorganized Otis from a partnership to a corporation, assumed the title of president, and personally selected a board of directors that rarely disagreed with him. While Eaton did not own any company stock until 1940, he never hesitated to shower Daley with advice on the firm's operations.

They were described as Mutt and Jeff, and it was more than their contrasting appearances. Eaton was the creative visionary; Daley, the methodical executor of his plans. While Eaton built his empire, Daley became one of the nation's leading experts on complicated stock offerings. And the two men were more than business partners; they were friends. They chatted at the office, exchanged regular telegrams when either traveled, and talked by phone on weekends. Daley once described Eaton as "the most prolific" user of the telephone he had ever seen. [8].

Together, they set about to rebuild Otis after the Depression and, not so incidentally, to beat out their hated rivals in New York. In 1938, Chesapeake & Ohio planned to raise money through a $30 million bond issue. Otis won the bond sale by underbidding Wall Street's Morgan Stanley & Co. by more than $2 million. Eaton used the proceeds to buy shares of C & O— a company he eventually controlled.

Harboring a deep distrust of their New York competitors, they delighted in outwitting them. In 1942, Eaton learned of a vast supply of iron ore under the deep Steep Rock Lake in Ontario. The ore was desperately needed for the Allied war effort, but steel companies had written it off as impossible to mine. The industrious Eaton paddled a canoe to the lake's center and concluded it could be drained and the ore recovered. [9] Handed Eaton's dream, Daley dutifully arranged the financing to dig a massive tunnel and dynamite the lake. They succeeded in mining the ore in what Daley would describe as "my most fascinating business venture." [10]

But Eaton and Daley also could be ruthless in defending their pursuit of wealth. A business deal gone awry in the late 1940s showed their style when their empire was threatened. Whether it was high finance in the 1940s or the Cleveland Indians in the 1950s, Daley played hardball. Neither he nor Eaton intended to ever be "broke" again.

Henry J. Kaiser needed help from Bill Daley and Cyrus Eaton. The man who helped overwhelm German submarines by building thousands of Liberty cargo ships during World War II wanted to challenge General Motors and Ford for automotive supremacy. Kaiser and his partner, Joseph Frazer of Detroit, turned to Otis for the financing, and in 1945 and 1946 Otis successfully underwrote millions of dollars in common stock for the new company.

Then, in May 1947, Frazer and Kaiser's son, Edgar, met with Daley and Eaton to ask if Otis could underwrite another stock offering. Edgar said the company would soon produce two new cars, but first needed fresh capital to pay off a $12 million loan.

Daley was cautious; he had watched in alarm as Kaiser-Frazer stock plummeted from $20 per share in 1946 to $6 a share on the day of the meeting. [11]

By December 1947, the stock had rebounded to $15. Henry Kaiser, still hopeful for help from Otis, telephoned Daley and predicted his company would show a profit of $20 million in 1947. [12] By mid-January, a deal was in the works where Otis and two other underwriters would buy 1.5 million shares of Kaiser's stock and sell it for a higher value on the market.

But the news at Kaiser-Frazer got no better. Otis attorney Carter Kissell warned Daley that Kaiser-Frazer's actual profit for December 1947 would be only $300,000—far short of the profits Henry Kaiser had promised Daley. The stock kept slipping, and Daley remained nervous until February 3, 1948, the day the contract was to be signed in New York. During the meeting with Henry Kaiser, Cyrus Eaton and two other investment bankers, Harold Allen of Allen & Co. and Ted Birr of First California, Daley suggested they instead put half the stock—750,000 shares—on the market immediately. Kaiser pushed for 900,000 shares, with an option for 600,000 later. If Otis backed out, Kaiser warned, he would turn to Dean Witter or any of a number of underwriters. [13]

"All right," Daley said reluctantly. "I will go ahead."

The next day when Otis offered the 900,000 shares, buyers had no interest. Otis faced catastrophe; the company would be stuck with hundreds of thousands of shares. An alarmed Cyrus Eaton, who had remained in New York, told Ted Birr he wanted to cancel the contract. "Anybody who goes through with a commitment when he is going to lose money is a sucker," Eaton snapped. [14] That evening, Eaton went to Henry Kaiser's office to announce his intention to withdraw from the deal. When Kaiser objected, Eaton angrily said, "I'm warning you that if you go through with this, you will be flooded with lawsuits and your stock will be driven down to $5 a share. All hell will be apoppin." [15]

Eaton telephoned Kissell in Cleveland to demand, "What sorts of outs do we have in this contract?" They concluded that a lawsuit filed by a Kaiser-Frazer stockholder would allow them to abrogate the agreement. Eaton telephoned Daley in Cleveland to advise him of the scheme. [16] There is no record of Daley objecting to using a technicality to evade the contract. As far as Daley was concerned, Kaiser-Frazer was at fault for being less than candid about its finances.

Eaton set in motion a series of telephone calls that culminated the following Monday when James Masterson, who owned 300 shares of Kaiser-Frazer stock, filed suit in Detroit. The timing was no accident. That very day, Daley and Eaton attended the closing in Cleveland with attorneys representing Kaiser-Frazer and the other underwriters. The meeting should have taken no more than two hours, but Eaton, Daley, and their lawyers pored over the papers so slowly that by lunchtime, they were barely half done. When they resumed in the afternoon, a staff member walked in and handed Daley a news report that a suit had been filed. That night Eaton terminated the contract, and Kaiser-Frazer struck back with its own lawsuit. [17]

Daley's role is murky. While telephone records introduced at trial make clear that Eaton helped initiate the Masterson suit, Daley was not directly involved in any of the numerous calls. During the 1951 trial in federal court in New York, Daley denied having advance knowledge of the Masterson suit. But there is evidence to the contrary. Not only was Eaton orchestrating the lawsuit, but Daley's old law partner, former Senator Bulkley, telephoned Masterson the Saturday before the suit was filed. Daley knew Masterson, who had served as an attorney for Otis in a case in Philadelphia. Moreover, Eaton and Daley so deliberately caused delay during the closing that Kaiser-Frazer attorney Mark Hughes told the court "they were just itching to know that the lawsuit was on file. They knew it was going on the A.P. wire." [18]

Eaton and Daley had played it hard and emerged as winners. U.S. District Judge John W. Clancy ruled in Kaiser-Frazer's favor in 1951, but a federal appeals court overturned the ruling in 1952. In the majority opinion, Judge Augustus Hand concluded the Masterson lawsuit was irrelevant. Eaton and Daley were justified in breaking the contract, Hand wrote, because Kaiser-Frazer had "stated its earnings in such a way as to represent that it made a profit of about $4 million in December 1947. This representation was $3.1 million short of the truth."

Eaton and Daley's tough tactics saved Otis from bankruptcy. "I would rather have a lawsuit on my hands than to be dead broke," Eaton said. [19] But their ruthlessness offended business competitors. With Eaton and Daley, one Cleveland businessman

later said, "everything was brinkmanship." The trick was to figure out when they were bluffing.

❖

The plan Nate Dolin brought to Daley and Eaton in the
Greenbrier Suite in 1955 had been born in 1949 when the Big
Seven was negotiating to buy the Indians from Bill Veeck. "What
am I getting for my $2.2 million?" Dolin asked Veeck over drinks
at Max Gruber's. Veeck replied that the Big Seven would obtain
the rights to player-manager Lou Boudreau "and the right to sign
39 other players." Any land, any buildings? Dolin asked. "No,"
Veeck answered. "That's it." [20]

Dolin was puzzled. Every corporation, he knew, had to have
assets, be it a blast furnace at Republic Steel or an assembly line
at General Motors. Assets could be depreciated, generating huge
tax savings. But if the city of Cleveland owned Cleveland Stadium, what on earth were the assets of the Indians? He finally
struck upon the obvious answer: The players. Dolin thumbed
through baseball history books and concluded that teams with
good players won more games and attracted more fans than
teams with bad players. Even though the players were human
beings and not machines, Dolin concluded they could be depreciated. In 1949, Dolin sketched out his ideas in a meeting with
Veeck at Cleveland Stadium. Then, Dolin took his case to the
Internal Revenue Service in Washington, the one city he regularly
traveled to so he could dine with *Washington Post* sports columnist Shirley Povich at Duke Zeibert's. Since 1935, the IRS had
permitted baseball teams to write off as a business expense for
one year the money used to buy a player from another team. But
the IRS had never extended the rule to Dolin's plan to buy the
entire roster of Indians players and depreciate them as assets.
After hearing Dolin's arguments, the IRS ruled that baseball
teams could depreciate their players over a five-year period,
known as a depreciation schedule. For the Big Seven, the ruling
was a windfall. To buy the Indians, they raised $1.2 million
among themselves and borrowed the remaining $1 million from
the banks. Within two years, they had paid back the entire loan.

By 1955, when the depreciation schedule was expiring on
many of the players, Nate Dolin's nimble mind devised a new
solution. Why couldn't the Big Seven sell the assets of the Indi-

ans to a brand-new corporation? The new company could depreciate the value of the same players all over again. Back he went to the IRS. The theory was fine, IRS officials told him. But the government would not permit the Big Seven to create another corporation and, in effect, sell the Indians back to themselves strictly for tax advantages. Instead, the IRS ruled that the Big Seven could control no more than 45 percent of the stock in the new company, and that new investors would have to own the rest. The Big Seven would have to yield control of the team. Harry Small and Donald Hornbeck, two of the original members of the Big Seven, suggested that Dolin contact Bill Daley and Cyrus Eaton. Daley, they told him, had plenty of money and would not be a hostile stockholder. He would fit right in with the Big Seven and allow Dolin, Hank Greenberg, and George Medinger to help direct the team.

Daley had never given up his hopes of owning the team. Sitting at the desk once used by firm founder Charles Otis, Daley could look down from his office on the 23rd floor of the Terminal Tower and watch the huge crowds file into Cleveland Stadium. No more the ragtag team he saw as an usher at League Park, the Indians were now big business. The Indians finished a strong second in 1955 and turned an impressive profit of $89,756. Only the three teams in New York City earned more broadcast revenue that year than Cleveland's $567,891. [21]

By February 1956, Daley and the Big Seven struck a deal. Although newspapers reported the transaction as a sale, in fact it was a reorganization. The Big Seven sold the Indians for $3.9 million to a new corporation headed by Daley, Hank Greenberg, and Ignatius O'Shaughnessy, Daley's old friend from Notre Dame. The new owners retained control of 55 percent of the stock and sold the rest back to Dolin, Harry Small, Don Hornbeck, George Medinger, Mike Wilson, and Charles and Andy Baxter.

For the Big Seven it was a financial coup; they had turned a $3 million profit since the 1953 buyout of Ellis Ryan. [22] Shares of stock they bought in 1949 for $100 had been sold to Daley for $1,550 a share. With Daley liquidating the assets of the old corporation, he and the Big Seven could look forward to five years of tax advantages worth millions. In 1956, for example, the Indians reported a loss of $167,110. But that was strictly on paper. The Big Seven wrote off in excess of $700,000 in player depreciation and other expenses, which meant the team earned more than $500,000. [23]

The new corporation looked much like the old: Wilson was named president, Dolin and Medinger vice presidents; Small was the treasurer and Hornbeck the secretary. Daley assumed the title chairman of the board, but he made clear that Hank Greenberg would have complete control of the baseball operations. Daley urged Greenberg to buy stock because of his belief that "anybody who runs a business should own a part of it." Daley told his family that while he was a baseball fan, he "didn't know enough to run the Indians." Greenberg had proven he could build a winning and profitable team. There was no reason to make a change. Daley's chief job would be "watching the box scores and attendance figures. Until now, I've been involved in three kinds of investment: conservative ones, highly speculative ones and in-between ones. This is a new kind. Call it a 'fun' investment." How much Daley intended to spend to have fun is unclear. O'Shaughnessy promised "we'll spend millions, if necessary, to win the pennant." As for Daley, there were limits. "Of course, you don't go wild," Daley said. "But we're willing to assume a reasonable cost in bringing a winner here." The Indians were still a powerful contender with a productive nine-team minor league system. There was no reason to believe that would change. [24]

Both Daley and O'Shaughnessy had the money to keep the Indians a winner. O'Shaughnessy had made a fortune as a tough wildcatter who founded his own company, Globe Oil and Refining Company. He delighted in handing out hundreds of thousands of dollars to his favorite universities. He gave Notre Dame $1.5 million in 1950 to construct a liberal and fine arts building, and when university officials told him a year later the costs had escalated, he wrote a new check for $670,000. A grateful Notre Dame named the building after him, and he continued to give money, including $1 million in 1962. "Money is like manure," he once told a friend after he saw *Hello Dolly* in New York. "It doesn't do any good unless you spread it around." [25]

By the time he invested in the Indians, O'Shaughnessy was past 70. With his rimless glasses and thinning white hair, he looked like a kindly grandfather. But I.A., as friends called him, could be blunt. During an audience with Pope Paul VI,

O'Shaughnessy offered $4 million to build the International Institute of Ecumenical Studies in Jerusalem. O'Shaughnessy then turned to his friend, Father Hesburgh, who was serving as translator. "Tell him I want some action on this project," O'Shaughnessy said. "I don't want these Vatican bureaucrats to sit on their hands." [26]

O'Shaughnessy had met Bill Daley on a train, and the two quickly discovered how much they had in common. They both adored Notre Dame and by the late 1940s were serving on the university's advisory council. They often met on Saturday afternoons in South Bend for a Notre Dame football game. Now they owned a baseball team. It was a fitting way to cap their careers.

For the first time, Bill Daley emerged from Eaton's shadow. The *Cleveland News'* Ed Bang published a major profile of Daley within a month of the sale of the team. The mayor of East Berlin personally greeted Daley on a visit to East Germany. Abe Fortas of the Washington law firm of Arnold, Fortas & Porter jokingly asked Daley in a letter if he needed any .400 hitters. Eaton himself felt compelled to congratulate his business partner. While on a visit to Rome in the spring of 1956, Eaton dashed off the following note: "This is the February 18 issue of the Rome *Daily American*, which gave me the first news that the Indians had a new Big Chief the morning after I arrived in Italy." [27]

But Daley's hopes of pennants and easy profits were quickly dashed. Although Early Wynn, Herb Score, and Bob Lemon each won 20 games in 1956, the Yankees hit 190 home runs and outscored the Cleveland offense by 145 runs. By July 1956, with the Yankees comfortably cruising toward another pennant, O'Shaughnessy complained, "I don't believe in being No. 2. I want those boys to get in there and fight like hell to win a pennant this year." [28] The Indians finished second for the fifth time in six years, nine games behind the Yankees. Worse, from Daley's point of view, Cleveland attendance dropped off dramatically. For the first time since 1945, the Indians failed to attract one million people to their home games. "Sure they're good," one Cleveland Stadium customer told Gordon Cobbledick. "But you can get tired of a good movie after you've sat through half-a-dozen showings. I used to think it was great stuff the way Lemon, Wynn and Garcia mowed down the bad guys and all we had to do was wait until Rosen and Doby or one of the other musclemen hit one out of the park. But I'll admit, the plot has become tiresome." [29]

The collapse in attendance was a shock to Daley and the Big Seven. Their fears went public in April 1957 when Mike Wilson appeared before a record crowd at the Cleveland Advertising Club. The huge turnout, Wilson told the audience, was a solid sign that people in Cleveland wanted the Indians to remain in the city. That comment produced a "What-in-the-World-Does-That-Mean" column the following Sunday by Gordon Cobbledick. It was the first time, Cobbledick wrote, that anyone "ever indicated officially that there was any question about the Cleveland Indians staying in Cleveland from now until the end of time." [30]

With Herb Score's eye-injury and Bob Lemon's arm giving out, the Indians fell to sixth place in 1957, and attendance plunged. During the All-Star Game in St. Louis, reporters picked up a story that the Indians planned to move to Minneapolis at the end of the season. "Frankly," Whitey Lewis of the *Cleveland Press* wrote, "I don't know whether or not it's too late to save the Indians for Cleveland." The next day, Daley felt obliged to issue a statement declaring that "the management and stockholders of the Cleveland Indians have never contemplated any transfer of this club to any other city." In the middle of September, Daley told a luncheon at the Hotel Manger that the Indians would be in Cleveland in 1958. Then, Daley and the Big Seven replaced Greenberg with Frank Lane at the end of the season. They wanted to liven up Cleveland baseball. [31]

Whitey Lewis was looking forward to spring training in 1958. Hank Greenberg was gone, and Lewis planned on a summer of fun with Frank Lane. No longer would Lewis have to deal with a general manager who loathed him.

On the morning of March 12, Lewis drove 120 miles from Tucson to cover an Indians' exhibition game against the Baltimore Orioles in Scottsdale. He interviewed Baltimore pitcher George Zuverink and returned to the stadium's open-air press box. As he typed, he glanced back at the dark clouds that suggested a desert storm would soon engulf the park. When he yanked the final page from his typewriter, rain fell and washed out the game. "Glad I got this one done," Lewis told another writer. "It's on George Zuverink, just so you don't duplicate." The tanned Lewis added, "It's not literature. But I talked with the guy."

Lewis drove back to Tucson where he joined Indians Publicity Director Nate Wallick for gin rummy. By the time the game ended at two in the morning, Lewis had won big. He then went back to his hotel room and fell asleep. Shortly before seven in the morning, Lewis walked into the bathroom, collapsed, and died of a heart attack. Nate Dolin accompanied Lewis' body by train back to Cleveland. Bill Veeck and Paul Brown of the Cleveland Browns hailed his memory. But Hank Greenberg could say little. The hostility had run too deep.

The team that Lewis had hoped to cover in 1958 excited nobody that season. Despite Lane's never-ending trades and the adoring attention he received from the press, attendance continued to sag. For the third consecutive season, the Indians would fail to attract one million fans. By August, the Indians were 18 games behind the first-place Yankees, and only 4,474 people showed up for one mid-month game. Frank Lane confessed that he was discouraged by the attendance, while stockholders were told to brace for a $300,000 paper loss that year. [32]

Lane complained that "only five or six downtown businesses" bought season tickets in 1958, but that was largely caused by Daley's unimaginative marketing approach. One businessman told Gordon Cobbledick that the Indians used to have their better players knock on the doors of Cleveland's biggest companies and sell season tickets. "I was glad to see one of them come into my office," the businessman recalled. "We talked some baseball, and I always wound up buying a box. Now, no one comes to see me and—you know how it is—I just don't get around to making the move myself. If I just opened my store and waited for people to come in, I'd be out of business in a hurry." [33]

Daley did not see it that way. Although he regaled friends with stories of watching the Indians play in the 1920 World Series at League Park, he now expressed doubts about Cleveland's ability to support major league baseball. He complained that the Cleveland area's seven racetracks were siphoning away his fans. "Maybe," Daley grumbled, "if we could send bookmakers running up and down the stadium aisle shouting, 'Three-to-one he doesn't get a hit,' we'd get the business back." [34]

Daley had said nothing publicly, but Cleveland City Council President Jack Russell was alarmed. In mid-August, he organized political and business leaders into a "Back the Indians" committee. Russell told Daley and Dolin that he wanted a special night in September and pledged to "draw the biggest crowd in the history of the stadium." He promised to pressure city ward leaders and suburban mayors to "get people down to the ballpark that night." He even suggested that team officials put on a spectacular fireworks show, harking back to the thrills of the Veeck era. [35]

Daley and Dolin agreed to support the special Cleveland Stadium night. But after meeting with Russell, Daley told a reporter, "We obviously can't continue this way. It's beginning to be evident that Cleveland won't support us." Daley said "we will continue to invest money in the improvement of the team, and if Cleveland won't support it, we may have to move." He warned that without an advance sale of 500,000 for 1959, it would not make financial sense to remain in Cleveland. He said he was under intense pressure from some of the stockholders to move the team. [36]

Daley's public pessimism echoed his private talks with stockholders. According to a written statement issued later that year by Hank Greenberg and the Baxter brothers, Daley summoned the stockholders to his office in late August and said he wanted to move the team. "I guess we better face up to it," Daley said, suggesting that he would open talks with civic leaders in Minneapolis and Houston. Greenberg released the statement as part of a bitter dispute among the stockholders, and it contained the strongest evidence that Daley was poised to give up his hometown in pursuit of greater profit. Daley controlled enough shares of stock to have the key vote in any decision to move. [37]

The fact that Daley issued his public warning on August 20 probably was no accident. Just one day earlier, Gerald Moore, chairman of the Minneapolis Metropolitan Area Sports Commission, had asked the Minneapolis City Council to approve a $9 million bond issue to modernize the city's minor league ballpark. "We are, right now, on the threshold of bringing a team to this area," Moore told council members. Moore did not identify the team, but he was referring to the Washington Senators. [38] By his comments, however, Daley clearly was suggesting that the Indians might have some interest as well.

If Daley wanted to move the team, he had one serious obstacle. The lease allowing the Indians to play in city-owned Cleveland Stadium appeared to preclude a transfer to another city. Don Hornbeck of the Big Seven negotiated the terms of the lease in the spring of 1950 with Joseph Rowley, chief counsel for the Cleveland City Law Department. The lease, still on file in Cleveland government archives, did not expire until the end of 1964, and contained two clauses that the city could have used to block the Indians' move. One section declared that the Indians "shall play all of [their] regularly scheduled home games at the Cleveland Municipal Stadium and no other place." Two paragraphs later, the team agreed to pay the city a minimum annual rent of $60,000 until the lease expired in 1964. [39] A partner at a Washington, D.C., law firm concluded in 1993 that it bound the Indians to Cleveland until 1964. If the team broke the lease, the Washington lawyer said, the city could have demanded at least $360,000 in damages—the minimum annual rent due from 1959 to 1964. [40]

It is almost inconceivable that the meticulous, well-prepared Daley did not take the simple precaution of examining the lease. Daley quickly would have realized that the city would have a powerful argument in court if the Indians moved. But Daley had been through this before with Kaiser-Frazer, and he knew that courts sometimes permitted contracts to be broken. In Cyrus Eaton's own words, anybody "who goes through with a commitment... when he is going to lose money, is a sucker." Bill Daley may have been "a sweet man," as Nate Dolin would say years later. But he was no sucker.

Al Rosen was worried throughout that summer of 1958. Since his retirement from the Indians, he had turned his attention full time to being a stockbroker. Daley's threat to move the team struck him as very real. Rosen telephoned his old friend, Bill Veeck, who was on the prowl for a ballclub. Rosen was confident the Indians could quickly be rebuilt into contenders, and Rosen already knew how he'd do it. He planned to bring back such former Cleveland stars as Bob Feller and Lou Boudreau to help run the team, while Veeck would turn loose his promotional skills on a city that had not seen his Barnum & Bailey style since 1949. Veeck and Rosen formed a syndicate that included Robert Black, president of White Motors in Cleveland. They offered Daley and the Big Seven $4 million, and Rosen produced a certified check for $100,000 to prove the offer was serious. "I believe deeply that the Indians belong in Cleveland, and to Cleveland," Rosen said. He was willing to show his "confidence in the future of baseball in this city by investing my money in the club. I'll be awfully disappointed if our offer isn't accepted." [41]

Daley, who was traveling in Detroit when Rosen's offer became public on Friday, August 22, rejected the bid, declaring that he "went into baseball to stay, and that's what I intend to do." Instead, Daley telephoned Cleveland Mayor Anthony J. Celebrezze and asked for a meeting at the mayor's office on Saturday morning.

Celebrezze, born in Italy before his parents immigrated to the United States, had been mayor since 1953. A lawyer and a Democrat, Celebrezze had big plans for Cleveland, hoping to turn a series of crumbling old buildings near the lake into office towers as the centerpiece of a new downtown. To lose the Indians would be a devastating blow to his plans. Celebrezze thought the real problem with the Indians' low attendance was Bill Daley, far too reserved to be an effective promoter. Celebrezze recalled the evenings in 1948 when Bill Veeck set off fireworks and entertained crowds with circus acts and midget races. Celebrezze knew Bill Daley was a shrewd businessman who often volunteered to help him on downtown projects. Daley was effective in private meetings with businessmen and political leaders. In public, he lacked Veeck's flair. [42] Moreover, Daley was incredibly busy with his other investments. Far too often, Daley was out of town when his team was playing. He once returned to Cleveland late in the evening after a game and telephoned the *Plain Dealer*. When a sportswriter told Daley the Indians had lost that night, he quietly complained, "Daggone it." [43]

Early that Saturday morning, Celebrezze asked Ralph Locher, the city's law director, to bring him a copy of the lease. They noted that the team had guaranteed the city $360,000 for the final six years of the lease. [44] Then Celebrezze, wearing a handsome gray suit, met Daley privately in his City Hall office. As reporters waited outside, Celebrezze told Daley that the city was about to embark on a "new era." The Indians were crucial to downtown Cleveland. Did Daley want to inflict such damage upon his hometown? Celebrezze asked. Daley countered by pointing to the team's declining attendance. The Indians' owners did not have the money to survive continued financial losses. "I'll give you a bit of advice," Celebrezze told Daley. "Your attendance will go up when your club starts winning."

"Well," Daley finally told Celebrezze, "you've given me a new light on the matter." [45] The two men emerged to speak with reporters. "I am convinced that Mr. Daley is sincerely interested in keeping the Indians in Cleveland, and that they will stay provided the community shows an interest in keeping them," Celebrezze said. The newspapers were puzzled. The *Cleveland News* ran an alarming headline, "Daley Keeps Moving Van Ready," while the *Cleveland Press* printed a more optimistic, "Want Tribe Here, Daley Tells Mayor."

The next evening, Daley and Celebrezze joined broadcaster Tom Manning for a radio interview at KYW. Both Manning and Celebrezze pressed Daley for a commitment to keep the Indians in Cleveland. "We're trying to sell boxes for next year's games," Celebrezze told Daley. "How can we sell them if we can't give assurances that the club will be here?" But Daley refused to budge. Unless the Indians' attendance increased, he told the radio audience, "the club would have no recourse but to go to other pastures." [46] Nobody seemed to know whether Bill Daley was playing the usual Eaton-Daley game of brinkmanship or if he truly wanted to move the team.

In Minneapolis, there was a frenzy of activity. On September 2, Minneapolis officials approved a $9 million bond issue to expand Metropolitan Stadium to 41,000 seats. Minneapolis Alderman Byron Nelson predicted it was a "dead cinch" that Washington owner Calvin Griffith would move the Senators there. [47] Griffith called for a special meeting of the American League owners on Monday, September 8, in Chicago, to ask for permission to move. Griffith flew to Chicago on Sunday, and at 6:30 in the evening abruptly advised Minneapolis officials he was staying in Washington. Griffith apparently succumbed to pressure from New York Yankee owners Dan Topping and Del Webb who opposed leaving the nation's capital. "They control enough votes to control any move," a league official told Sid Hartman of the *Minneapolis Morning Tribune*. [48]

Minneapolis, however, now had a stadium under construction and no team to play in it. The American League was particularly eager to have one of its clubs move into Minneapolis, lest the rival National League get there first as the league had done in Los Angeles and San Francisco. Charles Johnson, the *Minneapolis Star*'s influential sports columnist, wrote on September 9 that the Indians were the likeliest team to move into the new stadium. He wrote that the Cleveland owners "have insisted all year to Minneapolis people that they would not even talk about the subject at any time during the regular season." But the season would soon be over, and Johnson suggested that negotiations with the Indians might begin in October.

The very next night, 50,021 people—the largest single game crowd in Cleveland since 1955—filled Cleveland Stadium on "Back the Indians" night. The Yankees won, 8-3, but city officials were happy anyway. Arthur Haley, the director of public relations at Notre Dame and a longtime friend of Daley's, typed him a note saying, "I was glad to see in this morning's paper a good crowd had turned out for the game last night in Cleveland. It was unfortunate that the score was not different, and also that you did not have a bit warmer weather for the occasion. I do hope that good results were obtained publicity-wise." [49]

Hank Greenberg had never been through a more dismal summer than that season of 1958. He missed running the team, and league rules prohibited him from taking a front-office job with another club until he sold his Indians' stock. What hurt him even more was that friends throughout baseball ignored him. The only call he received that year was from Birdie Tebbetts, who asked him to become a batting instructor for the Milwaukee Braves.

His marriage to Caral Gimbel was crumbling. Although they were a striking couple, they had little else in common: She was bored with baseball and preferred to ride horses at the exclusive country clubs in the Chagrin Valley. By the end of the year, she made it official and filed for divorce.

Meanwhile, Greenberg hated what Frank Lane was doing to his team. He privately mocked the nickname "Trader Lane" and carped that Lane was "tearing the club apart." Greenberg was infuriated that the same Cleveland reporters who disliked him loved Lane, even though Greenberg thought that Lane's reputation was created "completely by his own comments to the press."

Greenberg's anger toward the city's reporters and the fact that his own money was at stake drove him toward the same drastic solution that Daley was considering: Moving the Indians to another city, preferably Minneapolis. Greenberg was convinced that Minneapolis was ideal for major league baseball, and that the Indians' farm system was capable of producing the players needed to win. The Minneapolis newspapers were enthusiastically seeking a major league team; their sportswriters would be far more supportive of the Indians than their Cleveland counterparts. [50] But Greenberg controlled only 20 percent of the team's stock and to move the team, he needed allies. The only major stockholders backing him were the investment brothers, Wing and Andy Baxter, and neither was particularly reliable. Wing Baxter was so well known in the Cleveland restaurants that he only had to walk in to be handed a tall glass of vodka with ice. Andy was younger and more impulsive; Nate Dolin tried to give Andy a crash course in baseball management by sending him one summer to the Indians' farm team in Reading. The next thing Dolin knew, Andy had gone right past Reading and did not stop until he reached South America.

But together, the Baxters and Greenberg controlled 38 percent of the team's stock. "The only way we can move this franchise is to buy the stock of the ballclub 100 percent and move it, or else offer to sell our shares of stock to the current management," Greenberg told them. That became Greenberg's plan of attack, and soon he got lucky. Craig Cullinan, Jr., whose family operated Texaco, sent Greenberg a telegram saying that he was interested in buying the Indians and moving them to Houston. Greenberg telephoned Cullinan and told him that "the club is for sale for $6 million as far as the Baxters and myself are concerned."

"Well, I'll agree to a $6 million price providing you can transfer the franchise," Cullinan replied. Just two years earlier, the Indians had been valued at $3.9 million.

"Send a telegram to Mr. Daley," Greenberg told him. "He will then be required to announce it at the directors' meeting." Greenberg explained that Daley would have only three choices: accept Cullinan's offer and allow the franchise to go to Houston; vote his shares of stock with Greenberg and the Baxters and move the Indians to Minneapolis; or buy Greenberg's stock at the hefty price Cullinan was offering.

Cullinan sent the telegram. Bill Daley now had two cities competing for his franchise. [51]

Bill Daley had to make a decision by October 31—the last day league rules permitted a team to move in time for the 1959 season. Daley flew to Milwaukee to watch the World Series between the Yankees and Milwaukee Braves. Frank Gibbons, who had taken over Lewis' column for the *Cleveland Press*, found Daley still pessimistic about the team remaining in Cleveland. "Frankly," Daley said, "I'm still very skeptical." Daley said the team's board of directors would meet in the next two weeks to decide the future of the franchise. [52]

Ever determined to be prepared, Daley wanted to learn more about Minneapolis. During the World Series, Cleveland newspapers reported that Daley would leave Milwaukee for a business trip to Canada. But Daley's real destination was Minneapolis; according to the Greenberg-Baxter statement, Daley "was in conference with a group in Minneapolis" during the World Series. [53] Their statement is supported by Sid Hartman, who said he showed Daley the Minneapolis ballpark during the Yankee-Braves series. Minneapolis officials promised Daley that the Indians would attract more than one million fans during their first year of operation. Daley finally told Hartman, "It's up to two guys, Nate Dolin and George Medinger. If they want to move, we're going to move." [54]

Forty years later, it is nearly impossible to untangle the twisted facts of who wanted to move the Indians. Nate Dolin, the only living member of the Big Seven, said he firmly opposed a transfer. George Medinger's son, Myron, declared that his late father also was against the move. Balanced against that is Gabe Paul's curious recollection that Medinger and Greenberg had rented apartments in Minneapolis, and Hartman said the Clevelanders were considering buying homes in Minnesota. Daley's thinking remains a mystery. In 1959, when the Indians were in a pennant race and attracting huge crowds, Daley publicly wrote off his actions of the previous season as "shock therapy" for Cleveland politicians and fans. "People had come to take the team for granted," Daley said. "It was popular to knock the ballclub. Even the mayor didn't give much thought to doing something about the complaints of the fans." [55] But that wouldn't explain his trip to Minneapolis during the World Series or the stockholders' meeting in August 1958, where he told colleagues he planned to move the franchise. Perhaps he was toying with the idea, but changed his mind after investigating all the avenues. Maybe he opposed the sale and used the lease restriction to face down the revolt by Greenberg and the Baxter brothers.

The most likely explanation, though, is that Daley wanted to move the team and was thwarted by the lease. While Minneapolis promised huge financial success, the cost of moving the Indians would be high. The Indians would have to pay $400,000 to the minor leagues for taking over the rights to Minneapolis. Cleveland officials almost certainly would sue, and a court might order the team to pay the city $360,000 for breaking the lease. Worse yet, a judge might even order the team back to Cleveland to fulfill the terms of the lease.

After checking with the board directors of the Indians, Daley met on October 16 with members of the "Back the Indians" committee at the Greenbrier Suite. The team, he told them, would remain in Cleveland. His public comments suggested that sentiment and hometown spirit motivated his decision to keep the team in Cleveland. "If this were strictly a business, and not a sport tied in with Cleveland, there would have only been one course I could have recommended to our shareholders," Daley said. "I would have said take one of the offers." [56]

Greenberg was infuriated. Daley's decision precluded the stockholders from either voting to move the Indians to Minneapolis or accepting Cullinan's $6 million offer. On October 21, at a board of directors meeting at Don Hornbeck's office in the Union Commerce Building, Greenberg and the Baxters demanded that Daley, Dolin, and Medinger resign. When Daley refused, Greenberg and the Baxters issued a detailed public statement charging that "for the past two months, we are informed, Mr. Daley has been conducting negotiations to move the club with groups from at least three different cities."

Greenberg handed Daley an ultimatum: Either sell him controlling interest in the Indians at $450 a share or buy out Greenberg and the Baxters at $400 a share. Daley had no real choice. On November 18, 1958, Daley and the Big Seven paid $800,000 to buy the stock owned by Greenberg and the Baxters. Just two years earlier, Greenberg purchased his stock for $50 a share; he earned a $350,000 profit on that investment. [57] Gordon Cobbledick wrote that Daley "proved himself a sportsman first, and an investor second."

After 10 turbulent years, Hank Greenberg was gone. The last great general manager of the Cleveland Indians was now without stock or a job, and ironically the sportswriters were pleased. Frank Gibbons of the *Press* said it would be "dishonest for me to say that I regret" Hank Greenberg's "passing from the Cleveland baseball scene." But Greenberg missed the game. When Bill Veeck asked him in 1959 if he wanted to help him buy the White Sox, Greenberg replied, "Sure, if you can get it, count me in." [58]

The price of Greenberg's departure haunted the Indians for years. Bill Daley had just shelled out hundreds of thousands of dollars to get Greenberg and the Baxters out of the organization. That was money that could have been invested in player development. Instead, Daley would embark upon a strategy designed to hold down the costs of operating the team. It was a decision that had far greater implications for the team's future than Frank Lane's 1960 trade of Rocky Colavito.

In addition, somebody connected with the Cleveland Indians learned a vital lesson. The next time the team threatened to move, it was 1964. This time, the lease would not be a problem.

Chapter 5

A Drink at Toots Shor's

"When the Russians drop that atomic bomb, I'm going to stand next to Gabe. He's a survivor." — David LeFevre

They both had been through disasters by the spring of 1961 when they bumped into each other at Toots Shor's in midtown Manhattan. Gabe Paul had left a job he loved in Cincinnati to become vice president and general manager of the expansion Houston Colts, mainly because he wanted to work for the team's owner, Craig Cullinan. But by the time Paul moved to Houston, Cullinan was being forced out by two partners who had little use for Paul. It was, Paul believed, the biggest mistake of his life.

Paul's drinking companion that evening, Nate Dolin, was in none too better shape. He and the Indians had just lived through the harrowing years of Frank Lane and his trades. After that experience, Dolin and Bill Daley had sworn off general managers. "There's no such animal anymore," Dolin announced. Instead of placing so much authority in the hands of one man, Dolin and Daley replaced Lane with Hoot Evers and gave him the less-than-imposing title of director of player personnel.

Paul's troubles gave Dolin an idea: "Are you telling me you're looking for a job?" Dolin asked Paul. With the answer in the affirmative, Dolin headed for a pay telephone to call Bill Daley in Cleveland. "I'm sitting here with a fellow named Gabe Paul," Dolin told the Indians' chairman. Paul, Dolin explained, would be a perfect replacement for Frank Lane. Gabe Paul would never trade Rocky Colavito. [1]

"Whatever you do is fine with me," Daley replied. The next day, Daley flew to New York to meet Paul, and, just before the Indians played the Yankees in Yankee Stadium, Gabe Paul was ushered in as the team's general manager. He was 51 years old, respected throughout baseball, and now would have the chance to become an Indians stockholder, an investment that promised to yield an enormous return.

Everybody liked Gabe Paul, the man with the always-present smile and the ever-ready joke. Dolin even enjoyed teasing Paul about his Cincinnati teams, which invariably led the National League in home runs. "You guys can win all the batting championships in the world," Dolin would chide Paul. "But you're never going to win the pennant because you don't have any pitching."

Despite Dolin's jokes, it was Gabe Paul who created the Cincinnati Reds' team that was winning the 1961 National League pennant. After assuming the general manager's job in Cincinnati in 1951, Paul methodically built a farm system that produced outfielders Frank Robinson and Vada Pinson, infielder Leo Cardenas, catcher Ed Bailey, and pitchers Jim Maloney, Claude Osteen, and Jim O'Toole.

Cunning and clever in his trades, Paul was nicknamed the "Smiling Cobra" by fellow general managers. His trademark tactic was to stand in the hotel lobby during the winter meetings and pounce. His favorite victim was Pittsburgh. He gave the Pirates three mediocre players in 1952 for outfielder Gus Bell, who four times drove in 100 runs for the Reds. Five years later, he dealt the Pirates an obscure left-handed pitcher for Bob Purkey, who developed into a 20-game winner. He persuaded the St. Louis Cardinals to part with pitcher Jim Brosnan, talked the Cubs out of pitcher Bill Henry, and conned reckless Frank Lane out of first baseman Gordy Coleman. Brosnan and Henry saved 32 of Cincinnati's 93 victories in 1961, and Coleman hit 26 home runs. Paul enjoyed driving a hard bargain, leading Bill Veeck to complain that Paul was dissatisfied with anything less than "grand larceny." Paul's style, Frank Lane would say with grudging admiration, was to tell other general managers, "Give me a major leaguer and I'll give you two minor leaguers in exchange." [2] Ed Linn once wrote, "Gabe purrs, speaks softly and walks away with the goods." [3]

But even the losers in those trades remained Paul's friends, perhaps mollified by his keen sense of humor. He could even turn it on himself. He traded Joe Adcock to the Milwaukee

Braves, where he quickly developed into a hard-hitting first baseman. When asked to explain the reasoning behind such a bad deal, Paul replied that Adcock "had no imagination. I saw him throw away a Marilyn Monroe calendar just because it was December 31." [4]

Reporters liked him, wrote Linn, because "he understands their problems. When it's on the line, he may not give them the whole story, but they know he'll always give them enough to keep their editors happy." Paul took reporters into his confidence and sometimes even accepted their advice; he once bought pitcher Art Fowler on the recommendation of *Atlanta Constitution* columnist Furman Bisher, who assured the Cincinnati general manager that Fowler had become more earnest in his work habits. Most Cleveland reporters wrote glowingly about Paul, although some questioned his sincerity. Frank Gibbons of the *Cleveland Press* liked to refer to Gabe Paul as the "man with the Mona Lisa smile."

Powerful and wealthy men gravitated to him. He developed a lifelong friendship in Cleveland with Steve O'Neill, the trucking executive who later bought majority control of the team. Bill Daley "loved Gabe," one reporter who covered the team later said. "And Gabe played on it. Gabe played Daley like you play a musical instrument. Gabe has that one great ability to deal with owners." [5]

The owners knew that Gabe Paul could deliver a decent team at little cost. His payroll at Cincinnati in 1953 was the lowest in either league, and the Reds that year were one of three National League teams to turn a profit. Graig Nettles claimed that Paul arranged to fly his teams to visiting cities late in the afternoon of game days to avoid paying the players' meal money. [6] Knowing that fans paid to see home run hitters, Paul built his teams around them. "I love power," Paul would say. [7] His 1956 Reds finished third, but they tied a league record with 221 home runs and showed a profit of $301,216. [8]

Given enough money, he could build a consistent winner. He helped craft the New York Yankee teams that swept to American League pennants from 1976 through 1978. Al Rosen, who joined the Indians' board of directors at Paul's request, described Paul as a "miracle man" who somehow kept the team in Cleveland and in business. But Paul was asked to produce in Cleveland with financial limitations that strained even his abundant skill.

❖

Gabe Paul learned his baseball from two of the best—Branch Rickey and Warren Giles. As a bat boy for the Rochester minor league team in 1919, he quickly impressed the team's general manager, Giles, with his energy and skill. Giles promoted him to direct public relations for the team, before advancing him to club secretary. It was during those years that Gabe Paul first came into contact with Branch Rickey.

No single individual had more influence on modern baseball than Branch Rickey. A mediocre catcher with the St. Louis Browns, Rickey demonstrated his real skills when he developed the modern player production system for the crosstown Cardinals in the 1920s. Before Rickey took control of the Cardinals, minor league teams were independent of the major leagues. They signed players from the sandlots, developed them, and sold them to the major leagues. The Baltimore Orioles of the International League in 1924 sold pitcher Lefty Grove to the Philadelphia Athletics for $100,000. The Indians in 1928 paid San Francisco of the Pacific Coast League $40,000 for outfielder Earl Averill.

Rickey's Cardinals could not afford such pricetags, so he struck upon a brilliant solution: "If we can't buy them," Rickey said of young players, "we'll develop them." [9] The Cardinals would sign players out of school, carefully advance them through a series of minor league teams they controlled, teach them the proper fundamentals, and send them to St. Louis. Within a few years, the Cardinals controlled 33 minor league teams including a Triple-A team in Rochester where Gabe Paul was learning the game. Paul was such a devoted follower of the Cardinals that he traveled to New York City to attend the seventh game of the 1926 World Series between St. Louis and the New York Yankees. From his seat next to the St. Louis bullpen, Paul watched in fascination in the seventh inning as the Cardinal coaches awoke Grover Cleveland Alexander from a sound sleep on the bench, warmed him up with a few pitches, and sent him into the game to strike out Tony Lazzeri.

In 1933, Giles went to Cincinnati to direct the Reds. Four years later, he brought Gabe Paul to the Cincinnati front office, where for a time Paul shared office space with Frank Lane. Giles, Paul, and Lane, the Reds' farm director, devoted their skills to developing pennant-winning teams in Cincinnati in 1939 and

1940. When Giles became president of the National League in 1951, Paul replaced him as general manager. "The job is yours and the responsibility is yours too," team owner Powell Crosley told him. "If you want to discuss anything with me, I'll be available. Otherwise, you'll find I won't interfere with you. If you do a good job, we'll want you to continue. If you don't, we'll get somebody else." That was fine by Paul. [10]

While controlling costs at the major league level, Paul spent lavishly on player development, adding six minor league teams, increasing the number of players in the Reds' system from 85 to nearly 400, and sending such brilliant scouts into the field as Bobby Mattick; it was Mattick who signed Frank Robinson and Curt Flood off the Oakland sandlots, although Paul later foolishly traded Flood to the St. Louis Cardinals. Paul hired Bill McKechnie, Jr., to run the farm system, explaining that "Bill never loses his enthusiasm. That's important because more great prospects are going to fold up on him than make good. And usually guys who do pan out eventually tend to sputter for a while." [11]

Paul proved to be a shrewd judge of front-office talent, always scouting about for bright, young people who would work long hours for little pay. He promoted Phil Seghi to farm director in 1958. In the summer of 1957, Tal Smith, a brash 24-year-old graduate of Duke University, pushed his way into Paul's office for a job interview. After dispelling Smith's illusions that front-office work with the Reds would be glamorous, Paul asked Smith if he could type or take shorthand. No, Smith replied. But when Smith returned to North Carolina, he enrolled in a special business school that taught young women to type and take rapid dictation. A suitably impressed Paul hired Smith as an assistant for $75 a week. Smith later became a Paul confidant and eventually advanced to become general manager of the Houston Astros.

Paul was a demanding taskmaster to those young men lucky enough to work for him. A stickler for detail, he insisted upon thorough scouting reports on players for all teams. He had a penchant for secrecy and constantly fretted about leaks to other teams. He instructed Tal Smith to close his office door during business hours, but even that did not meet Paul's exacting standards. One afternoon, Paul was astonished to discover he could hear Smith's voice booming through an air vent in Smith's office door. The next day, Paul ordered a carpenter to board up the vent. [12]

Paul loved Cincinnati and would have been content to remain there as long as he was in baseball. But, in 1960, the normally cautious Gabe Paul decided to risk it all for a fortune in Texas.

The man who lured Gabe Paul to Houston was George Kirksey, a peripatetic sportswriter turned public relations man with an appetite for high-class travel, beautiful women, and expensive cars. On the final day of his life in 1971, he had dinner near Cannes with a stunning French woman, drove her home, and at three in the morning accidentally plowed his Porsche into a Jaguar.

Kirksey had been a sportswriter for United Press in the 1930s in Chicago and New York, covering the World Series 12 times and heavyweight boxing championships six times. During World War II, as an editor of the Ninth Air Force, he became friends with General Lewis Brereton and later collaborated on the general's memoirs. In 1946, Kirksey opened a public relations firm in Houston and put his energy behind attracting major league baseball to the city. He persuaded 35 of the city's wealthiest men to attend a baseball meeting in 1957. His men of wealth included Craig Cullinan, Jr.; Judge Roy Hofheinz, the millionaire mayor of Houston by age 40; and R. E. "Bob" Smith, who made his fortune in oil and real estate. They formed the group that offered Daley and the Big Seven $6 million for the Indians in 1958. When that effort failed, they considered joining Branch Rickey's new Continental League. Alarmed at the prospect of competition from a third major league, the American League in 1960 expanded to Los Angeles and Washington, while the National League moved into New York and Houston. Kirksey had his team.

To run the franchise, Kirksey turned his charm on his closest friend in baseball, Gabe Paul. Kirksey had been a victim of Paul's devilish humor; Paul once hid Kirksey's shoes while they drank at a Tampa bar. Unable to find the shoes, Kirksey swore out a warrant for Paul's arrest. But neither man could stay angry with the other. When Kirksey left to join the Air Force, he had his last drink as a civilian with Gabe Paul. [13]

Kirksey and Cullinan offered Paul a three-year contract at a substantial increase in salary, a chance to buy stock, and a free hand in running the new Colts. On October 25, 1960, the Houston franchise announced they had hired Gabe Paul as vice president and general manager.

But Cullinan never owned more than 15 percent of the team, while Smith and Hofheinz combined to control more than 60 percent. Smith was content to allow Hofheinz to exercise control, and Hofheinz was eager to elbow Cullinan aside. Although Cullinan hung onto his shares until 1962, Paul ended up working for Hofheinz. Instead of having complete authority to run the team, Paul had to defer to Hofheinz. One afternoon, a dumbfounded Paul learned that Hofheinz had decorated the tiny Houston ballpark with streamers. "It looks like a used-car lot," Paul grumbled. He often poured out his complaints to Tal Smith, whom he lured away from Cincinnati with a front-office job in Houston. Over lunch, Paul would complain, "If I had known it was going to be like this, I wouldn't have accepted the job." By the spring of 1961, Paul was job-hunting and happened to run into Nate Dolin at Toots Shor's. [14]

Now, Gabe Paul had a new job in Cleveland. He had only one problem: Bill Daley did not want to spend any money on the Cleveland Indians.

On the eve of the 1957 winter meetings, while Frank Lane was attracting reporters with his efforts to pull off a glitzy trade for Minnie Minoso, the Los Angeles Dodgers were meeting secretly on a plan that would assure the team's success for the next 20 years.

That night in Colorado Springs, Dodger owner Walter O'Malley summoned his chief aides to his hotel room for a strategy session. The next day the 16 baseball owners planned to repeal the controversial bonus rule. The rule required a team to keep on its major league roster for two years any player signed to a bonus of more than $4,000. Although designed to discourage teams from paying huge bonuses, it also penalized player development. When the Dodgers signed 18-year-old Sandy Koufax to a huge bonus in 1954, they were forced to keep him in Brooklyn in 1955 and 1956 instead of developing him in the minor leagues. Because Koufax could not throw his overpowering fastball for strikes, Dodger manager Walter Alston rarely let him pitch.

O'Malley's advisers—Buzzie Bavasi, Fresco Thompson, and

Al Campanis—urged him to take advantage of the rule's repeal, which would allow teams to pay huge bonuses without penalty. The Dodgers, they reminded O'Malley, would be playing in the Los Angeles Coliseum with its 90,000 seats. They would break attendance records and could afford to outspend every team in baseball for young sandlot players.

"All right," O'Malley finally said. "Let's do it." [15]

In the next three years, the Dodgers spent $2 million for bonuses, including $108,000 for Frank Howard, a 235-pound first baseman who played basketball at Ohio State, and $75,000 for right-handed pitcher Joe Moeller. They also signed outfielder Ron Fairly, left-handed pitcher Pete Richert, right-handed pitcher Phil Ortega, and outfielder Willie Davis, the latter a $5,000 bargain from the Los Angeles sandlots.

The Dodgers hired better scouts and more of them. Davis had been a soft-tossing pitcher in high school, but Dodger scout Kenny Myers pursued him because of his speed in the 100-yard dash. Myers switched him from batting right-handed to left, converted him into an outfielder, and turned him loose. By 1962, Willie Davis hit 21 home runs and stole 32 bases for the Dodgers.

The Dodgers trained their new players at their elaborate Dodgertown facility in Vero Beach, Florida. Dodgertown had baseball diamonds, barracks, a basketball court, swimming pool, and movie theater; Hank Greenberg had been so impressed with Vero Beach that he used it as the model for his Indians' camp in Daytona Beach. Then the Dodger players would be assigned to one of the Dodgers' 11 minor league teams. The Dodgers insisted that every minor league manager teach the young players the fundamentals instead of trying to squeeze out a few extra victories. "Repetition, that's what we need," Al Campanis said in 1960. "You've got to condition a player until he makes the right plays automatically."

While the Dodgers were throwing money at their player personnel system, Bill Daley was pinching pennies. Still angry over the $800,000 payout to Hank Greenberg and the Baxter brothers, Daley suffered through the disastrous 1960 season. For the fourth time in five years, the Indians showed an operating loss, though in all probability it was a paper loss created by depreciating the players. But sooner or later, those tax advantages would expire, and Daley might have to pour additional money into the team. The time had come for cuts.

Daley's first target was Hank Greenberg's treasured farm system. The Indians reduced their minor league teams from nine in 1956 to five in 1961. At the end of 1963, the Indians lopped off another team to leave them with just four. By contrast, Baltimore, Minnesota, and the Angels each had six teams; the Orioles were busy developing the players who would help the team dominate the American League in the late 1960s. The Indians sent 26 scouts across the country compared to the Dodgers' 34.

Except for $40,000 handed to outfielder Paul Dicken in 1962, the Indians ceased paying hefty bonuses to high school and college players. The Indians watched as the Angels outbid every other team in baseball to pay a $200,000 bonus to outfielder Rick Reichardt. The Indians were without a team in the Florida Instructional League, where the best young prospects received intense training. Detroit's 1963 entry in the instructional league included catcher Bill Freehan, outfielders Willie Horton, Mickey Stanley, and Jim Northrup, and pitchers Denny McLain, Joe Sparma, and Pat Dobson. All would help the Tigers win the 1968 World Series.

To save even more, one of the Indians' bright ideas was to join a scouting combine with three other major league teams. Because each team would share its private scouting reports on the nation's best high school and college players, the Indians could save by dropping scouts. But when Hank Peters became farm director at the end of 1965, he discovered that some teams in the scouting combine were not sharing all their reports with Cleveland. He was particularly annoyed that in the first round of the June 1965 amateur draft one team selected a player on whom it had filed just one report with the Indians. Knowing full well that no team would base a first-round pick on a single report, Peters concluded this team was keeping much of its scouting data secret.

It quickly became apparent to Hank Peters that Bill Daley "wouldn't put up any money." It was folly, Peters thought, to operate a baseball team in such a penny-pinching manner. Without hiring good scouts, a team could not sign the best young players. Without developing the best young players, a major league team could not win. Without a winning team, a major league club could not attract enough customers to its home games to show a profit. By 1965, Cleveland's entire farm system consisted of a handful of prospects—pitcher Steve Hargan, catchers Ray Fosse and Fran Healy, first baseman Bill Davis, and outfielder Richie Scheinblum. The Indians did not have a single pitcher below Triple-A with major league ability. They did not have what Peters called "the flow of talent" necessary to have a winning team. Daley's cuts were far bigger blows to Cleveland baseball than Frank Lane's trades of Roger Maris and Rocky Colavito.

Gabe Paul privately disagreed with the cutbacks, but he was careful never to criticize Daley to others. When Peters urged the Indians to put a team in the instructional league, Paul lamely replied, "We really don't need an instructional team. It's an indictment of your player development program if you have to put a team in the instructional league." Peters knew that Paul was covering for Daley. "Cut the bullshit, Gabe," Peters said. "If we haven't got the money, that's one thing. But don't tell me that it's not a good thing for player development to have an instructional league team." [16]

By the time Gabe Paul arrived in Cleveland, Daley and the Big Seven were looking to sell. They had sound business reasons to unload the Indians. The depreciation schedule from the 1956 reorganization was expiring, which meant by the summer of 1962 they could no longer take advantage of this valuable tax break. Daley had poured hundreds of thousands of dollars of his own money into the Indians and was anxious to get some return. Dolin, Medinger, and Small had been involved financially with the Indians for a dozen years and wanted out. Dolin was already talking to his old friend, Bill Veeck, about buying the Washington Senators.

Don Hornbeck was even more eager to get out of the game. In the summer of 1962, his wife of 25 years, Jeannette Hornbeck, sued him for divorce, charging that Hornbeck drank too much and was dating another woman. During the highly publicized trial, Mrs. Hornbeck claimed to have found Hornbeck and the woman sipping martinis at Hornbeck's apartment. Hornbeck was so agitated during the trial that he challenged his wife's attorney to a fight. A judge ruled in Mrs. Hornbeck's favor and ordered Hornbeck to turn over $120,000 in household furnishings and pay her attorney fees of $25,000. Hornbeck needed cash. [17]

Gabe Paul was interested in buying the team. He knew that even if a team lost money annually, a stockholder could recoup the loss on appreciation. "I'll sell whatever number of shares are needed to give Gabe the amount he wants," Daley said. [18] Paul planned to invest $600,000 of his own money, raise $2.4 million from wealthy friends, and buy 55 percent of the team. For Daley and the Big Seven, the deal promised a vast return. Paul's offer established that the value of the Indians had increased from $3.9 million in 1956 to $5.5 million in 1962. At the World Series that fall in San Francisco, Dolin was so confident Paul had a syndicate that he told Daley, "We have a buyer." [19]

But the deal collapsed because Paul could not assemble enough investors. With Paul still willing to invest his $600,000, Daley reluctantly put together a completely new group. The same tax laws that required Daley to control 55 percent of the Indians in 1956 now prevented him from being the largest stockholder of the new company. He would have to prevail upon his closest friends in Cleveland to buy large shares of the team.

Some of them, such as Charles F. McCahill, he rounded up by phone the Sunday before the sale. McCahill, retired vice president of the company that published the *Plain Dealer*, was flattered when Daley called him and invited him to invest. The rest of the syndicate included Robert F. Black, chairman of White Motor Co.; former U.S. Senator Thomas A. Burke; John P. Murphy, president of the Higbee Co.; Edwin T. Jeffrey, chairman of the board of W.S. Tyler Co.; Timothy Conway, president of Fisher Foods; Steve O'Neill, chairman of the board of Leaseway Transportation; and Vernon Stouffer, one of the founders of Stouffer Foods. Their collective net worth was estimated at $100 million. Gabe Paul emerged as the largest stockholder with 20 percent, while Daley's holdings decreased to 18 percent. The *Plain Dealer* described Daley as the "key man in Indian deal," but Daley dismissed that by saying, "Gabe will run things."

The surviving members of the Big Seven earned handsome profits for their 14 years in baseball; Nate Dolin received $400,000 for his stock, while George Medinger got $200,000.

Daley announced that the new owners had two goals: To keep the Indians in Cleveland and produce a winner. While Daley spoke boldly of building a winner, his top priority was the bottom line. He and his partners made it clear to Paul that they would not contribute heavy capital to rebuild the team's minor league system.

Paul's first year as a stockholder was a disaster. The 1963 Indians finished 25 ½ games behind the first-place Yankees, attracted only 562,507 customers to their home games, and reported a paper loss of $1.2 million, although after the team wrote off its players, the actual out-of-pocket expenses for the stockholders was closer to $329,000. [20] An ambitious promotion by Kroger Grocery Store that involved thousands of trading stamps ended up drawing only 8,000 people. On Labor Day, the Indians played to just 4,858 in Cleveland Stadium. Fans were becoming captivated by the more exciting Cleveland Browns, who on a single October afternoon that year drew 84,684 people to Cleveland Stadium. The Indians performed so poorly that during the All-Star Game in Cleveland, writers picked up rumors that the team planned to transfer to Atlanta. Paul was required to kill the stories by declaring, "We're doing fine here and have no intention of moving." [21] But by the following January in a speech at the Cleveland Advertising Club, Paul sounded far more pessimistic. "We've got to have money to operate," Paul told the crowd. "I don't think the club's directors can be called on forever to be involved in an unprofitable operation. We must have the support to go on."

Daley and the wealthy stockholders raised the cash to cover the losses in 1963, but further cutbacks were in order. Paul admired Daley as a shrewd businessman and gentleman, but could not persuade him that "sometimes in baseball, bad business is good business and good business is bad business." [22] Paul warned that additional financial reductions would lead to continued losses on the field and more red ink.

When farm system cuts were not enough, Paul was expected to slash costs at the major league level. He sold future 20-game winner Jim Grant to the Minnesota Twins for $100,000 and two players, and followed by selling relief pitcher Pedro Ramos to the Yankees for $75,000. Both helped their new teams to future pennants. The Indians, meanwhile, continued to lose.

As attendance dwindled through the summer of 1964, so did Bill Daley's patience. The team struggled to break even on the field and was heading toward a paper loss of $1.1 million. [23] It was the same old story for Bill Daley. Everywhere he looked, people were flocking to baseball games. The Dodgers drew 2.7 million to their brand-new park in Chavez Ravine in 1962 and followed up with 2.5 million in 1963. The Giants, Yankees, Mets, Cardinals, and White Sox were consistently attracting one million customers every year to their home games. Even more galling was the performance of Calvin Griffith's Minnesota Twins, which drew 1.43 million fans to see a second-place team in 1962 and 1.4 million in 1963. Had Daley agreed to switch to Minnesota in 1958, he now would be making a fortune.

New stadiums were sprouting across the country. Atlanta officials broke ground that year on an $18-million stadium within sight of the city's gleaming new skyline; they expected the Milwaukee Braves to play in the stadium by 1965. Houston was set to open its $31-million air-conditioned domed stadium that sports reporters were proclaiming the "Seventh Wonder of the Western World." Judge Roy Hofheinz sold so many season tickets that the Astros expected to exceed two million in home attendance in 1965. Anaheim planned to lure the Angels from downtown Los Angeles with an $18-million stadium, while Oakland had completed plans to finance a $25-million coliseum for the Raiders of the American Football League and any baseball team willing to transfer. Dallas-Fort Worth hoped to break ground on a baseball park in nearby Arlington.

Meanwhile, Bill Daley was forced to play in aging Cleveland Stadium. In the days before television, the huge stadium had been an asset because, to see a game, people had to buy tickets. But by 1964, the stadium had become a liability. With its 70,000 seats, the stadium offered no incentive for anyone to buy a ticket in advance; the Indians could barely sell 2,800 season tickets. Throughout April and May, frigid winds blew off Lake Erie to chill customers in the stands.

Daley wanted to bring matters to a head. Unlike 1958, this time he had leverage. The lease expired at the end of 1964, and Daley was free to move the team wherever he wanted. The city was eager to negotiate a new lease, but Daley had steep demands: A $4 million overhaul of Cleveland Stadium. In a meeting in Mayor Ralph Locher's office, Daley was blunt: "I have a chance to move to Seattle. I'll move if I don't get what I want." Al Rosen later accompanied Daley on a business trip to Seattle and, as

Daley spoke of the Northwest, Rosen was convinced he was seriously thinking of moving the team. [24]

Seattle's allure had much to do with Gabe Paul. During his years in Cincinnati, Paul's Triple-A team had been in Seattle of the Pacific Coast League, where he developed a friendship with the team's general manager, Dewey Soriano. Paul made certain that the Seattle Raniers received his best prospects, including outfielder Vada Pinson, pitcher Claude Osteen, and first baseman Gordy Coleman. Every morning, Soriano telephoned Paul in Cincinnati to gush about Pinson and Osteen. At least twice a year, Paul flew to Seattle to watch the team. Now in 1964, Soriano had become president of the Pacific Coast League, and he and his brother Max were on the prowl for a major league team. [25]

Seattle officials formed a committee to find a team and William Wood left his post as president of the Seattle Chamber of Commerce to chair it. The goal: Lure a team by selling 8,000 season tickets. "A successful campaign," Wood said, "can have a lasting impact greater than the Seattle World's Fair. No other civic project in sight has the potential for bringing Seattle full national recognition." [26]

Otto Brandt, general manager of Seattle's ABC affiliate, flew to Cleveland and told Gabe Paul he could guarantee $1 million in television and radio rights—$200,000 more than the Indians earned in 1964. Gabe Paul listened carefully. He did not reject the offer. [27]

Hal Lebovitz was angry. He had just taken over Gordon Cobbledick's job as chief sports columnist of the *Plain Dealer*. It was one of the best sportswriting jobs in America in a city with professional baseball, football, and hockey. He had covered the Indians during their glory year of 1948 and helped Satchel Paige write a book about his rookie season in Cleveland. But Lebovitz knew the Indians were in trouble in 1964. The team was heading toward a sixth-place finish and attendance would barely break 650,000. Gabe Paul had conceded privately that he would have to dig up $60,000 of his own money to help cover the team's losses. Nor was there any reason to believe the Indians would soon improve. Except for a collection of young pitchers—Sam McDowell, Luis Tiant, Tommy John, and Sonny Siebert—the Indians lacked the talent to be anything more than a .500 team.

As a reporter with the *Cleveland News* in 1958, Lebovitz covered the Indians' near move to Minneapolis. This time, Lebovitz did not know whether Daley and Paul were bluffing to win concessions from the city or actually planning to move. Certainly it was unfair to ask Gabe Paul and Bill Daley to continue underwriting the team's financial losses.

Lebovitz went public with his fears at the end of August. In a front-page column in the *Plain Dealer*, Lebovitz announced that he was "scared stiff the team is going to be moved. I've done plenty of checking. The danger now is greater than 50-50...If the Indians leave, Cleveland becomes a bush league town. Cities spend fortunes to try and entice major league clubs. We're on the verge of letting ours get away." He urged Clevelanders to buy tickets to the Indians' home games in September. [28]

A week after he published his column, Lebovitz ordered sports reporter Russell Schneider to fly to Seattle and write about the city's effort to obtain a team. Schneider and Paul Wilcox of WEWS-TV in Cleveland both toured the city on September 8 and 9 and were impressed that Wood's committee already had sold $208,000 in season tickets. [29] Schneider wrote four articles suggesting that Seattle officials were confident of getting the Indians to move.

Ironically, the confidence of Seattle officials may have been inadvertently fueled by the pessimism of Schneider and Wilcox. On September 9—the very day that Schneider's first article appeared in the *Plain Dealer*—the *Seattle Post-Intelligencer* revealed that the Cleveland Indians were the target of Wood's committee. Their sources? None other than Russ Schneider and Paul Wilcox. The *Post-Intelligencer* even quoted Wilcox as saying that Gabe Paul had requested economic surveys of the Seattle market. [30]

Rumors of a franchise shift escalated on September 11 when veteran Associated Press baseball writer Joe Reichler wrote that the Indians would leave Cleveland at the end of 1964 and move to Seattle. A gloomy Gabe Paul told Reichler that he had not officially decided to move the team, but he warned, "I know one thing: I don't intend to go broke in Cleveland." Reichler added that the American League owners would unanimously approve the switch. In a revealing comment that suggested he had carefully studied the Seattle market, Paul said the tiny Seattle park was "no problem at all. There is only one problem: Making the decision whether to move or stay." [31]

The next day after a 90-minute talk with Paul in his office, Mayor Locher announced an aggressive campaign to boost the Indians' anemic season-ticket sales. Gabe Paul warned that the team's future was in jeopardy. "A shot of morphine," he told reporters, "was needed for a sick patient. If you operate at a loss year after year, you come to a point when you ask, how far can we continue in this method? We can't stand it for too long." [32]

Bill Daley and Gabe Paul were playing the game with skill. While never directly threatening to move the Indians, they refused to deny a transfer and fueled a bidding war by other cities. Paul was deluged with financial offers from as many as 12 cities. Oakland financiers topped Seattle's bid, offering $6.5 million to buy out the Cleveland stockholders. Lamar Hunt, eager to bring a team to Dallas, flew to Cleveland to meet privately with Gabe Paul. [33]

Cleveland officials also had increased their bid to keep the team. City Council President James Stanton urged Locher to negotiate a new lease and improve the stadium. The heads of more than 100 area companies pledged to Paul at a private meeting at the Union Club that they would buy 8,000 season tickets as part of a $4 million package to keep the team in Cleveland.

Paul was pleased. He was not eager to leave Cleveland, which he called a "sleeping giant." He was convinced that a winning team would make millions there. In interviews 30 years later, he insisted that neither he nor Daley intended to move the Indians to Seattle. While that may be true, the more likely explanation is that in the summer of 1964, Gabe Paul and Bill Daley forced a decision: Either Cleveland would offer major financial concessions or the Indians would accept an attractive offer from Seattle, Oakland, or Dallas. Any other business decision would have been foolish. Joseph Routh, chairman of the board of U.S. Trucking Co., and one of the few out-of-town shareholders, warned that while "many of the directors are Clevelanders and might be swayed to a certain degree by civic pride or patriotism or whatever you want to call it...they're also businessmen and they want out of this situation, too." [34]

To stay in Cleveland, though, Paul needed firm commitments from the city to upgrade the stadium. Paul had worked hard to cultivate the brash, young Stanton—a power in Cleveland politics. Stanton liked Paul much more than Daley. To Stanton, Daley was a cold businessman without a trace of sentiment for Cleveland, an "Irishman who acts like a WASP." Stanton was convinced that Daley would move the Indians, but he could not persuade Locher that the threat was genuine. [35]

To resolve the impasse, Paul and Stanton met for dinner on Monday, October 5 at Stouffer's Restaurant on Shaker Square. The team's board of directors would meet at 11 the next morning and Paul had promised to provide them with a new lease. During dinner, Paul and Stanton negotiated the outlines of an agreement. The Indians would sign a new lease and the city would guarantee $4 million in improvements, including new locker rooms, a fancy restaurant, more than 1,000 field-level box seats, new offices for the Indians and Browns, and a cleanup of the brick exterior. [36] Stanton also agreed to lower the team's rent from seven percent of the gross ticket sales to six percent. But, in return, Paul promised the team would pay the city a minimum of $60,000 a year for the stadium. Stanton promised to take the agreement to Locher, who would then telephone Paul the next day. "I'm confident the team will stay," Stanton told Hal Lebovitz that night. The rival *Cleveland Press* was convinced enough to print a large headline, "Indians decide to stay here," in its Tuesday afternoon home edition. [37]

On Tuesday morning, Paul waited in vain at his office for the telephone to ring. Finally, he telephoned Locher. "I don't make deals on dining room napkins," Locher told Paul. Paul was stunned. "Do you know what you're saying, Ralph?" Paul asked the mayor. [38] A discouraged Paul walked to the directors' meeting. Among the horde of newsmen covering the vote were two reporters from Seattle. Inside the room, a bowl with a red apple was placed in front of each board member's seat; someone joked they were apples from Washington state.

Paul reported to the shocked directors that Locher had not consented to the lease. Enraged, they felt the city was reneging on its commitment. "Let's get the hell out of here," one stockholder roared. Because of his private talks with Stanton, Paul was convinced the city eventually would relent, and the team would get the concessions it sought. But with tempers rising, Paul feared he would lose control, and the board would vote to move. Maurice Saltzman came to his rescue by introducing a motion: Delay action until Paul and Daley visited Seattle. Although Saltzman adamantly opposed moving the team, he calculated that the mayor would eventually agree to the improvements and the directors' anger would subside. [39]

Paul and Daley emerged from the four-hour meeting to read prepared statements. Paul said the directors "felt that Cleveland officials and civic groups should be given an opportunity to stimulate sufficient support to enable the club to remain here." Although the statement was a none-to-subtle jab at Locher, Lebovitz angrily wrote that "we can interpret yesterday's action by the board only one way: It was an attempt to put this city on the spot, while encouraging other cities to come and get our team—It's a sickening decision." [40]

After the vote, Lebovitz flew to St. Louis to cover the World Series between the Yankees and Cardinals. By chance, Paul and Daley were on the same flight. Paul walked over to Lebovitz' seat to object to his column. "You misinterpreted our statement," Paul complained. "If we did," Lebovitz replied, "so did everybody else in our office as well as the radio and TV announcers." Under questioning, Paul admitted that he and Daley planned to attend the World Series and then fly to Seattle to meet with city officials. But Paul told Lebovitz, "Look, stop this business with the directors. You're only going to hurt it. Just lay off a little bit."

Lebovitz thought for a moment and replied, "I'll cool it. Let's see what happens." [41]

Paul and Daley watched the Cardinals and Yankees split the first two games in St. Louis, then boarded a plane for Seattle. At the last moment, they were joined by Bob Sudyk, the 31-year-old baseball writer for the *Cleveland Press*. Sudyk had been covering the World Series, but *Press* Sports Editor Bob August told him to "forget the series and go with" Paul and Daley. "This is a bigger story than the series." [42]

At the Seattle airport, reporters and photographers mobbed them as they were greeted by Paul's old friend, Dewey Soriano, and William Wood. Paul was coy with reporters. "This is an inspection visit at the direction of our board of directors," Paul said. [43]

The next day, King County Commissioner Ed Munro explained to Paul and Daley that the Seattle commissioners were prepared to ask voters to approve a $25-million bond issue to build a domed stadium seating 50,000. Paul and Daley then met with Seattle Mayor Dorm Braman to discuss the city's tiny minor league stadium. "Nobody moves a ballclub," Paul told the mayor, "without a home to go to." The mayor offered to spend $800,000 to increase Sicks Stadium to 25,000 seats. The Indians could play there until the domed stadium opened in 1970, he told them. [44]

Finally, Soriano took Paul and Daley on a tour of Sicks Stadium. The size of the park jolted Daley; Cleveland Stadium had 60,000 more seats. As they walked about the tiny ballpark, Soriano became convinced that neither Paul nor Daley had any intention of moving; Soriano feared the small ballpark was a real obstacle. When baseball was ready to expand to Seattle in 1969, American League President Joe Cronin visited Sicks Stadium, too. "Have you considered," Cronin asked Max Soriano, "waiting until you've got the domed stadium built before starting in the American League? This is really a minor league ballpark." [45] Paul was saying little officially, but privately he warned Sudyk, "Bob, don't write that any of these cities are going to get this team. They're not." The longer Paul talked, the more Sudyk was convinced the trip to the West Coast was an effort to buy time in Cleveland. Sudyk caught the hint and on October 9 wrote, "It is a time of deep concern. It is not a time for total despair." [46]

Paul and Daley encountered the same problems in Oakland. Yes, Oakland Alameda County planned to build a coliseum. Architect John Merrill showed Paul and Daley the plans for the coliseum and the large hole in the ground that had been dug. He confidently predicted it would open by 1966. Until then, Daley and Paul were told, the Indians could play their home games in Frank Youel Field with its 22,000 seats. [47]

Paul had one more stop to make—Dallas. But the fact that Daley flew to Cleveland that night suggests that neither Paul nor Daley considered Dallas a realistic possibility. Paul went through the motions of meeting with Lamar Hunt and Tommy Mercer, the co-owners of the area's minor league team. Paul agreed to hold a one-hour press conference at a local hotel. The *Dallas Morning News* played the story on page four of its sports section, making clear the newspaper did not take Paul's visit seriously. [48]

Officials in Cleveland had stepped up their own efforts to keep the team. The Cleveland Growth Board and Chamber of Commerce launched an aggressive effort to sell tickets. In two weeks they sold $551,830 worth, including $16,000 apiece to Sohio and Higbee's Department Store. Only Locher's approval for the new lease was needed. Locher hesitated again during an October 15 meeting with Paul. An angry Stanton stormed out and complained that Locher was "procrastinating." Locher said he wanted to study the lease overnight and give his decision to the Indians when the board of directors met the next day. [49]

On an unusually sunny and warm fall afternoon, 16 of the team's 22 board members gathered at the stadium. As reporters waited outside, Locher told the board he would approve a new 10-year lease, the $4 million in improvements, and a reduction in the team's rent. Locher also gave in to the team's demand for a clause that would allow the Indians to cancel the lease on 90 days notice. At 4:46 in the afternoon, Paul and Daley emerged from the meeting to announce the Indians would stay.

Not everyone was satisfied. Vernon Stouffer, one of the founders of Stouffer Foods and a member of the board, sat through the meeting, glancing to his left to watch Paul and Daley. As long as the Indians continued to lose and pile up financial losses, they were likely to move. He was determined to prevent that.

Bill Daley's flirtation with Seattle in 1964 had lasting implications for the Cleveland Indians. Gabe Paul was under intense pressure to win immediately, even at the expense of the team's future. Paul knew that the easiest way to create interest was to trade for Rocky Colavito, still a hero in Cleveland.

Colavito remained a formidable home run hitter. After the 1963 season, the Tigers traded him to Kansas City where in 1964 he hit 34 home runs and drove in 102 runs for a team that lost 105 games. Charlie Finley was willing to deal Colavito, but he had no interest in the players Paul was offering. That led to a complicated three-way trade involving the Athletics, White Sox, and Indians. Finley would deal Colavito to the White Sox for outfielders Mike Hershberger and Jim Landis and pitcher Fred Talbot. The White Sox would then send Colavito to Cleveland. But their pricetag was high: catcher John Romano, pitcher Tommy John, and outfielder Tommie Agee.

Hoot Evers hated the thought of giving up Agee, whom he and Bob Kennedy literally snuck out of Alabama during the Freedom Riders' civil rights struggles of 1961. Agee quickly produced: A .258 average and 25 stolen bases for Burlington of the Carolina League in 1962; a .274 mark and 19 stolen bases for Charleston of the Eastern League in 1963; and 20 home runs and 35 stolen bases for Portland of the Pacific Coast League in 1964. He gave every indication of being an outstanding major league centerfielder.

For his part, Paul loathed trading John; quality left-handed pitching was always difficult to find. But Paul had paid high prices for power hitters in the past and now he desperately needed Rocky Colavito. What was the point in saving John and Agee? So they could play for the Seattle Indians? The Oakland Indians? In January 1965, Paul consented to the trade.

Cleveland had its first contender since 1959; the Indians led the American League as late as July 5, and finished with 87 victories. The team increased its home attendance by 43 percent to 934,786, and with the heavy tax write-off, stockholders earned a profit of $609,622. [50] But the price Paul paid for that one year of success was staggering. Agee and John developed into outstanding regulars for the White Sox, while Colavito was gone from Cleveland by 1967.

The years of cutting the team's farm system had taken their toll. There was no longer a quick fix for the Indians. Even Rocky Colavito could not save them.

Chapter 6

You're Committing Suicide

"Vernon's heart was certainly in the right place."
— Hank Peters

Vernon Stouffer loved new ideas. He turned an off-hand comment by a customer at one of his restaurants into an elaborate line of frozen foods. He was so impressed with the possibilities of microwave ovens that years before they were in common use, he installed one in the kitchen of his suburban Cleveland apartment. When he bought the Cleveland Indians in 1966, he championed the innovative idea of having regular season games between American and National League teams.

He was shy and modest except when he stumbled on a fresh idea. Then he would grow excited and confidently pronounce, "Yes, we can do that," no matter what dissenters said. When he wanted to open a restaurant in Manhattan in the 1930s, an adviser warned him, "Don't go to New York. There are already a lot of restaurants there, and there's a Depression on." But Vernon Stouffer shrugged off the advice and his ground-floor restaurant at 666 Fifth Avenue was a stunning success. [1]

Creative and determined, Vernon Bigelow Stouffer transformed a small restaurant at 9th Street and Euclid Avenue into Stouffer Foods—a nationwide corporation that by 1966 had 46 restaurants, five motels, 8,000 employees, and $79 million in gross sales.

As a young graduate of the University of Pennsylvania, Vernon Stouffer persuaded his parents to borrow $12,000 and open a 10-table restaurant called Stouffer's Lunch on a bustling downtown Cleveland corner. He picked up the idea on a family trip to the West Coast, where he noticed that small restaurants were succeeding by selling simple sandwiches to busy lunchtime crowds. At Stouffer's Lunch, the family served ham-and-cheese sandwiches, Mrs. Stouffer's deep-dish Dutch apple pie, and fresh buttermilk from the family's farm south of Cleveland.

104

You're Committing Suicide

While the recipes were his mother's and the seed money his father's, the menus and the concepts were the products of Vernon's fertile imagination. He was the innovative Mr. Inside, while his brother Gordon was Mr. Outside—the gregarious salesman of the family who recruited Stouffer managers from college. Under the direction of Vernon and Gordon, Stouffer's expanded to New York, Philadelphia, Pittsburgh, Detroit, Chicago, and Minneapolis. But even as the company grew, Vernon insisted that all food at Stouffer's be prepared by women, convinced that they would be more faithful to his mother's recipes. He was on a first-name basis with the cooks at every restaurant. When Vernon toured Stouffer's expanding empire, he never lost sight of the heart of the company's success. He would skip the front office and head directly for the kitchen to sample the soup.

Vernon was constantly on watch for new ideas to market his mother's food. He was among the first to recognize the possibilities of the suburbs. Although Cleveland's population continued to grow throughout the 1940s, Vernon Stouffer picked up on a new trend: People were seeking more space in the suburbs to the east. Ridership on the Shaker Rapids' bright red trolley cars that clanged from downtown to the east suburbs increased sharply from 2.9 million in 1939 to 7.2 million in 1946. Even though most successful restaurants were located in America's downtowns, Vernon Stouffer opened a restaurant on Shaker Square, an octagon of Georgian-style brick shops shaded by elm trees and located six miles east of the Terminal Tower. The Shaker Square restaurant quickly became a favorite of young suburbanites.

The restaurant also led to Vernon Stouffer's most brilliant innovation. When an elderly woman at his restaurant on Shaker Square told him, "If we could only have one helping of this and take it home," it sparked an idea. [2] Why not freeze spinach souffle, macaroni and cheese, and potatoes au gratin, and sell them at supermarkets? The only catch was proving to his mother that the frozen food would taste as good as fresh. After Mrs. Stouffer sampled both and found them to her satisfaction, Vernon excitedly told Stouffer's Vice President Margaret Mitchell, "Mother didn't know the difference." [3]

An early believer in microwave ovens, Stouffer was convinced that someday Stouffer's frozen food would be cooked in a matter of minutes. He envisioned a time when most American families

105

would buy a microwave for their kitchen, just as they bought a TV set for their living room. It was a major factor in his decision in the 1960s to merge his company with Litton Industries, a California conglomerate that manufactured microwaves. Roy Ash, president of Litton, told Vernon that "Litton microwave ovens and Stouffer Foods will go together like Gillette razor blades and Gillette razors." [4]

Not all of Vernon Stouffer's new ideas were as successful as frozen macaroni and cheese. Some bombed. As more people bought cars, Vernon conceived of selling Stouffer's frozen foods in coin-operated machines at gasoline stations. While filling a car with gasoline, a customer could heat up spinach souffle in a microwave oven. But to his consternation, Vernon discovered that people were too rushed to eat at a gas station, and the idea was dropped.

Although as a boy Vernon was photographed grasping a heavy baseball bat, he never had much interest in the game. He was barely 5-foot-4, and his field-hockey teammates at the University School in Cleveland cruelly nicknamed him "Shorty." [5] At the Wharton School of Finance, he lacked the skills to play most college sports, and instead served as manager of the junior varsity rowing crew. Unlike most prosperous businessmen, he shunned golf in favor of a rapid game of tennis.

His real passion was the water. The summer after he graduated from Penn, he hopped aboard a freighter on the West Coast for a trip to New York City. He even persuaded the captain to allow him to steer the ship briefly as it slid through the Panama Canal. He loved boats so much that near the end of World War II, he bought a 55-foot yacht from the Duke of Windsor, who had abdicated the throne of Great Britain in 1936 to marry an American divorcee, Wallis Simpson. Vernon retained the yacht's name, Gemini, which the duke personally chose because he and Mrs. Simpson both were born in June. Stouffer loved to take the 27-ton yacht, with its twin diesel engines, from its dock at the Cleveland Yachting Club onto the choppy waters of Lake Erie.

He and his wife Gertrude bought two apartments on the 19th floor of Winton Place, which towered above the shores of Lake Erie in suburban Lakewood. Stouffer knocked down the walls and created one enormous apartment that included a family kitchen and a personal kitchen for himself, where he installed the latest ovens and experimented with new recipes. From the spacious living room, he had a panoramic view of Lake Erie, its shoreline, and the twinkling lights of downtown Cleveland.

Like many of his prosperous business friends, he was solidly Republican. He played gin rummy with President Dwight D. Eisenhower, and once organized a 10-city birthday tribute to the president. His close friends included George Humphrey, the president of Cleveland's M.A. Hanna Co., and Eisenhower's first treasury secretary; and Frederick C. Crawford, a founder of TRW. When Henry Luce held *TIME*'s 40th anniversary party at the Waldorf, Stouffer was on the guest list. Vernon also entertained at his palatial apartment and once had Walt Disney as a special guest aboard the Gemini.

He served on the board of directors of United Air Lines, Republic Steel, Society National Bank of Cleveland, and the Consolidated Natural Gas Co. of New York. He was a member of the prestigious Union Club at 12th and Euclid in downtown Cleveland, where he enjoyed having lunch in the second-floor dining room with Louis Seltzer, the powerful editor of the *Cleveland Press*. Over cocktails, Stouffer would reveal inside information about trades and strategy contemplated by Indians President Gabe Paul. The team's secrets would soon show up on the sports pages of the *Press*, much to Paul's consternation. Where were these leaks coming from? the mystified Paul demanded. When Paul investigated and learned that Vernon Stouffer was the leak, one Indians executive teased him, "How are you going to plug that one?" [6]

For all his wealth and powerful connections, Vernon Stouffer still possessed a charming naivete. He had no idea of the tax advantages of owning the Indians and only called his tax lawyers after the deal was consummated. When Eisenhower invited him to visit the White House, Stouffer did what any good Midwesterner would do when asked to a neighbor's home. He brought along a gift: a collection of his favorite Stouffer frozen foods. [7]

Vernon gained a financial interest in the Indians in 1962 at the suggestion of William R. Daley, the chairman of the team's board of directors. From there, Vernon Stouffer's interest in the Indians intensified. It was born of civic pride; he adored the city where he spent most of his life and feared that, unless the Indians were dramatically improved, the team eventually would leave Cleveland. In 1964, he sat through the contentious meeting of the board of directors as they debated whether to transfer the franchise to Seattle. Stouffer had good reason to worry. It was the second time in seven years that the Indians appeared to be slipping from Cleveland's grasp.

He bought the Indians in a casual manner, almost like "buying something in a hardware store," his son-in-law, James Biggar, would later say. He bought 80 percent of the franchise for $8 million, personally contributing $5.5 million and borrowing $2.5 million to cover the rest. "This is the most exciting thing I've ever done," Stouffer said. [8] He was 65 years old, had built one of the country's most successful businesses, and now wanted to apply his talents to create a winning baseball team.

He had big plans and, of course, new ideas. More money to find talented players. Interleague play. Better marketing to attract customers. A long-term lease in Cleveland Stadium, and an end to talk of moving the Indians out of the city. Innovative as ever, Vernon Stouffer even asked one Cleveland engineering firm to draw up plans for a domed stadium. Vernon planned to succeed in the city he loved. "Whatever it takes to build a winner," Stouffer declared confidently, "we'll do it." [9]

His first move was to extend Gabe Paul's contract by 10 years, with an order to spend whatever he needed. Paul was eager to comply. Finally, he had the money to build a contending team in Cleveland. Paul had just hired Hank Peters from the Kansas City Athletics to rebuild Hank Greenberg's farm system. Others were just as enthused. Hal Lebovitz of the *Plain Dealer* described the sale to Stouffer as "the best thing that happened to Cleveland baseball since the 1948 World Series." Daley said, "I have a feeling I'm going to be very proud of this team." [10]

Hank Peters set about his task with fervor. He yanked the team out of the absurd scouting combine that was designed to cut costs, and hired his own scouts to comb the country. He added a fifth minor league team and entered the Indians in the Florida Instructional League. The Indians demonstrated greater skill in the June and January drafts of high school and college players. They drafted and signed pitchers Dick Tidrow and Ed Farmer in 1967, outfielder John Lowenstein in 1968, catcher Alan Ashby and third baseman Buddy Bell in 1969, and first baseman Chris Chambliss and catcher Jeff Newman in 1970.

Cleveland scouts also signed right-handed pitcher Jim Kern from the Michigan State campus. Kern had not been drafted, but he was 6-foot-5, and threw a powerful fastball. They very nearly signed right-handed pitcher Tom Seaver out of the University of Southern California. When Commissioner William Eckert voided Atlanta's signing of Seaver for $40,000 in 1966, the Indians, Philadelphia Phillies, and New York Mets were the only teams to enter a special drawing for Seaver's rights. The Mets won the drawing, but it was clear that Cleveland was back in the business of developing players. In the Florida Instructional League in 1969, Cleveland's entry of Tidrow, Farmer, Lowenstein, Ashby, catcher Ray Fosse, and infielder Jack Brohamer posted the best winning percentage.

To give himself more time for the Indians and to solidify his own vast holdings, Stouffer merged Stouffer Foods with Litton Industries of Beverly Hills, a sprawling conglomerate whose net sales in 1966 exceeded $1.7 billion. Stouffer and his family exchanged their Stouffer's stock for $21.5 million of Litton stock at $104.50 per share. The marriage brought together Stouffer's frozen dinners and the microwave ovens produced by Litton's Atherton Division in Cleveland.

Litton's success had been almost solely due to the energetic genius of Charles B. Thornton. Like Vernon Stouffer, Tex Thornton was a brilliant innovator with a firm belief that numbers and statistics always produced the correct answer. An Army Air Corps officer during World War II, Thornton was a disciple of Robert Lovett, an assistant secretary of war who later became secretary of defense in the Truman administration. Thornton headed a team of bright, young men—including Robert S. McNamara—at Harvard Business School, who sorted through the military chaos to produce rational solutions. For example, when the Army Air Corps wanted to bomb Japan with B-17s and B-24s, Thornton's team produced a study that showed that the new B-29s could drop 28,000 tons of bombs per month in just 15,000 combat hours compared to 90,000 hours for the B-17s and B-24s. By doing so, Thornton's group proved casualties among U.S. airmen would be reduced by 70 percent, and the Army Air Corps would save 250 million gallons of gasoline in one year. [11]

When the war ended, Thornton convinced young Henry Ford II to hire his military statisticians to reorganize the nearly bankrupt Ford Motor Co. and return it to profitability. Nicknamed the "Whiz Kids," the group included two future presidents of Ford—McNamara and Arjay Miller. Thornton's stay at Ford was brief; he joined Hughes Aircraft in 1948 at the personal invitation of Howard Hughes.

In 1953, Thornton and Roy Ash—whom he described as the only man he ever met as brilliant as Robert McNamara—purchased Litton, a small firm of 250 employees that produced electronics for U.S. Air Force air-to-air missiles. Thornton's dream was to create a mammoth electronics' company by purchasing other companies. By 1961, Thornton had engineered 25 different mergers to provide Litton with 48 plants in nine countries. Operating from a mansion in Beverly Hills, Thornton and Ash had created a conglomerate—or as Ash called it, a "multi-company industry"—that produced everything from typewriters to nuclear-powered submarines. An impressed Henry Ford said, "Boy, Tex is going to own everything one of these days." [12]

Thornton and Stouffer immediately liked each other. Both were convinced that the microwave oven would revolutionize cooking; Thornton even dreamed of the day when astronauts would cook frozen food in a microwave. In 1965, Litton began selling its own microwave oven at $1,000 per unit. But instead of selling microwaves to the average homeowner, most customers were schools and restaurants. By buying Stouffer Foods, Thornton hoped to marry the two concepts: Americans would buy Litton's microwaves to cook Stouffer's macaroni and cheese.

The merger seemed to assure even deeper pockets for the Cleveland Indians. But no one dreamed that the unpredictability of the stock market would ravage not only Litton, but Vernon Stouffer's dreams of a winning team.

In January 1968, Litton sent stock analysts a warning that after 14 consecutive years of increased profits, there would be a decline in the fourth quarter earnings for 1967. But the warning failed to buffer the effects when Litton in early February announced that fourth-quarter profit slid from $16.4 million in the final quarter of 1966 to $7.2 million in 1967. [13] The decline came as a number of key Litton executives were leaving; William R. McKenna to Hunt Foods and Industries, Seymour M. Rosenberg to Mattel, Inc., and Russell McFall to Western Union. The list grew so long that industry analysts nicknamed them Lidos— Litton Industries Drop Outs. [14]

Litton's stock tumbled from a peak of 120 at the end of 1967 to just $62\frac{1}{2}$ in March 1968. Stouffer's fortunes and that of the Indians plummeted with it. Under the terms of his agreement with Litton, Stouffer had agreed to hold the stock long term. His $21.5 million stake in the company was suddenly worth less than $9 million. He would have difficulty paying off the $2.5 million he borrowed to buy the Indians. Stouffer had assumed that he could survive years of small operating losses by the Indians. Now, that was out of the question.

He briefly toyed with selling the team; at one point a local florist expressed interest. A Texas group hoping to win the franchise for Dallas offered Stouffer $15 million for the team. "There's only one chance in 25 that the club will be sold to an out-of-town bidder," Stouffer declared. [15] That one chance was enough to set off another panic that the Indians might leave town. Then, just as abruptly, Stouffer took the team off the market. Instead, team costs would have to be slashed.

At the team's annual board meeting at Cleveland Stadium at the end of 1970, Stouffer called in Peters and delivered the news: Cut the team's annual $1 million budget for player development by 30 percent. [16] Peters was stunned. When the meeting ended, Stouffer naively asked Peters, "Is this going to hurt us?"

Peters had a question of his own: "Are you going to sell this club?" Stouffer bristled, but Peters wouldn't let go. "You don't have to answer," Peters told Stouffer. "Let me just tell you: In the area of player development, the things you do or don't do today are never reflected immediately at the top. It takes a period of three, four or five years before you feel the true effects. If you are going to sell the club in the next year or two, don't look back. It's not going to effect you." But Peters then delivered the verdict: "On the other hand, if you really intend to keep the Indians, you're committing suicide." [17]

Still, Stouffer's edict stood, and Peters complied. Peters

scaled back plans to spend bonus money in next year's drafts, released scores of players in the system, and reduced the number of farm teams to four. Even more painful, he slashed the scouting staff from 24 full-time scouts in 1970 to just nine. The Tigers, Yankees, Red Sox, and Orioles had six minor league teams each, while Kansas City had seven, and Minnesota eight. The Tigers and Yankees each had 31 scouts.

With these pathetic numbers, the Indians could not possibly compete. "Good scouts are the basis of any organization," Bob Kennedy liked to say. [18] As one of Cleveland's best scouts in the early 1960s, Kennedy watched 18-year-old Tommy John of Terre Haute, Indiana, warm up on the sidelines. On the basis of a handful of pitches, Kennedy gave John a $40,000 bonus to sign with the Indians. Kennedy also located and signed another 18-year-old lefthander, Sam McDowell of Pittsburgh. John and McDowell developed into 20-game winners in the major leagues.

Now even when the scouts stumbled across a good prospect, Peters did not have the bonus money to close the deal. The Indians picked left-handed pitcher Jim Umbarger in the second round of 1971, and in 1972 selected left-handed pitcher Rick Langford in the 36th round, right-handed pitcher Pete Redfern in the 10th, and second baseman Rich Dauer in the first round of the January draft. All chose not to sign with Cleveland, and all developed into major league players. The Indians were indeed slowly killing themselves.

Gabe Paul's ambitious plans to build a winner had now evaporated. He was back to cutting corners. Soon, though, he had an even greater worry: His job.

Vernon Stouffer was developing an enthusiasm for Paul's handpicked field manager, Alvin Dark. Stouffer wanted Dark to have a greater voice in running the team. As the Indians continued to lose on the field, Gabe Paul was losing an intense power struggle with Alvin Dark.

Although as a child Dark suffered from malaria and diphtheria, he developed into a remarkable athlete. At Louisiana State in the 1940s, Dark not only was a running and passing halfback on the football team, he started at guard for the basketball team. He had a knack for picking up any sport. One afternoon, he stopped into the office of LSU boxing coach Jim Owen and asked if he could borrow his golf clubs. "I didn't know you played golf," Owen said. Dark conceded he had never played the game. "But," he said, "I thought I'd try it once." Dark took the clubs and shot an 80. [19]

But his real talent was baseball. As a senior he played short-stop and led LSU in hitting. He was so highly regarded that the Boston Braves gave him $40,000 to sign a contract. By 1948, Dark was the Braves' regular shortstop, and he combined with second baseman Eddie Stanky to lead Boston to its first National League pennant since 1914. Dark covered wide tracts of ground at shortstop, ran the bases intelligently, bunted well, and rarely struck out. He played his best in the most crucial games. It was Alvin Dark's leadoff single in the ninth inning of the final playoff game in 1951 against the Brooklyn Dodgers that sparked the New York Giants to a four-run rally and the pennant. He batted .417 in the 1951 World Series against the Yankees, and followed with a .412 effort in 1954 against the Indians.

Like Leo Durocher, Alvin Dark played aggressive baseball and feared no one. He once knocked Jackie Robinson down at third base with a vicious slide. As manager of the Indians, Dark calmly folded his arms and stood his ground as an angry Lou Johnson stormed toward him during a game. "Take your uniform off," Dark told the Indians' outfielder. "You're through for the day." [20]

When Durocher was named manager of the Giants in 1948, one of the players he wanted was Dark. The Giants were domi-nated by brawny players who hit home runs, but could neither run nor field well. Durocher preferred speedy players who could bunt, execute the hit-and-run, and make the plays in the field. He quickly got lucky, because Dark and Stanky were in conflict with Billy Southworth, the manager who directed the Braves to the 1948 pennant. Southworth was known to enjoy a few drinks before and after a game, while Dark and Stanky were "malted milk and movie guys." [21] At the end of the 1949 season, Dark and Stanky both voted to deny Southworth a full share of the team's bonus money for finishing fourth.

Durocher heard of the nasty dispute and pressed for a trade. The Giants agreed to give up home run hitters Willard Marshall and Sid Gordon, and shortstop Buddy Kerr to the Braves for Dark and Stanky. "It's a hell of a deal," Durocher told Giants owner

Horace Stoneham. "We've got the maneuverability and defense the Braves had, and they've got to play long ball like we did. Now you can talk about the pennant, Horace." Durocher was right. Dark helped the Giants win pennants in 1951 and 1954. Durocher was so impressed, that he named Dark the team captain. [22]

When Dark finished playing in 1960, Stoneham snapped him up to manage his team. Dark directed a hard-hitting team to 102 victories and the National League pennant in 1962. San Francisco reporters nicknamed him the "Mad Genius" for his willingness to go against the book and try something outrageous. He once used four pitchers in the first inning in which the Phillies scored just two runs. "Baseball is a percentage game," Dark would explain, "but that doesn't mean each percentage is the same every day." Convinced that batting averages by themselves did not demonstrate a player's value, Dark invented his own system to rate his players. Dark issued high marks for advancing a runner and penalized a player for missing signs and throwing to the wrong base. Under Dark's system, ordinary hitting Jim Davenport earned a good score while heavy hitting first baseman Orlando Cepeda scored low. [23] Dark later moved to Kansas City to manage Charles O. Finley's youthful collection of rising stars. By the time Gabe Paul hired him in Cleveland in 1968, Dark was regarded as one of the ablest field managers in the game.

In his first year in Cleveland, Dark crafted a swift team that won with stolen bases and outstanding pitching. Fans loved his unorthodox approach; he once switched pitcher Sam McDowell to second base while he brought in a right-handed reliever to pitch to a right-handed hitter. That taken care of, Dark returned McDowell to the pitcher's mound.

The Indians finished third, and Vernon Stouffer was delighted. It was the best showing by the Indians since 1959, and attendance had climbed by 200,000. He liked Dark's daring style of field managing. Why not, Stouffer reasoned, combine the job of manager and general manager and hand it to Alvin Dark? Stouffer argued that the same system worked in football. Look at Vince Lombardi, Stouffer would say. He was both head coach and general manager of the Green Bay Packers. Stouffer broached his plan with Alvin Dark who enthusiastically agreed; he long had wanted the same sweeping powers Leo Durocher had with the New York Giants. But Dark failed to appreciate at the time that his promotion was at the expense of Gabe Paul, who brought him to Cleveland. [24]

Stouffer still had the job of breaking the news to the Cleveland front office. Stouffer telephoned Hank Peters, who had driven to South Carolina to watch one of the Indians' Class A teams in Sumter. Could you return to Cleveland as quickly as possible? Stouffer asked. Peters arrived in Cleveland on a Saturday afternoon, one day after violent thunderstorms had knocked down trees and power lines, and left the Coast Guard combing Lake Erie for missing boaters. The next day, Peters drove to the old Detroit Avenue bridge spanning the Rocky River, and down the winding road leading to the Cleveland Yachting Club. There, where the river washes into Lake Erie, Stouffer kept a small beachhouse.

Stouffer came right to the point. "I'll be making some changes. Alvin's going to be the general manager and the field manager. Gabe is going to stay on. He'll just be the president of the ballclub. I want you to help Alvin because there are a lot of things he doesn't know." [25]

Then, Stouffer tried to explain the move to skeptical newspaper reporters. Alvin Dark, he said, would now have the power to develop aggressive players throughout the Cleveland minor league system. "Until now, he hasn't had a free hand in bringing up more Alvin Darks, the kind of player he was," Stouffer said. "The Dark system of play should begin in the minors— and it will be his job to set it up. This is the way we do it in Stouffer restaurants. We fashion 'Stouffer' people all the way, and we have proven the system to be successful." [26]

But the innovations that made Vernon Stouffer millions of dollars in restaurants did not necessarily translate into baseball success. Gabe Paul privately warned Stouffer that the experiment with Dark would not work. But Stouffer ignored that advice, much as he shrugged off admonishments that opening a restaurant in New York would be a mistake. Vernon Stouffer's mind was made up, and Gabe Paul accepted the decision stoically.

Others were less docile. A disgusted Maurice Saltzman sold his $500,000 worth of stock. Hank Peters thought it was a ridiculous way to run a baseball team. Field managers were not like football coaches. Solid manager that he was, Dark had no clue about making trades, developing players in the farm system, and negotiating player salaries. The whole situation with the Indians had become a comedy, Peters thought. The club was just a ship adrift.

Dark's plan to rebuild the Indians was as unorthodox as his switch of Sam McDowell to second base. Instead of allowing young players to carefully develop throughout the Cleveland minor league system, Dark wanted to elevate to Cleveland any minor leaguer who displayed the slightest skills. "We're going to play anybody who can help us," Dark said. [27] Under Dark's tutelage, they would quickly develop into solid major leaguers.

The drawbacks were painfully evident. The Indians' farm system simply could not deliver enough young players to meet Dark's demands. At a time when the Athletics were developing Reggie Jackson, Catfish Hunter, and Vida Blue, the Indians were depending upon Rich Hand, Rick Austin, Steve Dunning, Vince Colbert, Jim Rittwage, Eddie Leon, Ted Ford, and Frank Baker. By the mid-1970s, all were out of the major leagues. The Indians staggered, losing 86 games in 1970, and 102 in 1971. Attendance dipped below 600,000 and the Indians lost $280,000. [28] To make ends meet, Alvin Dark was forced to sell pitcher Dean Chance to the New York Mets for $75,000.

Dark hated his new powers. Given the state of the team's finances, he could not grant players hefty raises. Instead of blaming Stouffer, the players were angry with Dark, the man who had to lead them on the field. Dark also found himself routinely second-guessed by a board of directors that knew little about baseball. One board member asked, "How about getting Nettles off third base? Put in someone else who can hit more?" Dark was stunned. Graig Nettles was one of a half-dozen quality players on Dark's team. Nettles was not hitting because opposing pitchers preferred to walk him and take their chances with the mediocre hitters in the rest of the Cleveland lineup.

"As long as I'm manager," Dark told the meddling directors, "Nettles will play third base." [29]

At first, Vernon Stouffer defended his move. He once engaged in a stormy argument with Hal Lebovitz outside the *Plain Dealer*. The ballclub was better, Stouffer insisted, than the sportswriters believed. "Vern, it's a terrible team," Lebovitz finally snapped. "You don't have any talent out there." [30] But as with selling frozen food at a gasoline station, Stouffer knew when to kill a bad concept. He recognized that he would have to jettison Dark and return to a more traditional form of baseball management with Gabe Paul in charge.

He still liked Dark and loathed telling him directly. Instead, he wanted Gabe Paul to deliver the bad news. Paul insisted, however, that Stouffer be present during the firing. Paul then telephoned Dark at his Mayfield Village apartment and tersely said, "Mr. Stouffer wants to see you." Dark knew what was happening. "Should I wear black?" he asked Paul, who replied, "I think so." Dark drove to Cleveland Stadium and went to Paul's office where both Paul and Stouffer waited. When Paul offered Dark a job as a scout, Dark replied, "Mr. Stouffer, I was hired as a manager and I will only manage." Paul glanced over to Stouffer who was so shocked that Dark had turned him down, his face turned ashen. [31]

Dark would later come to realize that Vernon Stouffer's experiment had been a horrifying mistake. He wrote a long letter of apology to Paul. Years later, Dark still blamed himself. He should have rejected Stouffer's offer. "A manager cannot handle that job," Dark said. "I found that out real quick."

What Hank Peters had described as a comedy had become a tragedy. In less than 20 years, the Cleveland Indians had crumbled from the mightiest team in baseball to a pathetic loser. A team that once had Bob Feller, Bob Lemon, Al Rosen, Bobby Avila, Early Wynn, and Larry Doby, now had five competent major league players on its roster—Chris Chambliss, Graig Nettles, Ray Fosse, Sam McDowell, and Ed Farmer. A team that routinely attracted well over one million fans a year, now was seeing 5,000 a night. A team that made millions was now losing a fortune. A team with a minor league system so potent it drew the attention of *Life Magazine* in 1954, was now unquestionably the worst in baseball.

Hank Peters knew it was time to leave. Even with Gabe Paul back running the Indians, Peters recognized that Stouffer lacked the money to make the team competitive. Peters let it be known that he was interested in the presidency of the minor leagues. He was easily elected and left Cleveland in the winter of 1971. There was no guarantee that the Indians would remain in the city much longer.

❖

Hank Peters had good reason to worry. Investors in other cities were eyeing the Indians with growing interest. Stouffer already had rejected the $15 million offer from Dallas in 1970, which would have provided him with nearly a 100 percent profit on his original investment. Others were certain to follow. At a special meeting of the American League, the owners voted—over the objections of Commissioner Bowie Kuhn—to move the Washington Senators to Texas. Kuhn, who had grown up in Washington, was so visibly upset over the decision that Gabe Paul told him, "Bowie, I've never seen you look so sad." [32] The transfer of the Senators enraged members of Congress. Joe Danzansky, who owned a supermarket chain in Washington, assembled a group determined to find a new franchise. "We're aware of the Cleveland situation," Danzansky said. [33]

Stouffer rejected all overtures throughout the summer of 1971 and set his creative mind upon a solution to the Indians' financial troubles. Since 1967, the team had suffered pre-tax operating losses of nearly $4 million. Depreciating the players had substantially reduced that loss, and Stouffer earned $1 million from the sale of players during the 1969 expansion draft to Kansas City and Seattle. [34] Stouffer had every reason to believe the huge losses would continue. The Indians were a bad team playing in what Stouffer knew was an antiquated stadium. Stouffer had argued that "Cleveland must have a new stadium." But politically, a new ballpark in 1971 was out of the question.

He was desperately unhappy at the turn of events. All he ever wanted was to keep the team in Cleveland. But as the team deteriorated, Cleveland newspapers stepped up their criticism of his leadership. "People are critical of me, but I'm for our town all the way," he complained. [35] He often felt physically ill and told friends that there were nights when he couldn't sleep. With the Indians in dreadful shape and his stock at Litton scraping bottom, Vernon Stouffer needed a novel solution.

In the summer of 1971, he thought he discovered one.

Like Vernon Stouffer, David Dixon of New Orleans was a man who loved new ideas. Friends joked that if they locked David Dixon in a room for an hour, he would produce 15 ideas. Throw out the 10 bad ones, they would laugh, and the remaining five would be sheer brilliance.

He played a major role in the city's efforts to win an expansion franchise in 1966 from the National Football League. He even thought of the nickname "Saints" while listening to a jazz band in Paris perform, "When the Saints Go Marching In." That, Dixon thought, was a great name for a football team. [36] In the 1980s, he helped found the United States Football League and its unusual concept of professional football in the spring.

Convinced that New Orleans needed an all-purpose stadium more versatile than the old Sugar Bowl, Dixon conceived of a huge dome that would dwarf Houston's Astrodome. He wanted massive TV screens inside the building to provide fans with instant replay. He even tried to design a small model out of cardboard. "They were grotesque and my cardboard models were silly," Dixon once explained. "I couldn't get the cardboard to form a circle or make a model dome." [37]

Armed with little more than his cardboard models and fertile imagination, Dixon approached Louisiana Governor John J. McKeithen, who was widely known as an enthusiastic football fan. McKeithen, a normally gregarious man with a booming voice, sat impassively as Dixon outlined his plan.

"Is that it, Mr. Dixon?" McKeithen finally asked. When Dixon nodded, McKeithen pounded his fist on the desk in excitement and proclaimed, "By gosh, that would be the greatest building in the history of mankind. And we'll build that sucker." [38] From then on, McKeithen became the dome's biggest booster. When he first visited the Houston Astrodome, McKeithen announced, "I want one just like this one, only bigger." He suggested opening the Superdome with "Billy Graham and the Pope. Put one in each end zone. There's room enough." [39]

Even though the Superdome was still three years away from opening, Dixon and other sponsors in 1971 desperately needed to find regular events other than the Saints for the huge facility. The obvious solution was baseball, but Dixon privately thought that New Orleans would have difficulty supporting major league baseball. In any event, it could take years to persuade an established team to move to New Orleans.

Instead, Dixon struck upon a wholly creative plan: Why not approach a team in financial difficulty and offer the owner a chance to play 25 of his home games in the Superdome? It seemed a perfect compromise. The owner could keep his franchise in his old city while playing to 25 sellouts in New Orleans.

The obvious team was Cleveland with its widely publicized financial troubles and its past links to New Orleans. As a boy growing up in New Orleans in the 1930s, Dixon had vivid memories of the Indians' spring training camp at Heinemann Park. There, he watched Bob Feller throw his powerful fastball, outfielder Jeff Heath hit screeching line drives, and first baseman Hal Trosky pound long home runs.

Dixon and Billy Connick, secretary treasurer of the Superdome, contacted Vernon Stouffer. Intrigued, Stouffer invited them to Cleveland, where they outlined the concept. Stouffer's frustration with Cleveland was evident to Connick. Stouffer explained that he did not want to abandon his hometown. But, he said, he was carrying the team at a huge personal sacrifice and nothing he tried had boosted attendance. Dixon's idea, he conceded, was a compromise he had never imagined. It appeared to be the best of all worlds and might even make the Cleveland Indians a national team.

"I'm for it," Stouffer finally declared. [40]

Dixon and Connick left Cleveland convinced that they had their team. In the next few months, a firm deal was negotiated: Beginning in 1974, the Indians would play between 27 and 33 games in the Superdome, while retaining 50 home dates in Cleveland Stadium. New Orleans investors would pay Stouffer $2.5 million for 25 percent of the franchise. [41]

The deal solved Stouffer's problems. He would receive enough cash to more than cover all his annual operating losses and retain control of the franchise. The games in New Orleans could boost the Indians' attendance by as much as 1.2 million, while providing the team with a vast source of new television and radio revenue. Most of the games in the Superdome would be played in the spring when the wretched weather in Cleveland normally held daily attendance to a few thousand. Stouffer, the visionary, proclaimed that the shared-city concept "will be the coming thing in baseball. Fifty home games are enough." [42]

Hal Lebovitz of the *Plain Dealer* and Bob August of the *Cleveland Press* were appalled. To them, playing a few games in New Orleans was only the first step toward permanently transferring the franchise to the Superdome. August wrote that Stouffer believed he would be a "pioneer breaking a new trail to baseball's future." But August warned that the "condition of baseball in

Cleveland is too perilous to survive such an experiment." [43] Stouffer was baffled by the criticism, but his real worry was persuading the American League owners to approve the transfer. Stouffer invited McKeithen, Dixon, and Connick to the 1971 winter meetings in Phoenix to personally lobby the league owners.

"Wait until you hear them," Stouffer said. "You'll be impressed." [44]

On Wednesday, December 1, McKeithen, Dixon, Connick, former Boston Red Sox pitcher Mel Parnell, and 17 other public officials from Louisiana posed in front of a DC-9 jet for a photographer from the *New Orleans Times-Picayune*. Then they flew to Phoenix. Stouffer already was waiting at his winter home in nearby Scottsdale.

The next morning, American League President Joe Cronin and the 12 league owners summoned them to a closed-door meeting at the Arizona Biltmore. McKeithen, who was so persuasive that one league owner complained he could "sell snow to an Eskimo," told the owners that the Superdome would be the "greatest arena of all time." [45] The split-city plan provided the least amount of turmoil because the Indians still would play most of their games in Cleveland.

Charlie Finley of the Oakland A's did not like what he was hearing. As the New Orleans delegation completed its presentation, Finley bluntly snapped, "I don't like approving the Indians tying up two cities. After all, I might want to move [to New Orleans] myself."

Stunned, Stouffer stood and weakly replied, "I thought you were my friend, Charlie." [46]

American League President Joe Cronin seemed dazed at the entire concept, referring to the Superdome as the Astrodome and garbling McKeithen's name. [47] Jerry Hoffberger of the Baltimore Orioles complained about receiving "a good sales pitch by a bunch of nice guys. But we have not been given any facts." Gene Autry of the California Angels said he had "mixed emotions." [48] The owners huddled privately before asking McKeithen, Connick, and Dixon to return for a brief seven-minute session. The owners explained there "were legal ramifications to be considered." They would form a special committee to study the proposal and issue a recommendation by the spring. "Give us the Christmas holidays and we'll give you the Mardi Gras," one owner told McKeithen. [49]

Stouffer invited McKeithen and the New Orleans' delegation to his Scottsdale home, where he had built a sparkling pool in the shadow of Camelback Mountain. There, they expressed confidence that by March the American League would reach the same conclusion: To survive financially, the Indians needed to play in New Orleans.

As the American League owners pondered the New Orleans proposal, Al Rosen, a prosperous stockbroker and member of the Indians' board of directors, was increasingly frustrated with the team's financial problems. Unlike the Cleveland teams he played on in the 1950s, the Indians of 1971 had no "focal point for the direction of the club," and he was appalled with Stouffer and what Rosen viewed as his drinking problem. "He was an embarrassment to go anyplace with," Rosen said years later. "First thing he'd do is put his head down on the table and go to sleep." Moreover, the old stadium had developed into a "black cloud" over the franchise. Rosen watched in admiration as Gabe Paul managed to keep the team operating. But eventually, a strong financial group would have to step in to rescue the franchise. [50]

Rosen and other young business executives in Cleveland were impatient with the older corporate elite that ran the city. In 1966, Rosen and 36-year-old shipping executive George M. Steinbrenner III formed an organization known as Group 66. They were young, ambitious Clevelanders eager to assume greater authority in managing the city's affairs.

Steinbrenner was brilliant, autocratic, and ever in the pursuit of wealth. Like many aggressive men, he loved sports. Steinbrenner ran track at Williams College, edited the sports pages of the college newspaper, and later served as an assistant football coach at Northwestern and Purdue. He bought the Cleveland Pipers of the old American Basketball League and quickly demonstrated his style by outbidding the National Basketball Association for Ohio State's All-America center, Jerry Lucas. The Pipers may have been the only failure in George Steinbrenner's life: They, along with the entire league, collapsed in bankruptcy.

Within a year, Steinbrenner had righted himself by assuming control of his father's Great Lakes shipping company, Kinsman Marine Transit Company. But Steinbrenner's ambition exceeded the Great Lakes, and in 1967 he organized a corporate takeover of the much larger American Ship Building Company. The city of Lorain agreed to expand the company's drydock facilities, and Steinbrenner was off. By 1968, *Fortune Magazine* named George M. Steinbrenner III as one of the 12 young "Movers and Shakers" in the country.

Steinbrenner had old ties with Vernon Stouffer; Steinbrenner and Stouffer's son, James, had attended Culver Military Academy together. It was clear by the fall of 1971 that Vernon Stouffer would listen to the right offer to sell the franchise.

Late in the summer of 1971, Rosen received a telephone call from Sheldon Guren, a wealthy partner at the Cleveland law firm of Godfrey, Ginsberg & Guren. Would Rosen attend a meeting at Cleveland Stadium with Art Modell, owner of the Cleveland Browns? When Rosen arrived, Modell explained that he was unhappy with aging Cleveland Stadium and wanted to move to the suburbs. Edward DeBartolo of Youngstown, who had earned a fortune developing shopping malls and racetracks, had assembled a large tract of land south of Cleveland and toyed with the idea of building two tracks. If the Indians and Browns were interested, perhaps they could finance two stadiums—one for baseball and the other for football. They would need to buy the Indians from Stouffer, and Guren asked Rosen if he would help put together a group of investors. [51]

The syndicate quickly expanded to Rosen, Steinbrenner, Guren; his law partner, Ed Ginsberg; Edwin T. Jeffrey, a current member of the board of directors; and Howard Metzenbaum and Alva T. Bonda, founders of APCOA parking.

Steinbrenner and Rosen also had an ally in Gabe Paul, still vigorous and relatively young. If the Indians were sold, Paul told them, he wanted to keep his stock and continue to direct the team's affairs. The deal promised that Paul could operate the Indians with substantial money for the first time. Paul was intrigued by Steinbrenner, once asking Rosen, "Is your friend Steinbrenner for real?" Rosen replied, "I like him a lot, and I think he can do whatever he says." [52] By joining the group, Paul would bring his close friend, Steve O'Neill, the chairman of Leaseway Transportation and a man of unlimited wealth.

They were wealthy, confident, and firmly convinced they could make the Indians profitable. Guren, who as a teenager sold hot dogs at League Park, thought the Indians' real problems could be traced to William Daley's unwillingness to commit money to build a competitive team. "We did not intend to build a loser," Guren said. "There was never any question that we were going to quickly re-invigorate the franchise and rebuild the team in a hurry. With Al's knowledge of baseball and our willingness to add the wherewithal, we thought we would be successful." [53]

Although Rosen was described in the newspapers as the titular head of the syndicate, Steinbrenner conducted most of the negotiations with James Stouffer. Steinbrenner made a firm offer of $8.6 million: $8.3 million in immediate cash, and forgiveness of a $300,000 debt the team had incurred by borrowing money against its 1972 television contract. Steinbrenner told Guren that he shook Vernon Stouffer's hand on the sale. [54]

Vernon Stouffer had remained in Scottsdale after the league meetings ended, but Rosen and Paul expected him to approve the sale by telephone. On a cold, drizzly December evening in Cleveland, Steinbrenner, Rosen, and Paul gathered in Steinbrenner's downtown office at American Ship. They telephoned Bob August to advise him the sale would take place that night. Steinbrenner and Rosen sounded so giddy to August, that he promised to remain by the phone. [55]

But when Steinbrenner telephoned Stouffer in Scottsdale later that night, Stouffer was angry. Details of the proposed deal had been leaked to the press. He thought the price of $8.6 million was ridiculous. He implied that Steinbrenner and Rosen were trying to take advantage of his financial difficulties. Enraged, Steinbrenner tried in vain "to argue Vernon out of it." But at the end of the conversation, Stouffer bluntly informed him, "There's no deal."[56]

Steinbrenner hung up and telephoned Bob August with the news. A discouraged Rosen released a written statement to reporters: "Today, a group of Clevelanders, of which I am the titular head, made an offer to purchase for cash the Cleveland Baseball Club, Inc. from Mr. Vernon Stouffer. It has been rejected. I am certain Mr. Stouffer, a civic-minded Clevelander, will continue to exercise his judgment in accomplishing what he feels is best for Cleveland." Rosen described the offer as "legitimate, reasonable, and realistic." He said that "financially, we cannot go any higher. It's a financial impossibility. If Mr. Stouffer wants to reconsider, we are here and the offer is, too." [57]

Privately, a number of members of the syndicate believed that anti-Semitism played a factor. "When Vernon Stouffer found who all the partners were, he backed out," one said. "He did not want to do business with Jewish people." Yet those close to Stouffer doubt that. Stouffer, they pointed out, sponsored an annual dinner promoting harmony between Christians and Jews. In addition, if Stouffer were anti-Semitic, why would he sell the Indians a few months later to a syndicate that included Ted Bonda and Howard Metzenbaum?

Others say that Stouffer was drinking heavily that evening. Gabe Paul remembered Stouffer as "belligerent" in his telephone conversation with Steinbrenner. "A lot of things," Paul said, "come out of a bottle." [58]

But Stouffer probably rejected the offer because he still believed the American League would approve his New Orleans' plan. Stouffer's telephone call to Steinbrenner took place just five days after the league meeting in Phoenix. Stouffer stood to make more money with the split-city scheme than by selling the team. Stouffer thought the $8.6 million offer was low. He had paid $8 million for the team in 1966, and New Orleans' offer of $2.5 million for 25 percent of the team's stock established that the entire franchise was worth $10 million. The Washington syndicate had offered Stouffer $12.5 million. When a *Cleveland Press* reporter reached him at his Scottsdale home that night, Stouffer was seething. As far as he was concerned, Steinbrenner and Rosen were trying to pressure him into handing over the Indians at a bargain price.

"I backed this team for five years with real money," he bitterly complained. "I have lost $1.5 million in the last five years. I have also spent my time and I have spent my energy. They think I'm desperate, but let me tell you: I am not. I am going right forward with New Orleans and I might even sell to Washington." [59]

Chapter 7

All the Glitter, But No Gold
"We had no business owning that club." — Armond Arnson

Nick Mileti confidently strolled through the Tampa International Airport. He was hard to miss on this March evening in 1972. His brown hair flopped about his ears, and he wore a checkered Edwardian sports coat over bell-bottomed slacks and black boots. One of his aides dutifully tagged along carrying Mileti's mink coat. An elderly woman from Cleveland approached. "You're Nick Mileti, the new owner of the Indians, aren't you?" Mileti nodded in approval. "So, you love baseball?" he asked, then added, "All beautiful women love baseball." [1]

It was quintessential Mileti—charming, outlandish, and the consummate promoter. He used that charm to persuade wealthy Ohioans to invest in his growing sports empire. Indeed there might not have been an empire without those investors. He bought the Cleveland Barons of the American Hockey League for $510,000; the Cleveland Cavaliers of the National Basketball Association for $3.7 million; the 11,000-seat Cleveland Arena for $1.4 million; and Cleveland Radio Station WKYC for $6 million. Mileti changed the station's name to 3WE and featured his basketball and hockey teams on the 50,000-watt clear-channel radio giant. He envisioned an $18 million basketball arena in the hills of Richfield, a small suburb between Cleveland and Akron. The new palace would be an enduring monument to Nick Mileti and his bold ideas.

He was a master of leverage, owning 51 percent of his enterprises, although he had little of his own money at risk. Sheldon Guren admired Mileti's resourcefulness in raising the money to finance his dreams, and Hal Lebovitz marveled at how Mileti could "do more things with other people's money." Even tough New York bankers succumbed to Mileti's sales pitch. One longtime associate said he knew why: Mileti "believed in what he was talking about."

126

Mileti's success was built on brains, personality, and a knack for making the right friends. In the Army in 1958, he befriended Leo C. McKenna, who later became a vice president of the New York investment firm of Lombardi, Vitalis & Paganucci. McKenna's client list included C.F. Kettering, Inc., of Dayton, a family-run investment house. Mileti convinced Kettering to finance one-half of his purchases, and he would raise the rest by juggling bank loans or turning to wealthy Democratic friends, such as Ted Bonda and Howard Metzenbaum.

To objections that Mileti was putting little of his own money into the teams, he had a quick response: "I put in work and talent. Sometimes you put in money, sometimes you don't." But the results were undeniable. "He has been phenomenal in producing... the profit he predicted," one banker told the *Plain Dealer*. [2]

He dazzled reporters, who regarded him as another Bill Veeck for his flair in promoting his sports franchises. He was an odd brew of old world and new. He loved to call up his "old Italian sayings" to explain his ideas, but often punctuated his sentences with an offhand, "We've been there, baby." When asked why he turned to old friends from Bowling Green State University to help him run his sports teams, Mileti quipped, "When you are a Sicilian peasant's son, you have a long memory." [3]

On this particular March afternoon in Tampa, Nick Mileti was at the pinnacle. He had climbed from working-class Italian roots to become the dominant sports figure in Cleveland. He owned a mansion encircled by lush greenery in Gates Mills, one of the right addresses in Cleveland's suburbs. When a high school chum came for dinner, he was astounded to see servants dashing about. Then, just like out of an old English movie, a butler appeared to solemnly announce: "Dinner is served." Little Nick Mileti, the friend thought, had come a long way from John Adams High School.

He was short and slender; so slight that his personal attorney, George Moscarino, thought he looked like a cheerleader. Moscarino was right. Mileti, one of three male cheerleaders at John Adams, had dazzled the crowd with tricky somersaults. He was known as Nicky then and "the girls loved him," recalled Shirley Kvet, a classmate. Dave Griffiths, an attorney in Chagrin Falls who attended John Adams, said that even as a teenager, Mileti "always was a bundle of energy and had a smile on his face." Mileti was popular, but few classmates predicted that he would build a vast business empire.

While they saw Mileti's energy, they missed his intense capacity for 14-hour workdays. "The old Puritan work ethic dressed up in a mod-striped suit," was the way a friend described Mileti to the *Plain Dealer*. [4] He delivered newspapers in grade school, put himself through Bowling Green, and earned a law degree from Ohio State. After the Army, he borrowed $500 to open a law practice in Lakewood. Friendships and hard work did the rest. Frank Celeste, the mayor of Lakewood and father of the future governor, took a liking to Mileti and named him to the city prosecutor's office. After Frank Celeste left office, he and Mileti formed a housing investment company. But Mileti quickly demonstrated that his ambitions went beyond one small housing firm.

Mileti got his chance to buy the Cleveland Arena in 1968 almost by accident. As chairman of the Cleveland chapter of the Bowling Green Alumni Association, Mileti organized a basketball game in Cleveland between Bowling Green and the University of Niagara. The only place to play was the aging downtown arena, and Mileti learned the facility and the Cleveland Barons of the American Hockey League were for sale. Mileti quickly grasped the advantages of owning both: By running the arena, he could pick the best dates for the Barons and save the remaining days for any shows and events he could entice to Cleveland.

His ownership of the arena logically led to his next acquisition —an NBA franchise. An NBA team would enable Mileti to double the number of regular events he could hold in his arena every year. When the NBA expanded in 1970, Mileti was first in line with his ever-ready investors and his fierce determination. He promised the NBA expansion committee that he would reserve Fridays, Saturdays, and Sundays for half the new team's home dates. He pledged to expand the arena's seating capacity to 19,500. Jack Kent Cooke, owner of the Los Angeles Lakers and chairman of the expansion committee, was impressed. "You've done your homework," he told Mileti. [5]

After winning his NBA franchise, Mileti named the team "Cavaliers," and shrewdly hired University of Minnesota basketball coach Bill Fitch to guide his new acquisition. Though Fitch would direct the players on the court, Mileti retained a strong hand. "The more I get into it," he explained, "I find more of my duties come under the realm of general manager." [6] One week after hiring Fitch, Mileti sat side-by-side with his new coach as the Cavaliers selected University of Iowa forward John Johnson as their first-round pick in the NBA draft.

Nick Mileti had succeeded where other prominent Clevelanders had failed: bringing an NBA team to Cleveland. In just two years he had risen from obscurity to become the best known sports promoter in Cleveland. But Mileti seemed to ricochet between apprehension and overconfidence. At one moment he would confide to his chief assistant, Steve Zayac, "Things are great at this moment, but we have to remember, at some point along the way, it can turn." Then he would reach out for the next dangerous challenge, perhaps another team or a grand arena. [7]

Mileti was well aware that the Indians and the Browns remained the city's prestige teams. While people might pay to see his Cavaliers and Barons, Cleveland fans were obsessed with baseball and football. One evening as he sipped a drink at the Theatrical Restaurant with Bob Dolgan of the *Plain Dealer*, Mileti said, "The Barons and the Cavaliers are my teams, and I own the arena." But, Mileti ruefully added, "Here we are, talking about the Indians and Browns." [8]

By 1972, Nick Mileti was poised to further expand his empire. He planned to drop the minor league Barons and finance a World Hockey Association franchise to directly compete with the National Hockey League. The new team, nicknamed "Crusaders" by Mileti, would join the Cavaliers playing in Mileti's proposed coliseum in Richfield Township, which he hoped would be a magnet for people from Cleveland, Akron, Canton, Columbus, and Youngstown. The old Cleveland Arena with its limited seating was too small for Nick Mileti. One afternoon, Mileti took George Moscarino and other friends to the site he had selected. They had a picnic lunch as Mileti described his palace. All anyone else could see was an empty field. But Nick Mileti saw his dream. [9]

Mileti had his chance for the Indians in the spring of 1972 after Vernon Stouffer rejected George Steinbrenner's offer.

Stouffer's plans to shift some home dates to New Orleans were stalled, and he was eager to find a buyer who would meet his price of at least $10 million. Stouffer knew Mileti by reputation and was intrigued by his promotional skills. One innovator was about to meet another.

With the Cavaliers, the Crusaders, and the coliseum, Mileti knew he ran the risk of overextending himself. Zayac feared the Indians would be a distraction. But Mileti was convinced that Stouffer's share-the-team plan with New Orleans would eventually lead to the Indians switching all their games to the Superdome. Mileti was still trying to gain the financial backing he needed to build his coliseum. "But nobody would listen to those ideas if Cleveland lost its major league baseball team," Mileti later said. Perhaps Mileti could put together a group to buy the team, then withdraw in a couple of years and focus on his coliseum. In early 1972, he set about to find investors and rounded up his usual suspects. [10]

Mileti visited Metzenbaum's corner office at 9th and Chester, with its view of Lake Erie and Burke Lakefront Airport. "I want to buy the Indians," Mileti told Metzenbaum. "I need half-a-million dollars. I need five guys who will come in with one hundred apiece." Metzenbaum never had been a baseball fan, preferring the swifter pace of basketball and hockey. But he liked Mileti and thought he was an "unbelievable promoter." Metzenbaum also knew first-hand about Vernon Stouffer's financial problems. Metzenbaum recalled sitting next to Stouffer at a board of directors' meeting at Society National Bank. The subject that day? A bank loan that Stouffer was having trouble repaying.

"OK," Metzenbaum told Mileti. "We'll go along." [11]

From there, Mileti expanded his group to trusted friends— Ted Bonda; Bruce Fine, the 35-year-old vice president of the Midwest Bank and Trust Co.; Fine's brother Marshall, the president of Associated Theaters; and Joseph Zingale, a business partner and cousin of Mileti's. The plan Mileti outlined would allow the group to buy a $10 million baseball team for only $1 million in cash. "Nick could perform miracles with nothing in the sense of money," Bonda later said. [12]

Mileti planned to personally borrow $500,000 from Bruce Fine's bank to control 51 percent of the team. Metzenbaum, Bonda, Zingale, and the Fine brothers would contribute $100,000 apiece. Mileti and his investors also would guarantee $3 million of Indians' notes held by the Society National and Union Commerce banks and borrow an additional $1 million to improve the Indians and their farm system. As for the rest, Mileti would sell $5 million worth of the team's stock to the general public for $5 per share. He had financed his purchase of the Cavaliers the same way, raising $1.8 million through the sale of 400,000 shares of stock. [13]

Stouffer agreed to the terms, which guaranteed him $1.4 million more than Steinbrenner's bid. But when Mileti presented his offer to the American League owners in Sarasota, Florida, they were horrified. The very idea of a public stock sale was out of the question. "It's like asking widows and babies to invest their money in Cleveland baseball," one owner sputtered. [14] The owners noted that Mileti planned on putting up only $1 million. That was nowhere near enough, they warned. Just two years earlier the league had been faced with the bankruptcy of the Seattle Pilots. Only the team's transfer to Milwaukee had saved the league from having to bail out Bill Daley and the other Seattle owners. Besides, the conservative league owners could hardly believe what they were seeing. "He looks like a hippie," one owner grumbled. [15]

The owners handed Mileti an ultimatum: Raise $3 million in the next two weeks and drop the public sale of stock or forget the deal. A frustrated Mileti had no choice but to accede to the owners' wishes.

But if there was one thing Mileti knew, it was how to raise money. The Blossom brothers, Dudley and Bing, and Richard Miller, a Cleveland lawyer and son of former mayor Ray Miller, agreed to contribute $500,000 apiece. Steve O'Neill, Gabe Paul, and Edwin T. Jeffrey would retain their 30 percent share of the team and provide the Indians with financial stability. Mileti would then transform the Indians from a corporation into a partnership, which would allow each partner the attractive option of writing off the team's financial losses against his personal income. Presented with the new financing arrangement, league owners approved the sale in St. Petersburg on March 22. [16]

That night, Mileti entered the crowded Theatrical to cheers and congratulations. He bantered with patrons and bartenders around the famed circular bar, sipping a drink that was wrapped in his customary napkin. A *Plain Dealer* editorial applauded Mileti's purchase: "If past performance is any measure, Mileti is capable of reviving the Indians' franchise, giving it fresh enthusiasm, drive and direction it so obviously needs." [17]

On Friday, March 31, Mileti told the Cleveland City Club that the split-city concept with New Orleans was dead. That afternoon, he flew to New Orleans to break the news to Billy Connick. The National Basketball Association's split-city schemes never worked, he told Connick. Mileti explained that he was a Clevelander. "We just are not going to play anywhere but in Cleveland," he told reporters. He later recalled that he "was a junior at John Adams High School here in 1948 when we drew two million six. We win, and we can do that again. Yet people wanted to move this team. I tell you, we took over to keep the Indians here. Before us, they were going, baby, going." [18]

Instead, Vernon Stouffer was gone. He never understood why he had been so unpopular. He thought that no one in Cleveland appreciated the agony he endured. The Indians could have been in Dallas in 1970 had Stouffer only given the word. All he ever wanted was to bring a winner to Cleveland. But, he said sadly, "things kept going the other way." [19]

Gabe Paul remained with the Indians, but was just as unhappy as Stouffer. He had planned to operate the Indians with Al Rosen by his side, and George Steinbrenner, Steve O'Neill, and Sheldon Guren supplying the money. Paul had survived Bill Daley's frugality, Vernon Stouffer's off-the-wall ideas, and Alvin Dark's scheming. But with Nick Mileti in charge, Gabe Paul had little to do except watch the games.

Paul groused that Mileti had bought the Indians with nothing more than green stamps. It should have been obvious to everyone in baseball, Paul thought, that Mileti did not have enough money to operate the franchise. The Indians would need to draw 1.2 million people to their home games just to break even. Fat chance with the ballclub Mileti had. Paul knew the organization had deteriorated. As far as he could determine, the Indians would lose money throughout the foreseeable future. Maybe the time had come for him to get out of Cleveland.

Paul soon had his chance when George Steinbrenner wandered into his office in the summer of 1972. Steinbrenner explained that he was eager to own a team and had heard from General Motors executive John DeLorean that the Detroit Tigers were on the market. Any truth to that one?

Paul shook his head no.

"What club is available?" Steinbrenner asked.

"Believe it or not," Paul replied, "the Yankees are."

Steinbrenner was astonished. Even though the Yankees had slipped dramatically during CBS's ownership and were projecting an $11 million loss in 1972, the team's name remained magic. Any fool could make a fortune in New York City with baseball's glamour team.

"Would you follow it up for me?" Steinbrenner asked. Paul telephoned Yankee President Mike Burke and they agreed to meet for breakfast at the Plaza Hotel in New York. As they ate, Burke told Paul that CBS President William Paley wanted to unload the team and had authorized him to find a buyer or put together his own syndicate. Paul promised to get him together with Steinbrenner. [20]

Steinbrenner and Burke agreed upon a price of $10 million, a steal for the nation's best sports franchise. Steinbrenner formed a syndicate that included John DeLorean; Cincinnati financier Marvin L. Warner; Jim Nederlander of Broadway's Nederlander Theater; Thomas Evans, a former law partner of Richard M. Nixon; and two members of the earlier group he had put together to buy the Indians from Vernon Stouffer—Sheldon Guren and Edward Ginsberg. Steinbrenner also lured Steve O'Neill and Gabe Paul into his group. O'Neill was the largest stockholder of the Indians and his loss would deliver a major financial blow to Nick Mileti. But O'Neill, like his close friend Gabe Paul, was unhappy that summer. The Indians were now Mileti's team. "The closeness is gone" among the Cleveland stockholders, O'Neill thought. [21]

Under the terms of Steinbrenner's purchase, Burke retained five percent of the Yankees' stock, and believed he would have clear authority to direct the team. But Steinbrenner wanted Gabe Paul to run the Yankees. When Burke learned that Paul was moving to New York City, he was enraged.

At a dinner in New York City honoring Toots Shor, Burke confronted Paul. "How would you feel if you got stabbed in the back?" Burke asked angrily. Paul shot back, "I didn't know you had any blood." [22]

❖

On the morning of January 10, 1973, Steinbrenner dropped the bomb: He told Nick Mileti that Paul and O'Neill were heading for New York. Mileti shouldn't have been surprised. Everybody else seemed to know how miserable Paul had been. Every time Mileti offered a suggestion on how to run the Indians, Paul seemed to resent it. But more than surprised, Mileti was worried. He knew that O'Neill and Paul would have to unload their $1.5 million worth of Indians' stock and that would rip a huge hole in the team's finances. Throughout that day, Mileti telephoned Paul in New York City and urged him in vain to stay in Cleveland. [23]

When the news broke, one team insider told Hal Lebovitz that it was "like taking one leg from a table. The table will stand. But it won't be as sturdy." [24] Those close to Mileti and Ted Bonda were angry. Paul's departure "was the one thing that made it impossible for Nick and Ted to be successful," one friend of Mileti's later said.

As he left, Gabe Paul mischievously created the impression that the Indians were about to become a contender. "The Cleveland club is on the move," Paul told reporters. "This is the first time in many years that we have a reservoir of players in the system." [25] Gabe Paul should have known better. He was leaving a franchise without money, scouts, or talented young players. But now when things went wrong, the public could blame Nick Mileti. Not Gabe Paul.

Armond D. Arnson, a Republican corporate and securities lawyer in Cleveland and a close friend of Hal Lebovitz, formed a group and bought O'Neill's and Paul's stock. Arnson was wealthy, but lacked the deep pockets of Steve O'Neill. Arnson's new status as a limited partner meant he had no legal say in directing the team. Still, Arnson, who had a mind of his own, wanted to offer his ideas on managing the Indians. But Arnson quickly discovered that Mileti resented any interference. "It was his baby and he ran it," Arnson said years later. [26]

To replace Paul, Mileti elevated farm director Phil Seghi, who had been recruited to Cleveland by Paul. Seghi, once one of Hank Greenberg's minor league managers, believed in developing players through a minor league system. Seghi had worked for Paul in Cincinnati as the Reds' farm director, and when Paul left for Houston, he advanced to assistant general manager of the Reds.

Then he moved to Oakland to direct Charles Finley's farm system, before rejoining Paul in Cleveland in 1971. Although some baseball executives such as Tal Smith had a high regard for Seghi's abilities, the players were not always as sure. He often had difficulty recognizing his own players; one agent swears that Seghi once approached a Cleveland pitcher with the words, "Hey slugger, how are you today?" Seghi obviously thought he was talking to an outfielder.

To Phil Seghi, a successful farm team and clever trades led to pennants. That took time and money, and by the summer of 1973 Nick Mileti had run out of both.

In the hills of Richfield, where work was proceeding on his new indoor arena, rising construction costs and interest rates were pushing the original $18-million pricetag to more than $30 million. Local residents objected to the new building, and Mileti devoted time and energy to fighting off lawsuits.

He also was trying to get the Cleveland Crusaders of the WHA off the ground. Unlike the old Barons, the Crusaders would be major league hockey, and Mileti was determined to go first class. He spent $1 million to sign Gerry Cheevers of the Boston Bruins, describing him as "the absolute foundation of our team." [27] But that too ended up in court when the Bruins filed suit to block the signing.

As Gabe Paul had anticipated, the Indians continued to lose in 1973, finishing last in the six-team American League East Division. No player drove in more than 68 runs, and, except for 19 victories from Gaylord Perry and 14 from Dick Tidrow, the team's pitching was nonexistent. In one of his last acts as general manager of the Indians, Paul traded third baseman Graig Nettles to the Yankees for catcher John Ellis, infielder Jerry Kenney, and outfielders Rusty Torres and Charlie Spikes. Paul liked Spikes, who hit 26 home runs for the Yankees Double-A team in the Eastern League. But as Nettles became the game's best third baseman, Spikes struck out too much, was slow afoot and clumsy in the field. The Indians tried to sell the fans on their young players—George Hendrick, Buddy Bell, Chris Chambliss, and Charlie Spikes. But the fans weren't buying. Attendance plunged to 605,073. Mileti needed at least double that figure just to break even. Instead, the Indians lost more than $1 million. [28]

Those close to Mileti, such as attorney Ted Garver of Jones, Day, Reavis & Pogue, worried that he was spread too thin financially. The Indians, they thought, had been too much for him. Because Mileti lacked a fortune of his own, he had to depend on others to bail him out. A cruel joke circulated in the city's elite bars about a new drink called the "Mileti Cocktail." According to the joke, a man would toss a quarter down for gingerale and ask everyone else at the bar to buy the scotch. "Nick once rode into town like gangbusters, performing near miracles and receiving much-deserved applause," Hal Lebovitz wrote. "Now jokes are being made about him. This has got to hurt." [29]

Mileti raised cash by adding limited partners. When that was not enough, he turned to the area banks for help. In the summer of 1973, Mileti arranged for a $2.5 million loan from National City Bank. But bank executives made clear they lacked confidence in Mileti's ability to pay back the money and urged that a wealthier man replace him. Unhappy limited partners, Armond Arnson for one, were pushing the same idea. The Indians, they argued, needed a full-time owner. Even Mileti's friends reluctantly agreed. Perhaps, Ted Garver advised, it would make sense to turn the team over to Ted Bonda, a trusted and longtime friend. The banks and limited partners were delighted with the selection. In August 1973—just 18 months after Mileti first appeared in Howard Metzenbaum's office—Mileti turned over his baby to Bonda, naming him executive vice president. [30]

Mileti retained the title of general partner, but Bonda had the power. "In many cases, the buck will stop here," Bonda told the *Cleveland Press*. In a none-too-subtle jab at his friend Mileti, Bonda said that the team's limited partners thought "the business end was not good. Nobody was minding the store. There was zero effort for years in selling tickets...I'd like to see dignity restored to the ownership. Our partners are winners in their fields and they hate to be connected with failure." [31]

Mileti clung to his figurehead status until March 1975 when he officially withdrew from the team. A year later, Chase Manhattan Bank forced Mileti to give up control of his dream in Richfield. Some were glad to see Mileti go: He promised far more than he could deliver. It was obvious he never had enough money to turn the Indians into winners.

Occasionally, Nick Mileti would second-guess himself. Perhaps he took on too much by trying to run the Indians, Cavaliers, Crusaders, and the coliseum all at once. "If I had stuck to just one or the other, and really concentrated on baseball, we might have made something out of it," Mileti mused a few years later to Peter Shimrak, a savings and loan executive and longtime friend. But Nick Mileti did bring the NBA to Cleveland and prevented the Indians from leaving for New Orleans. "Nick saved the Indians for Cleveland," Shimrak liked to say. David Griffiths, Mileti's high school classmate, agreed: "I think we have major league baseball in Cleveland because of Nick Mileti."

When Ted Bonda was a junior at Glenville High School, he and his buddy, Howard Metzenbaum, decided they could make big money selling class rings. They pooled their resources to buy 10 rings. But the business collapsed when a classmate broke into their locker and stole them. "We had no money and no sales," Bonda glumly recalled years later.

It was one of the few times the pair came out on the short end of a business venture. Smart, savvy, and hungry, they made a fortune in parking lots and car rentals and owned a large chunk of Society Bank. Bonda and his wife lived in a high-rise condominium overlooking Lake Erie and maintained a $400,000 winter home in Palm Beach. Bonda drove to Cleveland Stadium in a maroon Rolls Royce. When bored with the freeways, he would pilot his speedboat at 60 miles an hour to the stadium's lakefront dock.

Both Bonda and Metzenbaum gravitated toward Democratic Party politics. An early supporter of Carl Stokes, the first black mayor of Cleveland, Bonda also poured $100,000 into George McGovern's 1972 presidential bid. For that, he won a spot on the enemies list assembled by President Nixon's White House staff. Metzenbaum served as a Democratic state legislator in the 1940s and was denounced by conservatives as a Communist when he introduced a bill that would have outlawed racial and religious discrimination in hiring. He later was counsel to the Ohio AFL-CIO and brilliantly managed Democrat Stephen Young's 1958 upset over Republican Senator John Bricker. By 1970, Metzenbaum was running for the Senate himself, losing a close race to Republican Robert Taft, Jr., son of the legendary Ohio Republican senator. Three years later, Democratic Governor John Gilligan named Metzenbaum to fill a vacant seat in the U.S. Senate. Although he lost a primary to John Glenn in the spring of 1974, Metzenbaum doggedly ran again in 1976, defeated Taft, and won the Senate seat he would hold for two decades.

For all their passion for liberal causes, Bonda and Metzenbaum could be remarkably conservative when it came to their own money. When Metzenbaum owned a string of suburban newspapers in Cleveland, his management team opposed efforts by reporters to organize a union. "I think [Metzenbaum] got away with murder," one astonished Democrat said later.

In many ways, Alva Teddy Bonda was born to be president of the Cleveland Indians. His parents named him after Alva Bradley, who owned the building where Bonda's father worked. A decade later, Alva Bradley bought the Indians and served as the team's president until 1946. From the family's tiny duplex on Thornhill Drive in Glenville, young Bonda liked to hop on the yellow street cars that ran down to League Park. There he watched first baseman George Burns rocket doubles off League Park's left-field wall. Years later Bonda vividly recalled everything about those days, even that Burns "used to bat with his two feet together."

He was the son of hard-working Jewish immigrants, Jacob and Nettie Bonda. Jacob left the old Austro-Hungarian empire in the 1880s to become a dressmaker in Cleveland, but never made enough money to buy his family a house. Instead, they rented. Ted Bonda's friend, Metzenbaum, was just as poor, joking later that he thought "eating cream peas on toast was a normal diet." [32]

Ted Bonda grew up frail and had such a sleepy look about him that friends nicknamed him "Mopy." Far from it. He and Metzenbaum devised one money-making idea after another. Bonda caddied at Lake Shore Country Club for $1 per 18 holes and installed and maintained juke boxes. Metzenbaum hauled groceries in his wagon for 10 cents a trip, sold peanuts at the Cleveland air shows, and started a bicycle rental shop at Ohio State where he charged 25 cents a ride.

It was Metzenbaum who struck upon the plan that would

make a fortune for them both. In 1947, Metzenbaum telephoned Bonda and asked him to manage a car rental company he was starting. Bonda dug up two cars and a garage in downtown Cleveland to house them. Business expanded so fast that Bonda had more cars than garage space. He compensated by illegally parking his cars and hoping the police wouldn't notice. "That was not breaking the law," Bonda explained about the parking. "It was skipping it."

Their real break came a year later. As Metzenbaum flew from Cleveland to Columbus to attend the Ohio legislature, he looked down on hundreds of cars parked haphazardly in mudholes and unlit areas near the rapidly growing Hopkins Airport. He and Bonda offered the airport a deal: They would guarantee the airport $400 a month if they could charge people to park their cars in safe lots. From that grew APCOA, the largest company of its kind in the nation. In 1966, Bonda and Metzenbaum sold APCOA to ITT for $30 million.

But Bonda's and Metzenbaum's shrewd touch failed them with sports. They dropped $800,000 on the Cleveland Stokers, a professional soccer team in the 1960s. Bonda lost $100,000 when Mileti's Crusaders eventually collapsed, and Metzenbaum lost every penny of the $100,000 he put into the Indians. Years later, Metzenbaum laughed, "Soccer, I got clobbered. Hockey, I got clobbered." He could afford to chuckle. Between 1982 and 1987, Howard Metzenbaum showed an adjusted gross income of $5.2 million, making him one of the richest men in the Senate. [33]

Attendance was everything to Ted Bonda when he took over the Indians from Nick Mileti. To attract fans, he wanted big names on the roster, a manager with star appeal, and lively uniforms. He did get the uniforms: outlandish all-red jerseys and pants that he personally selected. The players were so embarrassed that they offered to spend $60 apiece to buy more conservative blue tops to wear with white pants.

Bonda saw himself as a visible promoter. Sportswriters might poke fun at George Steinbrenner's corny locker room speeches and Charlie Finley's perpetual firing of managers, but they motivated their teams, Bonda thought, and in the process sold tickets. For Opening Day in 1974, Bonda arranged for a human cannonball stunt and asked a tight-rope walker to traverse the huge field from one roof of Cleveland Stadium to the other. He organized a money scramble and promoted statewide baseball clinics. In 1974 alone, Bonda budgeted $200,000 for promotions.

Bonda insisted the heavy promotion schedule was necessary to fill the stadium because "we can't wait for a winning team." [34] And Bonda was indeed too impatient to wait while Phil Seghi reconstructed a Greenberg-style farm system. Bonda wanted immediate results. During spring training of 1975, he told manager Frank Robinson that he could boost attendance by winning a lot of exhibition games. "Do me a favor," Bonda asked Robinson. "Win three or four in a row." [35]

The Indians played competitive baseball in 1974 and as late as Labor Day were only six games behind the first-place Orioles. People in Cleveland responded to Bonda's colorful promotions, and the team's attendance leaped by half-a-million to 1,114,262. Though the Indians lost $100,000, Bonda envisioned the team breaking even in the next few years. [36]

Knowing that he lacked Phil Seghi's baseball expertise, Bonda deferred to his general manager at first. But by the fall of 1974, Bonda was growing more assertive. He blocked Seghi's plan to trade Gaylord Perry to the Boston Red Sox for three young pitchers—John Curtis, Marty Pattin, and Roger Moret. Seghi wanted pitching depth, but Bonda was appalled. Perry had won 24 games in 1973 and attracted large crowds to Cleveland's home games. "I'm a great believer in heroes," Bonda said. "He was the only hero we had." [37]

Instead, Bonda wanted more stars like Perry, and when a baseball arbitrator declared Oakland pitcher Catfish Hunter a free agent in December 1974, Bonda urged Seghi to sign him. Bonda reasoned that Hunter and Gaylord Perry would provide a potent starting staff. There was such a slim difference, Bonda thought, between a winning team and a losing one, and one pitcher like Hunter could make that difference for the Indians. Bonda even asked Perry to telephone Hunter and persuade him to sign with Cleveland. But the Indians could not match George Steinbrenner's offer of $3.75 million over five years and lost Hunter to the Yankees.

In the summer of 1976, when the major league owners and players union agreed to grant free agency to six-year players,

Bonda wanted to bid aggressively on more big-name stars. Bonda assumed that there would be a gentleman's agreement among the owners to control salaries of the new free agents, and every team would sign their share. Instead, the Yankees and Angels spent millions to reel in the best free agents. Salaries mushroomed. Bonda was forced to spend $2.3 million over a 10-year period to sign Wayne Garland, a 20-game winner for the Orioles in 1976. Bonda offered free agent first baseman Don Baylor $200,000 a year for 10 years and a $100,000 signing bonus. [38] Baylor rejected the offer. Still, Bonda was not discouraged. He wanted stars for Cleveland.

Ted Bonda had long been disappointed with the Indians' efforts to attract black customers to their home games. For the Indians to exceed one million in attendance, Bonda knew he had to spark interest in the black community, now 38 percent of Cleveland's population, according to Bonda's surveys.

The answer was obvious: The Indians, the first American League team to sign a black player, should now be the first to hire a black manager. It would generate massive and favorable publicity. And it would please Bonda's old friends in the civil rights movement, such as Howard Metzenbaum and Carl Stokes. It also would serve another purpose: Bonda wanted stars at every position and Ken Aspromonte, the Indians' solid, dependable manager, did not fit the mold. The time had come for a black manager, Bonda told friends.

Everybody's choice was Frank Robinson. For nearly 20 years, Robinson had been one of the game's best hitters and fiercest competitors. Everywhere he played, his teams won. His 37 home runs helped the Cincinnati Reds win the 1961 National League pennant. When the Reds foolishly traded him to Baltimore in 1966, Robinson responded by winning the Triple Crown. The Orioles won 97 games and swept the Dodgers four consecutive games in the World Series. Opposing managers were in awe. In 1972 when the Orioles were trying to trade him, Leo Durocher of the Cubs pleaded with Chicago General Manager John Holland to get him. "By accident he'll hit 35-to-40 home runs in our ballpark," Durocher told Holland. [39]

By 1974, Robinson's shoulder ached, and he was clearly in a

decline. But Robinson had always wanted to manage and tested his ideas by running his own team in Puerto Rico in the winter leagues. It was evident throughout baseball that he or Maury Wills would be the first black manager. Seghi was more than willing to pick up Robinson from the Angels for the final month of the 1974 season. Robinson understood the game and could still play well enough to be a designated hitter. But Seghi wasn't sure that Robinson, who had a ferocious temper, was ready to manage. Bonda, however, wanted Robinson, and Bonda got his way.

Bonda's sure sense of public relations paid off. Robinson's hiring as a player-manager was national news, and Commissioner Bowie Kuhn flew to Cleveland for the announcement. Holt, Rinehart & Winston teamed Robinson with Dave Anderson of *The New York Times* to write a book on Robinson's first year. Bonda invited Kuhn and Rachel Robinson, the widow of Jackie Robinson, to attend Opening Day in Cleveland in 1975. Years later, Kuhn would describe the frigid afternoon game as one of "most memorable" he ever attended. [40] During pre-game ceremonies, Rachel Robinson congratulated the crowd of 56,715 for "being the first to take this historic step. I've wished…that Jackie could be here, and I'm sure in many ways he is."

It was a coup, and Bonda could not have been more pleased. Robinson wrote himself into the lineup as the designated hitter and homered his first time up to help the Indians to a 5-3 victory. "A storybook debut," Hal Lebovitz wrote. This, Bonda thought, was the way to promote a baseball team. [41]

It could not last. The Indians' abuse of Hank Greenberg's farm system haunted Frank Robinson as it had his predecessors. Except for three young rookies—pitcher Dennis Eckersley, second baseman Duane Kuiper, and outfielder Rick Manning—the Indians did not get any help from players signed after Vernon Stouffer's 1970 purge. The Indians scored 108 fewer runs than the American League East champion Boston Red Sox, while their pitchers yielded 102 more earned runs than the second-place Orioles. It should not have been a surprise to anyone that the Indians finished fourth with 79 victories and 80 defeats.

Bonda's star system exploded the same year. His star manager, Frank Robinson, clashed with his star pitcher, Gaylord Perry.

The two nearly came to blows in the clubhouse in September 1974 after Perry told reporters that he wanted to be paid $1 more next year than Robinson's $175,000 salary. Brandishing a copy of the *Cleveland Press*, Robinson went to Perry's locker and asked, "Are these quotes straight?"

"Yes," Perry snapped.

"I don't want my name dragged through the papers," Robinson angrily told him. "I don't want my salary tossed around in the papers by someone else." [42]

Their relationship continued to sour the following spring. Robinson thought that Perry was a bad influence on the younger players, and privately scolded Perry for leisurely walking to the mound instead of running. "If you feel that way," Perry answered, "if you're watching every little move I make, maybe it's best that you trade me."

Forced to choose between Robinson and Perry, Bonda sided with his manager. On June 12, Seghi sent Perry to the Texas Rangers for pitchers Jim Bibby, Rick Waits, and Jackie Brown. Robinson was convinced that Perry would never be the "Great Gaylord Perry" again. But he was wrong: Perry won 21 games for San Diego in 1978.

By the fall of 1976, Phil Seghi was losing his patience with Frank Robinson. The Indians that year won 81 games and lost 78 —their first winning record since 1968. But Seghi thought the Indians should have finished higher in the American League standings. Seghi second-guessed Robinson so often that Bonda once had to break up a fight between the two or "Phil would have been killed." [43] Seghi wanted to replace Robinson with Dave Garcia, a competent strategist but a bit dull for Bonda's tastes. Bonda thought Robinson was doing a fine job with the talent he had and told Seghi to keep him. As far as Bonda was concerned, much of the criticism of Robinson was because he was black. "There was enormous prejudice against Frank in the media," Bonda said years later.

The following spring, though, pressure on Bonda intensified. The Indians had signed Wayne Garland to a 10-year contract and increased their annual payroll by $400,000 to $1.8 million. But the Indians lost 31 of their first 57 games, and Seghi again blamed Robinson. Bonda, who had just had eye surgery, weakened, saying in late May that Robinson would only remain as manager "with the help of a miracle." [44] Bonda knew that Phil Seghi was the experienced baseball man and he was not. In the early summer, Bonda "caved in" and consented to the firing.

But Bonda was furious with himself. Had he been more forceful, he thought, he would have waited until the end of the year before changing managers. Ted Bonda would never feel the same again toward Phil Seghi.

Watching from his perch as a limited partner, Armond Arnson was upset at the turn of events. Ever since buying Gabe Paul's and Steve O'Neill's stock in the winter of 1972, he and the other limited partners had continued to lose money. Nothing worked. Frank Robinson came, but still attendance never hit one million in 1975 or 1976. At the end of every year, Arnson and the other limited partners would receive a letter from Ted Bonda announcing that the team needed more cash. By the end of 1976, Bonda and the limited partners had lost $4 million since Nick Mileti bought the team from Vernon Stouffer.

Arnson was not even sure who to blame. He was good friends with Ted Bonda, but also admired Phil Seghi as a brilliant baseball executive. To Arnson, the real problem was the team ownership. None of the limited partners had as much money as the owners of the New York Yankees, Los Angeles Dodgers, Boston Red Sox, or California Angels. Those teams could afford to invest heavily in scouts and farm teams. By contrast, Arnson thought, the Indians operated on a "shoestring." They maintained just four farm teams and nine full-time scouts in 1976; their Double-A team did not have a single major league prospect, lost 85 games and finished $31\frac{1}{2}$ games out of first place. The Indians' lack of scouts showed in the annual draft of college and high school players; of the first 15 players the Indians selected in 1976, not one had major league ability.

The same tight budgets strangled the major league team. When Frank Robinson wanted to show his players videotapes of Maury Wills lecturing on baserunning, he was informed the Indians could not afford $2,600 for a new video machine. During spring training one year, the local dairy company refused to sell the Indians milk until the team paid its milk bill from the previous year.

Just to pay the players, Seghi often had to sell assets. In 1977, for example, Seghi sold his best relief pitcher, Dave LaRoche, to the Angels for $250,000. Seghi managed to convince the Angels to throw in left-handed Sid Monge, who developed into a dependable relief pitcher in Cleveland. But Monge did not compensate for LaRoche, who in 1978 won 10 games and saved 25 for the second-place Angels.

Sometimes, even cutbacks and selling players were not enough. One afternoon, Arnson got a desperate phone call from Bonda, who told him, "We're in a lot of trouble. We can't meet payroll." So, Arnson replied, go back to Cleveland Trust and ask for another loan.

"They won't lend us any more money," Bonda replied. The Indians already owed Cleveland Trust $6 million, their limit. There was no place else to turn.

Bonda and Arnson drove to Cleveland Trust and pleaded their case before a young bank executive. The Indians were not asking for millions, just a couple of hundred thousand dollars to meet payroll. They urged the executive to be reasonable. The banker coldly turned them down. "You've used up your line of credit," he told them. "That's all we're going to give you." As Bonda and Arnson turned to leave, Arnson asked Bonda for a set of keys. Then Arnson casually tossed them on the banker's desk. "Here, you own the club," Arnson snapped. "You make payroll." Arnson's bluff worked. Alarmed at the prospect of operating a baseball team, the banker handed over the money. [45]

Arnson thought the team's only hope was an owner with deep pockets and the political clout to force the city to build a new baseball park, someone tough enough to convince officials that he would move the team unless they met his demands. Arnson knew he was not the right man. He could not issue a threat to move the Indians out of his hometown and keep a straight face.

Despite dramatic charades at banks and fire sales of top players, Ted Bonda still wanted to retain control of the team. He loved the job. "There's nothing like the thrill of walking into that ballpark and knowing you are a part of this thing," he confided.

But most of the limited partners, fed up with digging in their pockets to cover the team's chronic losses, were eager to find a new buyer who could cover future deficits. The team lost $1.1 million in 1977 even after the player contracts had been depreciated. It was time for someone else to take over the team, and Bonda reluctantly hunted for a buyer. [46]

He could have sold the team to New York investor Donald Trump. Bonda flew to New York to meet with the brash young millionaire. There was no question that Trump had the resources, but Bonda could never win a firm pledge from him that the team would stay in Cleveland. Bonda suspected that Trump wanted to buy an existing team and move it to New Jersey. [47]

Next, Bonda thought he had a sale arranged with Edward J. DeBartolo, the Youngstown developer who had amassed a fortune by building shopping malls. Art Modell enthusiastically supported DeBartolo, whose son owned the San Francisco 49ers of the NFL and was highly regarded in football. Bonda and DeBartolo met in a Cleveland hotel and agreed upon a sale—DeBartolo would pay $10 million to acquire 80 percent of the team. Bonda was excited. DeBartolo was "on top of the world" and a man of "unlimited resources." He could finally put the Indians on solid financial footing; he could eliminate the team's $6 million bank debt just by signing a check.

All Bonda needed was approval from Bowie Kuhn and the American League. He met with Kuhn and American League President Lee MacPhail in Columbus. DeBartolo, they said, would not win approval from the league owners. Three years later, Kuhn and MacPhail used their power to block DeBartolo's efforts to buy the Chicago White Sox. Kuhn has heatedly denied that his opposition to DeBartolo was based on unproven rumors of ties to organized crime. "There is no basis for questioning the decency or ethics of this man," Kuhn said in 1980. Instead, Kuhn said he objected because DeBartolo owned racetracks in Ohio, Illinois, and Louisiana. Find another buyer, Kuhn and MacPhail told Bonda. [48]

A despondent Bonda returned to Cleveland to continue the search. Art Modell suggested Steve O'Neill, who, since selling his Indians' stock in 1972, had been one of Steinbrenner's limited partners in the increasingly profitable New York Yankees. Bonda liked the idea. O'Neill's family had made millions in trucking.

O'Neill loved his hometown and thought buying the Indians would be an act of civic responsibility. He just had one condition: His friend, Gabe Paul, would have to return to Cleveland and run the Indians.

The sale went through in rapid order. O'Neill paid off the team's $6 million debt and assumed control of IBC—the general partnership formed by Bonda to protect his own personal fortune in the unlikely event of the Indians declaring bankruptcy. IBC controlled 84 percent of the Indians' stock. Although O'Neill emerged as the largest shareholder of IBC, Bonda retained an 11.5 percent share and Gabe Paul purchased five percent. In addition to O'Neill, Bonda, and Paul, the other shareholders of IBC were prominent Cleveland businessmen who had been limited partners under Bonda—Dudley Blossom, Maurice Stonehill, and Carl Tippit. [49] The remaining 16 percent of the Indians' stock was distributed to 55 limited partners. Stonehill and Tippit, in addition to their holdings in IBC, held limited partnerships. O'Neill formed what proved to be an unwieldy board of directors that included Tippit, Paul, Bonda, Stonehill, and Armond Arnson, who also remained as general counsel.

Ted Bonda hated to yield control of the team. Years later, he would sit in his downtown office looking out over the light towers of the new downtown ballpark. He wished he had hung on to the team and "suffered a little while longer."

Chapter 8

A War Among Friends

"There would be no Cleveland Indians without [Steve O'Neill]."
—David LeFevre

On the wall of his suburban office in Beachwood, Steve O'Neill kept a large handwritten chart. The chart gnawed at the millionaire owner of the Cleveland Indians. To visitors, he said the chart represented the lease with Art Modell's Stadium Corporation that allowed the Indians to play their home games in Cleveland Stadium. The numbers on the chart, he explained, showed three things: Art Modell made money; the city of Cleveland made money; and Steve O'Neill lost money.

O'Neill calculated that since Art Modell assumed control of the stadium in 1974, the Browns' owner had earned $30 million from the Indians' use of the facility. Every year, according to O'Neill's chart, Stadium Corporation earned $2.2 million from the rental of luxury loges, $3.2 million from concession sales, $350,000 from the sale of advertising signs in the stadium, and $250,000 from parking.

And what did the Indians get? That too was memorialized on the chart: A mere $464,250 from those buying tickets to the loges, $650,000 from concessions, a paltry $25,000 from stadium advertising, and absolutely nothing from the parking revenues. Advertising revenue was a particular sore point to O'Neill; the Indians' farm teams in Charleston, West Virginia, and Buffalo, New York, made more money from their stadium advertising than the parent club in Cleveland. [1]

O'Neill could barely stand it. In the five years since he had assumed control of the Indians in 1978, the team broke the one-million mark in home attendance three times. But the Indians lost staggering sums: $11 million between 1978 and 1981; $2.5 million in 1981; $4.2 million in 1982. Now, in the summer of 1983, O'Neill was braced to lose an additional $3.96 million. [2]

Building a contender was out of the question. Gabe Paul,

who ran the team for O'Neill, could not bid for pitcher Tommy John of the Dodgers and outfielder Dave Winfield of San Diego when they became available as free agents. Nor could Paul expand the farm system. The Indians in 1983 operated only four minor league teams at a time when the St. Louis Cardinals carried seven clubs and 11 other major league teams had six.

To minimize losses, the Indians sold pitcher Sid Monge and his three-year, $1 million salary, to the wealthier Philadelphia Phillies. They sent pitcher John Denny and his $700,000 annual salary to Philadelphia for three marginal minor leaguers, and second baseman Manny Trillo to Montreal for $150,000 and a Double-A outfielder. [3]

The tight budgets imposed by Gabe Paul sparked friction between him and his longtime loyal general manager, Phil Seghi. During one game in Cleveland, team counsel Armond Arnson joined Seghi in his private box. The Indians performed so badly that Arnson slammed down his fist and shouted, "Phil, how can you sit here night after night and watch this shit?" Seghi, who in the past had never criticized Gabe Paul, finally replied, "Armond, you know that's not my team on the field." [4]

Now as he sat in his office, Steve O'Neill glared at the chart. It was Art Modell's fault. "Lease," the exasperated O'Neill sputtered. "We don't have a lease. We have the privilege to use the stadium." [5]

Art Modell had been his friend. Art Modell had put together the deal that allowed O'Neill to buy the Indians. But now, O'Neill was little more than Modell's prisoner. The lease would expire at the end of 1983, and O'Neill demanded changes. If it turned into a war against Modell, fine. O'Neill may have been a very private man, but on this one he was ready to do public battle.

The lease—that hated document that had almost become a living thing for O'Neill—was signed in the summer of 1974, years before O'Neill even thought of owning the Indians. At the time, the stadium was a decaying giant in need of an overhaul. The city of Cleveland—crippled by race riots and the exodus of 100,000 residents to the suburbs during the previous decade—did not have the money for repairs. The stadium was draining $300,000 annually from the city, and Council President James Stanton urged city officials to let the Indians or Browns operate the facility.

Art Modell, too, was fed up with the stadium and threatened to move his Cleveland Browns to the suburbs. He paid $800,000 for 192 acres of land in Strongsville where the Ohio Turnpike and Interstate 71 met and planned to build a 64,000-seat stadium. Cleveland officials and local business executives were alarmed. James Davis, a prominent partner of the Cleveland law firm of Squire, Sanders & Dempsey, recruited a delegation of businessmen and, over breakfast, they pleaded with Modell to stay in Cleveland Stadium. A move to the suburbs would be devastating to the downtown, they argued. Did Modell really want to torpedo any chance to revive the city?

All right, Modell said, he would stay if he could run Cleveland Stadium himself. He would form a new company, and the city would lease him the stadium for 25 years. In return, Modell would repair the aging structure and build luxury loges. His company would negotiate a lease with the Indians. The city wouldn't have to worry about operating deficits and could look forward to eventually earning real estate taxes. Years later, Ohio Governor George Voinovich was still grateful. "Art came in and bailed the city out on the stadium. I don't care what anybody said, he did the city a hell of a favor."

Modell and Sheldon Guren formed Stadium Corporation, borrowed $10 million, and plowed ahead. Modell replaced rusted girders and repaired the stadium's electrical system, plumbing, and roof. He installed a new scoreboard and built 108 luxury loges, which hung from the upper deck. Modell charged prosperous businesses as much as $15,000 a year to rent them.

Then he negotiated a lease with the Indians. The Indians would receive 20 percent of the food and beverage concessions and 27.5 percent of novelty concessions. Instead of a share from the rental of luxury loges, the Indians got $6 per loge ticket in 1975, which would increase to $7.50 per ticket by 1981. [6]

The lease had been negotiated before Ted Bonda replaced Nick Mileti in the late summer of 1973. Bonda not only examined the document, but asked his attorney, Ted Garver, to compare it with the Browns' lease. Bonda concluded that Modell was offering the Browns and Indians similar terms, although Modell owned both Stadium Corporation and the Browns. Bonda was dismayed. "I don't think it's a good lease for the Indians," Bonda told Hal Lebovitz. "I think it's a good lease for Modell, but we were probably willing to sign it, and we will probably next year." [7] Bonda felt he had no choice; the stadium was in bad shape, and neither the Indians nor the city had the money to repair it. [8] Bonda thought his only leverage was to threaten to move the Indians. For a time, he talked of a 40,000-seat baseball park in University Circle and managed to wring a few concessions out of Modell. But finally, Bonda signed the lease. He reasoned that if the Indians played well, the team would turn a profit. Put a winner in Cleveland, he thought, and those 78,000 seats would quickly fill. [9]

That, of course, did not happen. The Indians did not win and most seats remained empty. When Steve O'Neill bought the Indians in 1978, he inherited the lease and the empty seats. Now, they were his problems.

But Steve O'Neill did not intend to live with the lease. And though nobody realized it in 1983, Steve O'Neill set in motion the events that ultimately led to a new stadium in downtown Cleveland.

❖

Steve O'Neill loathed publicity. Once when Hal Lebovitz tried to interview him in his office, O'Neill instructed the *Plain Dealer* sports columnist to put away his pencil. Why? the incredulous Lebovitz wanted to know. "Because I don't want any publicity," O'Neill answered. "I'll tell you anything you want to know. But not for print." [10]

Though Steve O'Neill hated to have his name in the newspapers, he was not shy. He and his two brothers, Hugh and Bill, were tough-minded businessmen who expanded their father's horse-drawn transportation company into Leaseway Transportation, an international trucking conglomerate that by the 1980s produced annual revenues of $1.3 billion. All three brothers were robust; Hugh O'Neill, Jr., played football at Notre Dame, while Steve loved the polo fields. Bill O'Neill topped both his brothers when, at the age of 65, he was stabbed in the chest and robbed of $205 while waiting for a Rapid Transit train to the airport. Bill refused to be taken to a hospital and only grudgingly accepted first aid. Then he boarded the next train and got to the airport in time for his business flight. [11]

They inherited their spirit from their father, Hugh O'Neill, who even at age 75 loved to ride his favorite horse, Billy, in the jumping contests in Chagrin Valley. Hugh O'Neill's reputation as a horseman led Mark Hanna to ask him in 1897 to choose the team of black horses for President William McKinley's inauguration. When Hugh O'Neill died in 1948, the *Plain Dealer* devoted just one sentence in his obituary to his transportation company, choosing instead to pay tribute to his horsemanship.

Hugh O'Neill was born in Londonderry in Northern Ireland, although like a staunch Irish Catholic he called it Derry. At age 23 in 1882, he immigrated to the United States and settled in Cleveland where an uncle lived. He married Louise Bechtold, whose family had fled from German-controlled Alsace-Lorraine, and he found steady work managing the stables of Cleveland industrialist Jacob Perkins.

Hugh O'Neill's love of horses provided the inspiration for the family business that eventually became Leaseway: He would use horsedrawn wagons to pick up freight and deliver it throughout Cleveland. He was a persuasive man who easily convinced shippers in Cleveland that he could deliver their freight to customers more quickly than rivals. By 1908, his horses were delivering two of Cleveland's newspapers, and within four years he was replacing the horses with modern trucks.

Hugh O'Neill sent his three sons to Notre Dame, and after graduation they helped manage the family business. They developed a pattern of picking up small trucking companies and running them as separate entities. Hugh, Jr., for example, started a small auto garage, turned it into Superior Transfer in 1921, and won the contract to deliver the *Plain Dealer*. The brothers followed with one company after another: Anchor Motor Freight to deliver cars for General Motors; Signal Delivery Service, which handled merchandise for Sears; and Niagara Motor Express, which leased trucks to manufacturers who wanted to ship their own goods.

Bill and Steve were the driving forces behind the rapid growth of the O'Neill companies. In 1961, they merged 79 family companies into Leaseway, and the new conglomerate's growth was phenomenal: Revenues skyrocketed from $25 million in 1961 to $108 million in 1964, then to $475 million in 1975. The company ritually increased its earnings by an astounding 21 percent a year. When Leaseway went public in 1961, the company issued 150,000 shares of common stock at $15 per share. By 1965, the stock had split two-for-one and was still climbing at $28 per share. [12]

Their business concept was simple: While other trucking companies hauled a wide assortment of freight, the O'Neill brothers tailored each of their companies to a specific task. Bill O'Neill was convinced that one small company with one major customer provided better service than a giant firm dealing with scores of accounts. Yet Bill O'Neill pointed out to customers that Leaseway's nearby headquarters included an army of lawyers, auditors, and safety experts who could instantly supply high-class service to any of the O'Neills' smaller companies.

Bill, with his curly gray hair and ever-present bow tie, assumed the title of chief executive officer of Leaseway while Steve became chairman of the board. Bill handled the finances, and Steve devoted his energies to operations, particularly choosing able executives to direct his companies and permitting them to exercise broad authority.

Born Francis J. O'Neill in 1900, he was nicknamed "Steve" after Steve O'Neill, the tough Irish catcher for the Indians. "My first name is Francis," Steve explained. "That quickly gets changed to something." [13] As he watched his namesake Steve O'Neill and Tris Speaker at League Park, he developed a love for baseball and his hometown team.

Steve O'Neill was quiet, but what some mistook for shyness was something else: He always "would think before he talked," said one family member. Once he and a friend spotted a carved ivory tusk in a New York City shop. "How much is that?" O'Neill asked the shopowner. When the owner revealed the pricetag at $7,500, O'Neill said nothing. Anxious for the sale, the shopkeeper broke the silence by saying, "It's $6,000." Still, O'Neill stared at the tusk without saying a word. The anxious owner blurted out, "OK, you can have it for $5,000." Fine, O'Neill said. His silence saved him $2,500. [14]

O'Neill was thrifty, but if a friend or relative needed $50,000 for a business, he would hand it over without a question. When Leaseway's chief labor lawyer, Bernard Goldfarb, was building a house in the Cleveland suburbs, Steve O'Neill wandered by one afternoon for a look. O'Neill glanced at the ceiling in the entrance hall and noticed a large hole. "Have you bought a chandelier yet?" he asked. When Goldfarb said he had not, O'Neill replied, "Don't." A few days later, a beautiful chandelier arrived.

Steve O'Neill first became involved financially with the Indians in 1962 when Bill Daley persuaded him to invest in the franchise. Through the investment, O'Neill developed a lifelong friendship with Gabe Paul; the two often dined together and sat with each other during games. The outgoing Paul would regale O'Neill with inside baseball stories. "I trust Gabe," O'Neill would say. "Whatever he says, goes." [15] Years after Paul had retired, one of the few Cleveland mementos he displayed in his Tampa condo was a photograph of Steve O'Neill.

By the time O'Neill bought control of the Indians in 1978, he was 78, frail, and suffering from emphysema, the result of his heavy cigarette habit. He could have moved to Arizona where it was easier to breathe. But when friends or relatives would suggest it, O'Neill would invariably reply, "Cleveland's my home. It's my city."

Even as he complained about Modell's lease, O'Neill rejected one chance after another to sell the team at a substantial profit. In 1980, Broadway producer James Nederlander and Los Angeles attorney Neil Papiano offered to buy majority control. O'Neill was intrigued: Nederlander was an entertainer who knew how to sell tickets. "When you get right down to it," O'Neill said, "owning a baseball club is entertainment." [16] The sale appeared imminent. But O'Neill apparently was worried enough to seek advice from Armond Arnson, who predicted that "the team would be moved." O'Neill turned down the offer. [17]

Investors in cities seeking major league baseball put in their bids as well. Bernard Goldfarb brought him an offer from Indianapolis that could have made O'Neill millions. "Forget it," O'Neill told him. "This team is not going to move."

O'Neill could afford to lose money with the Indians. He had vast stock holdings in Aetna Life & Casualty, American Express, Anheuser-Busch, Pepsico, Pennzoil, Philip Morris, Revlon, R.J. Reynolds, Rockwell International, Shell Oil, and Standard Oil of California. His shares of Leaseway stock alone were worth $44 million. Steve O'Neill was a patient man who believed that, with proper management, the Indians eventually would make money. [18]

❖

When Steve O'Neill asked Gabe Paul in 1978 to run the Indians, Paul balked. George Steinbrenner warned Paul that leaving the Yankees was a mistake. The Indians had little money, a disastrous farm system, and an old stadium. Paul's wife was even more adamant; it was time to retire and live full time in warm Tampa, she said.

But Paul felt trapped. O'Neill would not buy the Indians if Paul refused to leave New York. [19]

True, in New York, Paul had to endure George Steinbrenner's constant putdowns: "Gabe's not what he used to be," Steinbrenner would tell friends. But Gabe Paul loved running the Yankees. He was a survivor who had waited his entire life to operate a team as rich as the Yankees in a market as vast as New York. The Yankees produced their own players through an elaborate minor league system, and Paul filled the gaps by spending millions on free agents.

The trades consummated by Gabe Paul between 1973 and 1978 vividly demonstrate how a shrewd operator can build a team. He remembered outfielder Lou Piniella from his days in the Cleveland farm system and picked him up from Kansas City for aging relief pitcher Lindy McDaniel. Piniella developed into a .300 hitter in New York, and McDaniel rapidly faded in Kansas City. A year later, Gabe Paul pounced on Cleveland to grab hard-hitting first baseman Chris Chambliss and pitcher Dick Tidrow in exchange for four pitchers. The deal was sharply criticized by the Yankee players, but Paul knew better: He had personally signed Chambliss for Cleveland and recognized his potential. The four pitchers he gave up were out of baseball by 1977. Paul traded outfielder Bobby Bonds with his 32 home runs and 137 strikeouts to the Angels for right-handed pitcher Ed Figueroa and outfielder Mickey Rivers. Then, after receiving a tip from an old friend about a young infielder in the Pittsburgh system, Willie Randolph, Paul acquired him and pitcher Dock Ellis for 16-game winner Doc Medich. Randolph tightened the Yankee defense and combined with Rivers to inject speed into the lineup. Ellis delivered 17 key victories for the Yankees in 1976, and Figueroa developed into a 20-game winner for the Yankees.

Paul also prevented Steinbrenner from impulsively giving up on Ron Guidry in the 1976 expansion draft. Steinbrenner could only rely on statistics: Guidry's 5.63 earned run average in seven games. Paul relied on scouts who assured him Guidry had a powerful left arm.

"Stick with Guidry," Paul advised Steinbrenner. "He's going to be the best left-handed relief pitcher in baseball within two years."

Steinbrenner yielded. "But this is on your head, Gabe." [20] Paul's only error was predicting Guidry would be a relief pitcher. By 1978, Guidry was the best starting pitcher in baseball, winning 25 games, striking out 248 batters, and posting a 1.74 earned run average.

Paul could be firm in a way that Steinbrenner understood. In a Boston hotel, they once quarreled over Yankee manager Billy Martin. Paul calmly left the hotel, went to the airport, and flew home to Tampa. Steinbrenner pleaded with Paul to return.

The Yankees won consecutive pennants from 1976 through 1978 and defeated the Dodgers in the 1977 and 1978 World Series. But by the time of their 1978 triumph, Gabe Paul was back in Cleveland. Steve O'Neill had made the move as attractive as possible to the reluctant Paul by lending him $250,000 without interest to buy stock. Although his friend O'Neill controlled the team, Paul had 50 other limited partners to contend with. Some, such as Ted Bonda, Paul frankly distrusted. Bonda, Paul complained, had become "a great friend of Art Modell." [21]

Steve O'Neill approached the lease in 1983 like he did any business problem. First, he needed the facts: How did the Indians' lease compare with other leases around the country?

O'Neill called in Michael Fetchko, a bright young attorney whom Gabe Paul hired in 1981 to handle the Indians' broadcast negotiations. Fetchko, a graduate of the law school at Temple University, had not yet turned 30, but clearly was a favorite of both Steve O'Neill and Gabe Paul. O'Neill assigned him to visit other major league cities and find out how their leases compared to the Indians'.

Fetchko visited 15 cities and conducted conference calls with the remaining teams. He was astonished to discover the Indians received so little from advertising, concessions, and parking, and concluded the Indians' lease was among the "least favorable to a ballclub in the country." [22] As Fetchko explained the report to Steve O'Neill, the Indians' owner did not explode in rage. Instead, he sat at his desk near his chart, calmly taking notes. But Fetchko could see O'Neill was determined to change the lease. He's really getting into this, Fetchko thought with admiration. The lease was strictly business to Steve O'Neill, and he wanted it fixed.

It was early 1983 and Steve O'Neill had less than a year before the December 31 expiration of the lease. He originally asked Armond Arnson to negotiate a more favorable agreement with Modell. But armed with Fetchko's study, O'Neill opted for a different approach. To execute his plan, O'Neill called on a trusted old friend, Bernard Goldfarb.

For more than three decades, Bernard Goldfarb had been the lawyer who fought management's trucking battles against the Teamsters in Cleveland. Every three years it was Goldfarb's job to confront Jimmy Hoffa and work out a new three-year labor agreement. In time, Goldfarb became Leaseway's chief attorney and twice argued on behalf of the company before the U.S. Supreme Court. Despite the rather tame nickname of "Bunny," Goldfarb was a blunt lawyer who wouldn't hesitate to offend the opposition if that's what the battle required. During one contentious deposition, Goldfarb turned to the opposing lawyer and snapped, "You're a snotty guy. You're a real pistol."

O'Neill asked Goldfarb to meet with him and Gabe Paul at Cleveland Stadium. When Goldfarb arrived, O'Neill did most of the talking. He explained that negotiations for a new lease were going nowhere. "Would you get involved?" O'Neill asked. When Armond Arnson learned that he had been pushed aside in favor of Goldfarb, he complained to a board member that O'Neill did not believe Arnson was "a big enough prick" for the job. [23]

Goldfarb was confident of his ability to bring about a quick resolution. He and Fetchko took the ritual walk from the Indians' offices on one side of Cleveland Stadium to those of Stadium Corporation on the other. Michael Poplar, executive vice president of Stadium Corporation, and James Bailey, the company's general counsel, were both cordial. But they never offered Goldfarb major concessions. Instead, they would politely point out that "we have a lot of maintenance and upkeep of the stadium."

Goldfarb was shocked. Talking to Modell's lawyers was like talking to the Sphinx, he groused. He thought Modell was being needlessly tough on the Indians. Goldfarb explained that O'Neill was not demanding major concessions, but only wanted a greater share of the revenues the Indians generated. He repeatedly asked to meet with Modell. "Let's talk to Art and we'll bring in Gabe," Goldfarb would implore. But Stadium Corporation was cool to the idea.

Modell said the Indians had only themselves to blame, writing Paul that "it should not surprise you that with the Indians' 1979 attendance ranking 22nd out of 26 teams, your gross concession revenues would rank at the low end of the chart." Modell reportedly told Paul if he did not like the lease, he could take his team to Edgewater Park, a swath of green parkland off Lake Erie. Stadium Corporation responded to O'Neill's study with its own survey of the leases for 14 other teams. It showed that the Indians' lease ranked in the middle. (24)

O'Neill's position hardened. "I don't want you to make any concessions at all," he told Paul.

"Steve," Paul protested, "this is not reasonable."

"I don't care," O'Neill retorted. "I don't want you to make any concessions." (25) O'Neill instructed Goldfarb and Fetchko that he wanted substantial changes in the lease. "Don't just throw me some dollars on the box seats and loges," O'Neill said.

O'Neill knew the ultimate answer was a new ballpark exclusively for the Indians. The Indians could never make money, he reasoned, until they had declared their independence from Art Modell. He even asked for drawings of the new domed stadium in Indianapolis and talked to associates about a 40,000-seat ballpark for Cleveland. Years before Richard and David Jacobs entertained thoughts of buying the Cleveland Indians, Steve O'Neill concluded the team needed a new park.

O'Neill even toyed with playing in the Rubber Bowl in Akron. But O'Neill's only realistic choice was to sue Modell and force him to negotiate a better lease. If he followed that course, O'Neill knew he would divide his board of directors and set off a public brawl with Modell. Even if Modell lost in the courtroom, Modell was likely to win publicly. While the reserved O'Neill seldom spoke with reporters, Modell avidly courted the Cleveland media, regularly serving up juicy quotes to enhance their stories. And because the Browns were consistent winners, Modell was far more popular than Gabe Paul, who was regarded by many as a relic.

On March 9, Modell offered a counterproposal: Stadium Corporation would hand the stadium back to the city if the city repaid Modell the $10.1 million he had spent on refurbishing the facility and building the loges. Then Modell would lease back the loges from the city for $1.25 million annually. Modell, in turn, would rent the loges to big companies and wealthy individuals and give the Indians 20 percent of the revenue he earned. Paul, pointing out there was no chance that the city of Cleveland wanted the stadium back, formally rejected the offer as a "sham." [26]

That word struck a nerve in Modell, who sent Paul a "personal and confidential" letter, charging that the Indians' president "misstated the facts in order to attack the proposal." Modell insisted that the Indians' claim that Stadium Corporation had made $30 million off the baseball team during the 10-year life of the old lease bore "no relation to reality." He added that "whatever our revenues from baseball, it was barely enough to cover our costs of maintaining and operating the stadium" and paying $6 million in interest on bank loans that had been used to rebuild the stadium in 1974. [27]

The day after Modell sent his letter to Paul, Bunny Goldfarb filed suit in Cuyahoga County court alleging that Stadium Corporation owed the Indians $1.25 million more in concession revenue from the past decade. Goldfarb demanded that the records for those years be opened. Modell erupted, denouncing the suit as a "sham and a disgrace. If the Indians have a complaint, where were they the last nine and one-half years? This is purely and simply a negotiating ploy for a lease." [28]

Bunny Goldfarb, in turn, was appalled at Modell's reaction. The Indians had filed their suit for purely business reasons. Art Modell's defense seemed to be that the lawsuit was hurting his feelings.

Bunny Goldfarb was right: Modell's feelings were hurt. He was shocked when his old friend Steve O'Neill filed the suit and was convinced that Gabe Paul had put him up to it. A friend of Modell's told him about a conversation over dinner one evening with Paul and O'Neill. "Gabe," O'Neill asked, "when are we ever going to win games?" Paul shrugged. "Steve, you know I can't win here with the lease Modell gave us." Even years later, Modell remained furious with Paul. "Gabe Paul?" he fumed. "Don't get me started on Gabe Paul."

Modell did not feel the need to apologize for Stadium Corporation. He had rebuilt the stadium by taking a huge risk: Borrowing $10 million at an interest rate that would float at one percent above prime. Throughout the late 1970s, interest rates increased, climbing to more than 20 percent; Modell calculated that with the loan and interest, as well as maintenance and repair, his investment in Stadium Corporation was $63 million. And it was all his money. No handouts from the state or city government.

The stress of the legal battle with Steve O'Neill proved too much. On June 11, Modell suffered a major heart attack. Doctors at the Cleveland Clinic performed a quadruple bypass on the owner of the Browns. But even as he recovered that summer, Modell vowed to beat Gabe Paul.

Although Ted Bonda was still a member of the Indians' board of directors, he learned of the lawsuit by reading Gary Clark's front-page story in the *Plain Dealer*. (29) Bonda thought the lawsuit absurd. He knew the lease was not perfect, but he had lived with it throughout the 1970s. If the Indians didn't like the lease, they should seek a compromise. Going to court was foolish. At an April 29 meeting of the board, including Steve O'Neill and Gabe Paul, Bonda exploded: "Why the hell are you doing this? What are you trying to gain?" (30) Watching Bonda pound the table with a newspaper, Bunny Goldfarb was reminded of Senator Howard Metzenbaum's typically fiery speeches. This guy, Goldfarb thought with amusement, thinks he's Howard Metzenbaum.

The bad feelings between Bonda and Paul had been bubbling along beneath the surface for years. Despite his seat on the board, Bonda had no say in running the team; Gabe Paul directed the franchise like a monarchy. Since Paul returned to Cleveland he had never as much as called Bonda to say, "Hey, come on over and let's talk about the Indians." (31) Often Bonda skipped board meetings because major issues were never discussed. The Nederlander offer was a good example: Bonda did not know about the bid until it was public. "Why didn't you tell us about the Nederlander offer?" Bonda complained at a board meeting. "Why didn't you tell us why you rejected it?" (32) Because his advice was shunned, Bonda refused to answer any of the six cash calls issued between 1978 and 1983, and his share of IBC slipped from 11.5 percent to just 2.9 percent.

Meanwhile, Bonda thought Paul's health was deteriorating and watched in alarm as the aging Paul nodded off in some meetings. [33] As the financial losses escalated, Bonda urged O'Neill to sell his share of the team to a younger and more vigorous man. Even though he had no authority to do so, Bonda solicited offers from Edward DeBartolo and New York real estate tycoon Donald Trump. Bonda handed Paul a $13 million offer from Trump. "If you want to go out and find someone, go ahead," Paul said curtly. "We're not going to accept any offers that we don't think are good ones." [34] Bonda thought he knew why Paul ignored the offers: Steve O'Neill ceded complete authority to Paul. "He does not want to sell this team," Bonda complained of Paul in 1983. "He owns it for nothing." [35]

Bonda also regarded Modell as a man of integrity and thought he had "been unnecessarily maligned" by Paul and the Indians. [36] When Bonda ran the Indians in the 1970s, he always could approach Modell for money to keep the team going. It had long been rumored that Modell had supplied some of the bonus money to help sign Wayne Garland—a story Bonda denied. [37]

Bonda was not the only member of the Indians' board uneasy with lawsuits. By the summer of 1983, Armond Arnson, Carl Tippit, and Maurice Stonehill were in full rebellion. Together, they controlled four of the nine votes on the board of directors. Tippit, a close friend of Steve O'Neill's, sided with Bonda, complaining that "these dumb lawsuits" could be avoided. [38]

As the dispute raged, Modell telephoned Tippit, trying to resurrect the city proposal that neither Paul nor the city wanted. When Tippit read the proposal in Modell's office, it appeared reasonable: The Indians stood to make an additional $500,000 a year.

Tippit immediately went to Gabe Paul's office to persuade him to reconsider. "What's wrong with this proposal?" Tippit asked. Paul dismissed it out of hand. [39] Tippit sharply disagreed. Having spoken directly with Modell, he was convinced the Browns' owner was eager for a peaceful resolution. At a contentious meeting of the nine directors in late May, Tippit launched a direct challenge to Gabe Paul, who headed the group trying to negotiate a new lease. The group should be enlarged, Tippit argued, to include himself, Bonda, and Maurice Stonehill.

"Why don't you let us do it, since all you are really interested in is having a good lease," Tippit told the directors. "Let's at least try to negotiate." Over Paul's objections, the board voted, 5-4, to accept Tippit's offer.

It was merely a temporary victory. What nobody seemed to appreciate was Steve O'Neill's determination to fight the lease. It was accepted among reporters and the rebellious board members that crafty Gabe Paul and Bunny Goldfarb had manipulated an aging and ill Steve O'Neill into a foolish lawsuit. Nothing could have been further from the truth: Paul and Goldfarb were doing O'Neill's bidding. At a June 10 directors' meeting, O'Neill added five loyalists to the board, including his nephew, Patrick O'Neill; Bunny Goldfarb; and Bob Quinn, the team's farm director.

Goldfarb walked out of the meeting of the newly reconstituted board and into the nearby federal courthouse where he filed a $25 million lawsuit, alleging that the Browns had violated the nation's antitrust laws. The suit declared that "by precluding the Indians' fair and equal access to an essential facility, the stadium—over which Stadium Corporation and Modell had complete control—and by negotiating on behalf of the Browns, Stadium Corporation and the Browns unlawfully established and maintained, or attempted to establish and maintain the predominance and monopoly power of the Browns" in Greater Cleveland. [40]

Tippit, who did not attend the meeting, learned of O'Neill's decision to enlarge the board in a phone call that night from Art Modell. Still, Tippit wanted to continue the negotiations. "I have already started this thing," he said to himself, "and I'm not going to drop it here." [41] The following week, Modell's aides gave Tippit four specific counterproposals. One was the old city proposal that Paul already had turned down. The second would have provided the Indians with a greater share of food, parking, and novelty concessions if the team surpassed the one million mark in attendance. The third would have essentially allowed the Indians to keep all the revenue they generated from baseball in return for paying Stadium Corporation $1.8 million in 1984, a sum that would climb to $2.6 million in 1994. The fourth proposal would permit the Indians to buy 50 percent of Stadium Corporation for $5 million. But Modell also insisted that before any new negotiations could begin, the Indians had to drop their lawsuits and formally apologize.

Paul handed the counterproposals to Fetchko, who wrote Stadium Corporation's James Bailey that the Indians might regard Nos. 2 and 3 as a basis for negotiation. But Fetchko added that the Indians would neither drop their lawsuits nor apologize before launching new lease negotiations. Bailey took the unusual step of writing Bonda that "we really do not see much substance" with the Indians' offer. [42]

Paul allowed Tippit to present the four offers to the full board on July 1. After Tippit spoke for an hour, O'Neill made clear he was not about to drop the suit or apologize to Art Modell. Tippit resigned, and told reporters, "I wish I knew the purpose behind the actions of Steve O'Neill and Gabe Paul. I keep asking and I get no answers. Steve and I are still good friends and we shook hands today. I'm not bitter, but I feel the Indians are wrong, wrong, wrong on this." [43]

Ted Bonda remained on the board, but his position was tenuous. Steve O'Neill's war against the lease had shattered his own board of directors, and provoked a vitriolic public feud with Art Modell. "I appreciate you taking these hits," O'Neill told Fetchko. "Bunny will take the hits. I will take the hits. But it's business."

Patrick McCartan resented the Indians' lawsuits. As a partner at Jones, Day, Reavis & Pogue, McCartan's job was to defend one of the firm's best clients, Art Modell and Stadium Corporation. As far as he was concerned, the antitrust lawsuit was "a waste of time." All the Indians were trying to do, McCartan thought, was use the courts to negotiate a more favorable lease. Although he did not know Steve O'Neill that well, McCartan doubted O'Neill was the driving force behind the legal action. [44]

On the same day that Tippit resigned from the board of directors, McCartan and Modell counterattacked with their own lawsuit, claiming the Indians' antitrust suit was "frivolous" and asking for $10 million in damages.

At 1:30 in the afternoon of Thursday, August 25, Ted Bonda was summoned to the Union Commerce Building, home to Jones, Day. Like all the major players in the dispute, Bonda was to provide a deposition, although Bailey apologized for calling Bonda and Tippit. "I hope that Ted and you will understand the necessity of doing this and that the deposition will be of minimum inconvenience," Bailey wrote in a "Dear Tip" letter to Tippit. [45]

Bonda appeared relaxed as McCartan questioned him. When Wayne Garland's disastrous $2.3 million contract came up, Bonda quipped, "I wish we hadn't been able to raise the money to pay him." As Bonda described negotiations in 1977 with Gabe Paul on the sale of the Indians to Steve O'Neill, he joked that Yankees' owner George Steinbrenner "was very anxious to have Gabe Paul leave" New York and return to Cleveland. [46]

But when it was Goldfarb's turn to question Bonda, the tension was apparent. At one point, Goldfarb asked to examine some Indians' documents that Bonda had in front of him. "I'd rather you didn't," Bonda said. "You have copies of those."

"You know I have copies of this?" Goldfarb asked innocently.

That was too much for Bonda. "Oh, come on. Don't give me that bullshit. Damn it, they're in Gabe Paul's files."

That day, as Bonda and Goldfarb snarled at each other, 76-year-old Bill O'Neill died. Four days later, on the morning of his brother's funeral, Steve O'Neill woke up and had difficulty breathing. An ambulance was summoned to rush him to St. Vincent Charity Hospital. As the ambulance raced through the streets of Cleveland, Steve O'Neill's heart gave out.

The Indians were playing the Angels in Anaheim. When *Plain Dealer* baseball writer Terry Pluto asked players for their reaction, most described O'Neill as a nice old man. Few understood that his death placed the franchise in jeopardy. But Gabe Paul knew. When he heard that his old friend had died, Paul wept. [47]

The elite of Cleveland attended Steve O'Neill's funeral in the century-old Calvary Cemetery, where his mother, father, and oldest brother were buried. The rolling hills and manicured grounds, dotted with pines and maples, looked a bit out of place now that the working-class neighborhood had fallen on hard times. As the mourners began to leave, Michael Fetchko and Tom Pulchinski, the team's director of marketing, walked to Fetchko's car. Like all the young executives working for the Indians, they had revered Steve O'Neill because of his tenacity in the struggle against Stadium Corporation. Fetchko had an idea: He reached into his car trunk and retrieved a baseball. Then he walked down a steep hill to Steve O'Neill's casket and tossed the ball into the grave.

A War Among Friends

❖

Steve O'Neill wanted to protect the Indians after his death by placing the team in the same revocable trust in which he put the bulk of his assets. That would have left his heirs with full control of the Indians' future. But the American League ruled that a trust could not own a baseball team. So O'Neill put IBC, the partnership that owned the Indians, in his private estate where his nephew, J. Andrew Kundtz, would serve as executor. The drawback was that estates are overseen by the courts, and Kundtz would have to answer to a Cuyahoga County probate judge for any sale of the Indians.

O'Neill's widow, Nancy, and two nephews, Patrick and Hugh III, served as the board for both the trust and estate. Pat assumed the most visible role among the three. The 59-year-old Patrick O'Neill looked the part of the button-down business executive. He shunned sports coats in favor of business suits, ties, and white shirts. But Pat was more gregarious than his uncle. He had what one friend described as a "terrific Irish laugh," and developed a fondness for talking to local reporters. [48]

Like his uncle, Pat O'Neill could be tough when necessary. He flew 11 combat missions in the Army Air Corps during World War II. As chairman of Anchor Motor Freight, he negotiated labor contracts with the Teamsters. "When you go to war," Pat once said, "you have to be pretty sure you're going to win. I've been through a lot of labor strikes and I know you have to be prepared to fight." [49]

Patrick was the son of Hugh O'Neill, Jr., who was Steve O'Neill's oldest brother. Like most O'Neills, Patrick loved polo and with other family members formed a polo team nicknamed the "Highway Men." He attended St. Ignatius High School and after World War II earned a degree from John Carroll University in Cleveland. From there, he moved into the O'Neill's trucking business, becoming a vice president of Leaseway in 1967. He always found time to raise money for St. Ignatius and Gilmour Academy, a private school in Gates Mills. Once, Peter Bavasi noticed a pick and shovel in the open trunk of Pat O'Neill's car. What on earth, Bavasi asked, were those for? "The pump house at Gilmour Academy is on the fritz," O'Neill explained, "and I have to fix it."

Patrick O'Neill quickly took charge of the franchise. He made clear that Gabe Paul would be retained as president through the end of 1984, when Paul planned to make good his promise to his wife and retire to Tampa. At a meeting of the board of directors on Saturday, September 10, O'Neill announced the lawsuits against Modell and Stadium Corporation would be pursued.

Armond Arnson objected. The legal squabbles should end, he advised. All the Indians were doing was "dragging the franchise through the mud." Patrick O'Neill rejected his entreaties. Arnson stood, picked up his papers, announced his resignation as team counsel, and walked out. [50]

Andy Kundtz, the executor of the O'Neill estate, was worried about the Indians. An attorney at the Cleveland law firm of Thompson, Hine and Flory, and the son of Steve O'Neill's sister, Kundtz and Pat O'Neill had a legal obligation to sell the franchise as quickly as possible. Although Pat O'Neill wanted to keep the Indians in Cleveland, Kundtz privately feared that investors from another city would step forward with a staggering offer. Kundtz would reject the bid, but the prospective buyers could plead their case in probate court. The judge might insist that Kundtz had a fiduciary responsibility to sell the Indians to the highest bidder.

Kundtz knew the city was filled with rumors that Patrick O'Neill would entertain bids from cities such as Tampa, Denver, and Phoenix—all searching for major league baseball. The last thing Kundtz wanted was to encourage investors from other cities. But the rumors persisted, partly, the tight-lipped Kundtz thought, because "I didn't talk enough and Pat O'Neill talked too much." [51]

Gabe Paul suggested that O'Neill and Kundtz call a press conference to flatly declare the team would only be sold to a Cleveland group. Kundtz welcomed the idea and enlisted the help of a public relations man to set up a press conference on September 15 at the Bond Court Hotel in the heart of the city's downtown. To the assembled reporters and television cameras, O'Neill and Kundtz announced the team was for sale "to the right buyer." Pat O'Neill insisted that "what we're attempting to do is keep this team in Cleveland, if it's at all possible." When reporters pressed O'Neill for details, he foolishly added, "In my judgment, anything can happen. The franchise could be lost. But we are going to make a sincere effort to keep the club here." [52]

The press conference was a catastrophe. As he watched from the rear of the room, Ted Bonda was depressed. Instead of scotching the rumors, Pat O'Neill had raised the possibility the estate would accept offers from other cities, Bonda thought. The reporters agreed. In a gloomy story, the *Plain Dealer* wrote that "the city's hold on the Indians seemed a little weaker" and that O'Neill's announcement was "good news to the Tampa Baseball Group." When he read the accounts the next day, Kundtz knew the press conference had only made things worse.

Patrick O'Neill was not nearly as perturbed as Andy Kundtz, for he already had a buyer in mind who would keep the team in Cleveland—David LeFevre, a 39-year-old lawyer who practiced in New York City.

LeFevre knew all the right people. As the maternal grandson of Cyrus Eaton, David LeFevre grew up in Greater Cleveland; as a boy his neighbor was Steve O'Neill, "a terrific guy," LeFevre would later say. Both Pat O'Neill and Gabe Paul liked LeFevre, although Paul was annoyed briefly when LeFevre was quoted as saying, "When the Russians drop that atomic bomb, I'm going to stand next to Gabe. He's a survivor." For a short time, Paul refused to return LeFevre's telephone calls. [53]

LeFevre also had the right connections in baseball. As a fledgling lawyer in the 1970s with the rapidly growing New York law firm of Reid & Priest, LeFevre developed a friendship with Tal Smith, whom Paul had recruited from Houston to help him run the Yankees. Smith moved back to Houston in 1976 to build the Astros into a contender, and in 1979 he asked LeFevre to invest in the team. LeFevre and John McMullen bought controlling interest, although McMullen had the larger share and greater voice in running the team.

Like his grandfather, LeFevre had a passion for international affairs. After graduating from Yale in 1967, LeFevre joined the Peace Corps and spent two years in Uruguay. Cyrus Eaton, who even in his 80s continued his crusade to end U.S. isolation of the Communist countries, twice took LeFevre to Cuba, where he met Fidel Castro. LeFevre toyed with signing young Cuban players for the major leagues until Bowie Kuhn blocked the idea.

LeFevre played basketball at Cleveland's Western Reserve

Academy and as a freshman at Yale, but he loved baseball, often racing down to Cleveland Stadium as a boy to watch Al Rosen, Larry Doby, and Bob Lemon help the Indians to the 1954 pennant. Now, he hungered to buy his hometown team.

LeFevre had first offered to buy the Indians when Steve O'Neill was still alive. Now in the fall of 1983, he moved rapidly to assemble a high-powered group of investors to purchase the team from the O'Neill estate.

He had two major obstacles. The first was the Indians' lease with Stadium Corporation, which he thought was "very, very bad" for the Indians, an assessment he would later change to "outrageous." LeFevre thought Steve O'Neill had been right in challenging the lease in court, and he had no intention of tying his team to a similar long-term deal at Cleveland Stadium. He knew the Indians eventually needed their own park. Ohio Governor Richard F. Celeste was pressing for a state-sponsored study to determine if a dome could be built at Cleveland State University for use by the Indians and the university. That, LeFevre thought, would make the Indians profitable. [54]

The second obstacle was more daunting. The Indians were owned by the limited partnership of IBC, which controlled 84 percent of the team's stock. The O'Neill estate owned 59.6 percent of IBC, while Walter Laich of Cleveland owned the second largest amount at 24.2 percent. The rest of IBC was held by Gabe Paul, Carl Tippit, Ted Bonda, Maurice Stonehill, and Dudley Blossom. The remaining 16 percent of the team, which remained outside IBC, had been distributed among 55 limited partners, some of whom owned only a few shares.

LeFevre faced the same problem Nate Dolin encountered 30 years earlier: How to save on taxes when buying a baseball team. LeFevre had two ways to buy the franchise. He could run the Indians by buying the shares of IBC controlled by the O'Neill estate, which the estate had valued at $16.5 million. [55] LeFevre would control a $30-million team for half the price. But because he was buying stock instead of assets, he could not depreciate the players and save millions in taxes.

LeFevre's other option was to buy all the assets of the Indians from each of the limited partners and enjoy five years of huge tax savings. That too had a drawback: Ohio law required the unanimous approval of every limited partner before the assets could be sold. If one limited partner objected—even if he or she held only a handful of shares—LeFevre's plan would be blocked.

LeFevre chose the first option, a stock purchase, and in the fall of 1983, he offered $18 million for all shares of IBC and $2 million to meet the cash calls for the 1983 season. He did not make a specific pledge to buy the stock held by the 55 limited partners.

Two other bids were made that fall. Donald Trump, who was preparing to add an Atlantic City gambling casino to his real estate empire, offered Patrick O'Neill $25 million for all the IBC stock. Laich, a self-made millionaire who owned two companies that produced baseball souvenirs, followed with a $22 million offer for IBC's stock. Like LeFevre, neither Laich nor Trump made any concrete promises to buy the stock held by the limited partners. [56]

Patrick O'Neill swiftly rejected LeFevre's and Laich's offers as far too low. Trump's was the highest, but Kundtz thought the American League would turn down the bid because of Trump's gambling casino. "He wasn't going to give that up to be the owner of the Indians," Kundtz later said. He suspected that the New York millionaire wanted to move the Indians to New Jersey to compete against the Yankees and Mets. Kundtz' suspicions deepened when Trump declined to sign an ironclad agreement to keep the team in Cleveland.

Pat O'Neill waited until May 1984 before asking LeFevre, Laich, and Trump to submit "their highest and best" offers. Trump offered $30 million for the IBC stock, but would only sign an agreement to keep the Indians in Cleveland for five years. Trump, apparently aware that his casinos could delay league approval, also suggested the O'Neill estate might have to retain control of the franchise for two more years. Those conditions eliminated Trump.

LeFevre offered $16.5 million for the IBC shares controlled by the estate and Gabe Paul—which worked out to $12,497 per share of stock. His bid did not include buying out the rest of the IBC shareholders or the limited partners. Laich countered with an offer of $11,716 per share for all IBC stock and a willingness to buy "on an equivalent basis" the limited partners' shares. Both Laich and LeFevre agreed to sign binding documents to keep the Indians in Cleveland. [57]

Privately, the O'Neills doubted that Laich could afford the team, and, on June 5, 1984, Patrick, Hugh, and Nancy O'Neill voted to accept LeFevre's offer. Laich, Arnson, Bonda, Stonehill, and Tippit were enraged; there was no guarantee that LeFevre would buy their shares at the price he paid the O'Neill estate. Ten days later, they filed suit in county court to block the sale, claiming that, before his death, Steve O'Neill had assured Laich that all IBC shareholders would receive the same price for their stock when the team was sold.

To counter Laich's suit, LeFevre decided to buy all the assets of the Indians, increasing his bid to $31.5 million and agreeing to assume responsibility for $9 million in team debt. Still, three limited partners popped up to object in court. In November 1984, LeFevre withdrew his bid in disgust and bought Gabe Paul's five percent of IBC for $1.5 million.

If Pat O'Neill was distraught over LeFevre's withdrawal, he hid it well. Throughout the 1984 season, he seemed more comfortable directing the team's financial affairs. "He was having fun running it," Kundtz later said. Pat O'Neill told one associate, "We don't have to sell this franchise. As long as it's not a cash drain [on the estate], we can keep this team indefinitely." [58] All he needed was an experienced hand to direct the baseball operations. Gabe Paul was retiring to Florida at the end of 1984, leaving O'Neill with the task of finding a new president. Ironically, O'Neill found his man with the help of David LeFevre.

The call to Peter Bavasi first came from LeFevre's friend in Houston, Tal Smith. After leaving the Astros in 1980, Smith formed his own consulting company in Houston, where he advised major league owners about staffing their front offices and winning salary disputes against their players at arbitration. Despite newspaper stories suggesting he would assume control of the Indians, Tal Smith had no intention of closing his company to run the Indians for anybody. But with LeFevre's bid still in limbo in the fall of 1984, Smith agreed to find a bright, young executive to run the Indians. Smith's choice was Peter Bavasi, the former president of the Toronto Blue Jays. "Would you have an interest in doing this?" Smith asked him in a phone call. Bavasi agreed to meet with LeFevre in New York and Pat O'Neill in Cleveland. [59]

Bavasi thought long about making the move. The Indians had just finished sixth in 1984, 29 games out of first place. It was a bad team, with an almost nonexistent farm system. The fans were sour, the news media disgruntled, and the front office exhausted. Still, he was intrigued. He had been forced out as president of the Blue Jays and was eager to redeem himself. Cleveland was the perfect place. The organization was so bad that any action Bavasi took would be an improvement. Pat O'Neill assured him he would have a free hand to staff the organization and select the players. What the Indians needed was an intense, vigorous young baseball executive. Peter Bavasi qualified. He was 42 and so addicted to work, he often could be found at his desk at four in the morning.

Bavasi was a child of baseball. His father, Buzzie Bavasi, had been general manager of the Dodgers in their final seven years in Brooklyn. Young Peter spent his days at Ebbets Field, watching Jackie Robinson, Gil Hodges, Roy Campanella, Pee Wee Reese, and Duke Snider. He would travel to baseball meetings with his father, and occasionally would sit in Buzzie Bavasi's office as he negotiated a contract with a player. After the Dodgers moved to Los Angeles, Buzzie Bavasi made certain his son received a proper baseball education: business manager for the Dodgers' farm team in Albuquerque; general manager of the Dodgers' minor league team in Santa Barbara; back to Albuquerque as general manager.

When Buzzie Bavasi left the Dodgers in 1968 to run the expansion San Diego Padres, he took his 26-year-old son with him to direct the new farm system. Four years later, Peter Bavasi advanced to vice president and general manager. Like all expansion teams, the Padres were pathetic; they finished last in the first six years of their existence. But by 1975, under the steady hand of manager John McNamara, the Padres improved to fourth place. They had developed a small group of talented players—outfielders Dave Winfield and John Grubb, and left-handed starting pitcher Randy Jones, who won 20 games that year.

Peter Bavasi was too restless to stay much longer. In the summer of 1976, he moved to Toronto to direct another expansion team, the Blue Jays. He was just 35 years old and had the chance to build his own organization. At Tal Smith's recommendation, Bavasi hired Pat Gillick of the New York Yankees to run the baseball team as executive vice president of baseball operations. Gillick later became one of the most respected front-office men in baseball. Like the Padres, the Blue Jays were pitiful in their early years. They lost 107 games in their 1977 inaugural year and did not escape last place until 1983. But Bavasi and Gillick created one of the most productive farm systems in the game, and within a short time the Blue Jays developed outfielders Jesse Barfield and Lloyd Moseby, first baseman Cecil Fielder, and pitchers Dave Stieb and Jimmy Key. They invested heavily in the Dominican Republic, and used the Rule V winter draft to literally steal outfielder George Bell from the Yankees and third baseman Kelly Gruber from the Indians.

Not everyone was captivated by Bavasi. A number of Toronto reporters privately believed that Gillick— not Bavasi—deserved the credit for putting together the Blue Jays. Some people found Bavasi impatient, prickly, and unable to deal with criticism. In 1981, Peter Bavasi, the loser in a power struggle with Pat Gillick, left the team. Resigned, he would explain. Fired, said others. "They got sick of me," Bavasi once said, "and I got sick of them." [60]

Peter Bavasi was starting at the bottom again. In many ways, the Indians in 1984 were worse than an expansion team. In 1983, the team tumbled to last place with 92 losses, followed by a sixth-place finish in 1984 with 87 defeats.

Hank Greenberg's farm system was in tatters. At the beginning of the 1980 season, there were only 10 players in the major leagues who had been scouted, signed, and developed by the Indians in the previous decade. Six of their seven first-round draft picks from 1977 through 1982 failed to play in the major leagues. Not one of the players the Indians picked from 1974 to 1983 in the first round of the January draft reached the major leagues. Player development in Latin America was a joke; the team that signed Bobby Avila in 1947 and Minnie Minoso in 1948 was a non-factor in baseball-rich Mexico, the Dominican Republic, Venezuela, and Panama.

Only four members of the 1984 Indians were developed through their own system—left-handed starting pitcher Neal Heaton, relief pitcher Mike Jeffcoat, reserve catcher Chris Bando, and part-time right fielder Carmelo Castillo. The only prospects in the Cleveland minor league system were outfielders Cory Snyder, Dave Gallagher, and Dave Clark, and catcher Andy Allanson. Except for Clark, not a single player on the Indians' two Class A farm teams would ever play in the major leagues. When Joe Klein, Bavasi's choice to head the farm system, first saw the Cleveland minor league pitchers in Tucson, he concluded that only John Farrell had a major league fastball. [61]

Without the money to build a farm system, Gabe Paul and Phil Seghi stuck with the high-risk strategy of trading established stars for a flock of young players. In 1983 and 1984, the strategy worked. Paul and Seghi traded away starting pitchers Rick Sutcliffe and Len Barker, and outfielder Von Hayes in three major transactions for third baseman Brook Jacoby, shortstop Julio Franco, and outfielders Joe Carter, Brett Butler, and Mel Hall.

Peter Bavasi planned big changes. He forced Phil Seghi into retirement and fired Bob Quinn, the farm director. Both were good baseball men who had labored under impossible conditions. But Bavasi wanted new people who would be loyal to him. He hired Dan O'Brien, former general manager of the Texas Rangers, as a senior vice president in charge of the front office, player negotiations, and final approval for all trades.

To direct the team's baseball operations and rebuild the farm system, Bavasi originally approached Joe McIlvaine of the New York Mets. When McIlvaine rejected the offer, Bavasi checked with his old friends in baseball. They suggested he contact Joe Klein, who had been fired as general manager of the Rangers in 1984. Klein had since joined the front office of the Kansas City Royals. Just 42 years old, Joe Klein possessed an extensive minor league resume: Manager, scout, and director of player personnel for the Rangers.

Klein was preparing to fly from Kansas City to the Royals' 1985 spring training camp in Ft. Myers, Florida, when he received word that Bavasi wanted to see him in Cleveland. He packed his golf clubs, flew to Cleveland, and landed at Hopkins Airport as a heavy snow pounded the city. A puzzled skycap saw Klein leave the plane with his golf clubs and said, "I don't think you'll be needing them here." Klein joined Bavasi for dinner at the Hollenden House. Bavasi warned him the Indians' situation was bleak. "I want you to know what you're getting into," Bavasi said.

"We've got a big job to do." Fine, Klein said, and flew to Cleveland's spring training camp in Tucson. [62]

Whatever Klein asked for, he got. He added a rookie league team and a coach to each minor league team. He hired new scouts, handed them radar guns, and ordered them to search for pitchers. He drafted young pitchers in hordes; his first six selections in both the 1985 and 1986 summer drafts were pitchers, and he followed by picking pitchers with four of the team's first five choices in 1987. They included left-handed starting pitcher Greg Swindell from the University of Texas, and right-handed pitchers Steve Olin from Portland State, and Tom Kramer from a Cincinnati high school. Klein and the Indians' public relations office exaggerated the ability of many of those pitchers. But they were clearly superior to the pitchers in the Cleveland farm system at that time.

Klein offered tryouts for veterans who had failed with other organizations. A month after he took the job in Cleveland, he signed 28-year-old Doug Jones, who had a sore right shoulder and a release from the Milwaukee Brewers. But Jones had spent his days in the minor leagues developing a clever changeup to go with his mediocre fastball. By 1988, that changeup saved 37 games for the Indians.

On a winter scouting trip to Puerto Rico, Klein was tipped off about Tom Candiotti, a right-handed pitcher for the Ponce team. Candiotti had been released by Milwaukee, but Orlando Gomez, a Cleveland minor league coach, told Klein that Candiotti had a good curveball, adding, "He's working on a knuckleball." Klein brought Candiotti to spring training the next year and American Leaguers were thoroughly baffled with his knuckler.

Klein took risks. In 1987, the best prospect in the draft was outfielder Albert Belle of Louisiana State. He had a powerful right-handed swing and crushed college fastballs. LSU baseball coach Skip Bertman called Belle the "most talented player I ever coached." Klein personally scouted him in the New Orleans Superdome that February, and, like all scouts, was impressed. But Belle had a fiery temper that he seemed unable to control. Bertman suspended him near the end of the 1987 LSU season. Major league teams shied away from him; Bobby Cox warned his Atlanta Braves player personnel director he would fire him if he drafted Belle. Cleveland did not have a first-round pick in 1987, but

Klein figured Belle would still be available in the second round. "Nobody's going to take him in the first round," Klein told Jeff Scott, the Indians' director of scouting. Klein was correct. By 1991, Belle became Cleveland's regular designated hitter and hit 28 home runs. The next three years, he drove in more than 100 runs apiece and developed into a dependable left fielder.

By 1986, Bavasi and Klein had assembled a young, exciting team that scored a lot of runs. Joe Carter drove in 121 runs, stole 29 bases, and batted .302; Cory Snyder batted .272 and hit 24 home runs; Brook Jacoby knocked in 80 runs; and Brett Butler stole 32 bases. Julio Franco, Pat Tabler, and Tony Bernazard all batted .300. The Indians won 84 games, and finished only 11 $\frac{1}{2}$ games behind the first-place Boston Red Sox. Gabe Paul's prediction of a sleeping giant came true. The Indians' home attendance of 1,471,977 was their best since 1959, and the team turned a $100,000 profit.

Things were falling in place, Joe Klein thought. *Sports Illustrated* picked the Indians to win the American League East title in 1987. Klein was convinced that by 1988 the Indians would be a contender. Brett Butler was the only player close to free agency, and Klein was confident he could sign him to a long-term contract. As long as Pat O'Neill kept the team, Klein thought that he, Bavasi, and O'Brien would be in Cleveland.

Pat O'Neill was delighted with the changes. The Indians were winning, the old stadium was filled with unexpected crowds and the estate did not have to worry about cash calls. He found he enjoyed operating a baseball team. Every Friday, a courier would deliver to his Beachwood office a complete report from Bavasi about the week's events. It would include cash-flow forecasts, a marketing analysis, promotional plans, and the latest sales of season tickets.

O'Neill did not keep an office at Cleveland Stadium, but made it a custom to watch each game from his private box. Often, he would be joined by Bavasi, either for dinner before, or just to chat during the game. He liked Bavasi and his energy. He even accepted Bavasi's recommendation to end the lawsuits with Stadium Corporation. Whatever the original merits of the suits, Bavasi argued, they had long been obscured by the increasing bitterness between the Indians and Art Modell. Bavasi and Modell finally reached a settlement in 1985 when the Browns' owner provided the Indians with $150,000 in concessions. Between that sum and savings in legal fees, Bavasi calculated he had saved the Indians nearly $500,000 annually.

The suits faded away with a whimper two years after Steve O'Neill's death. But Steve O'Neill had made his point: The Cleveland Indians could not last much longer as a tenant of Art Modell. Either they would get their own downtown ballpark or they would find one in another city.

The men who built the powerful Cleveland Indians of the 1950s—Hank Greenberg (left) and Bill Veeck. (Cleveland Press Collection, Cleveland State University)

Another 1954 victory: Catcher Jim Hegan (left) and third baseman Al Rosen (center) congratulate relief star Ray Narleski. (The Cleveland Press Collection, Cleveland State University)

Three reasons the 1954 Indians won 111 games: Outfielders Al Smith (left) and Larry Doby (right) flank 23-game winner Early Wynn. (Cleveland Press Collection, Cleveland State University)

Bobby Avila, a three-time .300 hitter in Cleveland, is safe at home in a cloud of dust in a 1953 game. (Cleveland Press Collection, Cleveland State University)

First baseman Luke Easter, one of the many black players shunned by the American League, but courted by the Indians. (Cleveland Press Collection, Cleveland State University)

With the Indians on the verge of a dynasty, Al Lopez joins 23-game winner Bob Lemon the day before the 1954 World Series opens against the
Giants in New York City. (Cleveland Press Collection, Cleveland State University)

The new fireballer meets the old: Rookie Herb Score (left) and veteran
Bob Feller. The same scout signed both. (Cleveland Press Collection, Cleveland State
University)

Two prized graduates of Hank Greenberg's farm system, Rocky Colavito (left) and Roger Maris (center). In 1961, Maris and Colavito combined to hit 106 home runs—for other teams. They are pictured here with out-fielder Gene Woodling in the spring of 1957. (Cleveland Press Collection, Cleveland State University)

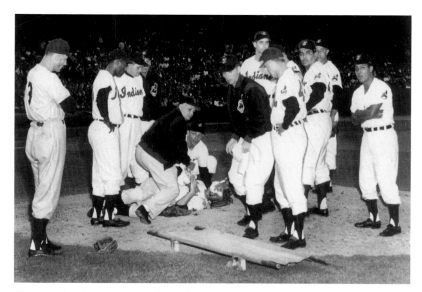

Teammates hover over a bleeding Herb Score just moments after Gil McDougald's line drive smashed into the right eye of the Cleveland lefthander. Although the injury often has been blamed for ending Score's career, Score was throwing as hard as ever the following spring. (Cleveland Press Collection, Cleveland State University)

A happy and prosperous Big Seven after buying the Indians in 1949. In the top row, left to right, are Harry Small, Nate Dolin, and Jack John. Lower row, left to right, are Don Hornbeck, Ellis Ryan, Guy Waters, and George Medinger. (Cleveland Press Collection, Cleveland State University)

Baseball Commissioner Happy Chandler with Ellis Ryan (right) at
Cleveland Stadium. (Cleveland Press Collection, Cleveland State University)

At the height of his power, Hank Greenberg (center) is flanked by Nate
Dolin (left) and George Medinger (right) in the top row, and Bill Veeck
(left) and Jim Gallagher, a partner in Veeck's company. (Cleveland Press Collection, Cleveland State University)

Hank Greenberg (left), William R. Daley (center), and Ignatius O'Shaughnessy are all smiles for the cameras as they emerge from a private meeting in the Terminal Tower. But the smiles are just for show: Greenberg has been fired as general manager of the Indians. (Cleveland Press Collection, Cleveland State University)

Confident and ready to deal, Frank Lane (left) joins Indians' President Mike Wilson. Despite Wilson's imposing title, he had little to do with the daily operations of the Indians. (Cleveland Press Collection, Cleveland State University)

Frank Lane (left) fired Joe Gordon in 1959, only to re-hire him a few days later when he could not hire Leo Durocher as Cleveland manager. (Cleveland Press Collection, Cleveland State University)

Gabe Paul prepares to fly to Seattle in 1964 to examine a new home for the financially troubled Indians. The near-departure of the Indians forced Paul to trade away the team's future to re-gain Rocky Colavito. (Cleveland Press Collection, Cleveland State University)

Vernon Stouffer relaxes in his high-rise apartment overlooking Lake Erie the day he buys the Indians, a dream that quickly turned into a financial catastrophe. (Cleveland Press Collection, Cleveland State University)

Ted Bonda hoped that splashy free agents, colorful uniforms, and Frank Robinson would attract huge crowds. He discovered that a team without a farm system cannot win or make money. (Cleveland Press Collection, Cleveland State University)

Talk about tension. General Manager Phil Seghi (left) joins manager Frank Robinson before a 1977 game. Three weeks later, Seghi fired Robinson. (Cleveland Press Collection, Cleveland State University)

F.J. "Steve" O'Neill, the reserved, publicity-shy trucking executive who saved the Indians for Cleveland. (Cleveland Press Collection, Cleveland State University)

Gabe Paul (left) enjoys a laugh with Cleveland Browns' owner Art Modell. The smiles would quickly turn into lawsuits. (Cleveland Press Collection, Cleveland State University)

Tom Chema used his political skills to persuade the most bitter of political enemies to back a tax increase to finance a new downtown ballpark.
(Photo © Mort Tucker)

Nobody drives a harder bargain in Cleveland than Richard Jacobs. He pushed hard for a new ballpark and, as usual, got his way. (Photo courtesy of the Cleveland Indians)

Hank Peters created the front-office in Cleveland that transformed the Indians from a 40-year loser into one of baseball's strongest teams. (Photo courtesy of the Cleveland Indians)

John Hart was handpicked by Hank Peters to become the new general manager of the Indians. Dick Jacobs was so impressed, he signed Hart to the job until the turn of the century. (Photo courtesy of the Cleveland Indians)

The crowd at Jacobs Field erupts as the Indians defeat the Braves in
game three of the 1995 World Series—the first time the Indians had won
a World Series game since 1948. (Photo © Mort Tucker)

Chapter 9

Finally, the Man With a Plan

"In baseball, your farm system is really your lifeblood."
— Herb Score

Let the other general managers squander their money and energy in search of the quick fix; Hank Peters built his baseball teams carefully and thoroughly by hiring the best scouts, signing the brightest young players, and choosing the wisest managers. "I believe in consistency, patience and fairness," he explained. He would methodically chart a long-term course and patiently stick with it. [1]

He believed that baseball teams should operate within their means. "You project your future attendance, then apply it to a budget and a payroll," Peters would say. [2] He was proud that his teams usually operated in the black and could not conceal his contempt for impatient owners who lavished millions of dollars on elderly free agents. "Baseball will be better off," he said in the early years of free agency, "when certain owners learn that it's not the worst thing in the world to lose a player to free agency and other owners learn it's not the best thing in the world to sign a free agent." [3]

In his careful manner, Hank Peters had little use for flamboyant trades. "You can only do so much with trades," he said. [4] Instead, like Hank Greenberg, he firmly believed that successful major league teams grew from a productive minor league farm system. It was a slow process, he admitted, but it always worked.

Like the frugal business executive he was, Peters wore conservative, blue business suits to his office and made certain that his tie was perfectly knotted. Rarely was a strand of his black hair out of place. He seldom raised his voice in anger and preferred to avoid the profanities that peppered the language of so many baseball executives. The ideal organization man, he surrounded himself with bright, young executives. "I believe in delegation of authority," he once said. "I don't believe in one man shows." [5] Those who worked for Peters admired him, and it was easy to see why. After his Baltimore Orioles won the 1983 American League playoffs from the Chicago White Sox, a reporter from the *Washington Post* congratulated Peters for the decision to place Tito Landrum on the team's post-season roster. Landrum hit a key home run during the series. "It was an organizational decision," Peters explained. "I had little to do with it. I'd never even seen Landrum in a uniform when he got here." [6]

That attitude often deprived him of public credit for his successes. When the Oakland A's swept to three consecutive American League pennants in the 1970s, they did so with players scouted, signed, and developed by an organization created a decade earlier by Hank Peters. Oakland owner Charles O. Finley earned raves for building the A's, but those in baseball realized that Peters "quietly knew how to spot and procure talent." [7]

This was the man Richard Jacobs set his sights on in the summer of 1986. Dick Jacobs and his brother, David, had just purchased the Cleveland Indians for $35 million and they wanted a talented executive to scrupulously protect that investment, someone who would carefully construct a winning organization while keeping a careful eye on the payroll. Shortly after he bought the team, Dick Jacobs telephoned Edward Bennett Williams, owner of the Orioles, whose disenchantment with Peters was known throughout baseball. Would Williams let Peters out of his contract and allow him to move to Cleveland? Jacobs asked. Williams said no. But the mercurial Williams fired Peters just one year later. And Dick Jacobs moved quickly to snare Peters for his Indians. [8]

Hank Peters had his doubts about returning to Cleveland. He was 63 years old and lived in a comfortable new townhouse in Baltimore. He did not need the job. Why make a move when he was so close to retiring?

But Dick Jacobs persisted, and persuaded Peters to fly to Cleveland for a chat. He told Peters that he and his brother had plenty of money to run a baseball team, but they needed an experienced baseball man to show them how. He offered Peters a three-year contract with an option for a fourth.

In his typical way, Peters counseled patience. "Hey, in three years you're not going to turn things around completely," Peters warned Jacobs. "You can get a start on it." Peters would recruit a new farm director, a new scouting director, new scouts, and new minor league managers. There would be no quick fixes, Peters said. Echoing the warning he delivered so many years ago to Vernon Stouffer, Peters said that "the things we start now aren't going to be evident for a few years. It's going to take a little time for these fellows to develop. You go through trial and error. When you've got that flow of talent, you'll be a successful team." [9]

That was fine, Jacobs responded. On a second visit to Cleveland, Peters agreed to take the job. "It's his ballclub to run," Dick Jacobs said in one of his rare appearances at a news conference. Hank Peters was relaxed. His first piece of advice to the reporters was predictable: "Be patient." [10]

Hank Peters knew that his own patience would be tested in Cleveland. All that he predicted to Vernon Stouffer in 1970 had come true. The Indians lost 101 games in 1987, and finished last for the fourth time in seven years. Team owners lost millions of dollars and, until Dick Jacobs bought the team, ownership had no interest in rebuilding Hank Greenberg's cherished player development system.

Cleveland players raced for the exit whenever they got the chance. Outfielder Brett Butler planned to sign with a National League team. Joe Carter, a powerful hitting outfielder, made it clear that when he became a free agent in 1990, no amount of money could persuade him to stay. Peters remembered his own description of the Indians he worked for in 1970: They were still a "ship adrift." [11]

Dick Jacobs liked to tell this story: When Arnold Palmer was playing in a Pro-Am, he grew increasingly impatient with his amateur partner who was smacking the golf ball all over the fairway. "For God's sake," Palmer finally snapped, "aim at something." [12]

As politicians and business executives learned, Dick Jacobs always aimed carefully at his objective and rarely missed. He began as a $1,500-a-year real estate salesman in Akron in 1950. By the time he and his brother bought the Indians, they had developed a sprawling commercial real estate company that owned 41 shopping malls in 14 states; hotels in Florida, Columbus,

South Bend, and suburban Cleveland; a string of Wendy's franchises in New York City; and a large chunk of downtown Cleveland. By the late 1980s, their combined wealth was believed to exceed $500 million.

Dick Jacobs' great advantage over his rivals was his ability to zero in on a target, then never pull back. He quickly concluded after buying the Indians in 1986 that the team needed a new baseball park, not some domed stadium that he would have to share with Art Modell and the Cleveland Browns. Instead, Jacobs wanted a small, traditional park designed strictly for baseball, one that he could control personally. In 1986, virtually every politician in Cleveland would have dismissed that concept as a fantasy. But Jacobs never wavered, and, on April 4, 1994, he moved his team into the most advanced outdoor baseball park in the United States; one that helped increase the value of the Indians from the $35 million he paid for the team to more than $100 million.

Standing just over 6-foot-3 with silvery white hair, Dick Jacobs cut an imposing figure, but he preferred to remain in the background of negotiations. Only at the last moment would he spring into action, usually to demand his way. More often than not, he got it. He entered any negotiation fully briefed and having mastered every detail. "I want no surprises," he would say. "His mind is like a dynamo," Marty Cleary, his chief associate, told a reporter. "He never forgets anything." Those less-prepared rivals would pay dearly. [13]

He worked hard to cultivate the leading Cleveland politicians, both Democrats and Republicans. While his brother David preferred crunching numbers and visiting construction sites, Dick Jacobs negotiated the deals with mayors and members of the city council. He gave $50,000 to Ohio Governor George Voinovich's 1994 campaign and developed ties with Democrat George Forbes, a man of such influence that *Cleveland Magazine* ritually placed him on its list of the 10 most powerful people in the city. Dick Jacobs invited other city politicians to his luxurious office in the 40-story Erieview Tower, where he enjoyed serving sweet rolls, fruit juice, and coffee. [14]

Despite his outgoing nature, Dick Jacobs intensely guarded his privacy and had no desire to see his name in the newspaper. "Some people need ink to live like others need a breath of air to live," Dick Jacobs said. "We are the latter of that group." George

180

Forbes thought Dick Jacobs was simply shy. [15] Dick Jacobs avoided reporters for so long that when he and his brother bought the Indians, news accounts raised questions about whether they could afford the team. "Make sure you point out that you sought this interview," Jacobs told a reporter from *Cleveland Magazine* in 1987. After buying the Indians, Dick Jacobs remained behind the scenes, while Hank Peters dealt with reporters. But after Dick Jacobs felt he had mastered the business of baseball, he engaged in a slightly more public role, attending owners' meetings and pointedly lecturing his colleagues that spending millions of dollars for broken-down free agents was financial folly.

Dick and David Jacobs grew up in a solid middle-class household. Their father worked in marketing for Goodyear in Akron, and moved the family into a house so close to the plant that Dick Jacobs later said he could smell the rubber burning. As a boy, Dick Jacobs worked at an assortment of odd jobs: selling window polish as a third grader; mowing lawns for 25 cents; waiting on cars and tables at a drive-in restaurant.

After serving as a lieutenant in the U.S. Army in World War II, Dick Jacobs rushed through college in three years. He briefly considered a job as an insurance salesman, but gravitated instead to real estate. In 1955, Dick and David Jacobs formed a partnership with Dominic Visconsi, whose family had been involved in the development of small shopping centers in Greater Cleveland. Within a decade, Jacobs-Visconsi-Jacobs was building a series of huge shopping malls to cater to the millions of Americans who fled the cities for the suburbs.

As Dick Jacobs' fortune multiplied into the hundreds of millions, he invested little of his money in the decaying downtown of Cleveland. When he was mayor of Cleveland, George Voinovich complained to Marty Cleary: "Marty, I don't understand you guys. You're from Cleveland and you haven't invested a dime. Not a dime in the city." [16] Dick Jacob's son, Jeffrey, considered by many of the Cleveland business elite to lack his father's intellect, actually started downtown Cleveland's renaissance in 1985 in the old industrial area known as the Flats. Jeffrey Jacobs paid $400,000 for an old U.S. Coast Guard station where the Cuyahoga River empties into Lake Erie. He built a dockside bar and restaurant looking out on the lake, the downtown skyline, and the iron bridges that spanned the river. Other restaurants quickly sprouted along both banks of the Cuyahoga, where thousands of pleasure boats bobbed at sunset and swarms of young people flocked for drinks and dinner. Albert Ratner, another major developer in Cleveland, later chided Dick Jacobs, saying that "kid of yours saved downtown."

Dick Jacobs, however, trumped his son's investment. In 1986, Dick and David Jacobs bought the Erieview Tower, long nicknamed "the Jolly Green Giant," for $43 million. That was only the beginning. They poured $45 million into building the Galleria, a glass-roofed shopping mall next to the Jolly Green Giant. They financed construction of the $330 million Society Bank tower. When it was completed in 1991, it eclipsed the Terminal Tower as the city's tallest building. The project included a new Marriott Hotel and the refurbishing of the century-old Society building adjacent to the new tower. "Cleveland's on the upswing," Dick Jacobs said. "And we want to be part of it." [17]

Dick Jacobs lived in a lavish, two-floor penthouse at Winton Place, where he spent $1 million to remodel the apartment to suit his taste. But he enjoyed flying to New York once a week in his company jet, often to visit the tony art galleries on the Upper East Side. He bought a large midtown townhouse and plowed $5 million into rebuilding it. [18]

Neither Richard nor David Jacobs showed much early interest in investing in baseball. During a black-tie event at the Union Club, Cleveland attorney David Weiner leaned over to David Jacobs to ask, "You and your brother are great Cleveland citizens. Why don't you save the Indians?" David Jacobs thought for a full minute and answered, "Why the fuck would we want to do that?" But the idea was forming. When David LeFevre put together his syndicate in 1984, an attorney recommended David Jacobs. LeFevre and Jacobs met for a drink at the Union Club, and, for 20 minutes, David Jacobs posed a series of questions about how LeFevre intended to run the team. Then, David Jacobs stood to leave. "Well, young man," Jacobs said, "you look like a good guy, and I think your program is right for the Indians. You can count me in for a couple of million. If you ever need more, come back and we'll have another drink." [19]

When Dick and David Jacobs did buy the Indians, they did so in typical fashion, avoiding the probing eyes of *Plain Dealer* reporters and operating behind the scenes with customary skill. Dick Jacobs turned to William Boykin, a partner in three Marriott Hotels with the Jacobs' brothers, to set up a meeting with Pat O'Neill in the summer of 1986. "Is this team for sale?" Jacobs asked. When O'Neill said yes, Jacobs took an option to buy the team for $35 million. Dick Jacobs insisted that every one of the 62 limited partners turn over their stock to him. This would be a Jacobs' operation, and he had no intention of debating strategy with meddling partners. Although Ted Bonda wanted to retain his share of the team, he realized he had little choice but to sell. After all, Bonda thought, Jacobs was making a very good offer. [20]

The deal was to be closed privately at an evening dinner at Dick Jacobs' favorite restaurant, Sammy's in the Flats. The high-powered dinner group included the Jacobs' brothers, Pat O'Neill, George Forbes, Indians President Peter Bavasi, American League President Bobby Brown, and Voinovich, who flew to Hopkins Airport that afternoon after a trip to Washington, D.C. But reporters and photographers from the *Plain Dealer* and local TV, tipped off about the secret rendezvous, showed up at the restaurant.

Dick Jacobs decided to do something no Cleveland Indians' owner had done since Nate Dolin: Run the baseball team like a business instead of a civic enterprise.

Hank Peters had worked for baseball's best and worst teams. He started in the front office of his hometown St. Louis Browns in 1947 at $150 a month. The Browns were, in the words of Bill Veeck, a "collection of old rags and tags." [21] Although Hank Peters admired the management skill of co-owner William O. DeWitt, he recognized that financially DeWitt and his brother "didn't have a pot to piss in." Just to meet payroll, DeWitt sold his best players to the Yankees, Red Sox, and Indians. In 1951, the DeWitts sold the dilapidated franchise to Veeck, who was just as underfinanced.

For eight years, Peters labored with a team that never finished above sixth place in the American League and ended in last place three times. When the Browns ran out of money in 1953 and the franchise was sold to a group in Baltimore, Peters expected to land a job in the Orioles' front office. Instead, at the last moment, Peters got the crushing news: He was not going with the team.

Peters briefly considered quitting baseball, but Bill DeWitt urged him to attend the winter meetings in Atlanta and find a new job. The only opening was in Burlington, Iowa, where the Three-I League team was in search of a general manager who could operate a team without money. Peters certainly knew how to do that. He did everything in Burlington: He hired a manager, signed the players, sold the tickets, operated the concessions, and searched for businesses willing to advertise at the ballpark. "I had to work my butt off," Peters later joked.

One year of Burlington almost drove Peters into the insurance business in St. Louis. But at the end of 1954, the Philadelphia Athletics moved to Kansas City and the team needed a farm director. Ray Kennedy, the team's director of player personnel, interviewed Peters. "If you want the job, it's yours," Kennedy told him. Like the Browns and Burlington, the old Philadelphia Athletics were bankrupt. Peters discovered he did not have scouts, minor league managers, or a spring training camp. All he had were "100 nondescript players" who had no chance of playing in the major leagues. Peters quickly went to work to build what would become the game's best scouting staff. Instead of hiring men with extensive scouting backgrounds, Peters preferred younger people who had managed a year or two in the lower minors. Peters reasoned they would be more likely to determine which sandlot players had the skills to move up in the Kansas City system.

Once again, Peters worked without financial resources. The team owner, Arnold Johnson, was a business partner of Dan Topping and Del Webb, the owners of the New York Yankees. Topping and Webb reportedly loaned Johnson $2.9 million to buy the minor league stadium in Kansas City. New York General Manager George Weiss sent Johnson an experienced Yankee hand, Parke Carroll, to run the daily operations in Kansas City, and suggested the Yankees would send surplus players as well. "I don't have to worry," Carroll said at a meeting with other teams. "Weiss has promised to take care of me." [22]

It was an open joke in baseball that the Athletics were nothing more than a farm team for the Yankees. Any player who displayed major league ability in Kansas City would soon be off to New York. The Yankees would even send promising players to

Kansas City for a little seasoning. In 1957, the Yankees traded 21-year-old pitcher Ralph Terry to the Athletics for hard-throwing relief pitcher Ryne Duren, who quickly developed into one of the game's best relief pitchers. Terry, meanwhile, learned how to pitch in Kansas City, and, in the middle of the 1959 season, the Athletics obligingly sent him back to New York. Peters was particularly proud of signing 17-year-old Clete Boyer. Young Boyer grew stronger and showed every indication of becoming a skilled major league third baseman when the Athletics sent him to the Yankees in 1957. Peters stormed into Parke Carroll's office. "Parke," Peters protested in vain, "we can't do that." [23]

Only Arnold Johnson's death ended the cozy relationship the Athletics had with the Yankees. In December 1960, Chicago insurance executive Charles O. Finley bought the team for $2 million from Johnson's estate. Finley intended to win, and quickly hired as his general manager Frank Lane, fresh from his disastrous tenure in Cleveland. Hank Peters remained as farm director.

Peters discovered to his consternation that it would be difficult to work for both Finley and Lane. During spring training of 1961, one of Peters' best scouts, Al Zarilla, called him about Bill Landis, a promising left-handed pitcher attending a California junior college. "His last game is on Thursday," Zarilla told Peters. "I'm going to be there, and I think I can sign him Saturday or Sunday night." Fine, Peters said. How much would he cost? When Zarilla suggested $25,000, Peters told him he would ask Lane to approve the money.

Peters then telephoned the Athletics' training camp in Florida. Nobody could locate Lane. Reluctant to lose a quality pitcher, Peters reached George Selkirk, the team's director of player personnel. "Unless you feel otherwise, I'm going to tell Al to go ahead and sign this guy," Peters told him.

Not until the following week did Peters advise Lane about the signing and the general manager approved. One month later, Finley telephoned Peters and hotly demanded, "Who gave you the authority to spend my money in signing this pitcher?" Peters was angry; it was obvious that Lane had not told Finley that he had approved the $25,000. Finley summarily fired Peters. Only at the end of the season did Finley call Peters back to apologize. Finley had discovered that Lane had approved the bonus. Finley wanted Hank Peters back as assistant general manager and farm director. [24]

Although Finley named a trusted friend, Pat Friday, as the team's official general manager, baseball executives quickly realized that Peters was running the team. Friday candidly admitted to a pitching prospect, "I don't know much about baseball, but you look like you throw the ball pretty hard." Ted Bowsfield, then a young pitcher with the A's and later an executive with the California Angels, once described Friday as "just a figurehead. But fortunately, they had Hank Peters in the front office." [25]

Finley wanted to spend money for young players, and Peters patiently created the scouting organization to find them. The A's paid $125,000 in 1961 for pitcher Lew Krausse, an 18-year-old righthander whose father served as a Kansas City scout. Krausse was the first of a long line of pitchers signed by Peters: Catfish Hunter from North Carolina; Jim Nash from Nevada; Paul Lindblad from Kansas; Chuck Dobson from Kansas City; John Odom from Georgia; and Fred Norman from Texas. Finley enjoyed personally signing the young players Peters' scouts discovered. Finley invited Hunter to his Indiana farm and fed him a steady diet of steaks and milkshakes until the pitcher signed for $75,000. Finley showed up at Odom's house in Macon, Georgia, helped his mother cook chicken, and signed the pitcher.

They joined a slew of position players signed and developed in Peters' system, including Cuban-born shortstop Campy Campaneris; outfielder Joe Rudi of Modesto, California; catcher Dave Duncan of Dallas; and third baseman Sal Bando and outfielder Rick Monday off the Arizona State University baseball team. After watching the Kansas City minor leaguers train one spring, Rex Bowen, a scout for the Pittsburgh Pirates, told Peters, "Boy, you guys are going to be good." When Alvin Dark took over as manager of the Athletics in 1965, he realized he had a potential All-Star at every position. [26] The players developed by Hank Peters helped the Athletics win three consecutive American League pennants from 1972 through 1974.

But Peters and Finley could not last; their styles were far too different. Peters wanted to take time to build a powerful team, while Finley's impatience was legendary. As the owner, Finley felt he had every right to meddle in the daily operations of the team. "The way you want to operate, Charlie, you should never have another general manager," Peters told Finley when he left at the end of the 1965 season. [27]

From Kansas City, Peters moved to Cleveland, where his efforts to build a strong farm system collapsed under the weight of Vernon Stouffer's financial problems. He served as president of the minor leagues for four years, but was eager to run his own team. He got that chance on December 15, 1975, when Baltimore owner Jerry Hoffberger asked him to become general manager of the Orioles. "Run the club like it's your own and spend the money like it's your own," Hoffberger advised Peters. [28]

For the first time in his career, Hank Peters was associated with a winning baseball team. The Orioles had won the World Series in 1966, three consecutive American League pennants from 1969 through 1971, and American League East titles in 1973 and 1974. The Orioles were committed to developing and keeping their own players. Baltimore's system had produced pitchers Jim Palmer, Dave McNally, Doyle Alexander, and Wayne Garland; first basemen Don Baylor and Boog Powell; second baseman Bobby Grich; shortstop Mark Belanger; and outfielder Paul Blair. By tradition, the Orioles traded cautiously; Hoffberger once vetoed a chance to get outfielder Billy Williams from the Cubs because he did not want to yield first baseman Mike Epstein, a player developed by Baltimore. Peters could confidently move into the general manager's office and, under baseball's existing rules, keep the best and the brightest of the Orioles for as long as he wanted.

Six days later, all that changed. Baseball arbitrator Peter Seitz ruled that pitcher Andy Messersmith of the Los Angeles Dodgers was a free agent and could bargain with any team in baseball. The ruling dealt a mortal blow to baseball's reserve clause, which held players to one team for life. Hank Peters, the Baltimore Orioles, and all of organized baseball were about to embark on a new era.

The owners in baseball were beside themselves. Their first reaction was to challenge the Seitz ruling in court and lock the players out of the spring training camps. But they had a losing hand. Two federal courts upheld Seitz' decision. When Commissioner Bowie Kuhn ordered the owners to open their camps, the owners had no choice but to negotiate a compromise with the players. The owners agreed to grant free agency to any player with six years of service in the major leagues.

Hank Peters would have to adjust. Peters could not keep the Orioles intact in the way George Weiss had kept the New York Yankees together throughout the 1950s. Garland, Baylor, Palmer, Grich, Alexander, and pitcher Mike Torrez would be free agents at the end of the 1976 season. "We can't sign a Brooks Robinson and have him for 23 years," Peters conceded with a touch of nostalgia. "Someone will buy him away after six years." [29]

Unlike the Dodgers, Yankees, and Angels, the Orioles had a limited budget for Peters to work with. Despite the Orioles' great baseball success, they had difficulty attracting customers to their home games in Memorial Stadium. The 1969 team, which won 109 games, had a home attendance of just 1,062,094. They barely exceeded one million in 1975 despite winning 90 games. The Orioles saved money by cutting their minor league teams from six in 1970 to just four in 1975, and slashing the number of scouts from 29 in 1972 to just 15 at the end of 1975.

Hank Peters realized he would have to win pennants without spending money. Except for signing Jim Palmer to a long-term deal, Peters could not afford to pay the rest of his free agents. But unlike many conservative baseball operators, Hank Peters was shrewd enough to adapt. "The game has changed in many ways," he said, "and you have to change with it." Rather than waiting for his free agents to leave, he would offer some to wealthier teams for younger players. [30] He traded Torrez and Baylor to the Athletics for outfielder Reggie Jackson and pitcher Ken Holtzman. Then he sent Holtzman and Alexander to the Yankees for veteran pitcher Rudy May and three young unproven players—left-handed pitchers Scott McGregor and Tippy Martinez, and catcher Rick Dempsey.

As Peters feared, the rest of Baltimore's free agents left at the end of the season. Grich signed with the California Angels, Jackson went to the New York Yankees, and Garland moved to Cleveland for a 10-year contract worth $2.3 million. A year later, pitcher Ross Grimsley signed with Montreal. Their defections infuriated Peters. "We've seen a handful of clubs that have been unsuccessful at building teams go out and use checkbooks to achieve things they couldn't accomplish through organizational efforts," he complained. [31]

But Peters had laid the foundation for the Orioles to quickly rebuild. McGregor developed into a 15-game winner by 1978,

Tippy Martinez became one of the game's best relief pitchers, and Dempsey assumed the regular catcher's job. In a vivid display of the value of a strong player development system, the Orioles' farm teams produced scores of replacements—first baseman Eddie Murray, second baseman Rich Dauer, and starting pitchers Mike Flanagan and Dennis Martinez. Peters traded cleverly, picking up relief pitcher Don Stanhouse from Montreal. He signed just one prominent free agent: pitcher Steve Stone.

By 1979, the Orioles won the American League pennant and lost a seven-game World Series to the Pittsburgh Pirates. They won 100 games the following year, only to lose the pennant by three games to the Yankees. Peters' farm system added shortstop Cal Ripken, Jr., and pitchers Mike Boddicker and Storm Davis, and by 1983 the Orioles won the pennant again and defeated the Philadelphia Phillies in five games in the World Series. For his efforts, Peters was chosen "Executive of the Year" by the *Sporting News.*

Like any good IBM executive, Peters aggressively tried to expand his budget by increasing sales. He signed a radio contract with WFBR Radio in Baltimore, which pledged to build a vast seven-state network. "I promised Hank Peters we'd put an extra 500,000 people in the stadium through our promotions," WFBR General Manager Harry Shriver said. [32]

Peters also pressed to expand the Orioles' marketing into nearby Washington. Surveys indicated that as much as 10 percent of Baltimore's home attendance came from Washington. Peters, in 1978, signed an agreement with WTOP Radio in Washington to broadcast the Orioles' games. The team's attendance rapidly climbed to nearly 1.7 million in 1979, and more than 2 million in 1983. By 1986, the team was attracting 400,000 people a year from Washington. A team that lost $102,531 in 1976 and $234,141 in 1978 turned a healthy profit of $1.5 million in 1979. [33]

Peters had learned to win under baseball's new rules. He had every reason to believe he would remain in Baltimore until his retirement. But this time, Hank Peters miscalculated.

Edward Bennett Williams did things his way. As a trial lawyer in Washington, he defended infamous clients shunned by other attorneys: Mobster Frank Costello, Teamsters President Jimmy

Hoffa, and Congressman Adam Clayton Powell. Brilliant and aggressive, Edward Bennett Williams founded what came to be one of the nation's most prestigious law firms, Williams & Connolly. In time, his close friends included President George Bush; Benjamin C. Bradlee, the executive editor of the *Washington Post*; Joseph Califano, the secretary of Health, Education, and Welfare under President Jimmy Carter; and CIA Director Richard Helms. He played as hard as he worked, drinking heavily and often flying to New York City to party with Leonore Lemmon, who served as the model for Holly Golightly in Truman Capote's "Breakfast at Tiffany's."

Edward Bennett Williams was an avid sports fan. He bought into the Washington Redskins of the National Football League in 1961. In 1978, Baseball Commissioner Bowie Kuhn asked former Treasury Secretary William Simon if he and Williams would buy the Orioles from Hoffberger. Williams enthusiastically bought the team himself, paying $11.8 million. He would be an activist owner. "I'll have a direct line to the Orioles' offices," Williams asserted. [34]

Despite that talk, Williams initially provided Hank Peters with a free hand. He had no reason to complain. The Orioles were winning and setting Baltimore attendance records. Following the Orioles' World Series triumph of 1983, Williams added five years to Peters' contract.

But by 1984, Williams began to grow disenchanted with Peters. Part of it was Williams' health; he was battling cancer of the colon and seemed impatient for another world title. "We have to win today," Williams told Peters on a trip to Japan in 1984. "I can't be worried about the long range." [35] He disliked Peters' management style and disdained Joe Altobelli, Peters' handpicked choice for field manager. Altobelli managed the 1983 team with considerable skill, but his remark that he had read only one book in his life appalled Williams, who called Altobelli "Cement Head." Soon his ire turned to Peters. "A nine-to-fiver," Williams carped, referring to Peters' office as "Sleepy Hollow." [36]

They clashed over free agents. Peters' methodical approach was too cautious for Williams. "Maybe I'm not emotionally suited to this game," Williams told reporters. "I have a hard time losing 62 times and saying I had a great year." After a fifth-place finish in 1984, Williams spent $12 million to sign aging outfielders Fred

Lynn and Lee Lacy, and relief pitcher Don Aase. Williams' approach was anathema to Peters, who had warned against heavy spending in 1979. To Peters, "Williams was an arrogant bull in a china closet that he only half understood," wrote Thomas Boswell of the *Washington Post*. Every time the Orioles signed a prominent free agent, baseball rules forced them to sacrifice a high selection in the June amateur draft. The Orioles' farm system would suffer, and, Peters knew, eventually so would the major league team.

He was right. The Orioles crumbled to last place in 1986, and sixth in 1987. The fault belonged to Edward Bennett Williams, but he could not see that himself. As soon as the 1987 season was over, Williams summoned Peters to his office and fired him. "I hope this doesn't affect our friendship," Williams said. Having never been invited to Williams' house socially, Peters could not see how they had a friendship to impact. [37] Always the gentleman, Hank Peters faced the press in a one-hour news conference. Peters resisted the chance to lash back at Williams, although reporters thought he went to extreme lengths to avoid even saying Williams' name. "I guess you could say I'm relieved to be relieved," Peters said. A National League executive told Richard Justice of the *Post*, "My understanding is that Hank's going to the Cleveland Indians." [38]

Hank Peters was aghast when he went to the 1988 Indians' camp in Arizona. Although the Indians had claimed to be developing a large number of talented young pitchers, Peters was unimpressed with what he saw. Throughout the entire organization, Peters thought, there was a lack of hard-throwing pitchers. The farm system, he concluded, was a "disgrace." [39] Like many baseball executives, he had privately laughed when *Sports Illustrated* picked the Indians to win in 1987. Peters was right. The Indians scored runs that year, but their pitchers were yielding five earned runs per game. No team could win with such poor pitching.

Nor was Peters impressed with many of Joe Klein's favorites. He told agent Scott Boras that Jay Bell was a Triple-A shortstop, and traded him to Pittsburgh. [40] He held a low opinion of catcher Andy Allanson's defensive skills, and released him. He did not believe that Klein draftees Rod Nichols, Jeff Shaw, or Kevin Wickander had major league arms.

Peters was unduly harsh in his criticism. Bavasi and Klein had taken control of baseball's worst franchise in 1985 and had initiated the transformation of the team. Klein's farm teams included such future major leaguers as pitchers Greg Swindell, Steve Olin, and Tom Kramer, and outfielder Albert Belle. Klein was one of the few top executives firmly convinced that Jay Bell would be an All-Star shortstop. But Bavasi knew the effort to rebuild the Indians was not completed. "I think we've got this thing halfway turned around," Bavasi confided to Hank Peters in 1987.

Peters scrapped the Indians' organization and replaced it with his own. He recruited John Hart from Baltimore to be a special assignment scout in Cleveland. Hart was young, bright, and so energetic that he kept a notebook by his bed to jot down ideas in the middle of the night. [41] Unlike Hank Peters, John Hart was intense and impatient. But Hank Peters always liked him and carefully promoted him through the Baltimore system. Peters discovered Hart when Tom Giordano, director of player development and scouting in Baltimore, scouted Ron Karkovice at an Orlando high school. "Watch how this club plays today," a scout told Giordano. "The fellow who manages the team does a real good job." The high school manager was John Hart, and an impressed Giordano hired him to manage an Orioles' Rookie League team.

When Peters brought Hart to Cleveland, he already was considering him as a possible successor. "The first year," Peters told Hart, "I want you to scout major league teams. It'll help you get to know the talent in the major leagues that you haven't seen. It also will give you the opportunity to go into other major league parks, introduce yourself, and get to know people at the major league level that you might have to deal with sometime in the future." Hart worked his way through a variety of chores in Cleveland until Peters elevated him to vice president of baseball operations in 1990. [42]

To direct the Indians' farm system, Peters brought Dan O'Dowd from Baltimore, where O'Dowd had spent two and one-half years as assistant director of player development. Like Hart, O'Dowd was young and ambitious; Peters was convinced that he would "be a general manager someday." Peters wanted to retain Jeff Scott as director of scouting, but when Scott took another job, Peters chose Chet Montgomery for the post. Peters added a new Class A team in the South Atlantic League. The Indians, who had just four minor league teams and 18 scouts in 1984, operated six minor league teams and had 29 scouts by 1992.

The additional scouts paid off quickly. While most teams choose wisely in the first and second rounds of the June free agent draft, clever scouts find players in the low rounds. Peters' scouts did exactly that. In 1989, the Indians drafted third baseman Jim Thome of Illinois Central Junior College in the 13th. By 1994, the left-handed batting Thome was the regular third baseman in Cleveland and hit 20 home runs. In 1990, the Indians plucked third baseman David Bell off the Cincinnati sandlots in the seventh round, and in 1991 selected right-handed pitcher Albie Lopez from Mesa Community College in the 20th round. Lopez was so highly regarded that when the Indians tried to obtain pitcher Bret Saberhagen in 1993, the New York Mets insisted on Lopez in return.

In particular, the Indians sought pitchers who could deliver major league fastballs of 88 miles per hour or more. They chose University of North Carolina righthander Paul Shuey in the first round of the 1992 draft after he topped 95 miles per hour on the radar gun. They selected Daron Kirkreit of the University of California at Riverside in the first round of 1993 because of his overpowering fastball; that year they chose pitchers in the first five rounds. "We felt we had to add pitching," Hart later said.

Peters also ordered O'Dowd and Tom Giordano to open a baseball school in the talent-rich Dominican Republic, home of such stars as Julio Franco, George Bell, and Tony Fernandez. For two decades, the Indians had made little effort to sign players in Latin America; Peters noted that the Indians' chief scout in Latin America spent most of the summer serving as a coach in Cleveland instead of scouting. That would end; for too long the Indians had simply allowed the Toronto Blue Jays and Los Angeles Dodgers to monopolize the Dominican Republic.

O'Dowd and Giordano hired Winston Llenas, a shrewd scout of Latin America talent. Instead of directly competing with Blue Jay and Dodger schools in the south of the Dominican, the Indians opened their school in Santiago in the north. Cleveland scouts fanned out across the Dominican Republic, Panama, and Venezuela in search of new talent. Those young players, many of them age 16, would be shipped to the Dominican school for development. Those deemed major league prospects would then be assigned to a Cleveland minor league team in the United States. Among those swiftly advancing was Julian Tavarez, a slender right-handed pitcher who earned brief promotions to Cleveland in 1993 and 1994, and was expected to compete for a starting job in 1995. Fifteen graduates of the Dominican school were scattered throughout the Cleveland farm teams in 1994. Compared to the $1 million bonuses handed to first-round draft choices, Hart calculated the Dominican school cost the Indians $300,000 a year. "For limited dollars," Hart explained, "we have a chance to develop quality players." [43]

Baseball executives were impressed. *Baseball America* magazine named the Indians the top organization of the year in 1992. The Indians showed they could develop players in their minor league system. But they had yet to demonstrate that they could keep them.

When Hank Peters returned to Cleveland, one of his first orders of business was to sign Indians' outfielder Brett Butler to a long-term contract. He asked his secretary to place a call to Butler's home, so he could introduce himself to the soon-to-be free agent. "I can't," she replied. "We don't have a phone number for him." She explained that Butler had not given the team his off-season phone number. "Send him a mail-o-gram," Peter instructed her, "and ask him to please call me collect."

Hank Peters knew it would take years for the Indians to rebuild their farm system. Until then, his goal was to keep the major league team as "competitive as possible." That meant he would have to sign any Indian approaching free agency.

Peters telephoned Dick Moss, who was Butler's agent. Moss told Peters that while he would listen to an offer from Cleveland, he already was in "deep conversations" with the San Francisco Giants. Still hoping for a hearing, Peters replied, "Well, I'd like to talk to Butler. I've never met him. I'm not going to negotiate with him. But I would like to introduce myself and tell him a little about the things we're going to be doing in the organization." Moss told Peters he would ask Butler to call him back. Peters never got that call. Instead, Butler signed a multi-year contract with the Giants. This embarrassing sequence would be repeated: Hank Peters discovered that once the better Cleveland players reached free agency, they wanted to leave the city. [44]

Nor could Peters find free agents from other teams willing to play for a bad team in a decrepit stadium. That was an old story. When Cleveland offered Don Baylor a 10-year contract in the mid-1970s, he flatly rejected it. Plenty of players, Baylor thought, had demanded throughout history to be traded. None, as far as he could tell, insisted upon Cleveland as a destination. Baylor thought if he wanted punishment, he could go to San Quentin. [45]

Once again, Hank Peters would have to adapt. And inadvertently, Joe Carter showed him how.

For six seasons, Joe Carter had been the best ballplayer on the Indians; perhaps the best player in a Cleveland uniform since Larry Doby and Al Rosen. He became the first Indian ever to steal 30 bases and hit 30 home runs in the same season, and three times he drove in more than 100 runs. He could play all three outfield positions and pitch in at first base.

Joe Carter should have been idolized in Cleveland. Instead, his years in the city often were stormy. He criticized Clevelanders as "fair-weather fans" who would heartily boo a player until he "hit three home runs." Then they would cheer and demand the player leave the dugout and tip his hat to the crowd. "When you're going bad," Carter asked, "what's wrong with cheering for someone to try and pick them up? But when you make a mistake, they just boo and boo and boo." [46] He said that Cleveland Stadium was not even a "20th century" ballpark. Like Hank Greenberg before him, Joe Carter bitterly decried the area sportswriters and sportscasters as hostile. "You guys have a lot to do with it," Carter told *Plain Dealer* baseball writer Paul Hoynes in 1989. "You have one newspaper in town and some people are going to believe whatever they read. When you guys get down on a player, it tears the team down." [47] *Plain Dealer* sports columnist Bill Livingston once wrote that Carter was "sounding like the epitome of the spoiled modern athlete." [48] Livingston wrote that Carter did not hit in pressure situations, did not steal enough bases, and played poorly in center field. Yet despite those flaws, Livingston urged the Indians to sign Carter to a long-term contract.

Carter also quarreled with Dan O'Brien, who had been Peter Bavasi's vice president. In 1986, Carter batted .302, hit 29 home runs, stole 29 bases, and drove in 121 runs. Had O'Brien been shrewder, he would have signed Carter to a multi-year contract. Instead, O'Brien, taking advantage of the fact that Carter had not been in the league long enough to qualify for either arbitration or free agency, renewed the outfielder's contract for $250,000.

Hank Peters was appalled. He thought Bavasi's front office had been foolish for renewing Carter's contract in such a high-handed fashion. He could not understand the reporters and sportscasters who criticized Carter. To Peters, Carter was one of the game's best ballplayers. Except for Albert Belle, the Indians did not have a player in its minor league system with Joe Carter's bat skills.

Carter was eligible for arbitration after the 1988 season, and Peters wanted to sign him to a long-term contract. He telephoned Carter's agent, Jim Turner of St. Louis, and offered a firm three-year contract worth $5 million with club options for an additional two years. Turner had always liked Peters as "upfront and honest." But Turner was dissatisfied with the two option years. If the Indians picked up the options, Turner knew, the value of Carter's contract would reach $9 million. But what if Carter suffered a serious injury and the Indians refused to pick up the options? Anyway Turner looked at it, the Indians were only committed to three years and nothing more.

With the arbitration hearings looming in early 1989, Turner presented Peters with a counterproposal: Three years at $6 million and a fourth year as an option. But if the Indians declined to pick up the option, they would owe Carter an additional $2 million. The day before the arbitration hearing was scheduled, Turner stopped at Carter's home in Kansas City, telephoned Peters, and urged the Indians to agree to the $8 million deal over four years. Peters declined. [49]

The arbitrator ruled in Carter's favor and awarded him a $1.64 million contract for 1989. But the entire arbitration process, combined with his clash with Danny O'Brien, convinced Carter that he would leave Cleveland when he was eligible for free agency at the end of 1990. Peters did not want to wait and, in fall of 1989, he telephoned Turner and offered what he thought was a "strong proposal"—$10 million for the next three years. But Peters wanted a quick answer. "I'm not going to keep Joe and let him become a free agent player," Peters told Turner. "That's not fair to the ballclub. If he's not going to sign here, then I'm going to trade him. Let's agree on a date." Peters and Turner settled upon the first week of November, which would allow Peters to head to the general managers' meeting in Palm Springs that month and open negotiations with other teams. [50]

Turner and Carter quickly replied. "My family's not happy here," Carter told Peters. "I'm not happy here. I'm not going to stay." Peters released a statement to the press on November 2, announcing that negotiations with Carter had collapsed and the Indians would trade him before the end of the year. Then Peters flew to Palm Springs for the general managers' meeting. There, every one of Peters' colleagues asked about Carter. They suggested they would offer Cleveland an excellent trade if Carter would agree to skip his free agent year and sign a long-term contract. [51]

Peters was pleased. Everything was falling into place. He could look forward to a number of teams all bidding against each other in their eagerness to offer Peters a package of young players for Carter.

But after the meetings, Peters' scheme collapsed: Turner telephoned and said Carter would only sign a long-term contract with the Dodgers, Angels, or Padres on the West Coast, or the Royals or Cardinals from his home state of Missouri. If the Indians traded Carter to any other team, he would not sign a multi-year deal. Peters was stunned. No team would offer Cleveland good players for the chance of having Carter for just one year. It meant that Peters would have to trade Carter to one of five teams: Padres, Dodgers, Angels, Cardinals, or Royals.

Peters shrewdly kept Turner's revelation out of the newspapers. He went through the motions of listening to offers from Toronto, Boston, San Francisco, Atlanta, and the New York Mets. Even up to the very end, newspapers reported that the Indians were in serious discussions with those teams. [52]

Peters spoke with John Schuerholz, the highly regarded general manager at Kansas City. Schuerholz wanted Carter, but he seemed reluctant to part with the type of players Peters wanted. He offered outfielder Danny Tartabull and little else. The more Peters thought about it, the more he became convinced that Schuerholz believed that Carter would only sign a long-term contract with his hometown team in Kansas City. Why offer Cleveland quality players for Carter when the Royals believed he eventually would sign with them as a free agent? [53]

The Dodgers expressed little interest, while the Cardinals offered outfielders Willie McGee and Vince Coleman. But Peters wanted younger players, much like when he traded for Scott McGregor and Rick Dempsey. His negotiations with the Angels came to a halt when Peters insisted they include center fielder Devon White in the trade.

San Diego General Manager Jack McKeon wanted Carter badly. The Padres had finished just three games behind the National League West champion Giants in 1989, and McKeon thought Carter could put the Padres over the top in 1990. McKeon, a short, friendly man who never was without a cigar, enjoyed orchestrating complicated trades involving scores of players. He would be willing to part with young players in return for Carter. Among those players McKeon dangled before Peters was Sandy Alomar, Jr., a 6-foot-5 catcher who drove in 101 runs at San Diego's Triple-A team in Las Vegas. But what scouts liked most about Alomar was his powerful throwing arm, his ability to handle a pitcher, and his skill at blocking curveballs in the dirt. Cleveland Manager John McNamara, who had personally scouted Alomar, described him as a "quality player who fills a position that's difficult to fill with skilled people." [54] Peters early on signalled his interest in Alomar. In late September—more than a month before Peters officially announced he would trade Carter—the *Plain Dealer* published a brief note saying the Indians would insist upon Alomar in return for Carter. The Padres, with young Benito Santiago as their regular catcher, could afford to part with Alomar. [55]

Peters flew to Nashville for the winter meetings in December at the sprawling Opryland Hotel, where he spotted McKeon and suggested they meet on Sunday morning. In addition to Alomar, McKeon offered the Indians a choice from a package of young players—outfielders Thomas Howard and Jerald Clark, and infielder Joey Cora. Peters was not interested: He told McKeon he wanted Carlos Baerga, a 21-year-old third baseman from Puerto Rico who was a switch hitter. He also wanted Chris James, a solid hitter who would replace Carter in left field. McKeon hesitated. He was willing to trade Alomar and James, but his minor league staff opposed including Baerga. Even though *Baseball America* had not placed Baerga's name on their list of top prospects in the Pacific Coast League in 1989, the Cleveland scouts were impressed.

Finally, the Man With a Plan

On Monday evening, Peters, McKeon, and the staffs from the two teams met in Peters' room. For a few moments, Peters and McKeon exchanged stories about Charlie Finley, before McKeon said, "OK guys, Hank is almost ready to fall asleep. Let's get something going." Peters said he wanted Alomar, Baerga, and James. "I can't do Baerga," McKeon protested. Peters would not yield; he was confident that McKeon "wasn't going to let a prospect stand in the way of making the deal." He was right. McKeon could only brood about the possibility of Joe Carter hitting 35 home runs for another team. At 11 that night, McKeon agreed to the deal. [56]

Peters personally hunted down Jim Turner at the hotel and advised him of the trade: Turner and the Padres would have until two in the afternoon Wednesday to agree to a long-term deal or the trade would fall through. Turner went to McKeon's suite. There, McKeon lit one cigar after another as he and Turner argued about a contract. Turner, a non-smoker, was convinced that McKeon was relying on his old ploy of filling the room with smoke, wearing out Turner, and negotiating a cheaper contract. But Turner was not about to give up: He knew McKeon had to sign Carter and figured he would be ready to agree on a contract when he stopped smoking. "When I finally can see the whites of your eyes," Turner joked with McKeon, "I know we're going to make a deal." [57] They finally agreed—$9.2 million during the next three years, including $2 million delivered before the end of the year. On Wednesday afternoon, Peters sent John Hart and Dan O'Dowd to knock on McKeon's door. Pointing to Turner, who was in the same room, McKeon replied, "We just shook on the deal." Turner left for Hank Peters' suite: He wanted to thank the Indians' president for orchestrating a deal that worked out well for the Indians and Joe Carter.

Turner was right; it was the best trade Peters ever made. He gave up a player he was going to lose as a free agent and received two future All-Stars in Alomar and Baerga. Alomar became the first outstanding defensive catcher to play regularly in Cleveland since Jim Hegan in the 1950s. Baerga, switched permanently to second base in the summer of 1991, batted .300 and drove in more than 100 runs in both 1992 and 1993. The night Peters completed the trade, he predicted that within a few years the regular Cleveland lineup would include Albert Belle in the outfield, Baerga in the infield, and Alomar catching. [58]

The trade also nudged the Indians in a different direction. Peters and Hart would part with overpriced veterans to make room for inexpensive younger players developed in the Cleveland farm system or obtained from other teams—outfielders Manny Ramirez and Kenny Lofton, first baseman Paul Sorrento, third baseman Jim Thome, and pitchers Charles Nagy, Albie Lopez, and Mark Clark.

The process was trying. "You go through trial and error," Hank Peters would tell Dick Jacobs. To rebuild the Cleveland Indians required a man with the seemingly infinite patience of Hank Peters. Others, however, did not see it that way. The Cleveland reporters, having devoted four decades to covering baseball's worst franchise, were slow to figure out the plan. Bill Livingston of the *Plain Dealer* assailed the Carter trade, writing that obtaining players such as James and Baerga does "not make the head whirl." [59] When the Indians traded another potential free agent, pitcher Tom Candiotti, to Toronto for young outfielders Mark Whiten and Glenallen Hill, Livingston denounced the move as the "Indians' latest abdication from competitive responsibility." [60]

Peters thought the Cleveland reporters were the most "negative" he had ever encountered. But he had his chance to respond. When Peters replaced McNamara as manager in the summer of 1991 with Mike Hargrove, he called a Saturday press conference. There, with the city's newscasters and sportswriters captive, Peters outlined his long-term plan for the Indians. In a parting salvo, the normally mild Hank Peters said, "I have tried very hard to explain to all of you what is going on with this club, but I'm sorry to say most of you don't have a clue." The next day, *Plain Dealer* sportswriter Tony Grossi suggested that Peters and Hart were the ones who "were clueless." [61]

Hank Peters knew better. "There's a pretty good flow of talent coming through the organization," he said after his retirement. "It's going to get better. Knowing what's on the horizon, their position players will be second to none."

Hank Peters retired at the end of 1991, just as he had planned. The transition went smoothly, as Dick Jacobs simply elevated John Hart to become general manager. Peters returned to his townhouse in Baltimore and a chance to spend time with his grandchildren. The fights with Charlie Finley, Vernon Stouffer, and Edward Bennett Williams were behind him. He had built a respected organization in Cleveland, operated the franchise in a fiscally responsible way, and pointed the team in the right direction. He would not be in Cleveland when the Indians finally won. But when they did win, it would be his team.

Chapter 10

A New Park in a
Very Old Place

"I felt from the very beginning that in order to keep the team in Cleveland…you needed a modern ballpark."
— Richard F. Celeste

Thomas V. Chema was not surprised to hear that Governor Richard F. Celeste was on the telephone that spring of 1989. For nearly 20 years, Chema had been a confidant of the Ohio governor. He had served in Celeste's cabinet and was considered one of its ablest members. Although he had left state government that April to return to the Cleveland law firm of Arter & Hadden, Chema remained in regular contact with Celeste.

Celeste wanted advice. He had less than two years to serve in his second term as governor, and the state constitution prohibited him from running for a third term. Like all governors in their final years, Celeste recognized his political power was eroding. But Richard F. Celeste had big plans after he left the statehouse: A visible role in national Democratic politics; a cabinet job in a Democratic presidency; or perhaps a run for the White House. That meant leaving Ohio with a series of major accomplishments. Would Chema join him for dinner with a few close associates the next time Celeste was in Cleveland?

Those invited to dinner were so close to Celeste that reporters nicknamed them "Celestials." In addition to Chema, the group included Helen Williams, manager of Celeste's Cleveland office and wife of Cleveland City Councilman Jay Westbrook; Mary Boyle, a Cuyahoga County commissioner with ambitions for the U.S. Senate; and Carolyn Lukensmeyer, who served as chief of staff for the governor and eventually would move to President Clinton's White House. They were devoted to Celeste and determined to do whatever was necessary to boost his career.

Boyle and Chema had the same idea: Celeste should place the prestige of the governor's office behind one last effort to build a new ballpark in downtown Cleveland. In his typical legalese, Chema warned Celeste: "If we don't get a new stadium, we think the Indians are going to move. We don't think they can economically stand to stay here in the face of a number of offers which are currently on the table and which we know will be on the table." Tampa, Miami, Phoenix, Washington, Buffalo, and Denver were frantically bidding for two expansion franchises in the National League, Chema reminded Celeste. The cities failing to win a team, Chema said, almost certainly would go shopping for an existing franchise and steal one from a city like Cleveland. [1]

This was not news to Celeste. He had grown up with the Indians as a kid in the west side suburb of Lakewood. For years, he had heard rumblings from organized baseball that the Indians were in danger of moving. In the fall of 1983, he was so worried that he asked Baseball Commissioner Bowie Kuhn, American League President Lee MacPhail, Cleveland Mayor George Voinovich, and Ted Bonda to the Tudor-style governor's mansion in suburban Columbus. Celeste put the question directly to Kuhn: "Are you going to take the team out of the city?" Celeste never received a direct answer, but as the meeting broke up and the governor escorted his guests to the front door, MacPhail hesitated. "The only way you're going to keep the club," MacPhail told Celeste, "is to get a new stadium." [2]

Despite that warning, Celeste went out of his way in 1984 to kill a county-wide ballot issue in Cleveland that would have raised property taxes to finance construction of a 72,000-seat domed stadium. The dome had been a favorite of Art Modell, owner of the Cleveland Browns, and Vincent Campanella, a Republican Cuyahoga County commissioner. Celeste thought using a property tax was a terrible way to finance a stadium, and, before the scheduled vote that May, Celeste denounced the project as "doomed." Defeat this proposal, Celeste promised, and he would offer a better plan. The county rejected the dome by 100,000 votes, and that November Mary Boyle ousted Campanella from the commissioner's office.

Since that vote, Celeste had done little to put forward a formula for building a new ballpark. Celeste and Voinovich both encouraged city officials and business executives to form the

Greater Cleveland Domed Stadium Corporation. By 1985, the organization was buying up a large tract of land in the city's old Central Market area, just to the southeast of the Terminal Tower.

But Celeste had other priorities. He won a smashing re-election victory in 1986 over an aging James A. Rhodes, and in the summer of 1987 he toyed with running for president, making a trip to Iowa where the first presidential caucuses would be held in 1988. But his administration had been plagued by a series of embarrassing scandals. One cabinet member went to jail on charges of bribery and theft. Marvin L. Warner, a close friend and major campaign contributor, was convicted of fraud for his role in triggering the state's savings and loan debacle. After mulling a run at the White House, Celeste decided to remain in Ohio.

Now during dinner, Celeste was noncommittal about Chema's stadium idea. He said he would return to Columbus before making a decision. Two months later, Celeste asked the Celestials to meet him again, this time at the Haymarket, a small restaurant behind the Terminal Tower.

"I think you were all right about the stadium," Celeste explained. "I think it's my responsibility to take another run at it. But the way to do this is not for me to just announce that I'm going to try again to get a stadium. It won't work." Turning to Chema, Celeste said, "The way I would like to do this is for you to go to the public sector players in town and try and develop a consensus behind putting public money in the pot. I think the only way to do this is to quietly, behind the scenes, try to get a consensus of all the public officials and get all the key players on the same page." [3]

That would be some trick. In its most tranquil moments, Cleveland seethed with political discord. The Democrats controlled most of the city offices, but that did not guarantee unity: Many Democrats barely spoke to one another. Then there were the Indians' owners, Dick and David Jacobs. Dick Jacobs was a demanding negotiator who considered any compromise in a business deal to be a failure.

If anyone could find common ground among these warring factions, Tom Chema could, or so Celeste believed. He viewed Chema as an indefatigable lawyer who would never take no for an answer. Chema personally knew the important political figures in the city, and he was one Democrat trusted by business executives in Cleveland. Like Celeste, Chema also was ambitious. He too wanted to be governor of Ohio.

Richard F. Celeste and Tom Chema came of age during the turbulent 1960s. Both were educated at prestigious universities; Celeste was a graduate of Yale and a Rhodes Scholar, while Chema attended Notre Dame and earned a law degree from Harvard. Like many young Democrats, Celeste and Chema passionately opposed the war in Vietnam.

They met in Chicago at the 1968 Democratic National Convention, where Chema worked as a public relations assistant for the Democrats. As protesters clashed with Mayor Richard Daley's police in the streets of Chicago, Chema joined a group of young Democrats hoping to persuade Senator Edward Kennedy of Massachusetts to challenge Vice President Hubert Humphrey for the nomination. Among those at the meeting was Richard F. Celeste.

Several years later, Chema moved to Cleveland, joining Arter & Hadden, where he represented corporations suing one another. The legal work was dull; Chema's cases rarely went to trial because his clients preferred to settle their differences privately.

As he practiced law, Chema kept up with politics. One day in 1974 he noticed that a young member of the Ohio House of Representatives, Richard F. Celeste, was running for the Democratic nomination for lieutenant governor. Intrigued, Chema went to Celeste's Cleveland headquarters, sought out the candidate, and announced, "I know you." Chema volunteered to help the 37-year-old Celeste in his longshot campaign. But Celeste won the crowded Democratic primary and that November defeated incumbent Republican John Brown.

While Celeste moved to Columbus, Chema remained in Cleveland and in 1976 managed the winning U.S. Senate campaign of Democrat Howard Metzenbaum. When Celeste was elected governor in a major landslide in 1982, Tom Chema joined Celeste's cabinet to direct the state's lottery, before advancing to chair the state's public utilities commission. In a cabinet filled with far too many mediocre managers and political rogues, Celeste's senior aides regarded Tom Chema as a trusted administrator whose legal skills and competence were unmatched. Perhaps Chema was too smart. One Celeste aide thought the governor regarded Chema as a competitor, and Celeste rarely sought his advice on broad statewide issues.

By 1989, Chema was ready to return to Arter & Hadden, where he planned to make the most of his years in government and develop a lucrative energy and telecommunications law practice. Dinner at the Haymarket changed that. Chema would have to visit every major public official and business executive, contend with fierce political ambitions, and forge a consensus on a new stadium. One thing was certain: Nobody in the summer of 1989 would have predicted success for Tom Chema.

Chema did have one advantage. Most people thought that the aging behemoth on Lake Erie needed replacing. Despite a sweeping series of improvements to stabilize the superstructure and build luxury loges, Cleveland Stadium in 1989 was hopelessly antiquated. More than 50,000 of the seats had been installed in 1931, and many were too far from the field of action. Massive steel girders that supported the roof obstructed views in the grandstand, and bathrooms were inadequate for large crowds. The choppy infield defied the best efforts of modern ground-skeepers. On cold spring and fall days, the crowds often fell below 6,000. Baseball players detested the environment. A standard joke was that only two players' wives would show up for every game: the wife of the starting pitcher and her best friend. Chicago White Sox catcher Carlton Fisk summed up the atmosphere: "It's depressing." [4]

It once was the showplace of baseball. In 1931, the *Plain Dealer* described the stadium as "a monument to the progressive spirit of the city's people." On the day it opened for baseball, National League President John Heydler called it the "last word in baseball parks." Thomas Shibe, president of the Philadelphia Athletics, was envious: "I wish we had this in Philadelphia." Judge Kenesaw Mountain Landis gazed at the massive grandstands. "This," Landis said, "is perfection." [5]

Until the Dodgers moved to the Los Angeles Coliseum in 1958, Cleveland Stadium held every conceivable attendance record. More than 80,000 people filled the stadium when the Indians and Athletics played the first game there in 1932. Cleveland Stadium in 1989 still held the American League records for the largest attendance at a night game, afternoon game, after-noon doubleheader, and World Series game.

A peculiar legend has emerged that Cleveland Stadium was a WPA project designed to attract the Olympics. In reality, work-ers completed the stadium nearly two years before Franklin D. Roosevelt, architect of the WPA, became president. Cleveland Stadium was built and paid for by the people of Cleveland.

Like the stadium Chema and Celeste wanted to build in the 1990s, the one that preceded it was far more than bricks and steel. It was built of political ambition, of the lust for money by team owners and the desire for lasting monuments. It was a pow-erful symbol of progress and economic might in a city enjoying what seemed to be limitless prosperity.

Cleveland Municipal Stadium was the creation of William R. Hopkins, a man so persuasive that Democratic City Councilman F.W. Walz complained that Hopkins "could sell brass door knobs for ostrich eggs." [6] With his rimless glasses and hair parted down the middle, Hopkins looked like a dull accountant. But he was a dynamic visionary who pressed for developments in air travel and dreamed of creating an underground subway throughout Greater Cleveland.

From the time of his appointment by the Republican city council as the city's first manager in 1924, Hopkins ruled Cleve-land with a strong hand, often ignoring the wishes of Republican leader Maurice Maschke for patronage appointments. Under his direction, the city paved miles of new streets, constructed new sewers, opened a huge airport, and devised a plan to develop the city's lakefront. Hopkins carefully balanced the budget and re-strained increases in city taxes.

William Rowland Hopkins was born in Johnstown, Pennsyl-vania, in 1869, the third child in a family of 10. His parents moved to Cleveland where he attended grade school. Although he was eager to attend college, he was forced to take a job as a "help-er boy" for American Steel & Wire Company in Cleveland. But William had no intention of spending the rest of his life in a wire plant; he devoted all his extra hours to learning stenography and frugally saved his money to attend Western Reserve University. He did post-graduate work at the prestigious University of Chica-go, before earning a law degree at Western Reserve in 1899.

Hopkins developed a passion for business and politics. As a law student, he won a seat on Cleveland City Council. He remained active in Republican politics, serving briefly as chairman of the county Republican party. But he was consumed by advances in modern transportation. He pushed for and developed the Belt Line Railroad, whose tracks circled the city and carried heavy freight. He became director of the Cleveland Short Line Railroad Company.

As city manager, Hopkins was particularly eager to complete work on the Mall, which was to run from Lake Erie to the heart of downtown. Cleveland Mayor Tom Johnson first conceived of the Mall in 1903; he wanted to transform an area of decrepit buildings just off Lake Erie into a park surrounded by elaborate government buildings. Between 1905 and 1922, some of those buildings were constructed—the Cleveland City Hall in 1916, the Cuyahoga County Court House in 1912, the Cleveland Public Library in 1925, and the Public Auditorium in 1922. Hopkins planned to finish work on the Mall, but with one key addition: A large, multi-purpose stadium on the lake. Hopkins wanted this stadium, unlike most others of the time, to be built with public money. Hopkins asked Peter Evans of the Osborn Engineering Company to sketch some plans of a new stadium, and showed them to Ernest Barnard, the president of the Cleveland Indians.

Over rummy with *Cleveland News* sports editor Ed Bang, Barnard often had talked of building a stadium much like the 50,000-seat Polo Grounds in New York City. [7] Barnard knew that the oddly shaped structure of brick, steel, and wood known as League Park was hopelessly obsolete for modern baseball. League Park had fewer than 30,000 seats, and because it was jammed into an East Side neighborhood of working class homes, there was no way to expand seating and provide parking. Barnard also reasoned that a new stadium would increase the value of the Indians, which were on the market. Barnard, who convinced the team to hire him as an office assistant in 1903, took control of daily operations of the Indians in 1922 following the death of owner James Dunn. Dunn's widow wanted to sell the team, and Barnard was eager for the sale so he could become president of the American League.

In a confidential letter to Hopkins, Barnard wrote that a large stadium would attract a minimum of 750,000 people a year to

Indians' home games, assuring the team an annual profit of $200,000. "In a stadium that would seat 70,000 people," Barnard wrote Hopkins, "Cleveland should play to one million paid admissions whenever its club occupies a position in the first division. With a club contending for first place as was the case in 1920 and 1921, it would not be impossible for the club to play to 1,250,000 paid admissions." [8]

By 1928, Hopkins was confident enough of the proposal to ask the voters for approval. City council approved placing a $2.5-million bond issue on the November ballot by a vote of 23-1. The sole dissenter was Walz, who warned that with Public Hall, the city had "one white elephant" on its hands. "Of course," Walz grumbled, "they say the stadium will pay for itself, but we've heard that story before. It's high time we called a halt to this." [9] Walz was a lonely voice lost in the rallying cry for the stadium. Cleveland was one of the nation's largest cities, and its public officials and citizens were in no mood to consider limitations. The city's elite pushed hard for voter approval. A committee headed up by Charles A. Otis—founder of Bill Daley's Otis & Co.—produced a report in 1928 suggesting a new stadium could be used for business gatherings, musical productions by the Cleveland Orchestra, boxing, soccer, and track and field. Supporters circulated sketches of the huge new stadium, looking very much like the Los Angeles Coliseum. It was advertised as seating nearly 100,000 people, and fireproof. "Cleveland must have this stadium," wrote Sam Otis, sports editor of the *Plain Dealer*. "It means more to sports here than any other project ever launched." [10] On the same November afternoon that Republican Herbert Hoover was winning 40 states in a landslide presidential election over Democrat Al Smith, more than 112,000 Clevelanders voted to support the construction of the municipal stadium.

Construction began on June 24, 1930, but, by then, the man responsible for the stadium was out of office. Hopkins sharply clashed with Maschke over patronage appointments. Maschke, a tough-minded politician who walked about Cleveland in a straw hat and dark-rimmed glasses, would not have his authority questioned. Maschke quietly instructed the Republican members of city council to get rid of Hopkins.

A list of trumped-up charges was drawn up and handed to Walz, the Democrat, who made them public. They included the accusation that Hopkins had agreed to pay an inflated price for a city playground site, and had "demonstrated an inherent and continuing incapacity for harmonious and effective cooperation with the council." The charges were preposterous. When Democratic councilman John L. Mihelich asked Walz who drafted them, Walz sheepishly replied, "I don't know." Councilman Conrad Krueck, a stout Hopkins' defender, complained that "this is the biggest farce I've seen in the 51 years I've been in this country." [11]

Hopkins demanded to appear before the council and rebut the charges in a speech broadcast throughout Cleveland. The broadcast was scheduled for a frigid afternoon in January 1930. To the roars of approval from his supporters, Hopkins strode to the clerk's desk where a microphone had been set up by WHK Radio. Holding a black leather looseleaf notebook in his right hand, Hopkins spoke for the next 90 minutes in a firm, clear voice, presenting a lawyerly defense of his six years as city manager. As Hopkins spoke, Walz scowled and angrily puffed on a series of cigars.

"The charges are not only improper in form, but untrue in substance and do not constitute the kind of reasons which justify a change in the office of city manager," Hopkins declared. Shortly after three in the afternoon, Hopkins concluded his address, and left the chamber amid applause and cheers from his supporters. His time was over. But his stadium would be built. [12]

Daniel Morgan, a Republican member of the Ohio Senate, replaced Hopkins as city manager and pressed for completion of the stadium. At various times during the 370 days it took for construction, as many as 2,500 workers were on the site. That December workers began erecting the massive steel structure that eventually took the shape of an egg and poured the concrete that would be the foundation of the grandstand seats. They covered the exterior of the stadium with what was described as "modeled-gray" brick, which was yellow in appearance.

Designers employed the most advanced construction techniques. Except for Yankee Stadium in New York and the Los Angeles Coliseum, Cleveland Stadium was unmatched anywhere in the world. It stood as high as an 11-story building and was more than 700 feet wide. The vast roof covering the upper deck was made of a lightweight sheet aluminum, in part because designers feared that the nearby lake water would cause rapid deterioration of a steel roof. On the very top of the roof, electricians installed 250 floodlights, each with 1,000 watts of power. At a time when every major league baseball game was played in daylight, designers of Cleveland Stadium demanded enough light to play baseball, football, and soccer at night. An awed *Plain Dealer* reporter described the lights as so "powerful that daylight is dull by comparison." [13]

City officials asked William Hopkins to help dedicate the new stadium when it officially opened on Thursday, July 2, 1931. They planned an elaborate two-day event highlighted by the heavyweight boxing championship fight between Max Schmeling of Germany and Willie Stribling of Georgia. The wealthy and elite from across the country decided that Cleveland was the place to be that weekend. Edsel Ford arrived by plane. A Detroit automotive rival, Robert Graham, crossed Lake Erie in his yacht Atrebor, with former heavyweight champion Gene Tunney as his guest. Others traveled by private Pullman cars: Will Hays, the censorship czar of Hollywood films; David Sarnoff, the president of RCA; R.W. Woodruff, the president of Coca-Cola; Chicago Mayor Anton Cermak; Wisconsin Senator Robert La Follette; former heavyweight champion Gentleman Jim Corbett; sportswriters Grantland Rice and Damon Runyon; and broadcaster Graham McNamee, who would describe the fight on radio.

The Midwest was near the end of an oppressive heat wave that had forced thousands of Clevelanders to sleep in city parks. Most visitors wore cool Palm Beach suits as they mingled in the lobby of the city's busy Hollenden House. Stribling, bored by the intensive training, borrowed a small biplane to fly about the city; he nearly killed himself when his plane just missed telephone poles along the Rocky River. [14]

On Thursday evening, with the setting sun splashing a red glow upon their faces, 1,500 singers officially opened the stadium with choral works. City officials were lucky. The heat wave broke and a cool breeze blew off the lake. Thousands of people wandered through the stands, their paths illuminated by the powerful new lights. Hopkins, never at a loss for words, took a microphone and told the crowd that the stadium would be an "enduring monument to the spirit and aspirations of our people," and would "take its place among the best known structures in the world, known to everyone who can read print, or hear the message of the radio, or see the pictures on the screen—the scene of great events inseparable from the name of Cleveland." [15]

The very next night before 35,000 people, Schmeling retained his title when the referee stopped the fight in the 15th round. Cleveland society watched from the best seats and the newspapers chronicled their every move. Mrs. Myron Wick stood out in a gown of printed tan and brown, with a small brown straw hat perched on her head. Mrs. Dan Hanna wore a pale blue chiffon with a matching hat. Mrs. Lawrence Lanier Winslow arrived in a black-and-white chiffon with floating cape, a black picture hat framing her face.

The stadium, however, needed one more year of work before it was ready for its chief tenant, the Indians. Under a sparkling blue Sunday afternoon sky, the Indians opened the stadium on July 31, 1932, against the defending American League champion Philadelphia Athletics. The largest crowd in the history of baseball, 80,184, arrived in 25,000 cars, 1,000 taxis, and scores of streetcars that clanged down Superior Avenue to East 9th Street. Ohio Governor George White, wearing a gray business suit and claiming to have pitched as a freshman at Princeton, tossed the first ball to homeplate where Mayor Ray Miller, smartly dressed in a brown sports jacket and white slacks, scooped it from the dirt. The Indians asked many of their old stars back, including second baseman Larry Lajoie, the most graceful infielder of his day; Tris Speaker, the swift center fielder who took the Indians to the 1920 pennant; Cy Young, the powerful righthander who pitched for the Cleveland Spiders of the National League in the 1890s; and second baseman Bill Wambsganss, who pulled off an unassisted triple play during the 1920 World Series.

A Goodyear blimp floated overhead. Lefty Grove of Philadelphia defeated Cleveland's Mel Harder, 1-0. Jimmie Foxx of Philadelphia smacked the game's only extra-base hit. The players complained that they could not see Grove's fastball because it blended into the sea of white-shirted spectators in the center-field bleachers. Cleveland General Manager Billy Evans promptly corrected that problem by placing a number of bleacher seats off-limits to customers.

To their chagrin, the hard-hitting Indians quickly discovered that Cleveland Stadium was a nightmare for the strongest of batters. The center-field wall was 450 feet from homeplate, and the playing field so vast that Babe Ruth once joked that the only way outfielders could catch up to flyballs was to ride polo ponies. Except for line drives down the right- and left-field lines, nobody could reach the seats. Earl Averill, the center fielder who hit 32 home runs in 1932, hit just 11 in 1933. Other Indians were just as frustrated; the team's batting average tumbled from .285 to .261, and the Indians scored 200 fewer runs.

In addition, the stadium opened at the worst possible time. The prosperity of the 1920s had given way to the Great Depression. Clevelanders did not have the money to spend for baseball, and home attendance sank to 387,936—a sharp drop from the 912,839 customers the team attracted in old League Park during the pennant-winning year of 1920. To the consternation of city officials, the Indians moved most of their 1934 games back to League Park, playing in the stadium only on Sundays and special events. When Hank Greenberg entered the final day of 1938 with 58 home runs, he was horrified to learn the season-ending doubleheader would be played in Cleveland Stadium. He hit a 420-foot single, but the huge stadium frustrated his best chance of tying Babe Ruth's single-season home run record of 60. Whitey Lewis of the *Cleveland Press* suggested to Indians President Alva Bradley and manager Roger Peckinpaugh that a temporary fence be used to make it easier to hit home runs. Bradley thought the idea was preposterous. [16]

That changed when Bill Veeck bought the team. To Veeck, it was a question of simple math: League Park had less than 30,000 seats; Cleveland Stadium had 80,000. In 1947, he signed a lease with the city to move all the Indians' games into Cleveland Stadium. Two weeks into the season, he installed a five-foot-high wire fence that cut down the size of the outfield. "This fence will stay permanently," Veeck declared. "Now our players will have a chance to hit some home runs at home like the Red Sox and Yankees." [17]

The Indians did just that, increasing their home run production from 79 in 1946 to 155 in 1948. Attendance increased from 558,182 in 1945 to 1.5 million in 1947, 2.6 million in 1948, and 2.2 million in 1949. The huge stadium was impressing other baseball owners. Walter O'Malley in Brooklyn suddenly regarded Ebbets Field and its 33,000 seats as woefully inadequate.

Everybody wanted a stadium as big as Cleveland's. O'Malley moved his Dodgers to Los Angeles where he personally approved the design and construction of the beautiful Chavez Ravine. Houston, plagued by brutal humidity in the summer, built the air-conditioned Astrodome. Shea Stadium in New York, Three Rivers in Pittsburgh, Riverfront in Cincinnati, Arrowhead in Kansas City, and Anaheim in southern California all pushed the design of modern stadiums well beyond Cleveland's. By the late 1960s, Cleveland Stadium was no longer the showplace. Instead, it was a relic from another era.

It was the spring of 1983, and Vince Campanella, one of the state's most ambitious Republicans, was fed up with years of empty talk about replacing Cleveland Stadium. Everyone agreed that the stadium was simply too old and worn out, but they never could agree on what to build and how to pay for it. Unless someone decided to take the lead, Campanella thought, it would remain nothing more than a "topic of discussion." He called in his budget assistant and abruptly announced, "We're going to do a stadium." Campanella could think of no way, other than public money, to finance a stadium. He knew he would have to take the risky course of proposing a tax increase. [18]

Campanella that spring was one of the best-known politicians in Ohio. He had been elected county auditor, before handily winning the county commissioner's race in 1980. He ran an effective race in 1982 for auditor of Ohio, but fell victim to Richard F. Celeste's landslide gubernatorial victory. Republicans considered him a possible challenger to Celeste in 1986, and he could boost his chances by becoming the architect of an impressive downtown project for Cleveland.

Like many city planners in the 1970s and early 1980s, Campanella preferred to build a large domed facility that could be used by the Browns, Indians, and Cavaliers every day of the year. He had visited the Silverdome in suburban Detroit and realized that a dome would allow Cleveland to host the Super Bowl. He even had a small model dome in his office to show to visitors.

Campanella's staff examined a number of downtown locations for a new stadium, before suggesting the Central Market area—a large tract of land at the southern edge of the city. Campanella took time to walk about the site before approving it. He dreamed of building a Rapid Transit station, which would allow visitors to fly into Cleveland, take a train downtown, and enter the dome without ever walking outdoors.

Campanella also was close to Art Modell, an influential player in Republican politics. Even though Modell's lease in Cleveland Stadium ran until 1998, he was willing to move into a brand-new dome as long as two conditions were met. First, he wanted at least 70,000 seats. Second, he insisted that the county repay his Stadium Corporation the $12 million Modell estimated he had spent renovating old Cleveland Stadium. "There is no question the city of Cleveland desperately needs a magnet, something to attract people downtown," Modell said. "A domed stadium, which has served that purpose elsewhere, will do the same thing for Cleveland." [19]

With Modell's support assured, Campanella proposed raising $150 million by asking the voters for an increase in the county's property tax for the next 25 years. He then aggressively lobbied the two other commissioners—Democrat Tim Hagan and Republican Virgil Brown—to place the issue on the May 8, 1984 primary ballot. Hagan agreed to do so, even though he thought Campanella had been captivated by Art Modell. [20] Campanella knew it would be difficult to win voter approval. During a private lunch at a Murray Hill restaurant, stadium architect Ron Labinski warned Campanella, "If this passes the first time, it will be the fastest stadium that ever went up." [21]

Any chance Campanella had of winning quickly evaporated. Mayor George Voinovich was appalled by the idea. He thought Campanella was foolishly asking taxpayers to shoulder the entire burden. He pleaded with Campanella to drop the property tax or, at the very least, secure a commitment from Cleveland business executives to assume half the cost. Only a month before the vote, Campanella signed a nonbinding agreement that the county would attempt to raise $75 million from private sources. Voinovich announced he would back the dome, but his support was half-hearted.

The other major political heavyweight, Richard F. Celeste, was hostile to the property tax and believed the commissioners had failed to build the necessary public support for the project. When Campanella heard Celeste's opposition, he knew the project was dead.

Except for Tim Hagan, not one major Democratic official in Cleveland supported the dome. Although Celeste insisted he wanted a new stadium for Cleveland, it also was clear that he intended to deliver a punishing political blow to Campanella. Mary Boyle, a member of the Ohio House of Representatives and a close friend of Celeste's, was challenging Campanella for election that fall. If Boyle defeated Campanella, she would have eliminated a major rival for Celeste in 1986. "The governor's opposition is purely politics," wrote Joe Rice of the *Plain Dealer*. [22]

Celeste and Voinovich disgusted Tim Hagan. He thought the governor had "sandbagged" Campanella for partisan gain, and that Voinovich "took a walk on us." Hagan campaigned hard, but he knew the effort was in vain. [23]

On election night, as voters defeated the issue by a 2-to-1 margin, Tim Hagan avoided reporters. It fell to a grim-faced Campanella to meet supporters at Stouffer's Inn on the Square, and declare, "The people decided they did not want this particular issue in the form it was presented. But I think the people in this community want public officials to assert some leadership, and I intend to do just that."

He never got the chance. The vote on the tax was a repudiation of his leadership. That fall, even as President Ronald Reagan rolled to a massive victory in Ohio, voters replaced Vincent Campanella with Mary Boyle. Campanella said there was no question he lost his seat because of his support for the dome. But he was convinced the idea would survive.

The Indians were beginning to worry George Voinovich. Although the Republican mayor was friends with the owners of the Indians, he was a casual baseball fan who only attended the obligatory Opening Day. He preferred detailed discussions on welfare reform and revenue sharing to the latest box scores. But he was shrewd enough to know that losing the Indians would be a catastrophe for Cleveland, and for George Voinovich.

Since his election as mayor in 1979, Voinovich had earned the reputation of a cautious executive who worked behind the scenes to secure consensus on controversial issues rather than taking flamboyant stands. As a Republican, Voinovich was welcome in the boardrooms of every major Cleveland corporation. But he also worked hard to develop political alliances with the city's most powerful Democrats, including City Council President George Forbes, City Councilman Mike White, Hagan, and Boyle. Hagan thought that Voinovich, more than anyone, ended the ceaseless confrontations among Cleveland public officials.

Voinovich had spent almost his entire life in Cleveland. He had earned a law degree from Ohio State in 1961, and served as a state assistant attorney general during the first term of Republican Governor James Rhodes. Then he returned to his hometown, where he was elected to the Ohio House of Representatives in 1967. From there, he won election after election: Auditor of Cuyahoga County in 1971; county commissioner in 1977; lieutenant governor in 1978.

His stay in Columbus was brief because, in 1979, alarmed business executives in Cleveland pleaded with him to return home and challenge Democratic Mayor Dennis Kucinich in the next election. Kucinich, elected as a brash boy wonder in 1975, had proved to be a failure. Kucinich enjoyed a fight, and his targets were big businesses, utility companies, and banks. His administration became a nationwide joke, and the city in 1978 was forced to default on its loans. Huge companies that had been in Cleveland for decades fled to the suburbs or the Sun Belt, and the city's population sagged from its postwar peak of nearly one million in 1950 to less than 600,000.

Voinovich easily defeated Kucinich in what was then a largely Democratic city. He pledged a new cooperative spirit and asked the major companies to pitch in and help. Voinovich quickly balanced the city's budget and presided over a major reconstruction of Cleveland's decaying downtown. More than $2 billion in new investment poured into the city, as massive office towers were erected on Public Square and East 9th Street. But those gains, Voinovich knew, would be jeopardized by the loss of the Indians. Voinovich held long talks with Baseball Commissioner Bowie Kuhn and American League President Bobby Brown. The rest of the American League owners, they told Voinovich, had lost their patience with Cleveland. They were fed up with playing before crowds of 5,000 in old Cleveland Stadium, losing money every time they came to town. Being in major league baseball was the same as being a member of a country club, they explained. There were dues to pay. The owners, they said, wanted the team to sell thousands more season tickets and were convinced such an increase would be possible only in a smaller park. With its vast size, Cleveland Stadium offered no incentive for anyone to buy a season ticket. People in downtown Cleveland on a July evening knew perfectly well they could walk down to the stadium and find a seat.

Kuhn and Brown never threatened to move the team, but Voinovich got the message anyway. For a time, he heard little else. He once hosted a cocktail party for some of the baseball owners during a Cleveland Browns' playoff game. Instead of talking football, the owners nagged Voinovich: "When are you going to do something? We're getting a little tired of this." [24]

Others were talking of a new stadium. Robert Corna, an architect from Westlake, proposed building a six-sided domed sports facility called the Hexatron. Among those intrigued by the odd-looking stadium was Jeff Jacobs, a member of the Ohio House of Representatives and Dick Jacobs' son. Jeff Jacobs suggested that a "sin tax" on cigarettes and beer could finance the project and proposed building it just off Lake Erie near City Hall. But to Voinovich, the whole project was out of the question. On April 23, 1985, Voinovich killed it, writing to Corna that the project would interfere with plans to develop the lakefront. [25]

George Voinovich had other ideas.

George Voinovich and Richard F. Celeste were not close politically, but they joined to support business executives and politicians who had formed a group known as the Greater Cleveland Domed Stadium Corporation. The impressive group was headed by Allen Holmes, the managing partner of the Cleveland law firm of Jones, Day, Reavis & Pogue, one of the largest in the nation. The corporation included representatives from the Indians, Browns, county board of commissioners, and executives from Cleveland's largest companies.

To direct the daily operations of the domed corporation, Holmes chose Dennis Lafferty, the 36-year-old vice president of government and community affairs at the Greater Cleveland

Growth Association. Lafferty, who never shed his harsh New York City accent despite living in Ohio for 20 years, established an office for the domed corporation in the Terminal Tower.

The corporation had two jobs: Decide what to build and where to put it. At a series of public hearings, suburban officials offered their own sites. But Lafferty and the domed corporation wanted to build downtown. They considered three sites, including two on the east side of downtown. But like Vince Campanella, they were attracted to the Central Market in the downtown's southern corner. During one meeting of the corporation at the National City Bank, Voinovich pointed out the window toward the Central Market and said, "It's got to be over in that area." [26]

The area was once the liveliest section of downtown, where just after the turn of the century thousands of people gathered to buy fresh meat and vegetables at two open-air markets on Sheriff Street. Just across the street was the Haymarket, the city's first slum, where Italian and Slavic immigrants crammed into brick tenements and rough boat men had their pick of saloons. One block north on Sheriff Street, fashionably dressed crowds flocked to Mark Hanna's Opera House, before finishing the evening with a drink at Otto Moser's Cafe. There, they could dine with the great stars who played on the Cleveland stage: W.C. Fields, Fanny Brice, and the Barrymores.

By the time Voinovich pointed out the window, the theater crowds were gone, the opera house had long since vanished. Except for the markets, the area was a sea of decrepit buildings and parking lots. Even so, the obstacles to assembling the 30 acres needed for a stadium were enormous. The city of Cleveland owned about six acres, but 60 other people owned the rest, and many were reluctant to move. Lafferty's group changed their minds with money, connections, and ingenuity. They borrowed $18 million from the city banks and convinced Celeste to hand over money from the state treasury. Voinovich agreed to find a new east side site for the owners of the Central Market. The Coast Guard, which owned a small piece of the land, swapped it for another piece of city-owned land on the west side. By late 1986, the corporation had control of more than 80 percent of the land.

Initially, they wanted to build a dome that would keep the Indians, Browns, and Cavaliers under one roof. They opted for a 70,000-seat facility that could be reconfigured to 40,000 seats during baseball season. With a retractable roof, the facility would cost at least $125 million. Unlike Campanella, they pledged to build the facility with a large infusion of private money. Lafferty flew to Toronto to meet with the planners of the Skydome, a new stadium with a retractable roof. He was horrified when designers told him the Toronto stadium's pricetag would exceed $400 million. Lafferty glumly returned to Cleveland and told board members, "It doesn't look like it's feasible for us." [27]

The Indians, meanwhile, were growing cool to playing under a dome. Pat O'Neill had been a key member of the domed corporation, but when he sold the team to Dick and David Jacobs in the summer of 1986, the team's attitude changed. It quickly became clear to Lafferty that Jacobs was more interested in an open-air, baseball-only park. Without a firm commitment from the Indians, the domed corporation's work could not proceed. Finally, on November 2, 1987, Dick Jacobs made public what Lafferty had suspected: The Indians would move to the Central Market, but only in a small, intimate ballpark. Real grass. No dome.

Tom Chema was making his rounds. He needed all his legal and negotiating skills to contend with the business and political rivalries that flourished even in the post-Kucinich age of Cleveland. He needed to forge an agreement between Mayor-elect Mike White and Tim Hagan, who competed with White for office. Chema had to convince Hagan and Boyle, who detested each other, to cooperate. Chema also would have to win the support of Dick Jacobs and Art Modell, whose interests were in sharp conflict. Finally, Chema would have to convince a public that was suspicious of tax increases to invest its money in a new ballpark.

He started with Mike White, who never had shown interest in a new ballpark. During the domed stadium campaign of 1984, White denounced the project as a "sports palace for the Republican privileged." [28] A year later, he told a Cleveland civic group that while a dome was "exotic," he placed greater emphasis on developing Cleveland's lakefront. He confided to Tom Chema, "Look, I'm not the greatest sports fan in the world. I think it's good that the Indians are here. But, it's not something that's visceral to me."

But without White's support, Chema's plan for a new stadium was doomed. Two days after White's election, Tom Chema visited him and explained the governor's proposal. What, Chema asked White, could you support? "I'm interested in an economic development project," White replied. "If you can show me that this makes sense from an economic development point of view in Cleveland, you'll have my support." [29] It was the same argument William Hopkins made half-a-century earlier when he contended the stadium would be one part of the huge downtown Mall.

White's comments cracked open a door. Clearly he would support a new ballpark under the right circumstances. But Chema was in a quandary. Even he realized that few permanent jobs would be created by moving the Indians from one downtown site to another. To be sure, there would be thousands of construction jobs. But they would vanish when the stadium was completed.

To Chema, the only possibility was to build a large indoor arena for basketball, ice hockey, and shows. Chema calculated that an indoor arena packed with nightly events would draw an additional 2.5 million people downtown every year. They would spend their money downtown for dinner, parking, and tickets to the arena, and satisfy White's demand that the project provide a long-term boost to Cleveland. Although Chema candidly admitted that adding the arena took "one tough project and made it one humongous and tougher project," he felt he had no choice. White would not support the ballpark without the arena, and White's support was crucial.

The drawback, however, was just as obvious. The Cavaliers were playing in the first-rate facility Nick Mileti had created just 15 years earlier. Although the Richfield Coliseum's luxury boxes were poorly situated, nobody could make the argument that the arena was obsolete. Moreover, the arena was providing hundreds of thousands of dollars in tax revenue to Summit County. Akron city officials would furiously object and launch a bitter battle with Cleveland.

But Chema became convinced the Cavaliers would switch. Chema believed the arena was built in the wrong spot. Few people from the west side of Cleveland made the lengthy drive to Richfield. Chema knew from experience that downtown business people in Cleveland had to leave their offices before five in the afternoon to see the opening tip-off in Richfield. Two freeways serviced the Coliseum, but the tiny country roads nearby always were choked with cars. The arena did not attract any new development; not one hotel or restaurant had opened in the area.

While Chema knew that the owners of the Cavaliers, the Gund brothers, were reaping large profits in Richfield, he concluded they had little prospect of making substantially more money in the future. The Cavaliers would draw crowds while they were winning, but if the team slipped in the standings, few people in Cleveland were going to drive down Interstate 271 to buy tickets.

Armed with those arguments, Chema approached Richard Watson, legal counsel for the Cavaliers. Watson was intrigued by the move. "You show us how we're going to be at least as well off economically as we are now," Watson told Chema. [30]

Tim Hagan was eager to build a stadium. Unlike Mike White, Hagan was a serious baseball fan. He paid close attention to the Indians and took in night games at the stadium. He was well aware of the stadium's defects, complaining that during a rain storm, baseball fans could never be certain whether "it was rainwater or urine falling on them as they walked out."

Unlike Voinovich and Celeste, Hagan was not convinced the American League would abandon Cleveland and the 13th largest market in the country. Hagan also doubted that Dick Jacobs would agree to sell the Indians to an out-of-town syndicate. Jacobs, Hagan reasoned, had invested hundreds of millions of dollars in downtown Cleveland. For Jacobs to allow the Indians to leave would be the same as driving the final nail in downtown Cleveland's coffin, Hagan thought.

Hagan, however, believed a new ballpark would be a badly needed stimulus for the downtown. Cleveland was known to the country as a city that couldn't pay its bills and whose rivers caught on fire. A brand-new baseball park would lure people downtown and provide a powerful symbol to the country that Cleveland was reviving itself. Hagan also thought it would satisfy former Ohio governor James Rhodes' chief rule of politics— "Show 'em something for their tax dollars."

The problem was that nobody in Cleveland regarded Tim Hagan as a consensus builder. Even in the contentious political environment of Cleveland, Tim Hagan stood out as blunt and divisive. Although a Democrat, he opposed Senator John Glenn's

1984 presidential bid and could barely conceal his disdain for Richard F. Celeste. Hagan himself conceded: "I'm known to be somewhat erratic." Hagan constantly griped that Dick Jacobs was demanding too much from the county in return for building a new stadium, and once quipped that it would be nice if Mother Teresa owned the Indians. During one meeting at Jacobs' office, Hagan finally lost all patience. As a startled Mike White and Tom Chema looked on, Hagan snapped at Jacobs and his partners, "You pigs." After a moment of embarrassed silence, Jacobs replied, "Maybe we can call this deal off."

"Let me tell you something," Hagan exploded. "You want to call this deal off? You think you'd win in the public against me? Call a press conference right now. Let's see who wins that deal." Hagan then stormed out of the meeting. [31]

Hagan also had a long political rivalry with White. In 1989, Hagan, White, and George Forbes, the powerful president of Cleveland City Council, had all run for mayor. Hagan hoped that Forbes and White would split the black vote and allow him to win. But he finished third, leaving White and Forbes to compete in a runoff.

But in Cleveland politics, there are no permanent enemies, just temporary allies. A few days after the election, Hagan asked White about a new stadium. "If we're going to do this, you've got to be with us," Hagan told the mayor-elect. "You've got to be a co-chair with me." White repeated what he already told Tom Chema: "I want to make sure we get the Cavaliers downtown as part of the deal."

Bringing the Cavaliers into the city appealed to Hagan, as it did to Chema. He had always thought that Nick Mileti made a terrible mistake by taking the team out to what Hagan derided as "that cornfield in Richfield." Putting a new ballpark and basketball arena next to each other in the Central Market would mean four million people entering the downtown each year. Hagan thought he could sell that to the voters.

Tom Chema conducted three rounds of meetings with Cleveland's business and political elite. During the first round, he politely asked if they wanted to build a ballpark. In the second round, he relayed suggestions that had been offered during the first round of talks. By December 1989, he was back for the third time, asking if they would support an open-air ballpark and an indoor basketball arena. One Cleveland pollster joked that Chema was a match for Henry Kissinger and his shuttle diplomacy.

Relying in large part on the proposals created by Lafferty's committee, Chema proposed building the two facilities in the Central Market. Public officials would raise half the money through a sales tax, while the owners of the Indians and Cavaliers would provide the other half. All he had to do was sell the taxpayers, Indians, and Cavaliers on the concept.

The teams should have been easy. But Chema discovered, as Cleveland city officials learned to their chagrin, that negotiations with Dick Jacobs were never easy. Jacobs would not even participate in early discussions, allowing his subordinates to engage in the negotiations. Only when both sides were at a stalemate would Jacobs summon everyone to his office in the Erieview Tower. Sternly, Jacobs would lecture Chema, Hagan, and White that "this is the way it's got to be. You guys are not living up to your word. You guys are putting it to me. What do you have against me?" Chema eventually concluded that Dick Jacobs enjoyed hardball negotiations and thrived on getting his way, whether it was over $500 or $500 million. [32]

Not until the spring of 1990 did the Indians and Cavaliers officially sign an agreement with Chema. The public would contribute half the estimated cost of $344 million for a 45,000-seat stadium and 20,000-seat arena. Chema also insisted that the teams manage the facilities and that taxpayers not be handed an annual bill to cover operating deficits. The rest would be raised by the teams through the sale and rental of luxury loges and club seats in the two facilities. The Indians would provide $20 million at the very beginning and nearly $3 million annually for the capital costs of construction.

Chema's options for finding tax money for the project were limited. A property tax was out of the question. So too was a county-wide sales tax. Voters would reject both out-of-hand. Chema turned to an idea originally suggested in 1985 by Jeffrey Jacobs as a way to finance the Hexatron—a sin tax on cigarettes and alcohol.

The Ohio legislature in 1986 authorized Cuyahoga County to impose a sin tax, but with so many restrictions that the tax raised only $7 million a year instead of the $15 million Chema needed. Chema turned for help to Richard F. Celeste, who pushed a bill through the legislature that would allow county officials to tax beer and wine at the retail level.

Chema had one final obstacle: Approval of the tax by the voters. Supporters of the project were sharply divided on when to spring it on voters: In the May primary, at a special election they would call in August, or the regular November election. Those who favored waiting argued that younger people were more likely to vote in November than in May. Primaries, they warned, were dominated by older voters, who distrusted tax increases.

But Chema pressed for what he called an early surgical strike. He thought voters could be quickly persuaded to support the project, but their enthusiasm might wane if they waited throughout the summer. In addition, Chema had to sell the bonds by year's end to take advantage of expiring federal tax breaks; a November election would make that virtually impossible. Bob Dykes, a Cleveland pollster who served as an adviser to the campaign, backed Chema. Why give opponents a chance to organize and defeat the project? "The longer we wait," Dykes said, "the more time we give them to coalesce." [33]

The county commissioners—Boyle, Hagan, and Republican Virgil Brown— agreed to a May election. Selecting a name originally suggested by the Greater Cleveland Domed Stadium Corporation, they called the campaign Gateway. Now Chema, Hagan, and White needed an experienced professional to run the campaign. They turned to Oliver Henkel.

Pudge Henkel, as his close friends called him, knew how to manage a campaign: He nearly guided Senator Gary Hart to the 1984 Democratic presidential nomination. He knew the right people: His law firm represented Jacobs-Visconsi-Jacobs. And he knew sports. As a boy in Mansfield, he was an all-state quarterback and such a skilled golfer that at age 16 he defeated young Jack Nicklaus in a golf tournament.

In the early 1980s, Pudge Henkel was a partner at Jones, Day, Reavis & Pogue, earned well in excess of $100,000 a year, and, with his wife Sally, bought a beautiful suburban home. But he gave up his law practice to manage the presidential campaign of Yale Law School classmate Gary Hart. Although Democratic pollster Pat Caddell denounced Henkel as "an amateur," Henkel directed Hart to a stunning second-place finish in the 1984 Iowa caucuses and an upset victory in the New Hampshire primary. With little money and haphazard organization, Hart nearly took the nomination from former vice president Walter F. Mondale.

By the time Chema was putting together the stadium project, Henkel was back in Cleveland practicing law. In the winter of 1990, his old friend Tim Hagan asked him if he would chair the campaign to win Gateway. Henkel enthusiastically agreed. He was close enough to the Jacobs brothers to realize how precarious the Indians' finances were. As far as he could determine, no team in the American League lost as much money annually as the Indians. He was convinced that without a new facility, the team was "on the verge" of leaving Cleveland. [34]

The campaign began with a myriad of advantages. The corporate community would raise $1 million, and opponents had no chance to match that amount. Gateway supporters could afford to produce clever commercials and blanket the area with literature. And, except for Democratic Congressman Louis Stokes, virtually every public official in Greater Cleveland supported the project. That meant the opposition would be disorganized.

But Dykes' surveys showed the issue losing by a substantial margin. It was clear people were not eager to pay more taxes, and they certainly did not want to pay for just a stadium. That led organizers to adopt the slogan, "More than a Stadium." The campaign would hammer home the point that the sin tax would help finance a stadium and arena that would provide a major boost to the downtown.

From the very beginning, Henkel and Dykes wanted Mike White to appear in the television commercials. Dykes' surveys showed that white voters in the suburbs liked White, and were anxious for White to succeed. They produced a commercial with White standing on a rooftop near the Central Market, pointing to the spot where the stadium and arena would be built.

When the opponents—who included the United Auto Workers and Dennis Kucinich—complained that the sin tax was regressive and would fall heavily on the poor, Henkel and Dykes had ready answers. The tax would add 4.5 cents to a pack of cigarettes and less than two cents to a glass of beer. "If you drink a beer a day for 365 days, it would cost you seven bucks," Tim Hagan said publicly. In private, he characterized the opposition's arguments as "bullshit." [35] They also pointed to the benefits of the project: 11,600 construction jobs and 17,000 permanent jobs. Mike White liked to remind inner city blacks, "We're bringing two million people with their wallets in their pockets into the middle of the city. Don't tell me I'm hurting the poor."

The campaign unfolded in nearly flawless fashion. Day after day, Henkel, Hagan, and White arranged for a series of county officials and organizations to endorse the project: Ohio Attorney General Anthony J. Celebrezze, Jr; City Council President Jay Westbrook; U.S. Rep. Edward Feighan; the AFL-CIO. Voinovich appeared at a press conference with Hagan and White to announce his support.

In the final days, the campaign orchestrated its most powerful message. Westbrook invited Baseball Commissioner Fay Vincent to appear before a city council finance committee. In clear language, Vincent warned that if voters defeated the sin tax, he would probably give the owners of the Indians permission to move the team to another city. Vincent suggested that the Indians might satisfy the four conditions he had established before granting permission for a team to move: If the team were losing money, had weak attendance, a poor stadium, and had lost the support of the community. "Should this facility not be available in Cleveland, should the vote be a negative one, we may be finding ourselves confronting a subject that we want to avoid," Vincent said. Vincent had done what Gateway organizers had been reluctant to do: Threaten Cleveland with the loss of its team.

The message was getting through. Dykes' surveys showed that once voters were persuaded that the tax was small and the benefits large, they tended to support it. A sizable number of east side suburban voters could be counted on to vote for it. His tracking polls, conducted every other day, showed momentum building for the project. But only on one night did the tracking polls show the issue winning. Moreover, voters in the city and the west side neighborhoods of Parma and Brook Park were not swayed. John Coyne, chairman of the Cuyahoga County Democratic Party, worried: "You can't get some of these areas to vote for their own school issues." [36]

❖

Neither Hagan nor Chema was very confident the morning of the vote. Like a good lawyer, Chema believed he had presented the best case. It reminded him of concluding his final argument at trial and waiting for the jury to return with the verdict. He knew that even when he offered the jury solid evidence to support his case, he still might lose. Whatever the verdict, though, it was out of his hands.

That morning, Chema passed out Gateway literature to voters in the suburbs of University Heights and Garfield Heights. Then he took time to vote in Shaker Heights, before driving downtown to his law office in the Huntington Building. By 11 in the morning, Chema was hearing alarming reports: voter turnout was extremely heavy. To Chema, that meant one thing. Older voters, suspicious of new taxes, were turning out in droves to vote down Gateway. It was one of the few times during the campaign that Chema miscalculated. Large numbers of young people were going to the polls; they wanted to make Cleveland a better place to live, and they believed Gateway was the solution.

Others were reading the returns more optimistically. Voinovich boarded a flight that morning for a gubernatorial campaign trip to Cincinnati. A number of business executives told Voinovich they almost missed the flight because they had to take time to vote. Later in the afternoon, while driving from Cincinnati to Columbus, Voinovich telephoned Mike White to tell him, "You're going to win." [37]

As he waited for the polls to close, Chema joined Mary Boyle and his staff for dinner in the British Petroleum building. Early returns filtered in, and by eight that night, the issue was losing by 3,000 votes. What Hagan and Chema suspected was true: city voters were rejecting Gateway. They would have to wait for the suburban vote later that night.

Hagan and White were meeting across Public Square in a suite at the Sheraton Hotel. For Hagan, this day meant more than just a stadium. If voters turned down Gateway, there would never be another effort to save the Indians. Word had circulated throughout Cleveland that Hagan had agreed to support the project in return for a promise from county officials that he would face token opposition for re-election. But Hagan was certain that if the issue failed, he and White "would have been history" politically.

Bob Dykes watched the returns at the county board of elections. Although early returns from the city wards and Parma showed Gateway losing, Dykes calculated the campaign had kept its losses to a minimum in those areas. "Look, we haven't seen Rocky River, Beachwood, and Solon," he told associates. "We're going to win this thing."

From all across the eastern suburbs of Shaker Heights, Euclid, and Beachwood, thousands of people were supporting the sin tax. Republican County Chairman Robert Hughes predicted shortly after 10 that the issue would win. A half-hour later, Chema was convinced as well. He telephoned Richard F. Celeste at the governor's mansion in Columbus. "We've won," Chema told the governor. "All of the city votes are in, and the outer suburbs are coming in the way we thought they were going to come in." Celeste replied, "Well Chema, it's a damn good thing we did, because your ass was on the line." [38]

An ebullient Hagan joined Mike White at a victory party in the British Petroleum building, where they donned sunglasses and did a Blues Brothers imitation for well-wishers. Then the huge crowd filtered out, and the television crews packed up their cameras and left. Chema's wife took one of their cars and drove home. Bob Dykes and his wife also went home, where he sat by himself and sipped a congratulatory drink.

But Tom Chema was not ready for sleep. He drove down to Dpoo's in the flats. Ahead of him was a year of tough negotiations with Dick Jacobs on a long-term lease, petty squabbles with the two teams over construction of Gateway, and a funding gap that had to be closed. But none of that mattered on this night. Tom Chema ordered a drink. It was fun, he thought, to win.

Chapter 11

Where Did It All Go Wrong?

"If [Dick Jacobs] makes the Indians one of the major priorities of his time, the Indians will be a winning team."
— Sheldon Guren

On an unusually cool, clear fall afternoon in 1993, Al Rosen returned to Cleveland. Four decades after he watched Vic Wertz hit his mammoth drive to center field in the Polo Grounds, Rosen donned his old Indians' uniform and stood near homeplate for the final time in Cleveland Stadium. The Indians were playing their last game in the stadium and had invited a number of their great players from the past: Mel Harder, sprightly and active at age 82; portly Bob Lemon, who jogged slowly to the pitcher's mound; and silver-haired Bob Feller, who enthusiastically waved his cap to the vast crowd of 72,390.

The Indians hoped to create some nostalgia for the relic they were leaving in favor of a new ballpark of glistening steel and brick on the other side of downtown. Bob Hope, who entertained another huge crowd in the same stadium in 1947, returned to his hometown to sing "Thanks for the Memories." The radio talk show hosts reminisced about Cleveland Stadium. But the crowd was not fooled; when asked to pick a song appropriate to the moment, the fans chose a 1965 hit by the rock group Animals—"We Gotta Get Out Of This Place." What Al Rosen once described as "this terrible period of Cleveland baseball" was coming to an end.

When Al Rosen was in his 20s, few teams played with the skill of the Cleveland Indians. They crushed most of their opponents, engaged in titanic struggles with the New York Yankees, and won two pennants during a decade of remarkable baseball success. Players did not regard a trade to Cleveland as the equivalent of being sent to San Quentin. Mickey Mantle looked upon the huge crowds in Cleveland Stadium with awe. The Indians negotiated lucrative television contracts, created a farm system without equal, and reaped huge profits.

Where Did It All Go Wrong?

Their collapse was rapid. By 1957, the Indians fell to sixth place and attendance slipped so sharply that Minneapolis and Houston tried to lure the Indians away. By 1960, the Indians ceased to be a contending baseball team and would not challenge for an American League pennant for the next three decades. Although William R. Daley complained about the disloyalty of Cleveland baseball fans, it is difficult to imagine residents of another city supporting such an inept product. Six times during the 1980s, the Indians attracted more than one million customers to their home games to watch a team that was never in contention. "I think," former *Cleveland Press* reporter Bob Sudyk said, "one of the miracles of baseball is that the team survived."

Where had it all gone wrong? Bad trades? Nobody could deny that the Cleveland front office orchestrated some ghastly deals. Frank Lane's decision to send Rocky Colavito to Detroit had catastrophic consequences for the Indians. But every successful general manager has approved a disastrous trade or two. To claim that one trade resulted in the 40-year collapse of a baseball franchise is absurd. Bad luck? Herb Score's eye injury; Tony Horton's illness, and the tragic deaths of pitchers Steve Olin and Tim Crews in a 1993 Florida boating accident. It is beyond dispute that Cleveland had its share of tragedies, but the New York Yankees survived the death of catcher Thurman Munson in an airplane crash. A curse? For years, Cleveland writers retold the fable that Bobby Bragan cursed the team when Frank Lane fired him in 1958. Peter Bavasi even jokingly asked Bragan to return to Cleveland and lift the spell. "I didn't put any curse on it," Bragan said. "I went away quietly." [1]

There is no mystery to the disintegration of the Cleveland franchise. As Gabe Paul once said, sports teams don't lose games and money by accident. They do so because of bad decisions by the owners and front office. The Cleveland Indians lost during the past 40 years for the same reason the Philadelphia Phillies and St. Louis Browns lost half-a-century ago: They were too poorly financed to produce a winning product. From the time Hank Greenberg was fired in 1957 until Dick Jacobs bought the team in 1986, the men who owned the Indians did not put enough money into the franchise to win. Vernon Stouffer, Nick Mileti, and Ted Bonda wanted to spend money, but could not afford to. William Daley could have, but did not. Steve O'Neill might have, but he insisted upon resolving the lease dispute with Art Modell first. Without ownership willing to commit major financial resources, the Indians never had a chance to field a contending team. The collapse of the farm system is almost entirely due to lack of money. Baseball teams before the era of free agency could not succeed without a productive player development system. Nate Dolin liked to describe the players in the Cleveland minor league system as inventory and the "only way your business grows is with inventory." [2]

The Indians, Yankees, Dodgers, and Giants were successful throughout the 1950s because they spent lavishly on player development. The casual fan may believe that slick trades create winners, but all the great dynasties of baseball—from the Yankees of the 1930s to the Cincinnati Reds of the 1970s—were built through intelligent front-office decisions, shrewd scouting, and a commitment to player development. "Scouting is the most important thing in baseball," said Bob Kennedy, who signed pitchers Sam McDowell and Tommy John. [3]

When players won the right to become free agents, many baseball operators—including Ted Bonda— rushed to spend millions for proven stars. They pointed to George Steinbrenner's success with the Yankees in 1977 and 1978, teams dominated by free agents Reggie Jackson, Rich Gossage, and Catfish Hunter. But the Yankees proved to be the exception rather than the rule. The Atlanta Braves, Toronto Blue Jays, Kansas City Royals, Pittsburgh Pirates, and Minnesota Twins won in the 1980s because they developed their own key players. The Braves won consecutive National League pennants in 1991 and 1992 with players their own scouts discovered—pitchers Tom Glavine, Steve Avery, Kent Mercker, and Mike Stanton; outfielders Ronnie Gant and Dave Justice; and infielders Jeff Blauser and Mark Lemke. Without an adequate minor league system, the Indians were forced to adopt a risky formula: Trading established players for a large crop of young, unproven prospects, hoping a few would grow to stardom. Such an approach is fraught with danger. As Hank Peters said, "Quantity never replaces quality." [4]

It is easy to blame Gabe Paul and Phil Seghi for the failures of the team, but the facts suggest they had little chance of winning with what they had. Paul, in fact, proved with the Yankees that given a strong financial situation, he could win. He never had that luxury in Cleveland. Nor should the parade of Indian managers be held responsible for Cleveland's horrendous teams. "A manager is no better than his players," Leo Durocher would say. "If you haven't got the talent, you can go home." [5] In that sense, Frank Robinson, Jeff Torborg, John McNamara, Birdie Tebbetts, Jimmie Dykes, Johnny Lipon, and Ken Aspromonte were doomed to fail before they managed their first game in Cleveland. A manager can win a few extra games with clever strategy. But no amount of managerial brilliance could have overcome the lack of playing talent in Cleveland from 1960 through 1990.

Those who shoulder the blame are the team owners who refused to act like businessmen when the business was baseball. The primary reason to be in business is to show a profit, but most owners of the Indians approached their task as if some heavy civic responsibility had been thrust upon them. Their objectives were limited to keeping the team in Cleveland and holding the annual losses to a minimum. In that sense, William R. Daley bears a particular responsibility. From the moment he assumed direction of the board in 1956, the Indians slashed spending on a farm system that had provided stockholders with winning teams and large profits. The Cleveland minor league system deteriorated so rapidly that when Hank Peters arrived in 1966, he discovered no more than half a dozen prospects. Vernon Stouffer delivered the final blow in 1970 when he demanded deep cuts in the scouting department instead of selling the ballclub. Prominent businessmen who made millions by packaging and marketing their own products somehow failed to take the same approach with the Indians. "A baseball team is a commercial venture, operating for a profit," Bill Veeck wrote. "The idea that you don't have to package your product as attractively as General Motors packages its product, and hustle your product the way General Motors hustles its product, is baseball's most pernicious enemy." [6] More than anything, the Indians illustrate the point that there is nothing worse than a businessman who behaves like a philanthropist.

The most critical blow was not the trade of Rocky Colavito or the eye injury to Herb Score, but the firing of Hank Greenberg in 1957. Hank Greenberg created the powerful Cleveland Indians of the 1950s. But Daley and the Big Seven, alarmed that the Cleveland newspapers and fans were unhappy, fired Greenberg, rolled the dice and hired Frank Lane. The story that the Big Seven fired Greenberg because he wanted to move the team is a fairy tale. The team's lease prohibited a transfer from Cleveland Stadium, and Greenberg never had the votes to move the team.

Contrary to the belief of Gordon Cobbledick and the other Cleveland sportswriters, the Indians in 1957 were not decaying. The team's strength throughout the 1950s—starting pitching—was decimated in 1957 by injuries to Bob Lemon and Herb Score. Had Lemon and Score been healthy, the Indians would have finished second that year to the Yankees. As poorly as they played that year, just six more victories would have propelled the Indians from sixth to third place. Even without Score and Lemon, Daley and the Big Seven should have recognized the team would rebound in 1958. They had a steady flow of young, talented players—Rocky Colavito, Roger Maris, Jim Grant, Jim Perry, Gary Bell, Gordy Coleman, Ron Taylor, Dick Stigman, Bud Daley, Hank Aguirre and Steve Hamilton. Combined with veterans Early Wynn, Cal McLish, Don Mossi, and Al Smith, those younger players would have made the Indians consistent contenders through 1965, and likely pennant winners in 1959, 1961, and 1962. Instead, the Big Seven hired Frank Lane—the wrong man to direct the wrong team at the wrong time. Though Daley and Dolin were astonished when Lane traded Rocky Colavito, he was running true to form. Frank Lane shook up a team that needed only a steady hand, and his reckless decisions haunted the team for years.

But what is not often recognized is that Lane only accelerated a process that was inevitable. Colavito, Maris, and the other graduates of Hank Greenberg's farm system were aging by 1966, and the Indians' owners declined to develop younger replacements. In particular, Cleveland failed to produce hard-hitting outfielders and quality left-handed pitching—the hallmark of Hank Greenberg's system. The years of minor league cutbacks became evident at the major league level by 1967.

The Cleveland sportswriters also are due a share of the blame. Sportswriters are not responsible for putting teams on the field, but they do contribute to the atmosphere. For decades, Cleveland sportswriters have been a sour lot. Gordon Cobbledick was a brilliant reporter, and even today it's a joy to read his old columns, brimming with information. But for some unfathomable reason, Cobbledick, Whitey Lewis of the *Press*, and other Cleveland sportswriters detested Hank Greenberg and liked

Frank Lane. They universally believed the Indians in 1957 were on the point of collapse, and in that judgment they were wrong. They rarely encouraged the Indians to undertake the gradual—but productive—process of building a strong farm system. By 1980, Cleveland had every conceivable disadvantage—a bad team, weak finances, an inept farm system, an obsolete stadium, and a grouchy press corps.

The franchise was revived in the late 1980s when the Indians' owners began to act like the businessmen they were. Although he often has been dismissed in Cleveland as a feeble old man, Steve O'Neill deserves credit for pointing the franchise in the right direction. O'Neill was among the first to recognize that the Indians could not prosper as Art Modell's tenant. Had Steve O'Neill been 10 years younger when he bought the Indians, he very likely would have forced the city and county to help build a new ballpark. Richard Jacobs agreed with O'Neill's conclusions about a new ballpark. Jacobs had the energy and clout to get city, county, and state officials to face the reality that the Indians would eventually leave Cleveland without a new stadium. From the time he bought the team in 1986 to the opening of the new park in 1994, Jacobs operated with skill and determination to make a reality of Steve O'Neill's dream. When the Indians win, Dick Jacobs will deserve much of the credit.

So too will Hank Peters. Like Edward Bennett Williams, the Cleveland sports reporters wrote off Peters as tired and unimaginative. They denounced him as "clueless." But they failed to appreciate the enormity of the job handed to him in 1987; John Hart thought the Indians resembled an expansion franchise when he joined the team in 1988. Hank Peters created the organization that was so widely praised in 1994.

Others baseball executives, however, recognized the change in Cleveland. As he operated the San Francisco Giants in the late 1980s, Al Rosen could see the difference in the team for which he was once a star. "Dick Jacobs really has got his act together," Rosen said. "He's got a bright young executive in John Hart who's done a terrific job. And they've got a direction. I think there is a new era coming." [7]

On Opening Day 1994, Dick Jacobs threw a party in his suite at the newly christened Jacobs Field. President Bill Clinton attended, accompanied by White House national security adviser Anthony Lake, and the president's chief political consultant, James Carville. Clinton wore a Cleveland baseball cap and, to the cheers of the crowd, tossed out the first ball. Later as he mingled with the crowds in the luxury boxes, the president mentioned he was flying to Charlotte that night for the NCAA basketball finals between Duke and Arkansas. Bob Weber, a brash Republican attorney at Jones, Day, Reavis & Pogue, threw his arm around Clinton and joked, "Another tough day at the office." [8]

To share his triumphal moment, Jacobs invited allies and foes, men who had played a role in the Indians' stormy history: George Voinovich, who as governor of Ohio steered millions of state dollars to help build the stadium complex; Tom Chema, who sold the crucial tax increase to skeptical voters; Art Modell, whose Browns were no longer the city's No. 1 team; Ted Bonda, longing to trade places with Jacobs and run the Indians again; Senator Howard Metzenbaum, fresh from his attempt to revoke the owners' prized antitrust exemption; and Tim Hagan, one of the few people in Cleveland who had sworn at Dick Jacobs.

Others could not make it that afternoon. Gabe Paul, requiring the help of a walker, stayed at his condo just off Tampa Bay. But he watched closely, declaring once again that "Cleveland is a sleeping giant. I think that new ballpark will prove it." [9] Nate Dolin remained at his Rancho Mirage home with its mountain view perfectly framed by stately palms. Just down the street from Dolin, Al Rosen was at home, too, already complaining that he was bored with retirement. Sheldon Guren rented a loge on the third-base line of Jacobs Field, but gave his tickets to his daughter and son-in-law, preferring the warm Caribbean sun to the frigid winds of Cleveland. Bunny Goldfarb missed the game, but, as he drove past Jacobs Field to his Public Square office, he thought with sadness of the name that wasn't mentioned anywhere: his old friend Steve O'Neill. Goldfarb recalled the battles in 1983 after O'Neill declared war on Art Modell. O'Neill, he thought, "really began this project." [10]

Even on this day, Dick Jacobs had difficulty relaxing. Jacobs is a blunt business executive, so uncomfortable with small talk that he rarely makes the effort. The script called for Jacobs to deliver a three-minute speech at homeplate before the game, but he chopped that to 20 seconds. Grasping the microphone,

Jacobs simply asked the crowd, "Are you ready?" During the game, he broke away from his own party to sit in the bleachers. [11]

In the eight years since he and his brother bought the Indians, Dick Jacobs had emerged as the heavyweight of Cleveland business and politics. The ballpark bore his name, although Tom Chema saw to it that Jacobs had to pay $14 million for the privilege. The baseball park and basketball arena increased the value of the Indians from the $35 million Jacobs paid in 1986 to $100 million in 1994. [12] After covering operating losses of $6.8 million in 1990 and $4.8 million in 1991, Jacobs expected 1994 profits of between $1.5 million and $7 million; the anticipated home attendance of 3.1 million would generate $34 million in ticket sales. Instead of earning a paltry $25,000 from scoreboard advertising in Cleveland Stadium, Dick Jacobs' take of advertising in Jacobs Field would be $1.5 million. [13]

Like any good businessman, Dick Jacobs could project the future costs of running his team, thanks to some ingenuity and tough bargaining by John Hart. Other baseball owners guessed at their future expenses, but Dick Jacobs did not believe in guesswork. Many of the important players who took the field—outfielders Albert Belle and Kenny Lofton, third baseman Jim Thome, second baseman Carlos Baerga, first baseman Paul Sorrento, catcher Sandy Alomar, and pitchers Charles Nagy and Mark Clark—were tied to multi-year contracts. The players earned more money than other young players throughout baseball, and the Indians avoided unexpected arbitration awards that would obliterate their budget.

John Hart concocted the plan after the Indians were hammered financially by salary arbitration in the winter of 1991. Players with three full years of major league experience were eligible to take their contract disputes to an arbitrator, who had to pick either the club's offer or the salary the player sought. Compromise was not an option. In 1991, eight key Indians were eligible for arbitration, including pitchers Greg Swindell, Tom Candiotti, Eric King, and Doug Jones. Their demands were steep; Candiotti wanted his salary boosted from $1 million to $3 million, while Swindell asked for an increase from $840,000 to $2 million.

The arbitrators were heavily influenced by what other teams were paying players with similar major league experience. In February 1991, the Boston Red Sox established the market price by signing pitcher Roger Clemens to a four-year extension worth $21.5 million. Hart was flabbergasted by what he considered Boston's "irresponsible" action. Hart knew that if Clemens was worth $5 million per year, then arbitrators would hand the Cleveland pitchers more than the Indians wanted to pay. [14] There was a brutal arbitration hearing between Swindell's agent and the Indians' lawyers. It ended with a baseball arbitrator awarding Swindell $2 million for his 1990 record of 12 victories and 4.40 earned run average. His bargaining position undercut, Hart gave Eric King $1.45 million and handed Candiotti $2.5 million. Hart was beside himself; the payroll had climbed from $7.5 million in 1988 to a projected $18 million. [15] After settling with Candiotti in Chicago, Hart and Dan O'Dowd caught a plane back to Cleveland, and started to wrestle with the concept of fielding a winning team at a reasonable cost. "We've got to figure out a better way," Hart told O'Dowd. [16] Dick Jacobs demanded a halt; within a year the Indians traded or released Candiotti, King, Jones, and Swindell to cut the team's payroll to just $9.2 million in 1992. But Jacobs was not slashing his payroll blindly as so many of his predecessors had done. The millions saved would be plowed back into the franchise to finance Hart's revolutionary idea: Tie talented young Indians to attractive multi-year deals before they had been in the major leagues long enough to qualify for arbitration. In return for long-term financial security, the player would have to yield his first year of arbitration. "If it's about making the last dollar, then you'll play in New York," Hart told his players. "You won't get that in Cleveland. But you'll get more money than you'll ever need in your lifetime." In the spring of 1992, John Hart set about to implement his plan and focused on three key players—Sandy Alomar, Carlos Baerga, and Charles Nagy. [17]

Scott Boras had his doubts about Hart's plan. Boras, an attorney in Southern California, represented Baerga and Alomar and knew they could make more money than John Hart could offer. Boras was considered baseball's most demanding agent and his list of clients was a testament to his abilities: Pitchers Greg Maddux and Steve Avery of the Atlanta Braves, Jim Abbott of the New York Yankees, Alex Fernandez of the Chicago White Sox, and Ben McDonald of the Baltimore Orioles. Boras relied upon his own background as a one-time Cardinal minor leaguer to per-sonally scout young players in high school and college, guide them through the June draft, and win huge signing bonuses for them. The family of pitcher Brien Taylor of North Carolina told Boras they wanted $250,000 when the Yankees made him the No. 1 pick of the 1991 draft. Boras easily topped that. By threat-ening to send Taylor to college instead of signing with the Yan-kees, Boras won a record $1.55 million bonus from New York. Convinced that owners had the advantage during any salary ne-gotiation, Boras used arbitration as a handy tool to win big raises for his clients. He was confident of his ability to win at arbitration and thought players made a serious mistake to yield that power.

Boras admired John Hart as a shrewd judge of young talent, but felt the Indians wanted to tie up players for years at below-market prices. Boras also was annoyed with Hart's habit of trying to negotiate directly with Boras' clients instead of going through him. Hart, Boras believed, was taking advantage of the fact that many players personally liked the Cleveland general manager. [18]

Hart offered Alomar an attractive three-year deal: $500,000 for 1992, $1.3 million for 1993, $2.3 million for 1994, and a club option for 1995 at $3.3 million. Boras quickly recognized that Hart had not manufactured the numbers out of thin air; he had closely followed similar payments to another Boras client, catch-er Benito Santiago of San Diego, who had just won $3.3 million at arbitration. Boras advised Alomar that if he did not accept Hart's offer, he probably could make an additional $3 million during those same four years. But Boras also made clear that "it's not a bad deal." Alomar signed.

Boras, however, adamantly opposed Hart's offer to Baerga: three years for $6.9 million. Boras reminded Baerga that few middle infielders hit for power and average as he did. In a few years, Baerga would easily command double what the Indians were offering. "This is a terrible deal," Boras told him. "It will cost you millions of dollars." But Baerga decided to take it. [19] Other young Indians also accepted Hart's terms—Charles Nagy in 1992, Albert Belle and Kenny Lofton in 1993, and Jim Thome and Mark Clark in 1994. Sometimes, Hart's strategy flopped: He gave two-year deals to pitchers Jack Armstrong, Scott Scudder, Dennis Cook, and Dave Otto, who in 1992 posted a combined record of 22 victories and 41 losses. But Hart's move sent a clear message that Cleveland intended to keep its better young players. "I like what the Indians are doing," said Lou Gorman, general manager of the Boston Red Sox. [20]

In 1993, Hart offered to extend Baerga's contract through the turn of the century for an additional $20 million. Boras opposed the deal: Baerga's statistics, he argued, were more impressive than Ryne Sandberg's at the same age. One of Boras' clients, Greg Maddux, had earned a $29-million contract from Atlanta just two years after turning down a $7-million deal from the Cubs. Just say no, Boras urged. A few days later, Baerga telephoned Boras: Hart had increased his bid to $26 million. "I really want to take it," Baerga said. "Carlos," Boras warned, "this contract will cost you $10 million. At least wait one year." But Baerga had an answer that Boras could not counter. "I could not play effectively during the season having turned down $26 million," he told Boras. He signed the extension and later that season assured Boras, "I'm still happy."

As far as Boras was concerned, the Indians saved millions of dollars with their long-term contracts. That money could be used by the Indians to sign free agents or pay huge bonuses to young high school players. In 1994, the Indians paid $1.15 million to sign hard-throwing California high school pitcher Jaret Wright, another Boras client. Boras did not like Hart's strategy. But he had to admit it was effective. [21]

Dick Jacobs flashed the green light to John Hart during the winter of 1994 to pursue free agents. Hart signed right-handed pitcher Dennis Martinez to a two-year deal worth $9.6 million, and designated hitter Eddie Murray to a one-year contract worth $3 million. Martinez stabilized a weak starting rotation, and Murray, by batting fifth, guaranteed that pitchers would not automatically walk Belle in the fourth spot. Hart then traded for Seattle's classy fielding shortstop Omar Vizquel. Not since Lou Boudreau in 1948, had the Indians fielded a quality defensive shortstop; even Hank Greenberg's vaunted farm system was noticeably deficient in producing middle infielders. Vizquel's soft hands and strong arm would dramatically improve Cleveland's defense. Vizquel also came with a $2.3 million salary, which fattened Dick Jacobs' team payroll to $28 million. But Jacobs was willing to go only so far and insisted that the Indians operate within a budget. He vetoed a trade for New York Mets' pitcher Bret Saberhagen because his contract called for payments through the year 2029. "We're not in the Social Security business," Jacobs told Hart. [22]

Jacobs was growing more assertive in running the team. On the final day of the 1992 season, he appeared in the Indians' locker room for the first time. Later that month, he attended the Indians' organizational meetings in Florida. Every day, he would talk to John Hart, either by telephone or in person. What players were the Indians thinking of trading? Jacobs wanted to know. Hart had complete authority, but he was careful never to leave Dick Jacobs in the dark.

To make it easier for his Indians to qualify for the playoffs, Jacobs agreed in September 1993 to transfer the team to the newly created American League Central Division. The owners wanted to change the two-division format in each league into three divisions. The league champions of the east, central, and west divisions would go into the playoffs along with a "wild card"—the club that had the best second-place record among the three divisions. Had Jacobs followed baseball tradition, he would have insisted the Indians remain in the American League East with New York, Toronto, Baltimore, Boston, and Detroit. Instead, the Indians joined the Chicago White Sox, Kansas City Royals, Milwaukee Brewers, and Minnesota Twins. Except for Chicago, the Indians played in the largest market in the division. With his new ballpark generating millions of dollars from attendance, advertising, concessions, and television, Dick Jacobs had every reason to believe that the Indians would dominate the new division.

The Indians won on that clear blustery opening day, defeating Seattle, 4-3, in 11 innings. But the low score was a fluke. Jacobs Field was a hitter's park; the power alleys were cozier than those in spacious Cleveland Stadium, and the Indian hitters regularly rocketed home runs over the high left-field wall. The Indians hit six home runs in a 9-8 victory over the White Sox in July, and, by August, seven Indians were heading toward 20-home run seasons; no team ever has had seven players with 20 or more home runs in a single season. Belle, Murray, and Baerga were on their way toward driving in more than 100 runs apiece and Belle seemed certain to break Al Rosen's 1953 team record of 43 home runs. Manny Ramirez, the Indians' No. 1 choice in the 1991 draft, claimed the right-field job, and his lightning quick bat smacked 17 home runs by August 12. At the top of the lineup, Kenny Lofton was batting .349 with 60 stolen bases, and, in Boston, he made a catch of a soaring flyball that was eerily reminiscent of Willie Mays' catch 40 years earlier.

The barrage of home runs obscured the fact that the Indians had assembled a competent starting rotation of Dennis Martinez, Charles Nagy, Mark Clark, and Jack Morris. In the team's first 84 games, the starters held opponents to three runs or less in six or more innings 47 times. Clark won 11 of 14 starts until he broke his right hand in July trying to field a groundball. Nagy recovered from shoulder surgery to win 10 games and lead the Cleveland starters in earned run average. But, by July, it was apparent that Martinez was the best: His curveball froze the game's best hitters. When Martinez pitched for Baltimore in 1979, Yankee scout Clyde King marveled at his ability to retire hitters on any of four pitches—fastball, curveball, slider, and change. Now at 39, Martinez had the control that had evaded him as a younger pitcher. [23]

Martinez and the Cleveland starters were largely responsible for an 18-game victory streak at Jacobs Field that began May 13 and did not end until June 25. Martinez won twice as Indian starting pitchers were 11-0 with a 2.81 earned run average during that streak. Meanwhile, opposing pitchers found it all but impossible to restrain the Indians' offense, particularly in the late innings. On June 16—Dick Jacobs' birthday—before 41,631 people, the Indians entered the bottom of the ninth trailing Boston, 6-4. With two out and Alomar on second, Vizquel singled off closer Jeff Russell to put runners at first and third. As Ruben Amaro ran for Vizquel, Russell poured two strikes past Baerga. But on the next pitch, Baerga scorched a double to right to score Alomar and send Amaro to third. With first base open, Russell chose to pitch to Belle and it was a mistake; Belle smacked a 1-and-1 pitch into left-center field for a game-winning double. "I should have a birthday every day," Jacobs joked. [24]

By the time the home streak ended, the Indians led the second-place White Sox by four games, and the city was responding. During the 18-game winning streak, the Indians attracted 704,087 people to Jacobs Field compared to a season-long attendance of 655,181 in 1985. After just 27 home games, the Indians surpassed the one million mark in attendance and expected to easily break the franchise's record of 2.6 million in 1948. The Indians were a major hit on TV; they averaged an 18.5 share on their local cable broadcasts during a four-game series in July against the White Sox in Cleveland. [25] National news organizations, such as *Sports Illustrated*, the *Washington Post*, *Business Week* magazine, *USA Today*, and ABC-TV shipped reporters to Cleveland to chronicle the revival.

Only the Cleveland bullpen and an unreliable infield defense stood between the Indians and the Central Division title. First, manager Mike Hargrove tried sore-armed Steve Farr, signed by Hart for $900,000, as the closer. With Farr's elbow aching, Hargrove next turned to Paul Shuey and his 95-mile per hour fastball. Shuey's talent was obvious, but so was his inability to find the strike zone. The Cleveland bullpen blew leads of 5-1 in Detroit and 8-3 at Jacobs Field against the Orioles. John Hart could have picked up Dennis Eckersley from Oakland, but, frugal as ever, Dick Jacobs was reluctant to guarantee his $5 million contract for 1995. Instead, on July 1, Hart traded Farr and Chris Nabholz and their combined salaries of $2 million to the Red Sox for Russell, who saved 33 games in 1993, but was laboring through a difficult year in 1994. "With so many teams in the pennant race, it's been difficult to find a closer," Hart explained. [26]

Russell added a strong right arm and an irritable disposition to a clubhouse already brimming over with grouchy players. Murray and Morris had long been known for their surliness, and when Morris left the team between starts to work his wheat ranch in Montana, Hart released him. Murray swore at reporters during a key series against the White Sox. Russell fit in nicely with this bunch. After winning a crucial game in relief for the Indians in Boston, Russell made clear that he loathed the months he pitched for the Red Sox. "I hate this town," Russell snapped. "I could care less if they bomb this town. The people have no manners. They have no respect for anything." [27]

The most difficult player was Belle. He should have been a public relations dream: He was a threat to win the Triple Crown and worked hard to improve defensively. Intelligent and ambitious, he earned an accounting degree in his off months and devoted long hours to the United Way, helping inner city youths transform a vacant lot into a baseball diamond. But Belle also snarled at reporters for asking the most innocuous questions. *Plain Dealer* sports columnist Bud Shaw wrote a laudatory column about Belle's extensive note cards on opposing pitchers. Shaw learned about the cards from the Cleveland coaching staff, but the day the column appeared, Belle charged that Shaw had found the cards by rifling his locker. In a game in Boston with the Indians comfortably ahead, Belle was ejected for arguing about a ground out. "He's a great player, but you can't act like that," umpire Rich Garcia said. [28] In defense of Belle, he played under intense stress. His seven-day suspension for using a corked bat in a July game provoked widespread coverage. When White Sox manager Gene Lamont demanded that umpires examine Belle's bat, league officials discovered it had been corked—a practice by which a player drills a small hole in the top of the bat and fills it with lighter material, such as cork. In theory, a corked bat is lighter, providing power hitters with more bat speed and greater distance on flyballs. Corking has been a fairly common practice; Norm Cash of the Tigers and Graig Nettles of the Yankees were notorious for using corked bats. But the incident provided sportswriters with an opportunity to write about the Belle incident as if it were original sin; *USA Today* ran a major cover piece under the headline, "Corked Bat Latest Flap in Career."

By the All-Star break, the Indians' lead over the White Sox had melted to two percentage points. Still, it was the first time Cleveland had been in first place this late in the season since 1959. With 51 victories, they were on pace to win 98 games—the most since 1954.

They opened the second half of the season in Chicago for the first of what would be eight games against the White Sox during the month of July. "The sense of things in Cleveland is that the next two weekends are Armageddon," wrote Bud Shaw of the *Plain Dealer*. The White Sox had beaten the Indians three of four times already, and on paper were a superior team. In a year of dreadful pitching, the White Sox offered four hard-throwing starters capable of winning 20 games apiece—Jack McDowell,

Alex Fernandez, Jason Bere, and lefthander Wilson Alvarez. With Roberto Hernandez, the White Sox had the reliable closer that Cleveland lacked, while Frank Thomas, Robin Ventura, and Julio Franco formed a potent offense. "We haven't played Cleveland in a while, but just from watching them on TV, you've got to like the way they come back late in the game," said White Sox manager Gene Lamont. "They're one of those teams you never feel real comfortable against." [29]

On Thursday evening, July 14, Fernandez struck out 12 Indians, won his eighth game, 6-3, and pitched the White Sox into first place by one-half game. Before 38,686 in Comiskey Park the next evening, Mark Clark and Jeff Russell held the White Sox to six hits as the Indians won, 3-2. Martinez shut out the White Sox, 2-0, on Saturday before 42,710, but Chicago evened the series on Sunday, hammering Jack Morris, 5-2, and the Indians left the city with a slim lead of two percentage points.

The Indians dropped two games to the Rangers before opening the rematch with the White Sox on Thursday, July 21. It was the most important series the Indians had played since the nightmarish four-game loss to the White Sox in the final days of August 1959. The first-place White Sox increased their lead over Cleveland to three games by defeating Martinez, 6-5, but the Indians hit seven home runs—including three by Jim Thome—and scored 20 times to defeat the White Sox on Friday and Saturday. The White Sox won the Sunday game and it was apparent that Cleveland and Chicago would engage in a brutal pennant battle all season long.

There was only one possible hitch: For the eighth time in 20 years, major league baseball was on the verge of a work stoppage.

The strike that shattered the 1994 season had its roots in the unusual financial disparity in major league baseball. The teams in the large markets of New York, Los Angeles, Chicago, Toronto, and Philadelphia had millions more to lavish on free agents and farm systems than clubs in the smaller markets of Montreal, Pittsburgh, Seattle, San Diego, and Milwaukee. Toronto won the 1993 World Series and led all baseball with a team payroll of $51.5 million, while the Atlanta Braves won 104 games with a payroll of $44.8 million. By contrast, the San Diego Padres lost

101 games with the game's lowest payroll—just $10.5 million. The 1994 dispute rested on a single question: Who should bear the brunt of creating a more competitive system? Should the players agree to limit their salaries so all the teams would have an equal crack at the best? Or should the owners share their revenues with each other, evening the monetary ability of each team to buy talent?

Teams in larger markets traditionally held major advantages. From 1920 through 1956, the New York Yankees, New York Giants, and Brooklyn Dodgers combined to win 39 pennants. Thirteen times in that span the nation watched an all-New York City World Series. Teams that broke the cycle tended to be exceptionally well operated, such as the Cleveland Indians under Bill Veeck and Hank Greenberg, or the St. Louis Cardinals with their vast farm system pioneered by Branch Rickey. Not all large-market teams won; the Phillies, Red Sox, and White Sox proved that inept management could overcome even the most overwhelming financial advantages.

The gap between the strong and weak teams widened in the 1950s as George Medinger in Cleveland and Walter O'Malley in Brooklyn realized the vast potential of broadcasting their games locally. Up until the day they moved to Los Angeles, the Brooklyn Dodgers were the most profitable team in the National League largely because O'Malley was televising more than 100 Dodger games every year in New York City. To counter that advantage, baseball in 1965 adopted the National Football League's policy of each team equally sharing revenue from the national television contract. Between 1969 and 1979, baseball earned $214 million from its contracts with ABC and NBC, and by 1980 the national contracts provided teams with more money than their local broadcasts. [30] In 1990, CBS and ESPN paid each team $14 million in television money; broadcast revenues now accounted for 50 percent of baseball's income compared to just 16.8 percent in 1956. [31] The huge influx of national TV money created a more competitive game throughout the 1980s, as the Royals, Twins, Cardinals, and Tigers won as often as the Yankees, Dodgers, and Mets. Baseball attendance skyrocketed from 22.4 million in 1965 to 57 million in 1991 as more teams had the finances to field competitive teams. [32]

But even as the game attained its competitive peak in the

1980s, the spread of cable television would allow the larger market teams to regain their dominance. Ratings for the national TV games declined sharply; ESPN lost $76 million in 1990 and 1991 on its baseball broadcasts while CBS lost $170 million during the four-year life of its baseball contract. [33] The national ratings plummeted because more viewers opted to watch their local team on cable instead of a national game they were not interested in seeing. The Braves developed a following throughout the South with Ted Turner's Superstation. In 1982, the New York Mets sold their local TV rights to a cable station for the then-unheard of price of $17 million. In 1988, that became small change as George Steinbrenner negotiated a 10-year deal with Madison Square Garden Network worth $486 million. Unlike the CBS and ESPN contracts, this deal did not force the Yankees to share their local broadcast money with other teams. In 1991, the Yankees earned a profit of $30.4 million—a sum nearly as great as the total revenues of the Indians at $46.8 million and the Montreal Expos at $43.6 million [34]

More importantly, this income gap grew as the average player salary mushroomed from $44,676 in 1975 to $371,157 in 1985 to $1.07 million in 1993. [35] Horrified owners tried every tactic—fair or foul— to restrict salaries. In 1981, owners provoked a 50-day strike with their demand that teams losing free agents be compensated with players from other organizations. Marvin Miller and Donald Fehr, the chief negotiators for the Major League Baseball Players Association, correctly viewed the owners' proposal as a scheme to restrict free agency. Would the Yankees sign Dave Winfield to a 10-year contract if they thought they might have to yield an equally talented player?

By 1985, Baseball Commissioner Peter Ueberroth sternly admonished the owners that they were inviting financial ruin if they continued to award lucrative contracts on a long-term basis. He pointed to Ted Turner's decision to give relief pitcher Bruce Sutter a $10 million contract; Sutter had labored throughout 1985 with arm trouble. The owners quickly responded to Ueberroth's appeal. Within a few short months, owners ceased bidding even for talented free agents; of 33 free agents, 29 signed with their old teams. The players' union filed a grievance, and the owners' strategy collapsed in 1987 when baseball arbitrator Thomas Roberts ruled the owners had colluded by not bidding for free agents. The owners handed over $280 million to the players in collusion payments.

Roberts' ruling set off a dizzying round of "Can you top this?" Jose Guzman signed a multi-year deal with the Chicago Cubs for $14.3 million; Rickey Henderson a four-year contract with Oakland for $12 million; Doug Drabek with Houston for $19.5 million over four years; Bobby Bonilla with the Mets for five years at $29 million; and Barry Bonds with the Giants for six years and a record $43.7 million. Even mediocre players suddenly found themselves multi-millionaires; Steinbrenner foolishly gave pitcher Pascal Perez $5.7 million for three years, while Al Rosen in San Francisco handed $10 million over four years to pitcher Bud Black, whose lifetime record was 83-82.

Teams in smaller markets saw their payrolls shoot into the stratosphere. The San Diego Padres' annual payroll nearly doubled from $16.7 million in 1990 to $32.7 million at the beginning of 1993 before beleaguered team owner Tom Werner insisted that costs be slashed. The Padres traded away high-salaried players Fred McGriff, Tony Fernandez, Gary Sheffield, Kurt Stillwell, and Craig Lefferts and made no serious effort to re-sign free agents Randy Myers and Benito Santiago. The Milwaukee Brewers watched helplessly as longtime star Paul Molitor signed a three-year, $9.1-million deal with Toronto. The Pittsburgh Pirates dismantled a team that swept to three consecutive National League East titles from 1990 to 1992. The Pirates could not afford to win; a 1993 study showed the team had not turned a profit since 1988 and had lost $40 million since 1986. The Pirates were in such dire straits that team officials asked the city of Pittsburgh in 1994 to bail them out with an $8 million loan. [36]

When Richard Ravitch accepted the $750,000-a-year job in 1991 as the owners' chief labor negotiator, he was appalled at the free-spending practices of many teams. Why, he would ask owners, are you spending millions you don't even have? "Well, the local press was really on me and we were having our season-ticket drive," they invariably would reply. [37] Nobody, Ravitch would say, ever ran a business like baseball owners.

A tough-talking, chain-smoking New York City Democrat, Ravitch throughout 1992 urged the owners to adopt a two-pronged strategy when they bargained for a new labor agreement with the players in 1994. First, the wealthier teams would agree to share some revenue with the poorer teams in smaller markets. Then, to mollify the large-market teams, Ravitch would demand the players accept a salary cap. Under Ravitch's proposal, the owners and players would divide the game's revenues evenly. "If baseball is going to survive, there will have to be some type of salary cap and revenue sharing," Carl Pohlad, owner of the small-market Minnesota Twins, said in 1992. [38]

A salary cap was anathema to the players and their chief negotiator, Don Fehr. The players already were getting 58 percent of the game's gross revenues instead of the 50 percent Ravitch offered, he pointed out. If the owners wanted to share revenue, they could do so on their own without concessions from the players. "We've had seven work stoppages in a row now—four strikes and three lockouts," Fehr complained in a July 31 interview with ABC. "And in every one of them...the issue has been the same. The owners make a series of proposals designed to interfere with the free market for players as much as they can, and the players would rather not do that." Fehr expected the owners to unilaterally declare a bargaining impasse after the World Series and, as permitted by labor law, impose the salary cap. The players' only weapon was to strike, but a strike in November after the season was pointless. Instead, the players' union pushed for a strike date near season's end when the owners would face losing millions by canceling the World Series.

The players set their date: August 12.

The looming strike date injected a sense of urgency in the games of late July and August. The Yankees were running away with the American League East and the Texas Rangers were all but certain to win the West with a sub-.500 record. Cleveland, Chicago, Baltimore, and Kansas City were fighting for the final two playoff spots. Looking ahead to August 12, everyone anticipated different season-ending scenarios. "Let's say the players go out on August 12 and don't come back until September 15," Hart explained to reporters. "We'd probably go to Florida for two weeks to get ready and then go into the playoffs. If a strike lasts longer than a week, I don't know how you could ask a pitcher to get right back into games." [39] For the Indians, the uncertainty fostered by the impending strike held special significance. It was, after all, their first season as a contender in almost four decades.

On July 26, the Indians went east for seven games against the Orioles and Yankees. Cleveland trailed the first-place White Sox by one and a half games, but led Baltimore by two games and Kansas City by five for the wild card spot. Martinez held the Orioles to seven hits and won his 10th game as the Indians split a doubleheader in Baltimore. Combined with Kansas City's 3-2 victory over the White Sox, the Indians were one game out of first place. Rain washed out the next Indians-Orioles game, but Cleveland gained a half game on the White Sox, who lost again to the Royals, 4-1. To make up for the rainout, the Orioles and Indians played a doubleheader on July 28. Eddie Murray homered twice, and Belle, Alomar, and Tony Pena added one each as the Indians won twice to surge ahead of the White Sox by one game.

They did not stay there long, losing three times over the weekend to the Yankees in New York. The Yankees won all nine games against Cleveland in 1994 by taking advantage of the one weakness in the Indians' offense—an inability to hit quality left-handed pitching. Yankee Manager Buck Showalter started three lefthanders—Sterling Hitchcock, Jim Abbott, and Jimmy Key—and left-handed closer Steve Howe saved all three games. With Belle's bat suspension taking effect on August 1, there were doubts that the Indians could hold off the Royals and Orioles for the wild card spot.

But Belle was hardly missed; the Indians won three of four games against Detroit. The unlikely hero of one of those games was Albie Lopez, the low-round draftee Hart refused to deal for Saberhagen. Only a collapse would keep Cleveland from the play-offs. Unlike the dreary finish to the 1955 season when the Indians fumbled away the pennant, this year was special. The Indians split four games in back-to-back Saturday and Sunday double-headers in Boston. In Sunday's second game, the Indians trailed, 9-5, after five innings. But they steadily whittled away the Red Sox lead and entered the top of the ninth, down 9-8. With one out, Murray singled, and Hargrove sent Amaro to run for him. Thome struck out, but Amaro advanced to second on a wild pitch. That left the game up to Wayne Kirby, whose single on Opening Day gave the Indians the victory. Kirby dropped a soft liner into center field to tie the game. The Indians had it won in the 11th when Amaro singled home Belle. All Jeff Russell needed to do was retire three batters. But weak-hitting Scott Fletcher elevated a flyball over Fenway Park's Green Monster, and the game proceeded to the 12th. Other Cleveland teams would have meekly surrendered. Not this version: The Indians scored five times in the top of the 12th, helped by a throwing error by first baseman Mo Vaughn. This time, Russell retired the Red Sox to give the Indians a 15-10 victory. "Things couldn't get much tighter," an exhausted Hargrove said after the eight-hour doubleheader.

The victory all but assured the Indians of qualifying for the playoffs if a strike ended the regular season; one victory in their final three games in Toronto would clinch the wild card and a sweep could tie them with the White Sox. On Monday, August 8, Nagy held the Blue Jays to six hits and one run for seven innings, and Thome hit his 20th home run for a 6-1 Cleveland victory. The Blue Jays won Tuesday, but Jason Grimsley recorded his fifth victory Wednesday to give Cleveland a 66-47 pre-strike record.

After the game, Mike Hargrove gathered his players about him in the Skydome locker room. They had, he told them, soared to heights no other Cleveland team had attained in 40 years. But it was the eve of the strike. If the players walked out the next day, he urged them to stay in shape. The Indians still had a chance to tie the White Sox for first place that night, but Chicago beat Oakland, 2-1, to finish one game ahead of Cleveland. "We knew Cleveland won, and we knew we had to win," White Sox starter Jason Bere said. [40]

The strike that began the next morning was pronounced as yet another example of the misfortune that has haunted the Cleveland franchise since Willie Mays' catch. "But There Is No Joy in Cleveland," blared a headline in *Business Week*. On ABC's "This Week With David Brinkley," reporter Dick Schaap noted that the strike would threaten "the Cleveland Indians' bid for their first World Series in 40 years." George Vecsey of *The New York Times* wrote that "the idea of Cleveland, far-away Cleveland, finally winning something seems innocent and romantic—so innocent and romantic that a strike must surely destroy it." When Bud Selig, owner of the Milwaukee Brewers and interim commissioner of baseball, appeared in July before the National Press Club in Washington, the second question asked of him was,

"How could you let a baseball shutdown occur in this of all years when the Cleveland Indians finally are contenders again?"

Forty years earlier after clinching the pennant in Detroit, the Indians returned home to an excited city that heralded their triumph. Tens of thousands of cheering Clevelanders shouted, applauded, and tossed confetti at the Indians as they were driven in open convertibles through the heart of the downtown. People stood five deep on either side of Euclid Avenue, while thousands of others escaped the day's swirling winds and waved from their office windows. An astonished City Traffic Commissioner John Sammon announced that the huge crowd easily exceeded the 200,000 who welcomed General Dwight Eisenhower downtown at the end of World War II.

The 1994 Indians were not welcomed with parades or speeches. Instead, they flew in from Toronto, drove to Jacobs Field, and cleaned out their lockers. "This is kind of hard for me," Carlos Baerga explained to reporters. "I've been here five years waiting for this kind of season. I know the people here have been waiting a long time." Then Baerga drove his Porsche convertible out of Jacobs Field and went home. (41)

George Hering was making his regular rounds of Jacobs Field on this chilly evening that hinted of the winter to come. Thick, gray clouds hovered over the ballpark and temperatures had plunged to 54 degrees. Five nights a week, Hering joined a small group of Burns' guards as they kept an eye on the ballpark.

On this particular evening at 7:15, Hering should have been a busy man. Thousands of people, bundled in heavy overcoats and warm sweaters, would have been filing down Ontario Avenue and East 9th Street, converging on the ballpark. The Cleveland Indians would have been finishing batting practice, as writers and broadcasters clung to the batting cage, seeking last-minute quotes for their stories. It was Tuesday, October 4, 1994, and the Indians and New York Yankees would have played the first playoff game in Cleveland in 40 years.

But there were no baseball players joking around the cage, no awkward pitchers shagging flyballs in the outfield, no coaches swatting groundballs to Jim Thome at third base. The rich green grass of the infield was still, tarps covered the pitcher's mound and homeplate, and the huge light towers were eerily dark. The entrance reserved for the press was locked tight, and the 14 ticket windows outside Gate A were shuttered. The only sign of life in the Indians' offices was a solitary guard sitting behind a huge desk. Near the larger-than-life poster of Al Rosen at Gate D on Carnegie Avenue, there were no delicious smells wafting from the pizza and hot dog stands. So much promise had come to nothing. A sign slapped on one of the ticket windows read, "Tours of Jacobs Field are no longer offered for the 1994 season."

Hering's chief task this evening was far simpler, keeping people out of the ballpark. But because the baseball strike had choked off the season, there were few to chase away, save for an occasional tourist gazing at the brilliant structure of steel and brick with its dark green seats. "One day, a gentleman from New York came down here," said Hering. "Five minutes later, a gentleman from California. Five minutes after, I ran into a couple from Michigan; all in town for other business, but all down here to see what might have been."

Hering had never been much of an Indian fan. Once in a while, he would buy a ticket for a game in the old stadium at the other end of East 9th Street. But in this magical season, it was impossible not to be swept up in the frenzy. Every night, the ballpark had been bursting with fans. "I think we had, what was it, 30 consecutive soldout home games?" Hering said. "It was unbelievable. That tells you right there. People were proud of their team. I call it the Cleveland curse. Every time something gets going good, something bad happens. No matter what it might be."

He heaved a loud sigh. "It's so depressing," Hering said softly. Then he continued his lonely night patrol down the side street past a sign declaring, "Road Closed to Through Traffic."

Hering was wrong. Luck had nothing to do with it, just as it had nothing to do with the fall of the Indians and their resurrection. Baseball had been plagued by seven other work stoppages since 1972, and none had prevented the Indians from winning pennants. Dick Jacobs staunchly supported the owners' position even though his team was on the verge of its first playoff appearance in 40 years. "We want to let the players and the union know we are in dire straits," Jacobs said. "This transcends the season. It's something that has to be worked out." [42]

Dick Jacobs quickly demonstrated that he would not be paralyzed by the strike. Near the end of October, he extended John Hart's contract beyond the turn of the century. Hart had been mentioned as a successor to Tom Grieve of the Texas Rangers, and Dick Jacobs had no intention of losing him. At the press conference announcing the extension, Jacobs was in an affable mood, taking time to banter with reporters. "Would John leave me?" he joked. "How could he even think such a thought?" Then he handed Hart a T-shirt with a tearful Chief Wahoo that read, "What a shame: 66-47." A nearby grill was selling the shirts for $13, Jacobs explained. "But," he said with a laugh, "I got a discount. I bought three thousand, and I got them for 12 bucks apiece." As reporters swarmed about the always-quotable Hart, Dick Jacobs quietly withdrew to the back of the room to chat with an old political ally, former Cleveland City Council President George Forbes.

Like any good business executive, Dick Jacobs could afford to be patient. During the next decade, the Indians and the White Sox would be the most profitable teams in the Central Division. Like the Indians of the 1950s, Dick Jacobs' Indians could hire better scouts, field more farm teams, and sign talented free agents. "On the business side, we have a winner," Jacobs said the day he extended Hart's contract. "We all want that ring on our finger, and we're going to have it very shortly, in my opinion." Baseball had not changed much from the days so long ago when Hank Greenberg organized his baseball school in Daytona Beach: Teams with money and brains won; those without lost. There would be plenty of time for Dick Jacobs.

Chapter 12

A Joke No More

"This town deserves it. They've been waiting a hell of a long time."— Rocky Colavito

Throughout the summer of 1995, Dick Jacobs was having the time of his life. The long-term plan he instituted a decade earlier with Hank Peters was now paying off handsomely: His team was winning the American League Central Division, crowds were flocking to the ballpark that bore his name, and the Indians were the talk of baseball. The reclusive Jacobs had become an unlikely celebrity; people sent him fan mail, thanking him for finally giving the city a winner. Jacobs carried some in his jacket and delighted in reading them to friends.

When the Indians played in Cleveland, Jacobs invariably started the evening with drinks at Johnny's, his favorite restaurant set among a block of gentrified warehouses from the city's industrial past. Each night, he would commandeer a huge, round table by the front window and drink his preferred vodka on the rocks, Stolichnaya, as cronies and acquaintances sat in court. Like a reigning monarch, Jacobs would benevolently pick up the dinner checks, sometimes for people he barely knew. He had one ironclad rule: No one was allowed to buy him a drink. One night, he bragged to a Cleveland reporter, "I can't be bought." He particularly liked handing out tickets to political allies, business associates, and sometimes, strangers. One story had Jacobs emerging from the Society Center— the 55-story office tower he had constructed—only to have a teenager ask for an autograph. Jacobs obliged and inquired, "Are you going to the game tonight?" When the teenager shook his head, Jacobs handed him three tickets so he could take his parents.

Reporters, however, received no such attention. With them, Dick Jacobs remained aloof; when he did grant interviews, his replies were cursory and mundane. No, Dick Jacobs was not good copy, but that, like so much else in Jacobs' life, was by design. Art Modell, he told friends, was too gabby with the press. Become familar, Jacobs would say, and you become vulnerable.

Dick Jacobs was becoming an expert on the game, too—quite a change from 1986 when he hardly knew rudimentary baseball rules. "I was on a learning curve," Jacobs explained. "I wanted to know what was going on before I began to rise a bit from the ashes." [1] By 1995, Jacobs was astounding his buddies; one friend swore that Jacobs could knowledgably discuss most of the players in the American League. His favorite was Kenny Lofton. "He's loose," Jacobs told Tim Hagan.[2]

Although Dick Jacobs had allied himself with the hardline owners in the player strike, he lobbied to end the impasse in the spring of 1995 when it became obvious that in their lengthy struggle with the players' union the owners had lost once again. With the owners threatening to field teams of replacement players, U.S. District Judge Sonia Sotomayor issued an injunction, requiring the imposition of the old system the owners loathed—salary arbitration and bidding on six-year free agents. The players offered to report to spring training, but many owners were in a hostile, combative mood. Lock the players out, they exhorted. But in typically pragmatic fashion, Dick Jacobs recommended opening the camps. His attorneys at the Cleveland law firm of Baker & Hostetler had warned him that the locked-out players could sue for backpay and damages. "For every day of the lockout, it would have cost me $195,000," Jacobs said in one of his rare public statements. "That got my attention." Jacobs did not allow his emotions to interfere with making money.[3]

With the strike over, Dick Jacobs increased John Hart's budget by $3 million, allowing Cleveland to sign free-agent starting pitchers Orel Hershiser and Bud Black, and left-handed relief pitchers Jim Poole and Paul Assenmacher, whose curveball and slider were so devasting that Sparky Anderson muttered, "That Assenmacher will get a left-handed hitter out before you can turn your head."[4] But though Dick Jacobs yearned to win, there were limits. When Florida offered Hart a chance at prized closer Bryan Harvey and his $4.5 million contract, Jacobs' response was chilly. "To me, the budget is etched in stone." Jacobs said.[5]

The Indians instantly made a shambles of the American League Central Division race, sweeping the White Sox in a four-game series in late May at Jacobs Field. By June 23, the Indians were seven games ahead of the second-place Royals and $17\frac{1}{2}$ ahead of the fourth-place White Sox. The Indians placed six players on the American League All-Star team—Kenny Lofton, Albert Belle, Carlos Baerga, Manny Ramirez, Dennis Martinez, and Jose Mesa. By midseason, the Indians were batting a hefty .294 with 95 home runs. They led the league with a team earned-run average of 3.68. Hart and Assistant General Manager Dan O'Dowd were so confident of the Indians appearing in post-season play that in July they traded three young minor leaguers for St. Louis starting pitcher Ken Hill, a 16-game winner in 1994. O'Dowd planned on Hill starting the fourth game of the post-season playoffs.

The fan apathy that left so many ballparks empty in the aftermath of the disastrous strike skipped Cleveland completely. Night after night, Jacobs Field filled to the limit; after waiting four decades for a winner, Clevelanders were not going to miss this season. The Indians specialized in those come-from-behind, late-inning victories that delighted even the casual fan. No lead was safe from the heavy-hitting Indians. During a Sunday afternoon game in Jacobs Field in June, the Blue Jays grabbed an 8-0 lead in the third inning, and, with David Cone pitching for Toronto, the game appeared over. But rookie Chad Ogea, a graduate of Hank Peters' farm system, held the Blue Jays to just one run in six and two-thirds innings of relief, and the Indians narrowed the lead to 8-6. In the bottom of the ninth, singles by Belle and Eddie Murray off relief pitcher Darren Hall put runners at first and third with one out. Jim Thome forced Murray at second, but Belle scored to cut Toronto's lead to 8-7. First baseman Paul Sorrento smacked a sinking fastball from Hall into the right-field stands for his 12th home run of the year and a 9-8 Cleveland victory. It was the 15th time the Indians had won a game with their final at-bat. Such exciting finishes attracted the attention of reporters from *Sports Illustrated*, *The New York Times*, and the *Washington Post*. Many of their stories credited the rebirth solely to John Hart, missing the pivotal role played by Hank Peters.

Just as Hank Greenberg's Indians drew upon a rich farm system to win a pennant a generation earlier, now the Indians' relentless drive for the divisional title depended upon the farm system created by Peters, particularly outfielders Albert Belle and Manny Ramirez, third baseman Jim Thome, first baseman Herb Perry, and pitchers Charles Nagy, Chad Ogea, Julian

Tavarez, and Alan Embree. At the All-Star break, Ramirez led the Indians in batting average and home runs, Ogea had won four big games and stabilized the starting rotation, and Perry was hitting .333 as a backup first baseman. All three had something else in common: They had been chosen by the Indians in the first three rounds of the 1991 draft of high school and college players.

A rhythmic rapping to the cadence of an Indian drum came from a suite on the top floor of the Sheraton Hotel in Cleveland, where Mickey White and the other Indians' scouts were huddled for the 1991 draft. *Thump*, thump, thump, thump. *Thump*, thump, thump, thump. One of the scouts tapped the table with his fists, as White and the others chanted war whoops.[6]

As the crucial first round of the draft unfolded, their top choice seemed almost within their grasp—a selection that carried both promise and risk. Most teams preferred to use their valuable first-round selection on experienced college players. And so it went: Arizona State University outfielder Mike Kelly to Atlanta; Stanford first baseman Dave McCarty to Minnesota; University of Alabama first baseman Joe Vitiello to Kansas City. Now, only the Seattle Mariners and Chicago Cubs, choosing 11th and 12th respectively, stood between the Indians and their No. 1 choice, Manny Ramirez, an untested high school outfielder from the Washington Heights section of New York City.

On this particular afternoon, as the 28 major league teams selected more than a thousand high school and college players, Mickey White was the single most important person in the Cleveland Indians' organization. Only the shrewdest scouts would recognize the handful of prospects among those drafted who would mature into major league players. White and his scouting staff—Tom Giordano, Jay Roberston, Tony DeMacio, and Buzzy Keller—had spent months in places like Mesa, Arizona, and Wichita, Kansas, checking every player who conceivably qualified as a prospect. Then they winnowed their list to 25, including Ramirez; Aaron Sele, a right-handed starting pitcher from Washington State University; Allen Watson, a left-handed pitcher from a small college in New York; Ogea and Paul Byrd, right-handed pitchers from Louisiana State University; and Perry, a power-hitting third baseman from the University of Florida.[7]

White had been trained in the Cincinnati Reds' system, an

organization that lived by scouting and player development. The fertile farm system developed by the Reds from the 1960s through the 1980s produced Johnny Bench, Pete Rose, Barry Larkin, Tony Perez, Ken Griffey, Sr., Eric Davis, and Paul O'Neill. Cincinnati scouts were respected throughout baseball; Chuck LeMarr, Chet Montgomery, Cam Bonifay, and Larry Doughty. These scouts learned their trade from the legendary Rex Bowen, who discovered Maury Wills simply by timing him in the 60-yard dash. Bowen was a key to the Reds' sweep of the Yankees in the 1976 World Series. During the final month of the season, Bowen scrupulously scouted the Yankees and concluded that the New York pitchers had what he called a slow release time — the amount of time the pitcher took between breaking his stretch and throwing the ball. The swift Reds could steal second or third whenever they wished, Bowen advised, because it would be physically impossible for Yankee catcher Thurman Munson to throw them out.

After nearly a decade with the Reds, White moved briefly to the Seattle Mariners in 1988. When the Mariners declined to renew his contract in 1990, John Hart immediately called him, saying he wanted White to replace Chet Montgomery as scouting director. White flew to Cleveland and joined Hart for a day-long talk. White told Hart that many of the younger Indian prospects were so slow and overweight, that past Cleveland scouting directors must have drafted by the pound. Impressed, Hart offered White the job within days. "My biggest ambition," White told Hart, "is to turn the doormat Cleveland Indians into a dynasty through scouting and player development."[8]

White plunged into the job, hiring nine scouts — men as assertive and aggressive as he, gutsy enough to challenge him when they thought he was wrong. Just before hiring DeMacio, White told him, "Tony, unless you can tell me I'm completely full of shit, I don't want to hire you."

As the Indians prepared for the 1991 draft, White clashed with Dan O'Dowd, the team's farm director and one of Hank Peters' favorites. O'Dowd agreed that Ramirez had the "God-given ability to bring the bat to the ball," but he was reluctant to gamble the Indians' No. 1 pick on a high school player. The Indians, O'Dowd argued, were rebuilding and needed college pitchers who would reach the major leagues faster. "The problem with a high school hitter is we may not be here when he gets to the big leagues," O'Dowd told White. The Indians, O'Dowd pointed out, had been burned in 1988 and 1989 when they drafted two high school players, shortstop Mark Lewis and outfielder Calvin Murray. Lewis never developed into a great player and Murray rejected their $250,000 offer in favor of a college scholarship. O'Dowd wanted White to choose Sele or Watson.[9]

No way, White retorted. Every time White had seen Ramirez, the ball had just exploded off his bat. "Everybody else we were talking about has good tools," White told his staff. "But Manny has a gift."

The day before the draft, the Mariners sent three scouts to check out Ramirez, and White's heart sank. If Seattle chose Ramirez, then the Indians would opt for Sele. But White knew he would be so upset at losing Ramirez, that another member of his staff would have to announce Sele's name.[10] White was spared that agony; Seattle took Sean Estes, a left-handed pitcher from a Nevada high school, and the Cubs chose Doug Glanville, an outfielder from the University of Pennsylvania.

The rest of the draft proceeded in orderly fashion. In the second round, White chose Perry, who played football and third base at Florida and exhibited the makings of a major league first baseman. In round three, White went for Ogea, a pitcher with a fastball of average velocity, but the "kind of guy you wouldn't want to get into a fight with. He's a very intense kid." In the fourth round, the Indians chose Byrd, a polished college pitcher. In round seven, Cleveland opted for Pep Harris, a high school pitcher from South Carolina. White's homework continued to pay off. In the 20th round, he went for Albie Lopez, a stocky righthander who had pitched for two years at Mesa Junior College in Arizona and been timed by one of White's scouts at 92 miles per hour. White finished his work in the 44th round by taking Damian Jackson, a speedy shortstop who had played one year of junior college baseball in Oakland.

Baseball experts ridiculed the choice of Ramirez, and some suspected that Dick Jacobs' frugality had forced Cleveland to choose an inexpensive players of limited ability. "Of all the kids taken with the top 15 picks, Ramirez' grades are such that he has little or no option but to sign," an unidentified agent told the *Plain Dealer*. "He has almost no bargaining position. Does it surprise you that the Indians took him?"[11] White later guessed the agent was Scott Boras of California.

White quickly signed Ramirez for $250,000, but within two

weeks, he appeared to have a full-blown disaster on his hands; Perry had injured his shoulder, Ogea delayed signing, and Ramirez was batting under .200. "I've warned you about those high school players," O'Dowd chided White.[12] Hank Peters ordered White to Watertown of the New York State League, where many of the young Indian draftees were playing. White assumed he was being punished.

But after his slow start at Burlington of the Appalachian League, Ramirez finished with a .326 batting average and 19 home runs. At the scouting director's meeting that winter in Boca Raton, Florida, Bob Engle of Toronto told White, "The best No. 1 pick this year was Ramirez. You took a kid that a lot of other people didn't even have in that round." O'Dowd would later credit Mickey White as the architect of "probably the best draft we ever had."[13] Not only were Ramirez, Ogea, Perry, and Lopez in Cleveland by 1995, but Byrd was pitching in relief for the New York Mets, and Jackson was stealing 40 bases for Cleveland's Double-A team in Canton.

Mickey White could not last long with the Indians. His bruising style clashed with the conservative, button-down organization put together by Peters. A telling example was White's fight with John Hart in the spring of 1991 to claim catcher Ed Taubensee off waivers. "John, I don't want to be a pain in the ass about this," White told Hart over dinner one evening in Tucson, "but I really think we ought to claim Taubensee." Hart's reply was terse: "Mick, you are being a pain in the ass, and unless you're willing to put your job on the line to claim this guy, then I'm not going to claim him." The next morning, White told Hart, "Here's my job. Take this kid."

White's affection toward Taubensee blinded him when the Indians had a chance to trade the catcher to Houston for outfielder Kenny Lofton, who started in center field for Houston's Triple-A team at Tucson. Hart had scouted Lofton and wanted to make the trade at the winter meetings in Miami in 1991.[14] White argued against the deal, but when he returned to his hotel room, he had second thoughts. Alex Cole was "dropping the ball" in center field for Cleveland, White told himself, and the Indians needed a replacement. Charlie Manuel, who managed Colorado Springs, "loved" Lofton. White was torn. "Is this an emotional decision or a rational decision?" he asked himself. At 2:30 in the morning, White wearily fell asleep. The next morning as he poured coffee and munched on a doughnut, White told O'Dowd, "We've got to make the fucking deal."[15]

But the back-and-forth proved wearisome to Cleveland's senior executives, who also expressed irritation with White's second draft in 1992. White chose hard-throwing relief pitcher Paul Shuey from North Carolina in the first round and outfielder Jon Nunnally from a Florida junior college in the third. But the rest of the draft was abysmal; six of the top 15 choices refused to sign. Among those six were four high school players, including Jeff Liefer, an outfielder from California. O'Dowd trusted Mickey White's ability to scout young players, but the Indians could not afford to waste six of their first 15 picks. Hart and O'Dowd decided White's talents were better suited as a special assistant in the front office. Annoyed, Mickey White decided the time had come to leave.

The crowd at Jacobs Field, oddly quiet throughout the evening, was now cheering with intensity as Jose Mesa strode from the Cleveland bullpen in center field to the mound. On this evening, Mesa's job as a closer was more crucial than ever. The Indians had entered the evening with 85 victories and just 37 defeats, giving them a $22\frac{1}{2}$-game lead over the second-place Royals. One more victory and the Indians would clinch their first baseball championship since that afternoon in Detroit so long ago when Early Wynn pitched the Indians to the 1954 pennant.

The man responsible for Mesa's success was Phil Regan, but ironically Regan watched his pupil from the Baltimore dugout as manager of the Orioles. A year earlier, as pitching coach for the Indians, Regan had urged that Mesa be converted from a starting pitcher to a reliever. Regan was convinced that Mesa's fastball, while overpowering, was too straight and by the fifth inning, major league batters hit him hard. By pitching just an inning or two in relief, Mesa could throw his fastball by the best hitters.[16]

Regan broached the idea with Hargrove and Hart. Persuading them was easy; Mesa was more difficult. Regan explained to the pitcher that he had "Lee Smith" stuff and a chance to become a dominant and wealthy relief pitcher. Plenty of starting pitchers, Regan pointed out, had become outstanding closers, Phil Regan among them. Regan, too, had made the transition reluctantly. While pitching in Detroit in 1965, Regan recalled watching a Tiger reliever and telling teammate Terry Fox, "I'd never want that job."[17] A year later, Regan had been traded to Los Angeles and sent to the bullpen. In an astonishing turnabout, Regan won 14 games and saved 21 for the pennant-winning Dodgers, earning the nickname, "Vulture."

Once Regan persuaded Mesa to move to the bullpen, he also changed Mesa's grip on the baseball. Mesa held the baseball across the seams, much like an infielder, who wants a straight and accurate throw to first base. Regan taught him to grip the ball where the two seams met, which caused a fastball to tail in on right-handed hitters. The results were devastatingly evident: Mesa pitched in relief 51 times in 1994 and won seven games. A suitably impressed Hart signed him to a two-year contract with club options for 1997 and 1998.

Regan had moved on to manage the Orioles by the spring of 1995, but his replacement, Mark Wiley, sketched what he and Hargrove envisioned as the typical Indians' game. Cleveland starting pitchers, relying on an assortment of sinkers, sliders, and curveballs, would work the first six innings and keep the game close. Then Hargrove would turn to a group of hard-throwing relief pitchers: Eric Plunk with a 93-mile-per-hour fastball; Tavarez with a 95-mile-per-hour fastball; and Alan Embree, who was timed during the World Series at 96. Tavarez would work the seventh, Plunk the eighth. "We can bring some power arms," Hart said.[18] All the Indians needed was a reliable closer to pitch the ninth.

The obvious choice was Mesa. Nobody doubted the firepower in Mesa's arm. His fastball zipped through homeplate at 98 miles per hour, and his slider reached 90. Mesa had pitched well in middle relief, but nobody knew if he could handle the pressure of closing. The transition was bumpy. During a game in New York as Mesa's attention wandered, catcher Tony Pena walked out to the mound and swatted him in the head with his glove. But by the end of May, Mesa was nearly unhittable. He saved three crucial games that month against the White Sox, made the All-Star team, and, on August 20, established a major league record with 37 saves in 37 consecutive chances. Even though his base salary was a relative bargain at $850,000, he was on pace to earn an additional $497,223 in performance bonuses, by far the largest on the team.[19]

Now Mesa was pitching the most important inning of Cleveland baseball since 1954. Down by one run, the Orioles had

Cal Ripken, Harold Baines, and Chris Hoiles scheduled to bat in the ninth. Mesa opened by firing a fastball for a strike past Ripken, before missing with a slider away. The next pitch was a burning fastball that Ripken nudged on the ground to Vizquel at shortstop. Baines, with a .188 lifetime average against Mesa, saw three fastballs, lifting the last one to Wayne Kirby in right field for an easy out. Mesa walked Hoiles on five pitches. Jeff Huson fouled off a Mesa fastball. On the next pitch, Huson lifted a weak pop to the left of third base. In the Cleveland dugout, coach Buddy Bell clapped his hands, while Mark Wiley calmly put away his pen and closed his notebook. Thome crossed just behind third base and snared the pop fly with one hand. Mike Hargrove raised both his arms in triumph. The Indians poured onto the field and savored the moment that had eluded them for so long. A woman in the stands held up a large, handmade sign: "Tell Me I'm Not Dreaming."

Most Monday afternoons, Carl Lupica joined his buddy, Elmer Balchick, for a brisk walk through the heavily wooded Chagrin Valley on Cleveland's east side. But today, the two retired draftsmen from Caterpillar decided to drive downtown and watch the Indians work out. Lupica had once been a devoted baseball fan; he could remember going to League Park to watch Bill Knickerbocker play shortstop for the 1936 Indians. His favorite players had been Lou Boudreau, Bob Feller, and Ken Keltner, who thrilled Clevelanders with his acrobatic play at third base. Lupica's cousin, Charlie, had been such an Indians' fanatic that in 1949 he climbed a small flagpole outside his office and vowed to remain there until the Indians went back into first place. Charlie waited in vain, but Bill Veeck, always in tune with a clever promotion, gave Charlie a new car when he climbed down. "He got a Pontiac and rheumatism out of it," cousin Carl often joked. But Carl's passion for baseball died with the Giants' 1954 sweep of the Indians. For years, like thousands of other Clevelanders, he shunned the local team. But Dick Jacobs' team was just too exciting to ignore.

On this sunny Monday afternoon, a welcome break from Cleveland's frosty October, Carl Lupica, Elmer Balchick, and more than 20,000 others scrambled through the lower decks to watch the Indians work out. The next evening, the Indians would open the five-game divisional playoff series against the Boston

Red Sox, champions of the American League East Division. The winner of the series would advance to the seven-game American League Championship Series against either Seattle, the winners of the West, or the New York Yankees, who entered the playoffs as the wildcard.

The entire city had come down with a virulent case of playoff fever. Whether it was Chuck's Beverage Shop in quaint Chagrin Falls or the towering British Petroleum Building on Public Square, the Indians' imprint was everywhere. Chief Wahoos hung from storefronts and living room windows; sparkling "Go Tribe" signs lit up skyscrapers. Even the stately Federal Reserve Building on Superior Avenue was not immune. There, a smiling George Washington sported an Indian feather above the inscription, "E. Pluribus Tribe."

The Red Sox had a strong team. First baseman Mo Vaughn drove in 126 runs to tie Albert Belle for the league lead; shortstop John Valentin hit 27 home runs; third baseman Tim Naehring batted .307, and designated hitter Jose Canseco smacked 24 home runs. Red Sox manager Kevin Kennedy had an outstanding closer in Rick Aguilera, and three solid starting pitchers in Roger Clemens, Tim Wakefield, and Eric Hanson. Mike Hargrove was particularly worried about Hanson, who had twice beaten the Indians that year with his changeup and reminded Hargrove of Milwaukee's Pete Vuckovich the year he won the Cy Young Award. "Hanson is tough because he throws his breaking ball when he's behind in the count," Hargrove explained. "That's a very difficult thing to adjust to."[20] But the Red Sox, overall, lacked Cleveland's offensive firepower and pitching depth.

Monday's brilliant Indian summer gave way on Tuesday to sullen clouds and a steady drizzle. By six in the evening, the rain still was falling and the game was in doubt. But the fans, many decked out in yellow slickers, still filed into Jacobs Field, and they were rewarded as a yellow-orange sun glinted through the clouds. At eight, about 20 minutes before the scheduled start of the game, Herb Score proclaimed on radio that there was "a good chance" the game would be played. Five minutes later, wild cheers erupted as the ground crew removed the tarp to reveal the velvety green infield. Dick Jacobs, Governor Voinovich, and Mayor White emerged from the dugout to throw out the first baseballs. The Cleveland Orchestra played the national anthem. Fireworks exploded in the night sky, and masses of red, white, and blue balloons floated out of the ballpark. At 8:42 in the evening, the players, wearing their starched white home jerseys with "Indians" scripted in red across the front, took the field. And 41 years of pent-up emotion spilled out in one thunderous, primal roar.

Dennis Martinez, his elbow tight and sore on this raw, damp evening, held the Red Sox to five hits and two runs through the first six innings. He handed the Cleveland bullpen a 3-2 lead, but Boston's Luis Alicea sent the game into extra innings with a home run in the eighth. In the 11th, the Red Sox took a 4-3 lead on Naehring's home run, but Belle responded with his own home run in the bottom half of the inning against Aguilera. Stung by Belle's blast, Kennedy asked homeplate umpire Tim Welke to confiscate Belle's bat to see if it had been corked. An infuriated Belle returned to the dugout, flexed his right arm and pointed to his biceps. Outgoing American League President Bobby Brown ordered the bat sawed in half and duly concluded it was legal.

The two teams slogged on, players on both teams slipping on the wet grass. Although thousands of people left for home, as many as 30,000 remained, some abandoning their upper-deck seats for cover in the lower deck. By the 13th inning, it was already two in the morning.

Boston relief pitcher Zane Smith retired Ramirez on a groundball and Perry on a line drive to right to open the 13th. Then, Tony Pena, who had replaced Sandy Alomar as the Cleveland catcher in the 10th, came to the plate to face his old teammates. Two years earlier, the Red Sox had allowed Pena to become a free agent because he no longer could hit on a regular basis. With the count 3-and-0, Smith heaved a fastball down the middle of the plate. Pena's bat flashed, and NBC announcer Bob Costas cried out, "Oh man!" At 2:08 in the morning, the ball barely cleared the 19-foot wall in left field for a home run and the first Indians' post-season victory in nearly half-a-century.

The second game of the playoffs began badly for Orel Hershiser. Belle dropped a line drive off the bat of Dwayne Hosey in the first inning, allowing Hosey to reach second. Vizquel then cleanly fielded Valentin's groundball, but Sorrento slipped off first base as he lunged to make the catch. The Red Sox should have had runners at first and second, but Hosey recklessly broke for third. Sorrento fired to Thome, who tagged the sliding Hosey. Hershiser then struck out Vaughn, and retired Canseco on a flyball to left field.

Orel Hershiser thrived on the pressure of post-season baseball, which was the reason John Hart signed him. The Cleveland farm system had produced a bevy of outstanding hitters, but many of the hard-throwing pitchers the Indians were developing were not ready for crucial post-season games. Hart refused to build a team with free agents, as other general managers foolishly attempted to do, but he would judiciously use them to fill the gaps. Hershiser had almost singlehandedly pitched the Dodgers to the 1988 World Championship, shutting out the Mets in the seventh game of the NLCS, and defeating the A's twice in the World Series. He overwhelmed opposing batters with his hard, sinking fastball and a sharp breaking curveball that drove right-handed power hitters to despair as it skipped over the outside corner.

Always analytical, he told reporters that the key to winning post-season games was to concentrate on executing a particular play instead of worrying about the results. He used the example of pitching in the ninth inning of a tense World Series game before a roaring hostile crowd, and facing a 3-and-2 count on a critical batter. To throw a curveball for a strike in that situation, Hershiser said, was the same as throwing a curveball during a quiet afternoon workout in the bullpen. "If I can do it in the bullpen, then there's no reason I can't block it out and do it again on the mound with everything happening," Hershiser said. [21]

Hershiser did not look the part of a major league pitcher. "Let's face it, I'm just a pale guy with glasses, long arms, and a sunken chest," he once told *Sports Illustrated*.[22] When major college baseball programs ignored him in high school, Hershiser went on to tiny Bowling Green State University in northwest Ohio, not far from his parents' home in Detroit. The Dodgers drafted him in the 17th round in 1979, and within four years he had advanced to Los Angeles. By 1988, he was the dominant pitcher in baseball, winning 23 games and shattering a major league record with 59 consecutive scoreless innings. A devout Christian who stayed calm by singing hymns to himself, Hershiser was brutally competitive on the mound, so much so that Dodger manager Tommy Lasorda nicknamed him "Bulldog."

His career nearly ended in the spring of 1990. He first noticed something wrong while driving his car one day. As he gestured with his right arm to the back seat where his two sons were sitting, he felt his shoulder click as if it were popping out of the socket. The same pain persisted during spring training. At first, Hershiser dismissed it as the normal soreness every pitcher feels in the spring. He gamely struggled through the early part of the season, but in late April the pain was bad enough that he left a game in the seventh inning against the Cardinals. The next day, team physician Dr. Frank Jobe performed an MRI. Thirty minutes later, Jobe called Hershiser and his wife, Jamie, into his office, where the X-rays were hanging on the wall. "Orel, I'm afraid this is very serious." Jobe explained that the shoulder was so badly damaged, that he would have to completely reconstruct it. It would be two years, Jobe predicted, before Hershiser could pitch again.[23]

Hershiser accepted the verdict stoically, praying in Jobe's office and vowing to quickly recover. That night, he and Jamie invited a few friends over for pizza. The next morning, though, in Centinela Hospital Medical Center, as a nurse gave him an anesthetic shot, Hershiser's calm demeanor faded. "Please, please, don't let them cut me!" he shouted at Jamie as he was wheeled into the operating room. [24] When Jobe opened up Hershiser's shoulder, the cartilage lining appeared as if it had been smashed over and over with a hammer.

Hershiser awoke to find his right arm in a brace, elevated above his head. "This is not going to work," a dejected Hershiser told himself. But that mood quickly passed. Within a week, he had discarded the brace in favor of a sling. Every morning, he rotated his right arm, then stood under hot showers and tried to touch the ceiling with his right hand.[25] He would lie on the family room floor and move his arm up to where it hurt, and hold it for 15 seconds. He devoted two hours a day to working with weights. Three months after the surgery, he tossed a baseball 30 feet, and by the middle of September, he was throwing off the mound.

The next season, he pitched 112 innings and won seven games, and by the spring of 1992 he showed signs of regaining his old sinking fastball. After facing Hershiser in batting practice,

Darryl Strawberry told reporters that "the ball moved. The ball did things. Last year, it was flat. This year, it ain't flat." [26] Hershiser pitched 211 innings and won 10 games that year, and by the spring of 1994, he was beginning to feel normal again. [27]

Knowing that Hershiser's contract expired at the end of 1994, John Hart asked Mark Wiley to scout Hershiser. As the season progressed, Wiley realized Hershiser was throwing harder and recommended that the Indians take him. [28] Days after the strike ended, Hershiser signed a one-year deal with Cleveland for $1.45 million, rejecting more lucrative offers from the Yankees and Giants. Hershiser thought the Indians had a better chance of reaching the World Series.

Hershiser pitched so well in the spring, that just before the team returned to Cleveland, John Hart asked him, "What was your best year?" When Hershiser answered 23 victories in 1988, Hart replied, "Set your sights on it. Because this club is going to score you runs." [29] By the late summer, the Cleveland radar guns regularly recorded Hershiser between 87 and 90 miles an hour, and occasionally nudging 93. He won 16 games, lost just six, and posted a 3.87 earned-run average.

Now in the second playoff game, the Red Sox were flailing away in vain at Hershiser's sinkers. In the third inning, Hershiser retired Valentin and Vaughn on groundballs and struck out Canseco. In the fourth, Greenwell flied to Belle, Naehring grounded out, and Willie McGee struck out. MacFarlane singled to open the fifth, but Hershiser neatly disposed of the next three hitters. He retired six consecutive Boston batters in the sixth and seventh.

Meanwhile, the Indians scored twice in the bottom of the fifth against Hanson. Hershiser took that 2-0 lead into the eighth inning, when with one out, he motioned to Hargrove in the dugout. His back was tightening, Hershiser explained. Perhaps it would be better for Hargrove to summon a fresh reliever. Tavarez and Assenmacher finished the eighth, Mesa the ninth. The Indians won, 4-0.

The teams moved to Boston. On a frigid night in Fenway Park, where the Indians won the 1948 playoff, Thome homered, Murray drove in three runs, and Nagy pitched seven innings as the Indians won, 8-2. In three games, Cleveland pitchers posted a 1.74 earned-run average, holding Vaughn and Canseco hitless in 27 at-bats. The Indians did not celebrate with champagne. Instead, they exchanged cordial handshakes with one another as they left the field. Vizquel knew the reason. "Our goal," he said, "is the World Series." [30]

Everyone had yearned for a Yankee-Indian matchup, reviving memories of their great rivalry in the pennant races of the 1950s. It also would allow Dick Jacobs and George Steinbrenner to match wits and drinks at Johnny's. Steinbrenner, the reckless big spender, and Jacobs, the meticulous long-range planner, were on friendly terms; Steinbrenner had recommended that Jacobs hire Hank Peters in 1987.

But after defeating the Mariners in the first two games of the divisional series, the Yankees lost all three games in the deafening din of the Seattle Kingdome. Inadvertently, Steinbrenner had done the Indians a favor; to beat the Yankees, Seattle manager Lou Piniella called upon hard-throwing lefthander Randy Johnson to start the critical third game and pitch in relief in the final game. Johnson already had pitched the playoff game against the Angels that gave the Mariners the Western Division championship. Worn out from the season's grinding conclusion, Johnson would be available to pitch only two games in the ALCS. The rest of the Seattle starting staff was right-handed and vulnerable to Cleveland's left-handed batters: Andy Benes, picked up late in the year from San Diego; Chris Bosio, whom the Indians hit hard earlier in the year; and Tim Belcher. Seattle could score runs with outfielders Ken Griffey, Jr., and Jay Buhner, who hit 40 home runs; designated hitter Edgar Martinez, who led the American League with a .352 average; and first baseman Tino Martinez, who hit 31 home runs.

The teams split the first two games in the noisy Kingdome. Although rookie pitcher Bob Wolcott scored a shocking victory over the hard-hitting Indians in the first game, Hershiser followed the next evening by limiting the Mariners to four hits in eight innings. He was particularly effective against the heart of the Seattle order, retiring Edgar Martinez, Tino Martinez, and Jay Buhner all nine times.

That set up the Friday night game in Jacobs Field where the Indians had to face Johnson, who during the season won 18 games, lost just two, posted a 2.48 earned-run average, and struck out 294 batters in 214 innings. By beating Johnson, the Indians could deliver a demoralizing blow to the Mariners, and perhaps avoid a return to the Kingdome for the sixth and seventh games.

Throughout the evening, the Indians flirted with victory. Nagy held the Mariners to two runs in eight innings, and a tired Johnson relied more on his slider than his fastball. The Indians tied the game, 2-2, in the eighth, and when Johnson was replaced in the ninth by Norm Charlton, it seemed the Indians had the game won. Instead, the Indians mangled their chance in the ninth, sending the game into extra innings. But for the Indians, the game ended all too abruptly. With two out and one on in the 11th, relief pitcher Eric Plunk threw what Buhner had waited all series for—a fastball out over the plate. Buhner extended his powerful arms, and the ball disappeared over the right-field wall. The Mariners led two games to one. Even worse for the Indians, no matter what happened in the next two games, they would have to return to Seattle and face Randy Johnson one more time.

The Cleveland locker room was eerily quiet. No bantering. No radios blaring the rhythm and blues of Montell Jordan. The players shed their uniforms in silence, as Hershiser and Martinez sat at a small table eating dinner. The only sound was the air-conditioning unit, which seemed to be operating a trifle too high.

Cameras surrounded Nagy as he pulled on his blue jeans. "It's a tough loss to take," Nagy admitted, but, he added with defiance, "one of the characteristics of this team is our resiliency. It's going to be a big test for us tomorrow, but I have no doubt in my mind that this team can come back and win tomorrow and the next night." [31]

By the following afternoon, the news had worsened. Albert Belle had twisted his ankle during his final at-bat and was on crutches. Sandy Alomar's neck was stiff, and he was out for the night. Martinez' shoulder was tender, forcing the Indians to push him back to the sixth game in Seattle and start Hershiser in the fifth game. Some reporters thought the Indians were dead. "Now, it's the Indians who look a little piqued," wrote Tom Boswell of the

Washington Post. But, as Nagy had warned, this team was resilient. Lofton opened the first inning with a single, stole second, and brazenly went to third on catcher Dan Wilson's throwing error. Vizquel walked, and Lofton scored on Baerga's groundball. Moments later, Eddie Murray smacked a two-run home run. Staked to a 3-0 lead, Ken Hill did what John Hart and Dan O'Dowd had hoped for when they picked him up from the Cardinals. Under Mark Wiley's tutelage, Ken Hill had increased the velocity of his fastball from 87 miles an hour to 95, and, in Wiley's words, Hill "blew Chicago away" in his final start of the season. The Indians won, 7-0, and the series was even at 2-2.

The pivotal game was Sunday evening. Hershiser held the Mariners to two runs in six innings. In the bottom of the sixth, Murray doubled off Bosio. Thome then drove a low fastball deep into the second deck in right field and the Indians led, 3-2. But nothing in this series would come easy. In the top of the seventh with Tavarez pitching for Cleveland, Sorrento lost control of Dan Wilson's groundball for an error. Sorrento then dove to grasp Cora's groundball, but his throw to second pulled Vizquel off the bag. Edgar Martinez forced Cora at second with a groundball, but the Mariners had runners at first and third with just one out. With the left-handed batting Griffey at the plate, Hargrove called for Assenmacher, and another John Hart investment paid off. Assenmacher struck out Griffey. Assenmacher had the choice of walking Buhner to face the left-handed batting Tino Martinez. He opted to pitch to Buhner, who swung and missed at two curveballs. Assenmacher planned to waste his next pitch, but instead threw a curveball higher than he wanted. Buhner, however, lunged for the ball, striking out to end the inning.[32] Mesa set the Mariners down in the ninth, and the Indians were just one victory from their first pennant in 41 years.

The two teams flew to Seattle where once again the 6-foot-10 frame of Randy Johnson loomed in the Kingdome. But Johnson was fatigued, while Martinez had had six days to shake the aches from his shoulder and elbow. "All through my life, this is the game I've been looking for," Dennis Martinez later said.[33] He baffled Seattle's power hitters with his sharp curveball and dazzling change of pace. He was at his best during a nervous sixth inning, with the Indians clinging to a 1-0 lead. Vince Coleman opened with a single, and stole second. Joey Cora's job was to bunt, but instead he popped to Herb Perry at first. Griffey advanced Coleman to third base with a flyball, and Martinez then hit Edgar Martinez with a pitch. With the winning runs on base, Dennis Martinez faced Tino Martinez, who had driven in 111 runs during the regular season. He worked the count to 2-and-2 before throwing a soft changeup that Tino Martinez helplessly swung at for a third strike. Watching from the dugout, an appreciative Orel Hershiser thought it was "the most professional pitch" he had ever seen.[34] In the eighth inning, the Indians broke through for three runs, the last on Baerga's home run.

Mesa made quick work of the Mariners in the ninth. Griffey grounded to second base, and Edgar Martinez struck out. From the dugout, Mike Hargrove recalled all the miserable Cleveland teams he had played for—teams best forgotten by everyone else. There were the 1985 Indians of pitchers Curt Wardle, Bryan Clark, Rich Thompson, and Roy Smith, a team that lost 102 times. The first Cleveland team he managed was even worse, losing 105 games in 1991. For a moment, Hargrove wondered, "Can this really be happening?"[35] Mesa walked Tino Martinez, but Buhner skipped a grounder to Alvaro Espinoza at third, who grasped the ball and fired crisply to Perry at first. The jubilant Indians carried Dennis Martinez off the field, and for the first time in four decades, champagne was spilled in a Cleveland locker room.

Half-a-continent away, Dick Jacobs watched the celebration on TV in his Winton Place penthouse. Jacobs had opted against flying to Seattle for the game, and, on this particular evening, he ordered a takeout dinner and ate by himself. John Hart telephoned from Seattle. So did Bill Bartholomew of the Atlanta Braves, the team the Indians would play in the World Series. It was a private triumph for a very private man.

The Braves were, in many ways, mirror images of the Indians. After years of pursuing broken-down free agents such as Al Hrabosky and Gary Matthews, Atlanta owner Ted Turner turned over daily operations of the team to seasoned professionals, general manager John Schuerholz and field manager Bobby Cox. Their focus on player development allowed the Braves' farm system to produce the heart of the team, starting pitchers Tom Glavine and

Steve Avery; relief pitchers Kent Mercker, Pedro Borbon, and Mark Wohlers, the latter with a fastball that topped out at 100 miles per hour; outfielders Dave Justice and Ryan Klesko; catcher Javier Lopez; third baseman Chipper Jones; shortstop Jeff Blauser; and second baseman Mark Lemke. Like John Hart in Cleveland, Schuerholz and Cox used trades and free agents to fill in the gaps. Righthander Greg Maddux, whose 19-2 record earned him a fourth consecutive Cy Young Award, had been signed as a free agent, while first baseman Fred McGriff, starting pitcher John Smoltz, and outfielder Marquis Grissom, whom Schuerholz called "the best center fielder I've seen since Paul Blair" were obtained through shrewd trades. The Braves had twice lost the World Series to Minnesota and Toronto; they were arguably the strongest team in baseball.

Freed from the job of trying to play general manager, Turner could play his favorite role, the flamboyant sportsman with the glamorous wife. Whenever the Braves scored, the cameras panned to Ted and Jane Fonda cheering. It was great theater. By contrast, when the spotlight shined on Dick Jacobs, nobody quite knew who he was; ABC showed Jacobs and Hart together behind the third-base dugout during the first game in Atlanta, but the announcer only mentioned Hart.

Before a crowd of 51,876, the World Series opened grimly for the Indians. Relying on his moving fastball and flawless control of four pitches, Maddux allowed just two hits and one earned run. In the second game, Glavine exploited Cleveland's vulnerability to left-handed pitching, holding the Indians to three base hits in six innings. As in 1954, the Indians returned to Cleveland, trailing two games to none, and facing the horrifying prospect of a sweep. "If a Cleveland team," wrote Tom Boswell, "with Bob Lemon, Early Wynn, Mike Garcia, Bob Feller, Don Mossi, Ray Narleski, Vic Wertz, Al Rosen, and Larry Doby can get swept by the likes of Dusty Rhodes, Don Liddle, Ruben Gomez, and Marv Grissom, then this Cleveland team shouldn't be too sure it will return to Atlanta this autumn."

In the Indians' climb to the 1995 World Series, each carefully chosen component in the strategic plan had contributed. Albert

Belle, developed in the Cleveland farm system, had saved the Indians from defeat in the opening playoff game against the Red Sox. Jim Thome, another homegrown product, hit the game-winning home run that beat the Mariners in the fifth game. Orel Hershiser, the free-agent pitcher chosen to add experience to the young team, had won three nerve-wracking post-season games. Now, Kenny Lofton, picked up from Houston for Ed Taubensee, would add a much-needed spark to the demoralized team.

Lofton played the kind of spirited, unpredictable baseball that was infectious on a team. It was Lofton who had provided the signature moment of the Indians sixth-game victory over Seattle: Randy Johnson, startled and gaping as Lofton lunged across homeplate on a wild pitch that started with Lofton at second base. Lofton continued his aggressive play into the World Series. In the first inning of the first game against Maddux, Lofton reached first on an error, stole second and third, and scored on a groundball. In the ninth, with Maddux leading, 3-1, Lofton singled with one out. Vizquel grounded out to Lemke at second, but Lofton, instead of holding at second, dashed toward third. McGriff threw wildly to Jones at third, and Lofton scored. The Indians' first-base coach Dave Nelson, noting that the Indians were down two runs at the time, conceded that "it wasn't the best of plays." But it was the kind of play that could throw opponents off-stride, the kind of play Nelson had come to expect from Lofton, his prized pupil.[36]

Nelson, Lofton's tutor in the fine art of basestealing, had watched Lofton hone his instinctive skills since 1992, when Nelson first saw him in spring training. Back then, Nelson thought Lofton had "a lot of speed and not a whole lot of basestealing knowledge." But Lofton was eager to learn, and Nelson predicted to Cleveland reporters that the new center fielder would rapidly improve. Nelson was correct: Lofton's batting average shot from .285 in 1992 to .349 in 1994 while he averaged 65 stolen bases a year. Lofton was beginning to learn what Nelson called "the little subtleties" of stealing. For example, right-handed pitchers often set up differently on the mound when throwing to first instead of home. Lofton picked that up, allowing him to take greater leads.[37]

Now, before the third game of the World Series, Lofton was worried enough about the Indians' play to give his teammates a pep talk in the clubhouse. Don't try and overdo things, Lofton advised. The Indians had too much talent to be swept. Lay off the bad pitches and make the Braves throw strikes.[38] When the starting lineups for the Indians were introduced before the game, it was a deadly determined Lofton whom the fans saw. Emerging from the dugout, Lofton turned toward Omar Vizquel and shouted, "Go."

Lofton singled off Smoltz to lead off the game, and scored when Vizquel tripled to right. The Indians increased their lead to 2-1 in the third, thanks to Lofton's double. Vizquel dropped a perfect bunt in the dirt on the third-base line for a single, allowing Lofton to scamper to third. Lofton then dashed home on Baerga's shallow line single to left. In the fourth, Lofton bounced a single over second base, but was thrown out by Javier Lopez attempting to steal second. But Nelson was not worried. As he liked to tell reporters, "Kenny is not afraid to fail." [39]

Lofton would have another opportunity with one out in the seventh, the Indians clinging to a 4-3 lead, and hard-throwing lefthander Kent Mercker pitching for the Braves. Lofton walked and advanced to second on Vizquel's ground out. With a one-ball count on Baerga, Braves shortstop Mike Mordecai broke behind Lofton at second for a pickoff attempt. Mercker should have either tossed to Mordecai or stepped off the rubber and called time. Instead, he committed a grievous error by pitching to Baerga with his shortstop out of position. Lofton instantly broke for third; he had such a lead that Lopez did not bother to throw. "A lot of people would say, 'He's stealing third base with two outs, that's a dumb play.' " Nelson said. "But it's easier to score from third base." [40] Nelson was right. Baerga pulled the next pitch to the right of Mordecai, who slipped and tumbled to the ground as he grasped the ball. Lofton, glancing at Mordecai, trotted home with Cleveland's fifth run. Although nobody realized it then, Lofton's run saved the game for the Indians.

In the eighth, the Braves took advantage of an error by Baerga to score three times for a 6-5 lead. But in the bottom of the inning, Sandy Alomar flicked a double to right field off Wohlers to drive in Ramirez and send the game into extra innings. In the bottom of the 11th, Baerga led off against Atlanta reliever Alejandro Pena. Baerga took the first pitch inside, and then fouled the next four fastballs down the left-field line. After two Pena changeups missed for balls, Baerga found the pitch left-handed hitters crave: a 92-mile-per-hour fastball at the knees. Baerga stroked it to deep center field where it bounced on the warning track for a double. As Hargrove sent Alvaro Espinoza to run for Baerga, Bobby Cox shouted to get the attention of Lopez. But the crowd was screaming so loud, that Cox had to emerge from the dugout and wave four fingers at his catcher: Walk Belle and pitch to Murray, who had struck out three times. But Pena's first pitch to Murray was a high fastball that the veteran designated hitter smacked into center field for a single. Grissom glided in, grabbed the ball, but his throw was to the left of homeplate. Lofton jumped from the dugout to urge Espinoza on. Espinoza slid home, touching the plate with his right hand, and then leaping into the waiting arms of Thome. The Indians had won their first World Series game since 1948. No matter what happened in the next four games, this World Series would not be like the 1954 debacle.

The next evening, the Braves increased their lead to three games to one as Avery held the Indians to just three hits and one run in six innings. An impressed Dennis Martinez explained that Avery had changed his pitching style since the days when Martinez pitched in the National League. Martinez thought Avery had "learned a lot from Glavine," becoming a "finesse pitcher," trading in a constant barrage of overpowering hard stuff for a variety of changeups and breaking balls. "That shows you he's learning." [41]

Avery's performance opened the way for Maddux to win the World Series in the fifth game, the final game of the year in Jacobs Field. But this time, the Indians were ready for him. From watching Maddux in the opener, Cleveland batting coach Charlie Manuel concluded that the best pitch the Indians saw was the first one. Once Maddux was ahead in the count, batters rarely saw a hittable pitch. Manuel urged his hitters to move up in the batter's box and swing at the first pitch, allowing them to reach Maddux' outside fastball. In the first inning, Belle swatted Maddux' first pitch over the right-field wall for a two-run home run. Maddux recognized the Indians' tactics, and, in frustration, aimed a fastball at Murray's head. Murray ducked, but when he gestured and swore at Maddux, players from both dugouts poured on to the field. There, in full view of the national TV audience, Hershiser admonished Maddux about throwing at opposing batters.

The Indians continued to hit the ball hard. In the sixth inning with one out and the game tied, 2-2, Baerga drove an outside pitch into left field for a double. Maddux intentionally walked Belle, and retired Murray on a flyball to right field, allowing Baerga to scramble to third base. The next hitter was Thome, who had been enduring a frightful series with just two base hits and a .143 average. With Thome looking for a pitch away, Maddux jammed him inside with fastballs and worked the count to 1-and-2. Catcher Charlie O'Brien called for a changeup away and set himself up on the outside corner of the plate. But Maddux' change floated across the middle of the plate and Thome lined the ball into center field for a single, driving in Baerga. In the Atlanta dugout, Bobby Cox folded his arms in dismay. Had Maddux thrown the same pitch low, Cox thought, Thome would have struck out.[42] Manny Ramirez followed by smacking Maddux' first pitch past Lemke for a run-scoring single and a 4-2 Cleveland lead.

Meanwhile, the Braves were coming up almost empty against Hershiser. Hershiser had yielded a home run in the fourth to Luis Polonia, and his wild throw on a groundball in the fifth gave Atlanta its second run. Between the seventh and eighth innings, Wylie asked Hershiser if he was tired. Hershiser's snap reply was, "I feel awesome." Then he went out and snared a line drive off the bat of Grissom for a doubleplay. "Finally!" Hershiser shouted out loud. The crowd of 43,607 stood as Hershiser struck out Polonia on a 2-and-2 pitch. In the ninth, Hershiser turned the game over to Mesa, who gave up a harmless two-run homer to Ryan Klesko. After the final Atlanta out and a 5-4 Cleveland victory, neither Hershiser nor the fans wanted to leave. Bruce Springsteen's "Glory Days" blared from the loudspeakers, people rang bells and cheered themselves hoarse. Hershiser told CNN that he had been "thanking God the whole way" on the line drive. "Finally I did something with my glove." Inside the clubhouse, Mark Wylie was bragging to reporters about the way the Indians hit Maddux. A great pitcher might beat the Indians once—but not twice, he said. During the year, the team had nailed every

American League pitcher: Mike Mussina, Roger Clemens, Kevin Appier, David Cone, Jimmy Key, Wylie said. "When you can get every great pitcher in [your] own league, we should have enough stuff to get somebody who's supposed to be the best pitcher in baseball." [43]

The reprieve sent the Indians back to Atlanta for the sixth game. But Glavine was at his best, holding the Indians to just one base hit. Dave Justice homered off relief pitcher Jim Poole in the sixth for the only run of the evening, allowing the Braves to leave the field as champions of baseball.

The Indians had lost the Series, but they were no longer a band of rag-tag losers. They were once again a baseball power. That was more than enough to content Cleveland fans and Dick Jacobs. A cheering crowd greeted the Indians at Cleveland Hopkins Airport and the city honored them with a downtown parade. When a friend consoled Jacobs over a drink at Johnny's, saying "Well, it's too bad," Jacobs shook his head. "We put this team together to win the division. We didn't put this together to win the American League." To Dick Jacobs, 1995 was only the beginning.

The morning after the Indians won the fifth game of the World Series, a Gulfstream jet roared from Hopkins Airport, glided over the empty Cleveland Stadium, and set a course east for Baltimore. The jet carried Art Modell, owner of the Cleveland Browns; Alfred Lerner, a minority shareholder and Modell's closest confidant; David Modell, stepson of the Browns' owner and his expected heir; and James Bailey, the Browns' lawyer who once tangled with Bunny Goldfarb over the Indians' lease. In Baltimore, the jet taxied to a private terminal, where Maryland Governor Parris Glendening and John Moag, chairman of the Maryland Stadium Authority, clambered aboard.

As David Modell poured coffee, Glendening sat on a leather couch opposite Art Modell, while Moag sat next to the Cleveland owner. Moag, an attorney with the influential lobbying firm of Patton, Boggs, was struck by how distraught Modell appeared. "This is the most traumatic thing that has ever occurred in my professional life," Modell told them. "What I'm doing is ending a life in Cleveland that has been long, and, in many respects, won-

derful. It's a city where I raised my children." But, Modell continued, he could not operate in antiquated Cleveland Stadium.
Cleveland officials had "failed" to produce a realistic plan to rebuild the mammoth stadium, Modell insisted. The time had
come, Modell said, to move his franchise. Modell appeared so
unhappy, that Moag wished to himself the conversation would
end. (44)

Suddenly it did, as Modell asked abruptly, "You have some
papers for me to sign?" Eight times, Modell scribbled his name.
With those brief strokes, Modell agreed to uproot the Cleveland
Browns from their home of a half century and take them to Baltimore. Glendening promised Modell a $200-million stadium and
all the proceeds from the luxury loges, club seats, parking, and
concessions—a fabulous deal that guaranteed a $30 million
annual profit for years to come. The $75 million from the sale of
personal seat licenses alone would enable Modell to build a practice facility, pay moving expenses, and handle what was expected
to be a hefty legal bill from Jones, Day. Modell's family would
have the money to pay estate taxes after his death, allowing David Modell to own an NFL franchise.

In many ways, the deal struck in Baltimore provided the cli-
max to the bitter war between Steve O'Neill and Art Modell that
began so many summers ago. Then Modell lorded it over the sickly Indians who were forced to lease space from him. But now,
Dick Jacobs operated the class team in Cleveland, playing in one
of the most envied parks in America, while Modell's franchise and
Cleveland Stadium had deteriorated. In a decade of ownership,
Dick Jacobs had managed to go where Art Modell had never
been: his sport's championship event. Modell, wrote John Helyar,
had been "outmaneuvered" by Dick Jacobs, "whose cool style
and commendable results made Mr. Modell's volatile, hands-on
proprietorship look anachronistic." (45) Many suspected that
Modell was jealous of Jacobs' success. "Art was yesterday's hero
and Dick Jacobs was today's hero," Al Lerner conceded.(46) David
Modell often "badmouthed" Dick Jacobs privately, according to
Cleveland business executives. One afternoon in front of reporters, he "launched into a profanity-laced tirade" against Jacobs,
then implored them to keep his remarks off the record.(47)

But there was more than simple envy involved. When Dick
Jacobs moved the Indians out of Cleveland Stadium, Art Modell

and Stadium Corporation lost their chief tenant and a big chunk of revenue. Without baseball, corporate demand for his luxury loges waned; by 1995, Modell could only lease 80 percent of the loges in Cleveland Stadium. Everyone knew the stadium needed a massive renovation, but Tim Hagan and the county commissioners first wanted to deal with paying off $28 million in construction cost overruns at Jacobs Field and Gund Arena. By the summer of 1995, Mayor White, Governor Voinovich, and Hagan agreed upon a plan to spend $175 million and meet Modell's demands to overhaul the old stadium. But covertly, Modell already was flirting with Baltimore. In late September, Modell and Lerner met secretly with Moag in Lerner's Manhattan office overlooking Central Park. Moag left the meeting convinced that Modell would make the move. Maryland's offer was so extravagant, Modell feared that if he hesitated, the owners of the Tampa Bay Buccaneers or Arizona Cardinals would snatch it out from under him.[48] Modell's choice was the same one Walter O'Malley faced 40 years earlier: O'Malley could make a fortune in Brooklyn or move to Los Angeles and make an even greater fortune.

While derision and threats rained down upon Modell after ths announcement, Dick Jacobs was careful not to criticize the Browns' owner. The Browns were Modell's private property and he could do as he wished, Jacobs said. He even ordered Indians executives to shut up if reporters asked for their comments on the deal. But Jacobs couldn't stop friends from issuing their own opinions. Many thought Modell had delivered a punishing blow to his longtime home and had done it in a particularly vengeful way, announcing his exit less than a fortnight after the World Series. "You go from the best sports story in this city in the last half-a-century to the worst sports story in this city in this century inside of one week," one friend muttered.

With the World Series behind them, John Hart and Dan O'Dowd quickly turned to the future, focusing anew on Cleveland's long-term strategic plan. Unlike other teams, whose budgets were haphazardly thrown together each year, the Indians could project their revenue streams through 1998 and their payroll to the turn of the century.

The plan was carried out by Hank Peters' boys, foremost among them Dan O'Dowd. "I was tied to the hip with Hank," O'Dowd would say, often regretting the fact that Peters wasn't receiving the credit he deserved for building the 1995 Indians. Peters had hired O'Dowd in Baltimore as assistant director of player development. When Peters moved on to Cleveland in 1987, O'Dowd was told by the new Oriole regime that he could stay, but in a lesser position and with a $20,000-a-year cut in pay. "If I wasn't fired in Baltimore," O'Dowd joked, "I was pushed out the fourth-floor window." Peters was there to catch him. He recruited O'Dowd as farm director, and, by 1995, O'Dowd had advanced to assistant general manager and director of baseball operations, and had become a sought-after commodity. When Baltimore owner Peter Angelos asked Dick Jacobs for permission to hire O'Dowd as the Oriole general manager, Jacobs said no. Reporters assumed that Jacobs was angry with Angelos because the Oriole owner had refused to use replacement players during the strike. But Dick Jacobs valued O'Dowd too much. Confident that some day he would attain his dream of being a general manager, the 36-year-old O'Dowd decided to "shut up and do my job." [49]

O'Dowd had cash to spend because the Indians had done something no other team in baseball had done: They sold all 3.3 million tickets to Jacobs Field for the 1996 season, months before the season's first baseball would be thrown out. Dick Jacobs approved an increase in the team payroll from $33 million to $43 million. [50]

But mindful of Dick Jacobs' spending edicts, O'Dowd and Hart established clear boundaries. They were willing to offer long-term deals to position players, such as Belle, Ramirez, Lofton, and Thome. But they generally refused to guarantee more than two years to pitchers, who were more fragile than position players. Anything longer than two years meant that "somewhere we'd be left with an injured guy on our hands," O'Dowd explained. [51]

So it unfolded. The Indians signed Manny Ramirez to a five-year contract worth $15 million; extended Vizquel's contract by six years for $18.3 million; agreed to a two-year, $5 million deal with free-agent first baseman Julio Franco; and signed Eddie Murray, Alvaro Espinoza, and Tony Pena to one-year deals. With Franco set for first base, the Indians refused to pick up Paul Sorrento's $1.5 million option for 1996; he signed with Seattle.

Pitchers, however, were another matter. When Ken Hill's agent demanded a four-year contract, O'Dowd and Hart said no, and allowed him to leave. Instead they signed free-agent starting pitcher Jack McDowell to a two-year contract worth $10.15 million, and a club option in 1998 worth $4.8 million. McDowell, a onetime Cy Young Award winner, won 15 games for the Yankees, including a shutout against the Indians in September. "That was the best pitching performance I've seen all season," one American League scout said.[52] The Indians then picked up Hershiser's $1.5 million option for 1996 and awarded him a second year in 1997 for $2.7 million. The Indians signed Nagy to a two-year deal worth $6.62 million, with the obligatory club option for $3.35 million in 1998. The only exception O'Dowd and Hart made was Julian Tavarez: They guaranteed him three years until 1998. But in return, the Indians insisted upon club options for 1999 and 2000.

"This has been by design," O'Dowd said. "We have now put together the entire core of our club." [53] Ramirez, Thome, Lofton, Baerga, Vizquel, Alomar, Franco, Nagy, McDowell, Hershiser, Mesa, Tavarez, and Assenmacher would be part of the Indians for at least the next two years. With that committed core, the Indians avoided the foolish bidding wars that George Steinbrenner and Peter Angelos engaged in for free agents such as Robby Alomar, David Cone, and Kenny Rogers.

Instead of lavishing millions of dollars on questionable free agents, O'Dowd could continue expanding the Cleveland farm system, much as Hank Greenberg had done four decades ago. Thanks in large part to Hank Peters, the Indians had increased their farm budget from $3.5 million in 1986 to $7 million by 1990. By 1995, the Indians spent a healthy $8.5 million on their minor league system; only the Blue Jays and Dodgers with their $12 million budgets dramatically outspent Cleveland. O'Dowd had opened a new baseball school in talent-rich Venezuela, where chief scout Luis Aponte would have $75,000 to sign young players. O'Dowd even discussed a possible joint venture with a team in Japan, the first step toward entering the lucrative baseball market in the Far East.

Few other teams were imitating the Indians; most organizations shied away from granting long-term deals to their younger players. Too much of a risk, they argued. The players, they said, would become complacent and lose their competitive edge. The

Indians success in 1995 had disproved that theory, but too many general managers seemed to ignore the lesson.

Perhaps it was the dawning of the Cleveland dynasty that Hank Greenberg envisioned so many years ago as he tracked the progress of his minor league empire from his office in the old stadium. Like Greenberg, Dick Jacobs knew that quick fixes would bring little more than fleeting success. If the Indians weren't in the World Series every year, so be it, Dick Jacobs told a friend. He wanted to build something that endured, a team that was always competitive. "As long as we're in the hunt," he said, "we're going to be all right."

The executives coming up in the Cleveland system shared that vision. Someday, Dan O'Dowd would direct his own major league team. During the fall of 1995, he vowed one thing: When he did become a general manager, he would run his team just like Hank Peters and John Hart ran the Cleveland Indians.

Cleveland Indians Team Lineups—1954 to 1995

1954 (111-43) first
1b Vic Wertz (14, 48, .275)
2b Bobby Avila (15, 67, .341)
ss George Strickland (6, 37, .213)
3b Al Rosen (24, 102, .300)
rf Dave Philley (12, 60, .226)
cf Larry Doby (32, 126, .272)
lf Al Smith (11, 50, .281)
c Jim Hegan (11, 40, .234)

Mike Garcia (19-8 2.64)
Bob Lemon (23-7 2.72)
Early Wynn (23-11 2.72)
Bob Feller (13-3 3.09)
Art Houtteman (15-7 3.35)
BULLPEN
Don Mossi (6-1 1.94)
Ray Narleski (3-3 2.22)
Hal Newhouser (7-2 2.49)

1955 (93-61) second
1b Vic Wertz (14, 55, .253)
2b Bobby Avila (13, 61, .272)
ss George Strickland (2, 34, .209)
3b Al Rosen (21, 81, .244)
rf Al Smith (22, 77, .306)
cf Larry Doby (26, 75, .291)
lf Ralph Kiner (18, 54, .243)
c Jim Hegan (9, 40, .220)

Early Wynn (17-11 2.82)
Herb Score (16-10 2.85)
Bob Lemon (18-10 3.88)
Art Houtteman (10-6 3.99)
Mike Garcia (11-13 4.01)
BULLPEN
Don Mossi (4-3 2.41)
Bob Feller (4-4 3.47)
Ray Narleski (9-1 3.70)

1956 (88-66) second
1b Vic Wertz (32, 106, .264)
2b Bobby Avila (10, 54, .224)
ss Chico Carresquel (7, 48, .243)
3b Al Rosen (15, 61, .267)
rf Rocky Colavito (21, 65, .276)
cf Jim Busby (12, 50, .235)
lf Al Smith (16, 71, .274)
c Jim Hegan (6, 34, .222)

Herb Score (20-9 2.53)
Early Wynn (20-9 2.72)
Bob Lemon (20-14 3.04)
Hank Aguirre (3-5 3.74)
Mike Garcia (11-12 3.77)
BULLPEN
Ray Narleski (3-2 1.53)
Don Mossi (6-5 3.58)
Cal McLish (2-4 4.94)

1957 (76-77) sixth
1b Vic Wertz (28, 105, .282)
2b Bobby Avila (5, 48, .268)
ss Chico Carresquel (8, 57, .276)
3b Al Smith (11, 49, .247)
rf Rocky Colavito (25, 84, .252)
cf Roger Maris (14, 51, .235)
lf Gene Woodling (19, 78, .321)
c Jim Hegan (4, 15, .216)

Herb Score (2-1 2.00)
Cal McLish (9-7 2.75)
Mike Garcia (12-8 3.75)
Early Wynn (14-17 4.31)
Bob Lemon (6-11 4.62)
BULLPEN
Ray Narleski (11-5 3.10)
Don Mossi (11-10 4.13)
Bud Daley (2-8 4.45)

1958 (77-76) fourth
1b Vic Power (12, 53, .317)
2b Bobby Avila (5, 30, .253)
ss Billy Hunter (0, 9, .195)
3b Billy Harrell (7, 19, .218)
rf Rocky Colavito (41, 113, .303)
cf Larry Doby (13, 45, .283)
lf Minnie Minoso (24, 80, .302)
c Russ Nixon (9, 46, .301)

Cal McLish (16-8 2.99)
Herb Score (2-3 3.95)
Gary Bell (12-10 3.31)
Jim Grant (10-11 3.84)
Ray Narleski (13-10 4.08)
BULLPEN
Hal Woodeshick (6-6 3.63)
Don Ferrarese (3-4 3.69)
Don Mossi (7-8 3.88)

1959 (89-65) second
1b Vic Power (10, 60, .289)
2b Billy Martin (9, 24, .260)
ss Woodie Held (29, 71, .251)
3b George Strickland (3, 48, .238)
rf Rocky Colavito (42, 111, .257)
cf Tito Francona (20, 79, .363)
lf Minnie Minoso (21, 92, .302)
c Russ Nixon (1, 29, .240)

Jack Harshman (5-1 2.59)
Jim Perry (12-10 2.65)
Cal McLish (19-8 3.64)
Gary Bell (16-11 4.04)
Jim Grant (10-7 4.15)
Herb Score (9-11 4.70)
BULLPEN
Bobby Locke (3-2 3.12)
Don Ferrarese (5-3 3.20)

1960 (76-78) fourth
1b Vic Power (10, 84, .288)
2b Ken Aspromonte (10, 48, .290)
ss Woodie Held (21, 67, .258)
3b Bubba Phillips (4, 33, .207)
rf Harvey Kuenn (9, 54, .308)
cf Jimmy Piersall (18, 66, .282)
lf Tito Francona (17, 79, .292)
c John Romano (16, 52, .272)

Jim Perry (18-10 3.62)
Barry Latman (7-7 4.04)
Gary Bell (9-10 4.12)
Jim Grant (9-8 4.39)
Dick Stigman (5-11 4.50)
BULLPEN
Frank Funk (4-2 1.97)
John Klippstein (5-5 2.92)
Bobby Locke (3-5 3.37)

1961 (78-83) fifth
1b Vic Power (5, 63, .268)
2b Johnny Temple (3, 30, .276)
ss Woodie Held (23, 78, .267)
3b Bubba Phillips (18, 72, .264)
rf Willie Kirkland (27, 95, .259)
cf Jimmy Piersall (6, 40, .322)
lf Tito Francona (16, 85, .301)
c John Romano (21, 80, .299)

Jim Grant (15-9 3.86)
Barry Latman (13-5 4.02)
Wynn Hawkins (7-9 4.06)
Gary Bell (12-16 4.11)
Jim Perry (10-17 4.70)
BULLPEN
Frank Funk (11-11 3.33)
Bob Allen (3-2 3.73)
Bobby Locke (4-4 4.55)

Cleveland Indians Team Lineups—1954-1995

1962 (80-82) sixth
1b Tito Francona (14, 70, .272)
2b Jerry Kindall (13, 55, .232)
ss Woodie Held (19, 58, .249)
3b Bubba Phillips (10, 54, .258)
rf Willie Kirkland (21, 72, .200)
cf Ty Cline (2, 28, .248)
lf Chuck Essegian (21, 50, .274)
c John Romano (25, 81, .261)

Dick Donovan (20-10 3.59)
Pedro Ramos (10-12 3.72)
Jim Perry (12-12 4.13)
Barry Latman (8-13 4.17)
Jim Grant (7-10 4.26)
BULLPEN
Frank Funk (2-1 3.22)
Gary Bell (10-9 4.25)
Ron Taylor (2-2 6.00)

1963 (79-83) fifth
1b Fred Whitfield (21, 54, .251)
2b Woodie Held (17, 61, .248)
ss Dick Howser (1, 10, .247)
3b Max Alvis (22, 67, .274)
rf Willie Kirkland (15, 47, .230)
cf Vic Davalillo (7, 36, .292)
lf Tito Francona (10, 41, .228)
c John Romano (10, 34, .216)

Jack Kralick (13-9 2.92)
Pedro Ramos (9-8 3.11)
Jim Grant (13-14 3.69)
Dick Donovan (11-13 4.24)
Barry Latman (7-12 4.95)
BULLPEN
Ted Abernathy (7-2 2.90)
Gary Bell (8-5 2.95)
Jerry Walker (6-6 4.91)

1964 (79-83) sixth
1b Bob Chance (14, 75, .279)
2b Larry Brown (12, 40, .230)
ss Dick Howser (3, 52, .256)
3b Max Alvis (18, 53, .252)
rf Woodie Held (18, 49, .236)
cf Vic Davalillo (6, 51, .270)
lf Leon Wagner (31, 100, .253)
c John Romano (19, 47, .241)

Sam McDowell (11-6 2.71)
Luis Tiant (10-4 2.83)
Jack Kralick (12-7 3.20)
Sonny Siebert (7-9 3.23)
Tommy John (2-9 3.93)
BULLPEN
Don McMahon (6-4 2.41)
Ted Abernathy (2-6 4.32)
Gary Bell (8-6 4.33)

1965 (87-75) fifth
1b Fred Whitfield (26, 90, .293)
2b Pedro Gonzales (5, 39, .253)
ss Larry Brown (8, 40, .253)
3b Max Alvis (21, 61, .247)
rf Rocky Colavito (26, 108, .287)
cf Vic Davalillo (5, 40, .301)
lf Leon Wagner (28, 79, .294)
c Joe Azcue (2, 35, .230)

Sam McDowell (17-11 2.18)
Sonny Siebert (16-8 2.43)
Steve Hargan (4-3 3.45)
Luis Tiant (11-11 3.54)
Ralph Terry (11-6 3.69)
BULLPEN
Gary Bell (6-5 3.03)
Don McMahon (3-3 3.28)
Lee Stange (8-4 3.34)

1966 (81-81) fifth
1b Fred Whitfield (27, 78, .241)
2b Pedro Gonzales (2, 17, .233)
ss Larry Brown (3, 17, .229)
3b Max Alvis (17, 55, .245)
rf Rocky Colavito (30, 72, .238)
cf Vic Davalillio (3, 19, .250)
lf Leon Wagner (23, 66, .279)
c Joe Azcue (9, 37, .275)

Steve Hargan (13-10 2.48)
Luis Tiant (12-11 2.79)
Sonny Siebert (16-8 2.80)
Sam McDowell (9-8 2.88)
Gary Bell (14-15 3.22)
BULLPEN
John O'Donoghue (6-8 3.83)
Jack Kralick (3-4 3.84)
Dick Radatz (0-3 4.58)

1967 (75-87) eighth
1b Tony Horton (10, 44, .281)
2b Vern Fuller (7, 21, .223)
ss Larry Brown (7, 37, .227)
3b Max Alvis (21, 70, .256)
rf Chuck Hinton (10, 37, .245)
cf Vic Davalillio (2, 22, .287)
lf Leon Wagner (15, 54, .242)
c Joe Azcue (11, 34, .251)

Sonny Siebert (10-12 2.38)
Steve Hargan (14-13 2.62)
Luis Tiant (12-9 2.73)
John O'Donoghue (8-9 3.23)
Sam McDowell (13-15 3.85)
BULLPEN
Stan Williams (6-4 2.62)
Steve Bailey (2-5 3.88)
George Culver (7-3 3.96)

1968 (86-75) third
1b Tony Horton (14, 59, .249)
2b Dave Nelson (0, 19, .233)
ss Larry Brown (6, 35, .234)
3b Max Alvis (8, 37, .223)
rf Tommy Harper (6, 26, .217)
cf Jose Cardenal (7, 44, .257)
lf Lee Maye (4, 26, .281)
c Joe Azcue (4, 42, .280)

Luis Tiant (21-9 1.60)
Sam McDowell (15-14 1.81)
Stan Williams (13-11 2.51)
Sonny Siebert (12-10 2.97)
Steve Hargan (8-15 4.16)
BULLPEN
Vincente Romo (5-3 1.63)
Horacio Pina (1-1 1.74)
Eddie Fisher (4-2 2.84)

1969 (62-99) sixth
1b Tony Horton (27, 93, .278)
2b Vern Fuller (4, 22, .236)
ss Larry Brown (4, 24, .239)
3b Max Alvis (1, 15, .225)
rf Ken Harrelson (27, 84, .222)
cf Jose Cardenal (11, 45, .257)
lf Frank Baker (3, 15, .256)
c Duke Sims (18, 45, .236)

Sam McDowell (18-14 2.94)
Luis Tiant (9-20 3.71)
Stan Williams (6-14 3.94)
Dick Ellsworth (6-9 4.13)
Steve Hargan (5-14 5.69)
BULLPEN
Juan Pizarro (3-3 3.14)
Mike Paul (5-10 3.62)
Horacio Pina (4-2 5.17)

Cleveland Indians Team Lineups—1954-1995

1970 (76-86) fifth
1b Tony Horton (17, 59, .269)
2b Eddie Leon (10, 56, .248)
ss Jack Heidemann (6, 37, .211)
3b Graig Nettles (26, 62, .235)
rf Vada Pinson (24, 82, .286)
cf Ted Uhlaender (11, 46, .268)
lf Roy Foster (23, 60, .268)
c Ray Fosse (18, 61, .307)

Steve Hargan (11-3 2.90)
Sam McDowell (20-12 2.92)
Rich Hand (6-13 3.83)
Dean Chance (9-8 4.24)
Steve Dunning (4-9 4.98)
BULLPEN
Steve Mingori (1-0 2.70)
Phil Hennigan (6-3 4.00)
Denny Higgins (4-6 4.00)

1971 (60-102) sixth
1b Chris Chambliss (9, 48, .275)
2b Eddie Leon (4, 35, .261)
ss Jack Heidemann (0, 9, .208)
3b Graig Nettles (28, 86, .261)
rf Vada Pinson (11, 35, .263)
cf Ted Uhlaender (2, 47, .288)
lf Roy Foster (18, 45, .245)
c Ray Fosse (12, 62, .276)

Sam McDowell (13-17 3.39)
Vince Colbert (7-6 3.97)
Alan Foster (8-12 4.15)
Steve Dunning (8-14 4.50)
Steve Hargan (1-13 6.21)
BULLPEN
Steve Mingori (1-2 1.42)
Ray Lamb (6-12 3.36)
Ed Farmer (5-4 4.33)

1972 (72-84) fifth
1b Chris Chambliss (6, 44, .292)
2b Jack Brohamer (5, 35, .233)
ss Frank Duffy (3, 27, .239)
3b Graig Nettles (17, 70, .253)
rf Buddy Bell (9, 36, .255)
cf Del Unser (1, 17, .238)
lf Alex Johnson (8, 37, .239)
c Ray Fosse (10, 41, .241)

Gaylord Perry (24-16 1.92)
Dick Tidrow (14-15 2.77)
Ray Lamb (5-6 3.08)
Steve Dunning (6-4 3.26)
Milt Wilcox (7-14 3.40)
BULLPEN
Tom Hilgendorf (3-1 2.68)
Phil Hennigan (5-3 2.69)
Ed Farmer (2-5 4.43)

1973 (71-91) sixth
1b Chris Chambliss (11, 53, .273)
2b Jack Brohamer (4, 29, .220)
ss Frank Duffy (8, 50, .263)
3b Buddy Bell (14, 59, .268)
rf George Hendrick (21, 61, .268)
cf Rusty Torres (7, 28, .205)
lf Charlie Spikes (23, 73, .237)
c Dave Duncan (17, 43, .233)
dh Oscar Gamble (20, 44, .267)

Gaylord Perry (19-19 3.38)
Dick Tidrow (14-16 4.42)
Brent Strom (2-10 4.61)
Tom Timmerman (8-7 4.93)
Milt Wilcox (8-10 5.84)
BULLPEN
Ken Sanders (5-1 1.67)
Tom Hilgendorf (5-3 3.13)
Ray Lamb (3-3 4.60)
Jerry Johnson (5-6 6.15)

1974 (77-85) fourth
1b John Ellis (10, 64, .285)
2b Jack Brohamer (2, 30, .270)
ss Frank Duffy (8, 48, .233)
3b Buddy Bell (7, 46, .262)
rf George Hendrick (19, 67, .279)
cf John Lowenstein (8, 48, .242)
lf Charlie Spikes (22, 80, .271)
c Dave Duncan (16, 46, .200)
dh Oscar Gamble (19, 59, .291)

Gaylord Perry (21-13 2.52)
Jim Perry (17-12 2.96)
Fritz Peterson (9-14 4.35)
Dick Bosman (7-5 4.11)
Steve Kline (3-8 5.07)
BULLPEN
Tom Buskey (2-6 3.19)
Bruce Ellingsen (1-1 3.21)
Tom Hilgendorf (4-3 4.88)
Fred Beene (4-4 4.93)

1975 (79-80) fourth
1b Boog Powell (27, 86, .297)
2b Duane Kuiper (0, 25, .292)
ss Frank Duffy (1, 47, .243)
3b Buddy Bell (10, 59, .271)
rf George Hendrick (24, 86, .258)
cf Rick Manning (3, 35, .285)
lf Charlie Spikes (11, 33, .229)
c Alan Ashby (5, 32, .224)
dh Rico Carty (18, 64, .308)

Dennis Eckersley (13-7 2.60)
Rick Waits (6-2 2.96)
Jim Bibby (5-9 3.20)
Fritz Peterson (14-8 3.95)
Roric Harrison (7-7 4.79)
BULLPEN
Dave LaRoche (5-3 2.20)
Tom Buskey (5-3 2.57)
Jim Kern (1-2 3.75)
Don Hood (6-10 4.40)

1976 (81-78) fourth
1b Boog Powell (9, 33, .215)
2b Duane Kuiper (0, 37, .263)
ss Frank Duffy (2, 30, .212)
3b Buddy Bell (7, 60, .281)
rf George Hendrick (25, 81, .265)
cf Rick Manning (6, 43, .292)
lf Charlie Spikes (3, 31, .237)
c Alan Ashby (4, 32, .239)
dh Rico Carty (13, 83, .310)

Jim Bibby (13-7 3.20)
Dennis Eckersley (13-12 3.44)
Pat Dobson (16-12 3.48)
Rick Waits (7-9 3.99)
Jackie Brown (9-11 4.25)
BULLPEN
Dave LaRoche (1-4 2.25)
Stan Thomas (4-4 2.29)
Jim Kern (10-7 2.36)
Tom Buskey (5-4 3.64)

1977 (71-90) fifth
1b Andre Thornton (28, 70, .263)
2b Duane Kuiper (1, 50, .277)
ss Frank Duffy (4, 31, .201)
3b Buddy Bell (11, 64, .292)
rf Jim Norris (2, 37, .270)
cf Rick Manning (5, 18, .226)
lf Bruce Bochte (5, 43, .304)
c Fred Kendall (3, 39, .249)
dh Rico Carty (15, 80, .280)

Dennis Eckersley (14-13 3.53)
Jim Bibby (12-13 3.57)
Wayne Garland (13-19 3.59)
Rick Waits (9-7 4.00)
Al Fitzmorris (6-10 5.41)
BULLPEN
Larry Anderson (0-1 3.21)
Jim Kern (8-10 3.42)
Pat Dobson (3-12 6.16)
Sid Monge (1-2 6.23)

Cleveland Indians Team Lineups—1954-1995

1978 (69-90) sixth
1b Andre Thornton (33, 105, .262)
2b Duane Kuiper (0, 43, .283)
ss Tom Veryzer (1, 32, .271)
3b Buddy Bell (6, 62, .282)
rf Paul Dade (3, 20, .254)
cf Rick Manning (3, 50, .263)
lf John Grubb (14, 61, .265)
c Gary Alexander (17, 62, .235)
dh Bernie Carbo (4, 16, .287)

Rick Waits (13-15 3.21)
Mike Paxton (12-11 3.86)
David Clyde (8-11 4.29)
Rick Wise (9-19 4.33)
Don Hood (5-6 4.47)
BULLPEN
Sid Monge (4-3 2.75)
Jim Kern (10-10 3.09)
Paul Reuschel (2-4 3.10)
Dan Spillner (3-1 3.70)

1979 (81-80) sixth
1b Andre Thornton (26, 93, .233)
2b Duane Kuiper (0, 39, .255)
ss Tom Veryzer (0, 34, .220)
3b Toby Harrah (20, 77, .279)
rf Bobby Bonds (25, 85, .275)
cf Rick Manning (3, 51, .259)
lf Mike Hargrove (10, 56, .325)
c Gary Alexander (15, 54, .229)
dh Cliff Johnson (18, 61, .271)

Rick Wise (15-10 3.72)
Rick Waits (16-13 4.44)
Len Barker (6-6 4.93)
Wayne Garland (4-10 5.21)
Mike Paxton (8-8 5.91)
BULLPEN
Sid Monge (12-10 2.40)
Victor Cruz (3-9 4.22)
Dan Spillner (9-5 4.61)
Larry Anderson (0-0 7.41)

1980 (79-81) sixth
1b Mike Hargrove (11, 85, .304)
2b Duane Kuiper (0, 9, .282)
ss Tom Veryzer (2, 28, .271)
3b Toby Harrah (11, 72, .267)
rf Jorge Orta (10, 64, .291)
cf Rick Manning (3, 52, .234)
lf Miguel Dilone (0, 40, .341)
c Ron Hassey (8, 65, .318)
dh Joe Charboneau (23, 87, .289)

Len Barker (19-12 4.17)
John Denny (8-6 4.38)
Rick Waits (13-14 4.46)
Wayne Garland (6-9 4.62)
Dan Spillner (16-11 5.29)
BULLPEN
Victor Cruz (6-7 3.45)
Sid Monge (3-5 3.54)
Bob Owchinko (2-9 5.29)
Mike Stanton (1-3 5.44)

1981 (52-51) sixth
1b Mike Hargrove (2, 49, .317)
2b Duane Kuiper (0, 14, .257
ss Tom Veryzer (0, 14, .244)
3b Toby Harrah (5, 44, .291)
rf Jorge Orta (5, 34, .272)
cf Rick Manning (4, 33, .244)
lf Miguel Dilone (0, 19, .290)
c Bo Diaz (7, 38, .313)
dh Andre Thornton (6, 30, .239)

Bert Blyleven (11-7 2.89)
John Denny (10-6 3.14)
Len Barker (8-7 3.92)
Rick Waits (8-10 4.93)
Wayne Garland (3-7 5.79)
BULLPEN
Dan Spillner (4-4 3.15)
Tom Brennan (2-2 3.19)
Sid Monge (3-5 4.34)
Mike Stanton (3-3 4.40)

1982 (78-84) sixth
1b Mike Hargrove (4, 65, .271)
2b Jack Perconte (0, 15, .237)
ss Mike Fischlin (0, 21, .268)
3b Toby Harrah (25, 78, .304)
rf Von Hayes (14, 82, .250)
cf Rick Manning (8, 44, .270)
lf Miguel Dilone (3, 25, .235)
c Ron Hassey (5, 34, .251)
dh Andre Thornton (32, 116, .273)

Rick Sutcliffe (14-8 2.96)
Len Barker (15-11 3.90)
Bert Blyleven (2-2 4.87)
John Denny (6-11 5.01)
Rick Waits (2-13 5.40)
Lary Sorenson (10-15 5.61)
BULLPEN
Dan Spillner (12-10 2.49)
Ed Whitson (4-2 3.26)
Ed Glynn (5-2 4.17)

1983 (70-92) seventh
1b Mike Hargrove (3, 57, .286)
2b Manny Trillo (1, 29, .272)
ss Julio Franco (8, 80, .273)
3b Toby Harrah (9, 53, .266)
rf George Vukovich (3, 44, .247)
cf Gorman Thomas (17, 51, .221)
lf Pat Tabler (6, 65, .291)
c Ron Hassey (6, 42, .270)
dh Andre Thornton (17, 77, .281)

Bert Blyleven (7-10 3.91)
Neal Heaton (11-7 4.16)
Lary Sorenson (12-11 4.24)
Rick Sutcliffe (17-11 4.29)
Len Barker (8-13 5.11)
BULLPEN
Mike Jeffcoat (1-3 3.31)
Bud Anderson (1-6 4.08)
Juan Eichelberger (4-11 4.90)
Dan Spillner (2-9 5.07)

1984 (75-87) sixth
1b Mike Hargrove (2, 44, .267)
2b Tony Bernazard (2, 38, .221)
ss Julio Franco (3, 79, .286)
3b Brook Jacoby (7, 40, .264)
rf George Vukovich (9, 60, .304)
cf Brett Butler (3, 49, .269)
lf Joe Carter (13, 41, .275)
c Chris Bando (12, 41, .291)
dh Andre Thornton (33, 99, .271)

Bert Blyleven (19-7 2.87)
Roy Smith (5-5 4.59)
Don Schulze (3-6 4.83)
Neal Heaton (12-15 5.21)
Steve Comer (4-8 5.68)
BULLPEN
Ernie Camacho (5-9 2.43)
Mike Jeffcoat (5-2 2.99)
Tom Waddell (7-4 3.06)
Jamie Easterly (3-1 3.38)

1985 (60-102) seventh
1b Pat Tabler (5, 59, .275)
2b Tony Bernazard (11, 59, .274)
ss Julio Franco (6, 90, .288)
3b Brook Jacoby (20, 87, .274)
rf George Vukovich (8, 45, .244)
cf Brett Butler (5, 50, .311)
lf Joe Carter (15, 59, .262)
c Jerry Willard (7, 36, .270)
dh Andre Thornton (22, 88, .236)

Vern Ruhle (2-10 4.32)
Neal Heaton (9-17 4.90)
Roy Smith (1-4 5.34)
Don Schulze (4-10 6.01)
Curt Wardle (7-6 6.68)
BULLPEN
Dave Von Ohlen (3-2 2.91)
Jamie Easterly (4-1 3.92)
Jerry Reed (3-5 4.11)
Tom Waddell (8-6 4.87)

Cleveland Indians Team Lineups—1954-1995

1986 (84-78) fifth
1b Pat Tabler (6, 48, .326)
2b Tony Bernazard (17, 73, .301)
ss Julio Franco (10, 74, .306)
3b Brook Jacoby (17, 80, .288)
rf Cory Snyder (24, 69, .272)
cf Brett Butler (4, 51, .278)
lf Joe Carter (29, 121, .302)
c Andy Allanson (1, 29, .225)
dh Andre Thornton (17, 66, .229)

Tom Candiotti (16-12 3.57)
Greg Swindell (5-2 4.23)
Phil Niekro (11-11 4.32)
Ken Schrom (14-7 4.54)
Scott Bailes (10-10 4.95)
BULLPEN
Ernie Camacho (2-4 4.08)
Bryan Oelkers (3-3 4.70)
Frank Wills (4-4 4.91)
Rich Yett (5-3 5.15)

1987 (61-101) seventh
1b Joe Carter (32, 106, .264)
2b Tommy Hinzo (3, 21, .265)
ss Julio Franco (8, 52, .319)
3b Brook Jacoby (32, 69, .300)
rf Cory Snyder (33, 82, .236)
cf Brett Butler (9, 41, .295)
lf Mel Hall (18, 76, .280)
c Andy Allanson (3, 16, .266)
dh Pat Tabler (11, 86, .307)

John Farrell (5-1 3.39)
Scott Bailes (7-8 4.64)
Tom Candiotti (7-18 4.78)
Greg Swindell (3-8 5.10)
Ken Schrom (6-13 6.50)
BULLPEN
Doug Jones (6-5 3.15)
Mark Huisman (2-3 5.09)
Rich Yett (3-9 5.25)
Darrell Akerfelds (2-6 6.75)

1988 (78-84) sixth
1b Willie Upshaw (11, 50, .245)
2b Julio Franco (10, 54, .303)
ss Jay Bell (2, 21, .218)
3b Brook Jacoby (9, 49, .241)
rf Cory Snyder (26, 75, .272)
cf Joe Carter (27, 98, .271)
lf Mel Hall (6, 71, .280)
c Andy Allanson (5, 50, .263)
dh Ron Kittle (18, 43, .258)

Greg Swindell (18-14 3.20)
Tom Candiotti (14-8 3.28)
John Farrell (14-10 4.24)
Rich Yett (9-6 4.62)
Scott Bailes (9-14 4.90)
BULLPEN
Doug Jones (3-4 2.27)
Brad Havens (2-3 3.14)
Don Gordon (3-4 4.40)
Bud Black (2-3 5.03)

1989 (73-89) sixth
1b Pete O'Brien (12, 55, .260)
2b Jerry Browne (5, 45, .299)
ss Felix Fermin (0, 21, .238)
3b Brook Jacoby (13, 64, .272)
rf Cory Snyder (18, 59, .215)
cf Joe Carter (35, 105, .243)
lf Oddibe McDowell (3, 22, .222)
c Andy Allanson (3, 17, .232)
dh Dave Clark (8, 29, .237)

Tom Candiotti (13-10 3.10)
Bud Black (12-11 3.36)
Greg Swindell (13-6 3.37)
John Farrell (9-14 3.63)
Rod Nichols (4-6 4.40)
BULLPEN
Jesse Orosco (3-4 2.08)
Doug Jones (7-10 2.34)
Steve Olin (1-4 3.75)
Scott Bailes (5-9 4.28)

1990 (77-85) fourth
1b Keith Hernandez (1, 8, .238)
2b Jerry Browne (6, 50, .267)
ss Felix Fermin (1, 40, .256)
3b Brook Jacoby (14, 75, .293)
rf Cory Snyder (14, 55, .233)
cf Alex Cole (0, 13, .300)
lf Candy Maldonado (22, 95, .273)
c Sandy Alomar (9, 66, .290)
dh Chris James (12, 70, .299)

Bud Black (11-10 3.53)
Tom Candiotti (15-11 3.65)
John Farrell (4-5 4.28)
Greg Swindell (12-9 4.40)
Charles Nagy (2-4 5.91)
BULLPEN
Doug Jones (5-5 2.56)
Steve Olin (4-4 3.41)
Jesse Orosco (5-4 3.90)
Rudy Seanez (2-1 5.60)

1991 (57-105) seventh
1b Carlos Martinez (5, 30, .284)
2b Carlos Baerga (11, 69, .288)
ss Felix Fermin (0, 31, .262)
3b Brook Jacoby (4, 24, .234)
rf Mark Whiten (7, 26, .256)
cf Alex Cole (0, 21, .295)
lf Albert Belle (28, 95, .282)
c Sandy Alomar (0, 7, .217)
dh Chris James (5, 41, .238)

Charles Nagy (10-15 4.13)
Greg Swindell (9-16 3.48)
Eric King (6-11 4.60)
Rod Nichols (2-11 3.54)
Dave Otto (2-8 4.23)
BULLPEN
Steve Olin (3-6 3.36)
Jeff Shaw (0-5 3.36)
Shawn Hillegas (3-4 4.34)
Doug Jones (4-8 5.54)

1992 (76-86) fourth
1b Paul Sorrento (18, 60, .269)
2b Carlos Baerga (20, 105, .312)
ss Mark Lewis (5, 30, .264)
3b Carlos Martinez (5, 35, .263)
rf Mark Whiten (9, 43, .254)
cf Kenny Lofton (5, 42, .285)
lf Glenallen Hill (18, 49, .241)
c Sandy Alomar (2, 26, .251)
dh Albert Belle (34, 112, .260)

Charles Nagy (17-10 2.96)
Dennis Cook (5-7 3.82)
Jose Mesa (7-12 4.59)
Jack Armstrong (6-15 4.64)
Scott Scudder (6-10 5.28)
BULLPEN
Derek Lilliquist (5-3 1.75)
Steve Olin (8-5 2.34)
Ted Power (3-3 2.54)
Eric Plunk (9-6 3.64)

1993 (76-86) sixth
1b Paul Sorrento (18, 65, .257)
2b Carlos Baerga (21, 114, .321)
ss Felix Fermin (2, 45, .262)
3b Jim Thome (7, 22, .266)
rf Wayne Kirby (6, 60, .269)
cf Kenny Lofton (1, 42, .325)
lf Albert Belle (38, 129, .290)
c Sandy Alomar (6, 32, .270)
dh Reggie Jefferson (10, 34, .249)

Tom Kramer (7-3 4.02)
Mark Clark (7-5 4.28)
Jose Mesa (10-12 4.92)
Jason Grimsley (3-4 5.31)
Charles Nagy (2-6 6.29)
BULLPEN
Derek Lilliquist (4-4 2.25)
Jerry DiPoto (4-4 2.40)
Eric Plunk (4-5 2.79)
Jeremy Hernandez (6-5 3.14)

Cleveland Indians Team Lineups—1954-1995

1994 (66-47) second
1b Paul Sorrento (14, 62, .280)
2b Carlos Baerga (19, 80, .314)
ss Omar Vizquel (1, 33, .273)
3b Jim Thome (20, 52, .268)
rf Manny Ramirez (17, 60, .269)
cf Kenny Lofton (12, 57, .349)
lf Albert Belle (36, 101, .357)
c Sandy Alomar (14, 43, .288)
dh Eddie Murray (17, 76, .254)

Charles Nagy (10-8 3.45)
Dennis Martinez (11-6 3.52)
Mark Clark (11-3 3.82)
Jason Grimsley (5-2 4.57)
Jack Morris (10-6 5.35)
BULLPEN
Eric Plunk (7-2 2.54)
Jose Mesa (7-5 3.82)
Derek Lilliquist (1-3 4.91)
Jeff Russell (1-6 5.09)

1995 (100-44) first
1b Paul Sorrento (25, 79, .235)
2b Carlos Baerga (15, 90, .314)
ss Omar Vizquel (6, 56, .266)
3b Jim Thome (25, 73, .314)
rf Manny Ramirez (31, 107, .308)
cf Kenny Lofton (7, 53, .310)
lf Albert Belle (50, 126, .317)
c Sandy Alomar (10, 35, .300)
dh Eddie Murray (21, 82, .323)

Chad Ogea (8-3 3.05)
Dennis Martinez (12-5 3.08)
Orel Hershiser (16-6 3.87)
Ken Hill (4-1 3.98)
Charles Nagy (16-6 4.55)
 BULLPEN
Jose Mesa (3-0 1.13)
Julian Tavarez (10-2 2.44)
Eric Plunk (6-2 2.67)
Paul Assenmacher (6-2 2.82)

Cleveland Indians Home Attendance

Year	Attendance	Finish	Year	Attendance	Finish
1948	2,620,627	first	1972	759,871	fifth
1949	2,233,771	third	1973	605,073	sixth
1950	1,727,464	fourth	1974	1,114,262	fourth
1951	1,704,984	second	1975	977,039	fourth
1952	1,444,607	second	1976	948,776	fourth
1953	1,069,176	second	1977	900,365	fifth
1954	1,335,472	first	1978	800,584	sixth
1955	1,221,780	second	1979	1,011,644	sixth
1956	865,467	second	1980	1,033,872	sixth
1957	722,256	sixth	1981	661,395*	sixth
1958	663,805	fourth	1982	1,044,021	sixth
1959	1,497,976	second	1983	768,941	seventh
1960	950,985	fourth	1984	734,269	sixth
1961	725,547	fifth	1985	655,181	seventh
1962	716,076	sixth	1986	1,471,977	fifth
1963	562,507	fifth	1987	1,077,898	seventh
1964	653,293	sixth	1988	1,411,610	sixth
1965	934,786	fifth	1989	1,285,542	sixth
1966	903,359	fifth	1990	1,225,241	fourth
1967	667,623	eighth	1991	1,051,863	seventh
1968	857,994	third	1992	1,224,274	fourth
1969	619,970	sixth	1993	2,177,908	sixth
1970	729,752	fifth	1994	1,995,174*	second
1971	591,361	sixth	1995	2,842,745	first

* Strike-shortened seasons

1995 Division Playoffs

Game One   Cleveland 5, Boston 4 (13 innings)
Game Two   Cleveland 4, Boston 0
Game Three   Cleveland 8, Boston 2

1995 American League Championship Series

Game One   Seattle 3, Cleveland 2
Game Two   Cleveland 5, Seattle 2
Game Three   Seattle 5, Cleveland 2 (11 innings)
Game Four   Cleveland 7, Seattle 0
Game Five   Cleveland 3, Seattle 2
Game Six   Cleveland 4, Seattle 0

1995 World Series

Game One   Atlanta 3, Cleveland 2
Game Two   Atlanta 4, Cleveland 3
Game Three   Cleveland 7, Atlanta 6 (11 innings)
Game Four   Atlanta 5, Cleveland 2
Game Five   Cleveland 5, Atlanta 4
Game Six   Atlanta 1, Cleveland 0

Notes

Notes to Chapter 1

1. The *Cleveland Plain Dealer*, September 28, 1954.
2. The *Plain Dealer*, September 19, 1954.
3. The *Plain Dealer*, September 28, 1954.
4. The *Plain Dealer*, September 21, 1954.
5. Interview with Rosen.
6. *The Story of My Life*, by Hank Greenberg and Ira Berkow, page 217.
7. Interview with Rosen.
8. *Veeck as in Wreck*, by Bill Veeck and Ed Linn, page 142.
9. *Baseball's Great Experiment*, by Jules Tygiel, page 243.
10. *Ibid*, page 240.
11. *The Story of My Life*, page 216.
12. Interview with Rosen.
13. *When the Cheering Stops*, by Lee Heiman, Dave Weiner, and Bill Gutman, page 70.
14. "Low Pressure Lopez," by Ernest Havemann, *Sports Illustrated*, September 6, 1954.
15. *Ibid*.
16. *Veeck as in Wreck*, page 334.
17. Interview with Al Smith.
18. Interview with Lopez.
19. The *Plain Dealer*, April 12, 1954.
20. The *Plain Dealer*, September 19, 1954.
21. The *Plain Dealer*, April 11, 1954.
22. Interview with Lopez.
23. The *Plain Dealer*, September 26, 1954.
24. The *Plain Dealer*, September 28, 1954.
25. "The World Series is a Wonderful Moment," by Roger Kahn and Gordon Cobbledick, *Sports Illustrated*, September 27, 1954.
26. *When the Cheering Stops*, page 223.
27. Interview with Rosen.
28. *Say Hey*, by Willie Mays with Lou Sahadi, page 118.
29. The *Plain Dealer*, September 30, 1954.
30. The *Plain Dealer*, September 30, 1954.
31. The *Plain Dealer*, September 30, 1954.
32. "One, Two, Three, Four & Bingo," by Roger Kahn, *Sports Illustrated*, October 11, 1954.

33. Interview with Dolin.
34. The *Plain Dealer*, October 2, 1954.
35. The *Plain Dealer*, October 3, 1954.

Notes to Chapter 2

1. "Cleveland's Left-Handed Lightning," by Hal Lebovitz, *The Saturday Evening Post*, May 11, 1957.
2. "Here's the Score on Herb Score," by Lester Koelling, *Baseball Digest*, April 1955.
3. Interview with Altobelli.
4. Interview with Lopez.
5. "With St. Jude's Help, Hard-Luck Herb Is Back," *Life Magazine*, May 18, 1959.
6. "How we got into the Series," by Hank Greenberg and Arthur Mann, *Life Magazine*, September 27, 1954.
7. *Ibid.*
8. "What you learn in the Big Leagues," by Rocky Colavito and Furman Bisher, *Sport Magazine*, July 1961.
9. *Roger Maris, A Man for All Seasons*, by Maury Allen, pages 50 and 51.
10. Eulogy of Hank Greenberg by Walter Matthau, reprinted in *The Story of My Life*, page 282.
11. *Ibid*, pages 283 and 284.
12. *Ibid*, page 198.
13. *Veeck as in Wreck*, page 294.
14. Interview with Dolin.
15. Interview with Lopez.
16. The *Cleveland Press*, January 8, 1945.
17. The *Press*, March 23, 1954.
18. The *Plain Dealer*, September 19, 1954.
19. The *Press*, April 14, 1956.
20. Interview with Dolin.
21. Greenberg's tape-recorded recollections.
22. Interview with Colavito.
23. Interview with Lopez.
24. Interview with Lopez.
25. Interview with Lopez.
26. Interview with Colavito.
27. The *Plain Dealer*, March 4, 1956.
28. The *Plain Dealer*, September 12, 1955.
29. The *Plain Dealer*, September 13, 1955.
30. Interview with Dolin.
31. Interview with Lopez.
32. The *Plain Dealer*, September 30, 1956.
33. "Bat Title for Rosen," by Franklin Lewis, *Baseball Digest*, May 1951.

34. Interview with Rosen.
35. Interview with Rosen.
36. The *Plain Dealer*, April 2, 1957.
37. Interview with Rosen.
38. Interview with Rosen.
39. The *Plain Dealer*, April 2, 1957.
40. Interview with Lopez.
41. The *Plain Dealer*, April 16, 1957.
42. The *Plain Dealer*, May 1, 1957.
43. The *Plain Dealer*, April 17, 1957.
44. The *Plain Dealer*, April 28, 1957.
45. The *Plain Dealer*, April 25, 1957.
46. *Roger Maris*, page 77.
47. The *Press*, May 8, 1957.
48. *My Favorite Summer, 1956*, by Mickey Mantle and Phil Pepe, page 143.
49. Interview with Smith.
50. The *Press*, May 8, 1957.
51. The *Plain Dealer*, May 8, 1957.
52. The *Press*, May 8, 1957.
53. The *Plain Dealer*, May 10, 1957.
54. The *Press*, May 23, 1957.
55. Interview with Bragan.
56. The *Plain Dealer*, March 6, 1958.
57. The *Plain Dealer*, April 24, 1958.
58. Score is convinced that the eye injury has always been overplayed by reporters and that in the spring of 1958, he was throwing the ball as hard as ever. Score pitched an extraordinary number of innings at a very young age, increasing the possibility that he would have suffered from elbow or shoulder problems.
59. Interview with Score.
60. Interview with Rosen.

Notes to Chapter 3

1. Interview with Devine.
2. The *Plain Dealer*, April 3, 1958.
3. The *Plain Dealer*, April 15, 1958.
4. The *Plain Dealer*, December 3, 1952.
5. *Veeck as in Wreck*, page 298.
6. The *Plain Dealer*, April 28, 1958.
7. Interview with Bragan.
8. Interview with Bragan.
9. Interview with Dalton.
10. The *Press*, November 13, 1957.

Notes

11. "Frank Lane: Baseball's Busiest Dynamo," by Tim Cohane, *Look Magazine*, June 12, 1956.
12. The *Press*, November 13, 1957.
13. The *Chicago Tribune*, October 15, 1948.
14. The *Tribune*, December 7, 1948.
15. Interview with Dalton.
16. Interview with Rosen.
17. *Organized Professional Team Sports Hearings, House Subcommittee on Antitrust*, July and August 1957, page 2053.
18. The *Tribune*, September 18, 1955, quoting from a speech by Chuck Comiskey in Waterloo, Iowa.
19. The *Tribune*, September 17, 1955.
20. "Baseball's Busiest Dynamo."
21. The *Tribune*, September 19, 1955.
22. House antitrust hearings, page 2053.
23. The *Press*, November 13, 1957.
24. "Baseball's Busiest Dynamo."
25. The *Plain Dealer*, November 13, 1957.
26. Interview with Devine.
27. Interview with Dolin.
28. The *Plain Dealer*, November 21, 1949.
29. Interview with Dolin.
30. The *Plain Dealer*, December 6, 1952.
31. The *Plain Dealer*, December 7, 1952.
32. Interview with Dolin.
33. The *Plain Dealer*, December 19, 1952.
34. House antitrust hearings, page 2053.
35. The *Press*, October 17, 1957. The reported loss does not reflect the financial realities of the Indians. The Big Seven claimed a $700,000 depreciation on the player contracts that year, turning a reported $150,000 loss into a probable profit of $400,000. Nate Dolin con firmed in 1994 that throughout the time he held stock from 1950 through 1962, the team's cash flow was positive.
36. *Organized Professional Team Sports Hearings, Senate Subcommittee on Antitrust and Monopoly*, July and August, 1958, page 802.
37. The *Press*, September 18, 1957.
38. Interview with Dolin.
39. The *Plain Dealer*, October 17, 1957.
40. The *Plain Dealer*, November 13, 1957.
41. The *Press*, December 5, 1957.
42. The *Plain Dealer*, November 22, 1958.
43. Interview with Frank Lane for *Roger Maris*, page 82.
44. Interview with Dolin.
45. *Veeck as in Wreck*, page 269.
46. The *Plain Dealer*, June 16, 1959.
47. The *Plain Dealer*, August 27, 1959.
48. *Sports Illustrated*, September 7, 1959.

49. The *Plain Dealer*, August 30, 1959.
50. The *Plain Dealer*, August 30, 1959.
51. The *Plain Dealer*, September 19, 1959.
52. The account of the Indians' efforts to hire Leo Durocher comes from an interview with Nate Dolin, page 336 of *Nice Guys Finish Last*, and articles from the *Plain Dealer* on September 18 and 19, 1959. The *Plain Dealer* indicates that Lane personally traveled to Pittsburgh to meet Durocher, but Dolin revealed that he drove to Pittsburgh by himself. That is confirmed by Durocher in his autobiography. Durocher and Dolin agree they discussed an offer that would have paid Durocher at least $50,000 after taxes. Dolin said he refused Durocher's request for such a salary, while Durocher wrote the Indians offered $53,000 after taxes.
53. The morning telephone conversations between Lane and Gordon are taken from an excellent story by Harry Jones of the *Plain Dealer*, September 24, 1959.
54. Interview with Milkie.
55. Interview with Colavito.
56. Interview with Kennedy.
57. Dolin is quoted nearly one year later in the January 6, 1961 edition of the *Plain Dealer* as saying he spoke to Lane before the trade was made. But in a 1994 interview, Dolin flatly declared he could not physically speak to Lane because of his surgery. I have chosen to accept the latter explanation.
58. The account of Colavito being told of the trade is re-created from interviews with Colavito and Score, and Joe Gordon's explanation in the *Press*, April 18, 1960.
59. The *Plain Dealer*, April 18, 1960.
60. Interview with Kathleen Daley.
61. Interview with Peters.
62. Interview with Paul.
63. Interview with Dolin.
64. The *Plain Dealer*, January 4, 1961.
65. Interview with Frank Lane for *Charlie — Charles Oscar Finley vs. the Baseball Establishment*, by Herbert Michelson, page 96.
66. Interview with Milkie.
67. Interviews with Bragan and Milkie provided details of Lane's funeral.

Notes to Chapter 4

1. Interview with Dolin.
2. The *Cleveland News*, February 15, 1956.
3. The *Cleveland News*, February 15, 1956.
4. University of Notre Dame Archives.
5. Interview with Kathleen Daley.
6. The *Plain Dealer*, February 17, 1922.

Notes

7. Opening argument of Kaiser-Frazer attorney Mark Hughes in U.S. District Court in New York in 1951, Kaiser-Frazer Corp. vs. Otis & Co., page 21.
8. Daley's testimony at Kaiser-Frazer trial, page 1795.
9. *The World of Cyrus Eaton*, by Marcus Gleisser, pages 86-87.
10. The *Press*, February 15, 1956.
11. Daley testimony at Kaiser-Frazer trial, page 1679.
12. Daley testimony, page 1683.
13. Daley testimony, page 1742.
14. Hughes' opening argument at Kaiser-Frazer trial, page 17.
15. Hughes' opening argument, page 18.
16. Hughes' opening argument, page 19.
17. Daley testimony, page 1775.
18. Hughes' opening argument, page 32.
19. Hughes' opening argument, page 21.
20. Interview with Dolin.
21. Senate antitrust hearings, page 802.
22. The *Plain Dealer*, March 1, 1956.
23. House antitrust hearings, page 363.
24. The *Press*, February 15, 1956.
25. Eulogy of I.A. O'Shaughnessy in 1973 by James Shannon, courtesy of Notre Dame archives.
26. *Ibid.*
27. Both the Fortas letter and Eaton telegram are in the personal papers of Cyrus Eaton, courtesy of the Western Reserve Historical Society.
28. The *Press*, July 16, 1956.
29. "Is Cleveland Mad at the Indians," by Gordon Cobbledick, *Sport Magazine*, June 1956.
30. The *Plain Dealer*, April 21, 1957.
31. The *Press*, September 16, 1957.
32. The *Youngstown Vindicator*, August 21, 1958.
33. The *Plain Dealer*, August 24, 1958.
34. The *Plain Dealer*, August 22, 1958.
35. The *Plain Dealer*, August 21, 1958.
36. Daley's comments first appeared in the August 21, 1958, afternoon edition of the *Cleveland Press* and followed up by the *Plain Dealer* on August 22.
37. Statement of Hank Greenberg, Andy Baxter, and Wing Baxter, published in the *Press*, October 22, 1958.
38. *Minneapolis Tribune*, August 20, 1958.
39. Cleveland City archives.
40. Allen R. Snyder, of the Washington law firm, Hogan & Hartson.
41. The *Plain Dealer*, August 23, 1958.
42. Interview with Celebrezze.

43. The *Plain Dealer*, September 13, 1962.

44. That both Celebrezze and Locher realized the Indians would owe $360,000 is confirmed in an August 25, 1958 story in the *Press*. "It is a firm contract and naturally the city expects the baseball club to fulfill it," Locher told the *Press*. The story, however, did not specifically mention the clause that the Indians could play in "no other place" than Cleveland Stadium.

45. Interview with Celebrezze.

46. The *Plain Dealer*, August 25, 1958.

47. The *Minneapolis Star*, September 2, 1958.

48. The *Minneapolis Tribune*, September 8, 1958.

49. The files of William R. Daley, courtesy of the University of Notre Dame archives.

50. *The Story of My Life*, pages 213-214.

51. The Cullinan offer was revealed by Greenberg in his own taped recollections, and not used in his book with Ira Berkow. Greenberg describes the Houston bid as part of a plan he "concocted," but it is unclear whether his goal was to gain control of the Indians or simply sell his stock at a large profit. It very well could be that Greenberg's sole intention was to force Daley and the Big Seven to buy his stock. That theory is supported in a July 4, 1960 article in *Sports Illustrated*, "Master of the Joyful Illusion," in which Bill Veeck flatly declared he offered to buy the Indians in 1958 only as part of a strategy to set a price for Greenberg's stock.

52. The *Press*, October 9, 1958.

53. The *Press*, October 22, 1958.

54. Interview with Hartman.

55. The *Press*, September 8, 1959.

56. The *Press*, October 17, 1958.

57. The *Plain Dealer*, November 19, 1958.

58. *Veeck as in Wreck*, page 321.

Notes to Chapter 5

1. Interview with Dolin.

2. "I'm Here To Win A Pennant," by Frank Lane as told to Roger Kahn, *Look Magazine*, June 23, 1956.

3. *Steinbrenner's Yankees*, by Ed Linn, page 63.

4. *Baseball Digest*, April 1955.

5. Interview with Lebovitz.

6. *Balls*, by Graig Nettles and Peter Golenbeck, page 50.

7. *Sports Illustrated*, July 1958.

8. House antitrust hearings, page 358. Only the Brooklyn Dodgers ($487,462), the Milwaukee Braves ($414,398), and Frank Lane's St. Louis Cardinals ($329,495) made more money in the National League that year than Paul's Reds. It was the fourth consecutive year that the Reds turned a profit, a mark equaled in the league only by the Dodgers and Braves.

9. *Baseball Story*, by Fred Lieb, page 242.

10. "Next Year's Team, The Story of the Cincinnati Wrecking Crew," by Ed Linn, *Sport Magazine*, February 1957.

11. *Ibid.*

12. Interview with Tal Smith.

13. *The George Kirksey Story*, by Campbell Titchener, page 52.

14. Interview with Tal Smith.

15. "How the Dodgers are building a Dynasty," by Myron Cope, *Sport Magazine*, July 1961.

16. Interview with Peters.

17. The *Plain Dealer*, August 23, 1962.

18. The *Plain Dealer*, September 26, 1962.

19. Interview with Dolin.

20. In a March 20, 1972 article, *Press* sports columnist Bob August reported the Indians' financial record between 1963 and 1971. The story shows how much stockholders saved through depreciation.

21. The *Press*, July 9, 1963.

22. Interview with Paul.

23. The *Press*, March 20, 1972. The Indians were fortunate to have a heavy writeoff that year, which reduced the stockholders' out-of-pocket loss to $90,716.

24. Interview with Rosen. His belief that Daley planned to move the team is shared by then-Cleveland City Council President James Stanton.

25. Interview with Dewey Soriano.

26. The *Seattle Post-Intelligencer*, September 2, 1964.

27. The *Plain Dealer*, September 11, 1964.

28. The *Plain Dealer*, August 30, 1964.

29. The *Post-Intelligencer*, September 9, 1964.

30. The *Post-Intelligencer*, September 9, 1964.

31. The *Post-Intelligencer*, September 11, 1964.

32. The *Plain Dealer*, September 12, 1964.

33. The *Press*, October 8, 1964.

34. The *Press*, October 9, 1964.

35. Interview with Stanton.

36. *Cleveland Stadium, Sixty Years of Memories*, by James A. Toman, page 30.

37. Paul and Stanton, in separate interviews, provided the details of their dinner meeting at Stouffer's Restaurant on Shaker Square. Stanton's comment to Lebovitz was published on the morning of October 6, 1964.

38. Interview with Paul.
39. Interview with Paul.
40. The *Plain Dealer*, October 7, 1964.
41. Both Paul and Lebovitz agree on the substance of their exchange on the plane. The conversation also was reported by Lebovitz in his column in the *Plain Dealer* on October 8, 1964.
42. Interview with Sudyk.
43. The *Post-Intelligencer*, October 9, 1964.
44. The *Post-Intelligencer*, October 10, 1964.
45. Interviews with Dewey Soriano and Max Soriano.
46. Interview with Sudyk.
47. *United Press International Dispatch*, Oakland, October 11, 1964.
48. The *Dallas Morning News*, October 13, 1964.
49. The *Plain Dealer*, October 16, 1964.
50. The *Press*, March 20, 1972.

Notes to Chapter 6

1. Interview with Atkinson.
2. Interview with Atkinson.
3. Interview with Margaret Mitchell Gannon.
4. Interview with Biggar.
5. "Vernon Stouffer," *Cleveland Plain Dealer Sunday Magazine*, February 26, 1967.
6. Interview with Peters.
7. Interview with Biggar.
8. The *Plain Dealer*, August 15, 1966.
9. The *Plain Dealer*, August 15, 1966.
10. The *Plain Dealer*, August 14, 1966.
11. *The Whiz Kids*, by John Byrne, page 51.
12. *Ibid*, page 416.
13. *New York Times*, March 22, 1968.
14. *New York Times*, March 22, 1968.
15. The *Plain Dealer*, September 8, 1969.
16. In a July 10, 1969 interview with Lebovitz, Stouffer said the team's farm budget was $1 million. Lebovitz pointed out that most teams spent an average of $1.5 million on their farm system in 1969 and that Cleveland's $1 million budget was "among the lowest" in baseball. Stouffer proposed to reduce it below $700,000.
17. Interview with Peters.
18. Interview with Kennedy.
19. "Tall, Dark and All-Around," by Francis Stern, *Baseball Digest*, May 1951, condensed from an article originally published in the *Washington Star*.
20. The *Plain Dealer*, January 30, 1969.

Notes

21. "The Dark that Shines," by Tom Meany, *Baseball Digest*, April 1955.
22. *Nice Guys Finish Last*, page 295.
23. "Time of Trial for Alvin Dark," by Robert H. Boyle, *Sports Illustrated*, July 6, 1964.
24. Interview with Dark. In his 1980 autobiography, *When in Doubt, Fire the Manager*, Dark concedes he aggressively sought out both jobs, hoping to have complete authority over the Indians.
25. Interview with Peters.
26. The *Plain Dealer*, July 5, 1969.
27. "The Time is Now for Indians," by Bob Sudyk, *Sporttime* published by *The Cleveland Press*, April 2, 1970.
28. The *Press*, March 20, 1972.
29. Interview with Dark.
30. Interview with Lebovitz.
31. The scene of Dark's firing is re-created through interviews with Paul and Dark, and from Dark's autobiography. All versions agree that Dark rejected a chance to remain as a scout.
32. *Hardball, The Education of a Baseball Commissioner*, by Bowie Kuhn, page 98.
33. The *Press*, December 2, 1971.
34. The *Press*, March 20, 1972.
35. The *Press*, December 2, 1971.
36. Interview with Dixon.
37. *Sports Illustrated*, July 22, 1974.
38. Interview with Dixon.
39. *Sports Illustrated*, July 22, 1974.
40. Interview with Connick.
41. The *Press*, December 2, 1971.
42. The *Press*, December 2, 1971.
43. The *Press*, March 20, 1972.
44. The *Press*, December 2, 1971.
45. The *Plain Dealer*, December 3, 1971.
46. The exchange between Finley and Stouffer is reported by Bob Sudyk of *The Press*, December 3, 1971.
47. The *New Orleans Times-Picayune*, December 4, 1971.
48. The *Plain Dealer*, December 3, 1971.
49. The *Times-Picayune*, December 3, 1971.
50. Interview with Rosen. Rosen was among four men close to the Indians who said that Stouffer had a drinking problem. Except for Rosen, only Gabe Paul was willing to be quoted directly.
51. Rosen is the first member of the group to declare that buying the Indians was part of a more elaborate plan to build two new stadiums in Greater Cleveland, much like the Kansas City complex which was under construction at the time. Art Modell and Sheldon Guren both said in interviews that Rosen was mistaken and that nobody in Cleveland was planning a twin-stadium complex.

52. Interview with Rosen.
53. Interview with Guren.
54. The actual offer varies with the news account. Rosen said he clearly recalls that the whole package was $8.6 million, of which $8.3 million was in cash. In addition, Rosen said that Steinbrenner told him he shook James Stouffer's hand on the deal. James Stouffer is now deceased.
55. The *Press*, October 27, 1977.
56. Paul and Rosen offered the same version in separate interviews. Rosen said that Steinbrenner was angry with Stouffer.
57. The *Plain Dealer*, December 8, 1971.
58. Both Paul and Rosen say Stouffer was drinking that evening, although only Steinbrenner spoke on the telephone with Stouffer.
59. The *Press*, December 7, 1971.

Notes to Chapter 7

1. The *Press*, March 8, 1972.
2. The *Plain Dealer*, February 3, 1972.
3. "Whooping It Up With The Indians," by Ron Fimrite, *Sports Illustrated*, July 29, 1974.
4. The *Plain Dealer*, February 3, 1972.
5. The *Plain Dealer*, January 19, 1970.
6. The *Plain Dealer*, March 6, 1970.
7. Interview with Zayac.
8. The *Plain Dealer*, 1980.
9. Interview with Moscarino.
10. "How Cleveland Almost Lost The Indians," by Bob Sudyk and Edward P. Whelan, *Cleveland Magazine*, April 1978.
11. Interview with Metzenbaum.
12. Interview with Bonda.
13. The *Plain Dealer*, March 12, 1972.
14. The *Plain Dealer*, March 10, 1972.
15. The *Press*, March 9, 1972.
16. The *Plain Dealer*, March 12, 1972.
17. The *Plain Dealer*, March 7, 1972.
18. "Whooping It Up With The Indians," July 29, 1974.
19. The *Press*, March 6, 1972.
20. Interview with Paul.
21. The *Plain Dealer*, September 30, 1983.
22. Interview with Paul.
23. The *Plain Dealer*, January 11, 1973.
24. *Ibid.*
25. The *Press*, January 10, 1973.
26. Interview with Arnson.

27. The *Plain Dealer*, August 5, 1972.

28. The *Press*, September 13, 1973.

29. The *Plain Dealer*, July 8, 1973.

30. Bonda in an interview declared that Mileti asked him to take over. Zayac said Mileti's original plan was to eventually turn the team over to someone like Ted Bonda.

31. The *Press*, September 13, 1973.

32. Interview with Metzenbaum in 1989 for the *Toledo Blade*.

33. Interview with Metzenbaum.

34. The *Plain Dealer*, March 3, 1974.

35. *Frank, The First Year*, by Frank Robinson and Dave Anderson, page 38.

36. The *Plain Dealer*, March 20, 1975.

37. Interview with Bonda.

38. *Don Baylor*, by Don Baylor and Claire Smith, Page 97.

39. *Nice Guys Finish Last*, page 372.

40. *Hardball*, page 115.

41. The *Plain Dealer*, April 9, 1975.

42. *Frank, The First Year*, page 5.

43. Interview with Bonda.

44. The *Plain Dealer*, May 21, 1977.

45. Interview with Arnson.

46. "How Cleveland Almost Lost The Indians." The Indians reported a net loss of $2 million, but wrote off $900,000 in player depreciation.

47. Trump later made a well-publicized bid for the Indians in 1984, but Bonda revealed he also met the New York real estate tycoon in 1977.

48. *Hardball*, page 217.

49. The estate of Francis J. O'Neill's in Cuyahoga County probate court lists how many shares of IBC each investor owned.

Notes to Chapter 8

1. A version of Steve O'Neill's chart was filed in federal court as part of Cleveland Indians vs. Cleveland Stadium Corp. Bernard Goldfarb and a September 6, 1983 article in the *Plain Dealer* also described O'Neill's chart.

2. The *Plain Dealer*, October 20, 1984.

3. The *Plain Dealer*, September 20, 1983.

4. Interview with Arnson.

5. The *Plain Dealer*, September 6, 1983.

6. A copy of the Indians' lease was filed in federal court as part of Indians vs. Stadium Corp. The prices of the loge tickets and numbers sold were included as exhibits for Bonda's deposition in Indians vs. Stadium Corp., on August 25, 1983.

7. The *Plain Dealer*, March 3, 1974.
8. Bonda's deposition, Indians vs. Stadium Corp.
9. Interview with Bonda.
10. *The Plain Dealer*, August 30, 1983.
11. *The Press*, May 26, 1972.
12. *The Plain Dealer*, December 20, 1965 and May 14, 1975.
13. *The Plain Dealer*, February 4, 1978.
14. Interview with Goldfarb.
15. *The Plain Dealer*, August 30, 1983.
16. *The Press*, October 31, 1980.
17. Interview with Arnson.
18. Estate of Francis J. O'Neill, Cuyahoga County probate court.
19. Interview with Paul.
20. *Steinbrenner's Yankees*, page 81.
21. Interview with Paul.
22. Internal Status Report for the Indians, page 5, filed in federal court as part of Indians vs. Stadium Corp.
23. Deposition of Tippit, Indians vs. Stadium Corp.
24. *The Plain Dealer*, September 6, 1983.
25. Interview with Paul.
26. Internal Status Report, page 5.
27. The letter from Modell was included among Bonda's depositions exhibits.
28. *The Plain Dealer*, April 27, 1983.
29. Bonda's deposition, page 76.
30. *Ibid*, page 68.
31. *Ibid*, page 148.
32. *Ibid*, page 149.
33. *Ibid*, page 58.
34. *Ibid*, page 127.
35. *Ibid*, page 149.
36. *The Plain Dealer*, April 30, 1983.
37. Modell's lawyers repeatedly asked Indians' stockholders if Modell helped finance the signing of Garland. Bonda in an interview, however, said the Indians paid Garland's entire contract.
38. *The Plain Dealer*, July 2, 1983.
39. Tippit's deposition, page 26.
40. Indians vs. Stadium Corp., page 8.
41. Tippit's deposition, page 30.
42. Letter from Bailey to Bonda, June 24, 1983, included among Bonda's deposition exhibits.
43. *The Plain Dealer*, July 2, 1983.
44. Interview with McCartan.
45. Letter from Bailey to Tippit, July 29, 1983, included among Bonda's deposition exhibits.
46. Bonda's deposition, pages 24 and 28.
47. Interview with DiBiasio.

48. Interview with Bavasi.
49. The *Plain Dealer*, April 24, 1986.
50. The *Plain Dealer*, September 15, 1983, and from an interview with Arnson.
51. Interview with Kundtz.
52. The *Plain Dealer*, September 16, 1983.
53. The *Plain Dealer*, November 14, 1983.
54. Interview with LeFevre.
55. Estate of Francis J. O'Neill.
56. The exact offers are included in papers filed with Cuyahoga County common pleas court in Laich vs. O'Neill.
57. *Ibid*.
58. Interview with Bavasi.
59. Interview with Bavasi.
60. The *Plain Dealer*, February 4, 1985.
61. Interview with Klein.
62. Interview with Klein.

Notes to Chapter 9

1. The *Washington Post*, October 16, 1983.
2. The *Post*, April 12, 1977.
3. *The Baseball Business, Pursuing Pennants and Profits in Baltimore*, by James Edward Miller, page 254.
4. Interview with Peters.
5. The *Post*, October 16, 1983.
6. The *Post*, October 16, 1983.
7. *Charlie O*, pages 97-98.
8. Interview with Peters.
9. Interview with Peters.
10. The *Plain Dealer*, November 3, 1987.
11. Interview with Peters.
12. "Top Gun." by Edward P. Whelan, *Cleveland Magazine*, March 1987.
13. *Ibid*.
14. Interview with Hagan.
15. The *Plain Dealer*, September 19, 1992.
16. Interview with Voinovich.
17. *Top Gun*.
18. *Ibid*.
19. Interview with LeFevre.
20. Interview with Bonda.
21. *Veeck as in Wreck*, page 11.
22. *Ibid*, page 269.
23. Interview with Peters.

24. Interview with Peters.
25. *Charlie O*, pages 97 and 100.
26. Interview with Dark.
27. Interview with Peters.
28. Interview with Peters.
29. The *Post*, April 12, 1977.
30. The *Post*, October 16, 1983.
31. *The Baseball Business*, page 226.
32. The *Post*, February 15, 1986.
33. The Orioles' financial performance is detailed in *The Baseball Business*, pages 227, 232, and 250.
34. *Ibid*, page 250.
35. Interview with Peters.
36. *The Man to See, Edward Bennett Williams*, by Evan Thomas, page 447.
37. Williams' firing of Peters is from page 480 of *The Man to See*, and an interview with Peters.
38. The *Post*, October 4, 1987.
39. Interview with Peters.
40. Interview with Boras.
41. The *Plain Dealer*, March 20, 1994, and May 3, 1992.
42. Interview with Peters.
43. Interview with Hart.
44. Interview with Peters. When asked about the story, Dick Moss said he did not recall it, but confirmed that Butler was eager to leave Cleveland before Peters became team president. Moss said that Peters never made a competitive offer to keep Butler.
45. *A Baseball Life*, page 97.
46. Interview with Carter in the *Plain Dealer*, September 4, 1989.
47. The *Plain Dealer*, December 7, 1989.
48. The *Plain Dealer*, March 3, 1989.
49. Interview with Turner.
50. Interview with Peters. Turner agrees with Peters' version except to add that Carter by then had firmly decided against staying in Cleveland.
51. Interview with Peters.
52. Paul Hoynes of the Plain Dealer, who had excellent sources, reported on December 4, 1989, that seven teams were in the running for Carter. While he correctly identified San Diego, California, Kansas City, and St. Louis as four of them, he also reported that Boston, Toronto, and Chicago White Sox were still in the competition. He reported that San Diego was the "No. 1 contender" and that catcher Sandy Alomar would be included in the trade.
53. Interview with Peters.
54. The *Plain Dealer*, December 6, 1989.
55. Russell Schneider's Plain Dealing column in the *Plain Dealer*, September 27, 1989.

56. The exchange between Peters and McKeon is re-created from interviews with Peters and Hoynes' excellent account in the *Plain Dealer*, December 10, 1989.
57. Interview with Turner.
58. The *Plain Dealer*, December 10, 1989.
59. The *Plain Dealer*, December 6, 1989.
60. The *Plain Dealer*, June 28, 1991.
61. The *Plain Dealer*, July 7, 1991.

Notes to Chapter 10

1. Interview with Chema.
2. Interview with Celeste.
3. Interview with Chema.
4. The *Plain Dealer*, April 26, 1984.
5. The *Plain Dealer*, August 1, 1932.
6. The *Plain Dealer*, January 21, 1930.
7. *The Cleveland Indians*, by Franklin Lewis, page 166.
8. The papers of William Hopkins, courtesy of the Western Reserve Historical Society.
9. The *Plain Dealer*, August 25, 1928.
10. The *Plain Dealer*, November 6, 1928.
11. The *Plain Dealer*, January 17, 1930.
12. The *Plain Dealer*, January 22, 1930.
13. The *Plain Dealer*, July 4, 1931.
14. The *Plain Dealer*, July 1, 1931.
15. The *Plain Dealer*, July 3, 1931.
16. *The Cleveland Indians*, page 245.
17. *Ibid*, page 245.
18. Interview with Campanella.
19. The *Plain Dealer*, March 16, 1984.
20. Interview with Hagan.
21. Interview with Campanella.
22. The *Plain Dealer*, May 6, 1984.
23. Interview with Hagan.
24. Interview with Voinovich.
25. The *Plain Dealer*, April 24, 1985.
26. Interview with Voinovich.
27. Interview with Lafferty.
28. The *Plain Dealer*, April 5, 1984.
29. Interview with Chema.
30. Interview with Chema.
31. Interviews with Hagan and Chema.
32. Interview with Chema.
33. Interview with Dykes.

34. 1990 interview with Henkel for an article that was published in the *Toledo Blade* and *Pittsburgh Post-Gazette*.
35. Interviews with Hagan, 1990 and 1993.
36. 1990 interview with Coyne.
37. Interview with Voinovich.
38. Interview with Chema.

Notes to Chapter 11

1. Interview with Bragan.
2. Interview with Dolin.
3. Interview with Kennedy.
4. Interview with Peters.
5. *Nice Guys Finish Last*, page 138.
6. *Veeck as in Wreck*, page 104.
7. Interview with Rosen.
8. Interview with Weber.
9. Interview with Paul.
10. Interview with Goldfarb.
11. Interview with Chema.
12. "The $11 Billion Pastime," by Michael K. Ozanian, *Financial World Magazine*, May 10, 1994.
13. *Business Week*, August 15, 1994.
14. The *Plain Dealer*, February 18, 1991.
15. The *Plain Dealer*, June 26, 1991.
16. "Tribe of the Future," by Peter King, *Sports Illustrated*, March 30, 1992.
17. Interview with Hart.
18. Interview with Boras.
19. Interview with Boras.
20. The *Plain Dealer*, May 3, 1992.
21. Interview with Boras.
22. Interview with Hart.
23. When the author covered the New York Yankees Triple A team in Columbus between 1979 and 1983, Yankee scout Clyde King repeatedly praised Martinez for having "four out-pitches."
24. The *Plain Dealer*, June 17, 1994.
25. The *Plain Dealer*, July 28, 1994.
26. The *Plain Dealer*, July 2, 1994.
27. *USA Today*, August 8, 1994.
28. The *Plain Dealer*, August 8, 1994.
29. The *Plain Dealer*, July 14, 1994.
30. *Lords of the Realm*, by John Helyar, Page 366.
31. *Baseball and Billions*, by Andrew Zimbalist, Pages 149-150.

32. *Ibid*, Page 52.
33. *Ibid*, Page 159.
34. *Financial World Magazine*, July 7, 1992.
35. *Baseball and Billions*, page 85. The 1993 figures are from *Baseball America's 1994 Almanac*, page 13.
36. The Pittsburgh law firm of Buchanan Ingersoll conducted an audit of the Pirates for the city of Pittsburgh.
37. The *Washington Post*, August 10, 1994.
38. The *New York Times*, December 1, 1992.
39. The *Plain Dealer*, August 2, 1994.
40. *Associated Press Dispatch*, August 11, 1994.
41. The *Plain Dealer*, August 12, 1994.
42. The *Plain Dealer*, September 15, 1994.

Notes to Chapter 12

1. The *Plain Dealer*, October 3, 1995.
2. Interview with Hagan.
3. The *Plain Dealer*, April 16, 1995.
4. *Akron Beacon Journal*, June 7, 1995.
5. The *Plain Dealer*, April 16, 1995.
6. Interview with White.
7. Interview with White.
8. Interview with White.
9. Interview with White. O'Dowd confirmed in an interview that he originally wanted to choose a college pitcher.
10. Interview with White.
11. The *Plain Dealer*, June 4, 1991.
12. Interview with White.
13. Interview with O'Dowd.
14. Interview with Hart after the third game of the World Series.
15. Interview with White.
16. Interview with Regan.
17. Interview with Regan.
18. Interview with Hart before the divisional playoffs.
19. *USA Today*, November 17, 1995.
20. Post-game interview with Hargrove, October 1, 1995.
21. Interview with Hershiser before divisional playoffs.
22. The *Plain Dealer*, July 30, 1995.
23. *Los Angeles Times*, May 29, 1991.
24. *Ibid*.
25. *Los Angeles Times*, March 19, 1991.
26. *Los Angeles Times*, March 17, 1992.
27. *Los Angeles Times*, April 4, 1994.
28. Interview with Hart.
29. Interview with Hart.
30. The *Plain Dealer*, October 7, 1995.

31. Post-game interview with Nagy.
32. Post-game interview with Assenmacher.
33. *Toledo Blade*, October 18, 1995.
34. The *Plain Dealer*, October 19, 1995.
35. *Toledo Blade*, October 18, 1995.
36. Interview with Nelson before the fourth game of the World Series.
37. Interview with Nelson.
38. Sandy Alomar told of Lofton's talk in a post-game press conference.
39. Interview with Nelson.
40. Interview with Nelson.
41. Post-game interview with Dennis Martinez.
42. Bobby Cox in a post-game press conference.
43. Interview with Wylie after the fifth game of the World Series.
44. The scene in the plane is re-created through an interview with Moag and an article published in the *Baltimore Sun*, December 17, 1995.
45. The *Wall Street Journal*, December 15, 1995.
46. The *Plain Dealer*, December 24, 1995.
47. David Modell was temporarily successful. The *Plain Dealer* printed the tenor of his attack upon Dick Jacobs on December 26, 1995, after Art Modell decided to move the Browns.
48. The *Baltimore Sun*, December 17, 1995.
49. Interview with O'Dowd.
50. Peter Gammons baseball column, *Boston Globe*, December 10, 1995.
51. Interview with O'Dowd.
52. Gammons column, *Boston Globe*, September 17, 1995.
53. Interview with O'Dowd.

Bibliography

Books

Allen, Maury. *Roger Maris, A Man for All Seasons*. Donald I. Fine Publishing, 1986.

——————. *Baseball, The Lives Behind the Seams*. MacMillan Publishing Company.

Baylor, Don and Claire Smith. *Don Baylor*. St. Martin's Press, 1989.

Byrne, John. *The Whiz Kids, The Founding Fathers of American Business and the Legacy They Have Left Us*. Doubleday, 1993.

Dark, Alvin and John Underwood. *When in Doubt, Fire the Manager*. E.P. Dutton, 1980.

Durocher, Leo and Ed Linn. *Nice Guys Finish Last*. Simon & Schuster, 1975.

Feller, Bob and Bill Gilbert. *Now Pitching, Bob Feller*. Harper-Perennial, 1990.

Feller, Bob. *Strikeout Story*. A.S. Barnes & Co., Inc., 1947.

Golenbock, Peter. *Bums*. Pocket Books, 1984.

Greenberg, Hank and Ira Berkow. *Hank Greenberg, The Story of My Life*. Times Books, 1989.

Halberstam, David. *The Summer of '49*. William Morrow & Co., 1989.

Hano, Arnold. *A Day in the Bleachers*. Da Capo Press, 1955.

Heiman, Lee and Dave Weiner and Bill Gutman. *When the Cheering Stops*. Macmillan Publishing Co., 1990.

Helyar, John. *Lords of the Realm, The Real History of Baseball*. Villard Books, 1994.

Kerr, Jon. *Calvin, Baseball's Last Dinosaur*. William C. Brown Publishers, 1990.

Koppett, Leonard. *The Man in the Dugout*. Crown Publishers, 1993.

Kuhn, Bowie. *Hardball, The Education of a Baseball Commissioner*. Times Books, 1987.

Lewis, Franklin. *The Cleveland Indians*. G.P. Putnam's Sons, 1949.

Lieb, Frederick G. *The Baseball Story*. G.P. Putnam's Sons, 1950.

Linn, Ed. *Steinbrenner's Yankees*. Holt, Rinehart & Winston, 1982.

Mantle, Mickey and Phil Pepe. *My Favorite Summer, 1956*. Dell Publishing, 1991.

Mays, Willie and Lou Sahadi. *Say Hey*. Pocket Books, 1988.

Mead, William B. *Even the Browns*. Contemporary Books, 1978.

Michelson, Herbert. *Charlie O, Charles Oscar Finley vs. the Baseball Establishment*. Boobs-Merrill Co., Inc., 1975.

Miller, James Edward. *The Baseball Business, Pursuing Pennants and Profits in Baltimore*. University of North Carolina Press, 1990.

Miller, Marvin. *A Whole Different Ballgame*. Carol Publishing Group, 1991.

Minoso, Minnie. *Just Call Me Minnie, My Six Decades in Baseball*. by Minnie Minoso with Herb Fagan, Sagamore Publishing, 1994.

Nettles, Graig and Peter Golenbock. *Balls*. G.P. Putnam & Sons, 1984.

Pluto, Terry. *The Curse of Rocky Colavito*. Simon & Schuster, 1993.

Ribalow, Harold U. and Meir Z. Ribalow. *The Jew in American Sports*. Bloch Publishing, 1966.

Robinson, Frank and Dave Anderson. *Frank, The First Year*. Holt Rinehart & Winston, 1976.

Smith, Curt. *The Voices of the Game*. Diamond Communications, 1987.

Sullivan, Neil J. *The Dodgers Move West*. Oxford University Press, 1987.

————. *The Diamond Revolution*. St. Martin's Press, 1992.

Thomas, Evan. *The Man To See, Edward Bennett Williams*. Simon & Schuster, 1991.

Titchener, Campbell B. *The George Kirksey Story, Bringing Major League Baseball to Houston*. Eakin Press, 1989.

Tygiel, Jules, *Baseball's Great Experiment*. Oxford University Press, 1983.

Veeck, Bill and Ed Linn. *Veeck as in Wreck*. G.P. Putnam's Sons, 1962.

—————————. *The Hustler's Handbook*. Simon & Schuster, 1965.

—————————. *Thirty Tons A Day*. Viking Press, 1972.

Voigt, David Quentin. *American Baseball, From the Postwar Expansion to the Electronic Age*. Penn State University Press, 1983.

Westcott, Rick. *Diamond Greats*. Meckler Books, 1988.

Young, A.S. *The Mets From Mobile, Cleon Jones and Tommie Agee*. Harcourt, Brace & World, Inc., 1970.

Zimbalist, Andrew. *Baseball and Billions*. BasicBooks, 1992.

Magazine Articles

Cobbledick, Gordon. "Is Cleveland Mad At The Indians," *Sport Magazine*, June 1956.

Cobbledick, Gordon and Roger Kahn. "The World Series is a Wonderful Moment," *Sports Illustrated*, September 27, 1954.

Cohane, Tim. "Frank Lane: Baseball's Busiest Dynamo," *Look Magazine*, June 12, 1956.

—————. "Will The Indians Fold Again," *Look Magazine*, August 10, 1954.

Colavito, Rocky. "What You Learn In The Big Leagues," *Sport Magazine*, July 1961.

Fimrite, Ron. "Whooping it up with the Indians," *Sports Illustrated*, July 29, 1974.

—————. "Circle the Wagons, Indian Uprising," *Sports Illustrated*, May 29, 1972.

Furlong, William Barry. "Master of the Joyful Illusion," *Sports Illustrated*, July 4, 1960.

Gibbons, Frank. "Ruth Didn't Do It, But Luke Easter Will," *Baseball Digest*, May 1951.

Greenberg, Hank. "How We Beat The Yankees," *Life Magazine*, September 27, 1954.

Havermann, Ernest: "Low Pressure Lopez," *Sports Illustrated*, September 6, 1954.

Kahn, Roger. "The Twilight of the Gods," *Sports Illustrated*, September 20, 1954.

—————. "One-Two-Three-Four & Bingo," *Sports Illustrated*, October 11, 1954.

King, Peter. "Tribe of the Future," *Sports Illustrated*, March 30, 1992.

Koelling, Lester. "Here's the Score on Herb Score," *Baseball Digest*, April 1955.

Lane, Frank, as told to Roger Kahn. "I'm Here To Win A Pennant," *The Saturday Evening Post*, June 23, 1956.

Lebovitz, Hal. "Cleveland's Left-Handed Lightning," *Saturday Evening Post*, May 11, 1957.

—————. "The Story Behind the Rosen Headlines," *Sport Magazine*, February 1957.

Lewis, Franklin. "Bat Title For Rosen," *Baseball Digest*, May 1951.

Linn, Ed. "Next Year's Team: The Story of the Cincinnati Wrecking Crew," *Sport Magazine*, February 1957.

Meany, Tom. "The Dark That Shines," *Baseball Digest*, April 1955.

McDermott, John. "With St. Jude's Help, Hard-Luck Herb is Back," *Life Magazine*, May 18, 1959.

Ozanian, Michael K. "The $11 Billion Pastime," *Financial World Magazine*, May 10, 1994.

Reed, J.D. "Superdome," *Sports Illustrated*, July 22, 1974.

Roberts, Michael D. "Of Time and Table 14," *Cleveland Magazine*, June 1990.

—————, and Rory O'Connor. "The 10 Most Powerful," *Cleveland Magazine*, October 1988.

Ross, Stephen F. "Monopoly Sports Leagues, *University of Minnesota Law Review*, February 1989.

Schiller, Zachary. ". . . But There's No Joy in Cleveland," *Business Week*, August 1994.

Schlemmer, Jim. "Lane's Best Deal," *Baseball Digest*, February 1958.

Smith, Gary. "The Ripples from Little Lake Nellie," *Sports Illustrated*, July 12, 1993.

Sudyk, Bob and Edward P. Whelan. "How Cleveland Almost Lost The Indians," *Cleveland Magazine*, April 1978.

Terrell, Roy. "Doom Around the Corner: A Report on Minor League Baseball's Sad Plight," *Sports Illustrated*, December 16, 1957.

Underwood, John and Morton Sharnik. "Look What Louie Wrought," *Sports Illustrated*, May 29, 1972.

Whelan, Edward. "Top Gun," *Cleveland Magazine*, March 1987.

"Why The Ballclubs Want To Move," *Business Week*, June 8, 1957.

"Indian Sign," *Newsweek*, May 16, 1966.

Newspapers

Baltimore Sun
Chicago Tribune
Cleveland News
Cleveland Plain Dealer
Cleveland Press
Dallas Morning News
Los Angeles Times
Minneapolis Star
Minneapolis Tribune
New Orleans Times-Picayune
New York Times
Seattle Post-Intelligencer
Toledo Blade
USA Today
Washington Post

Index

Index

Index

Index

Index

Index

Index